Governing through Regulation

Over the past forty years, the science and practice of regulation has evolved rapidly. Numerous theoretical advances have been made. From Ayres' and Braithwaite's ground breaking work on 'responsive regulation', we have seen models of 'smart regulation', 'regulatory governance' and 'regulatory capitalism' emerge to capture the growing prevalence and importance of regulation in modern liberal Western capitalist societies. Important advances also have been made in the practice of regulation, with regulators evolving from traditional enforcement focused 'command and control' models to being 'modern regulators' with a suite of diverse and innovative regulatory tools at their disposal.

This book presents and critically examines these theoretical and practical developments from the perspective of governments who design regulations and the regulators that deploy them. In doing so, the book examines the various forces and interests that influence and shape the regulatory endeavour, and the practical challenges facing governments and regulators when deciding whether and how to regulate.

This volume is a study of regulation in context: in the context of the public policy it is designed to deliver; the law that enables, shapes and holds it to account; and the evolving societal and institutional frameworks within which it takes place.

This volume aims to provide innovative cross-disciplinary conceptual frameworks that regulators, regulatees, those whom regulation is intended to benefit and academics might employ to better understand and undertake the regulatory endeavour. This will be of great interest to researchers, educators, advanced students and practitioners working in the fields of political science, public management and administration, law and public policy.

Eric L. Windholz is a Senior Lecturer and Research Associate with the Monash Centre for Regulatory Studies, Monash University, Australia.

Routledge Critical Studies in Public Management
Edited by Stephen Osborne

For a full list of titles in this series, please visit www.routledge.com

The study and practice of public management has undergone profound changes across the world. Over the last quarter century, we have seen

- increasing criticism of public administration as the over-arching framework for the provision of public services,
- the rise (and critical appraisal) of the 'New Public Management' as an emergent paradigm for the provision of public services,
- the transformation of the 'public sector' into the cross-sectoral provision of public services, and
- the growth of the governance of inter-organizational relationships as an essential element in the provision of public services.

In reality these trends have not so much replaced each other as elided or co-existed together—the public policy process has not gone away as a legitimate topic of study; intra-organizational management continues to be essential to the efficient provision of public services, whist the governance of inter-organizational and inter-sectoral relationships is now essential to the effective provision of these services.

Further, whilst the study of public management has been enriched by contribution of a range of insights from the 'mainstream' management literature, it has also contributed to this literature in such areas as networks and inter-organizational collaboration, innovation and stakeholder theory.

This series is dedicated to presenting and critiquing this important body of theory and empirical study. It will publish books that both explore and evaluate the emergent and developing nature of public administration, management and governance (in theory and practice) and examine the relationship with and contribution to the over-arching disciplines of management and organizational sociology.

Books in the series will be of interest to academics and researchers in this field, students undertaking advanced studies of it as part of their undergraduate or postgraduate degree and reflective policy-makers and practitioners.

Public Policy, Governance and Polarization
Making Governance Work
Edited by David K. Jesuit and Russell Alan Williams

Business and Government Relations in Africa
Edited by Robert A. Dibie

Governing through Regulation
Public Policy, Regulation and the Law
Eric L. Windholz

Governing through Regulation

Public Policy, Regulation and the Law

Eric L. Windholz

LONDON AND NEW YORK

First published 2018 by Routledge

2 Park Square, Milton Park, Abingdon, Oxfordshire OX14 4RN
52 Vanderbilt Avenue, New York, NY 10017

Routledge is an imprint of the Taylor & Francis Group, an informa business

First issued in paperback 2019

Library of Congress Cataloging-in-Publication Data
A catalog record for this book has been requested

ISBN: 978-1-138-93558-7 (hbk)
ISBN: 978-0-367-24308-1 (pbk)

Typeset in Sabon
by Apex CoVantage, LLC

To Rhoda

Contents

Figures and Tables

Figures

Tables

Preface and Acknowledgements

This book has been thirty years in the making. That is the length of time I have been working with regulation. My first experience with regulation was as a junior lawyer in private practice. My clients included pharmaceutical companies navigating the intricacies of the patent system and credit-card issuers working out how best to comply with the complexities of Australia's consumer credit laws. From there I moved into an in-house counsel role with a fast-moving consumer goods company. Food, beer and tobacco were its staples; all regulatory mine fields. Working first in Australia, and then in Asia and the United States, I came to see first-hand how different regulatory and political systems worked. My third incarnation was back in Australia, and this time as a workplace health and safety regulator, first as its General Counsel and later as the General Manager responsible for its compliance framework and strategic prevention programs. I quickly learned that applying the law fairly and consistently can be just as difficult as—if not more difficult than—complying with it. And now I am an academic studying regulation and regulators.

This book seeks to impart to the reader some of the things I have learned over these thirty years. The book examines the regulatory endeavour through the eyes of both the regulator and the regulatee, and with the assistance of the more neutral perspective of an academic. By merging my coal face experience with academic perspectives, this book seeks to marry theory and practice into a holistic examination of the science and art of regulation, and to present it in a manner that is intelligible and intuitive to regulators, regulatees and regulatory practitioners, as well as academics and their students.

A number of people have been instrumental to the writing of this book. I would like to thank them. First, I would like to thank my friend, colleague and 'rock-climbing' guide, Professor Graeme Hodge. His time, encouragement, counsel and comments on drafts of some of the earlier chapters have been invaluable and are greatly appreciated. Second, I would like to thank Miriam Kolacz, Benjamin Needleman and Emily Domingo for their research assistance and editorial help. I also would like to thank the team at Routledge who helped with this book. Next, I would like to thank my family, friends and colleagues at Monash University's Faculty of Law. To all the people from whom I have learned, on whom I have leaned, and with whom I have laughed, I say a very heartfelt 'thank you'.

And finally—but by no means least—I would like to thank my wife, Rhoda. Without her love, patience and humour, this book would never have been written.

Eric Windholz,
Melbourne, March 2017

Part I

Introduction

1 Introduction

This book is a study of regulation in context: in the context of the public policy it is designed to deliver; and the law that enables, shapes and holds it to account. It also is a book for its time: a time when regulation has come of age as a primary tool of governance; and a time when those charged with its formulation and implementation are facing unprecedented challenges and pressures.

The past forty years has seen a dramatic increase in both the volume and breadth of regulatory activity.[1] In traditional economic areas of commerce and competition, and traditional social areas of health, safety and consumer protection, regulation has increased in number and complexity. At the same time, new regulatory arenas have emerged in areas as diverse as the environment, biotechnology, the internet, equal opportunity, privacy, human and animal rights, and human reproduction, to name but a few. This same period also has seen increasing use by governments of independent regulatory agencies to govern these areas.[2] Perhaps, as some commentators have observed, we are living in the 'golden age of regulation'.[3]

But what explains this dramatic growth in regulation? The answer to this question lies in the complex and complicated world in which we live. Increasing reliance on market mechanisms to deliver government services, rapidly evolving social mores and the pace of technological change have combined to fundamentally alter the nature of commercial and social activity, creating both new opportunities and new risks. Governments find themselves simultaneously being asked to create an environment in which innovation, new technologies and markets can flourish while protecting citizens from the worst excesses of these forces; to safeguard an ever-increasing array of rights and to provide protection from an ever-increasing array of risks; to balance market efficiency with societal demands for justice, equity and fairness; and to do so in a manner that minimises the compliance burden on regulatees, the fiscal burden on taxpayers and the regulatory burden on society generally.[4] And all of this at a time when many people's confidence in governments' ability to address the challenges of the 21st century is diminishing.[5]

The growth and increasing complexity of regulation inevitably attracted the attention of academics from different disciplines, including public policy, law, public administration, politics, economics and sociology. It also has seen the study of regulation evolve from an issue on which these disciplines have something to say to become a discrete discipline with its own theories, concepts, technical language and accumulated body of specialist knowledge. Numerous theories have been developed to explain the growth, nature and importance of regulation in modern democratic liberal capitalist societies,[6] with terms such as the 'regulatory state', 'regulatory capitalism' and 'regulatory governance' entering our lexicon. Important advances also have been made in the practice of regulation, with regulators evolving from traditional prescriptive 'command and control' models to become 'modern regulators' employing a range of 'responsive', 'smart' and 'better' regulatory techniques designed to persuade, assist, incentivise and nudge regulatees to comply with standards that are performance-based and outcome-orientated.[7]

The rich body of knowledge that has developed explaining the regulatory endeavour contains valuable lessons, insights and perspectives to assist us to better design and deploy regulation in the public interest. At the same time, however, this body of knowledge has become increasingly complex and contested. For every theory, there are one or more alternate or counter-theories, and numerous critiques. Moreover, many academics are more inclined to write for other academics than for policy-makers, regulators, practitioners and students of the area.[8] The typologies and classification systems they develop to explain and differentiate between aspects of the regulatory endeavour often employ labels and terms, and draw distinctions, that are not intuitive to the regulatory community.[9] In this regard, it is not surprising that the theoretical advance to gain the most traction amongst them is Ayres' and Braithwaite's enforcement pyramid that is inductively based on the practice of regulators and expressed in language familiar to them.[10]

The aim of this book is to assist people to understand and navigate the regulatory endeavour without being overwhelmed by its complexity. The first step in achieving this aim is to define the terrain being navigated, being the core concepts that give the book its title: governance; public policy, regulation and law.

Core Concepts

Defining the book's core concepts would not be necessary if these terms had universally accepted meanings. This is not the case, however. These are concepts about which many disciplines have many different things to say, with different disciplines using alternative words to describe the same thing, and the same word to describe different things. Moreover, new labels and buzzwords are constantly being devised—sometimes to describe a new (or newly discovered) phenomena, or to rebadge an existing phenomena with a new but not always significant edge. The semantic confusion this creates is further complicated by the tendency, once a label gains traction and currency, 'to affix to it all of the other fashions of the day'.[11]

No attempt is made here to cover all the different meanings ascribed to each concept, or to explain the nuanced differences between them. Nor will we attempt to craft definitions capable of universal application. Their variability is such that any attempt to do so would be an exercise in futility. Rather, this book's approach is guided by the practical advice of Black that what is important is what we want to do with a concept rather than what a concept 'means' in some fundamental sense.[12] We also are guided by Jordana's and Levi-Faur's advice that rather than look for exhaustive and consensual definitions across different disciplines and research agendas, we should allow the specific context and goal to shape the particular meanings given to concepts.[13] Our goal here is to examine the phenomenon of governing through regulation; its context is the public policy it is designed to deliver and the law that enables, supports and holds it to account. It is this goal and context which underpins the meanings given to the book's core concepts.

Governance

The term 'governance' derives from the Latin *gubernor*, meaning to 'pilot, steer or direct'.[14] The act of steering or directing is central to its meaning. However, it also allows for great variation with respect to what should be steered or directed, by whom, and how, leading some to 'lament the multiple and sometimes ambiguous meanings given to it'.[15] The term has been used to describe an ever-increasing variety of decision-making methods,[16] and has been applied to nearly every aspect of collective life from countries and societies through to universities, clubs and corporations. Indeed, Hughes observes that 'corporate governance' is one of the more theorised applications of the concept.[17]

This book is concerned with the governance of societies through regulation. The governance with which it is concerned is 'public governance'. Public governance generally gives government a privileged role, placing it at or near the centre of the endeavour. However, 'government' is not the same as 'governance'. 'Public governance' is the manner, method or system by which a particular society is steered or directed;[18] and 'government' is the set of institutions that steer or direct (or coordinate the steering or direction) of that society. This is not to suggest that government is the only institution steering or directing society. Governance increasingly is understood as requiring 'the active participation of a range of actors in addition to government itself'.[19]

Within the realm of 'public governance', many typologies or systems of classification exist, each with its own focus and emphasis. Some typologies classify governance by the instruments or tools employed to govern;[20] and some by the resources of government.[21] Two classifications of particular relevance for the focus of this book are those that classify governance by the mode of steering and by the functions of government.

Knill and Tosun identify three principal modes by which societies are steered and directed: hierarchical governance, governance by markets and governance through networks.[22] Hierarchical governance has the state steering directly and from above, either through the provision of common goods (e.g., infrastructure, education, health services), or by controlling societal behaviour and conduct though rules and regulation. Governance by markets, on the other hand, sees societies steered by the 'invisible hand' of the market aggregating individual preferences expressed in the market place. Under this mode of governance, the market (not government) is considered the best vehicle for delivering outcomes in the public interest. This is not to say that there is no role for government, however. In modern societies, markets cannot function effectively without some laws and regulations to ensure that contracts are honoured, consumers are protected and businesses are constrained from engaging in anti-competitive conduct. The third mode, governance through networks, challenges the assumption that either governments or markets alone can best order society. Rather, it envisages governments collaborating through networks of public, non-government and private actors to address public problems and pursue public opportunities with respect to which they have mutual or interdependent goals.[23]

An alternate but equally useful lens through which to view governance is the functional classification employed by Braithwaite, Coglianese and Levi-Faur.[24] They conceive of government and governance being about three things: providing goods, services and infrastructure; distributing and redistributing wealth; and regulating behaviours.[25] They further observe that of these three functions, regulation is the expanding part of governance, a theme to which we will return in the next chapter.

If governance is the manner, method or system by which a particular society is steered, this leaves open the question—how are decisions made about which method of steering to use, and in which direction? This is where public policy comes in.

Public Policy

Numerous definitions of the term 'public policy' exist.[26] Maddison and Denniss classify these definitions into two categories.[27] The first category represents what Maddison and Denniss term the 'classical view'. According to this view, public policy is an authoritative choice of government based on plausible hypotheses designed to deliver the government's objectives and desired outcomes. This view presents public policy as a rational, systematic and hierarchical process in which problems and/or opportunities are defined, options developed and evaluated, and rational, evidence-based choices are made by a government or a government official in an authoritative position. The second category is in many ways the antithesis of the first. According to the second view, government is less the decision-maker and more the arena or space in which a range of actors with divergent positions and interests interact. This view presents public policy as an inherently political process through which competing interests and values are weighed and balanced and compromises made. In this book, we take the position that public policy has elements of both views—that it is an authoritative choice of government based on plausible hypotheses designed to deliver the government's objectives and desired outcomes; that (in most cases) it employs rational, evidence-based processes; but that it also is informed and influenced by interested actors with different degrees of power and influence; and that the final outcome is the product of evidence rationally assessed, societal values and realpolitik.

Like governance, many systems of classifying public policy exist.[28] Some classify public policies according to subject-matter. Thus, policies often are classified into economic and social policies; or industry and welfare policies; and each with its own sub-policies. Economic policy, for example, often is sub-divided into monetary, fiscal and competition policies. Subject-matter classification systems, while descriptively useful, say little about how the policy functions, which is where our interest lies. A useful functional classification is provided by Lowi's policy typology that classifies public policy into four categories—distributive, redistributive, constituent and regulatory.[29] Distributive policies distribute new state resources to citizens. Examples of distributive policies include farm subsidies, education and infrastructure such as schools, hospitals and roads. Redistributive policies modify the existing distribution of resources. Taxation and the provision of welfare payments are the most common examples of redistributive policies. Constituent policies create or modify state institutions, and the rules and processes pursuant to which these institutions operate. Administrative tribunals, ombudsmen and other forms of alternative dispute resolution mechanisms are examples of these. And finally, regulatory policies seek to modify individual and collective behaviour in accordance with specified conditions. Consumer protection, environmental and workplace health and safety policies are examples of regulatory policy. Regulatory policy is the focus of this book, and it is to the means by which regulatory policy is effected—regulation—that the chapter now turns.

Regulation

The definition of regulation is heavily contested. As Levi-Faur observes, regulation 'means different things to different people' with definitions varying according to professional discipline, political ideology and even geography.[30] 'Definitions of regulation vary from the legalistic that confine regulation to legal rules promulgated by a sovereign state, to more expansive but still state-centred definitions that include all forms of government intervention, through to decentred definitions that include all activities designed to influence behaviour regardless of source and intent'.[31] This book's definitions of governance and public policy emphasise the centrality of government and conceptualise regulation as being about behaviour change or modification. Consistent with these definitions (and the book's purpose), the following definition of regulation is adopted:

> Regulation is a structured process undertaken by or under the auspices of government designed to modify the behaviour of persons or entities according to defined standards.[32]

As with governance and public policy, different systems of classifying regulation exist. Like public policy, regulation can be classified by the nature of the activity or industry being regulated. Thus, regulation often is classified into economic regulation and social regulation, with sub-categories within each. Economic regulation, for example, can be broken down into financial, corporate, utilities and telecommunication regulation; and social regulation into environmental, workplace health and safety, equal opportunity (anti-discrimination) and privacy regulation. And like governance, regulation also is classified by reference to its modes, with commentators differentiating between state-centred or government regulation, laissez-faire or market-orientated regulation, and networked, cooperative or collaborative regulation.[33] Other commentators classify regulation according to the resources, capacities, instruments or tools employed by governments to influence behaviour. Freiberg, for example, identifies six categories of regulatory tools: economic tools (such as taxes, quotas and pricing); transactional tools (such as contracts and grants); authorising tools (such as registration, licensing and accreditation); informational tools (such as product labelling and disclosure regimes); structural tools (of physical design or processes); and legal tools (such as laws, rules and regulations).[34] Finally, there are classifications according to the style of the regulator—for example, command and control, responsive, smart and risk-based regulation.[35] As will be seen, this book employs and borrows from each of these classification systems, at different places and for different purposes.

A number of commentators have opined that broad conceptions of governance and regulation such as those employed in this book pose challenges for the law and for those who tend to view the world through a legal lens.[36] But this presupposes we know what law is and what it does. It is to these questions that the chapter now turns.

Law

What is 'law' is a question that has occupied the minds of philosophers for centuries. Plato and Aristotle, for example, saw law as the embodiment of reason. Others such as Rousseau and Kant viewed the law in terms of morality, ethics and justice; and others still such as Bentham, Austin and Hart eschew connections between law and morality, and view law positively in terms of binding commands emanating from a socially recognised, legitimate legal authority. This book's focus is on what law does rather than what it is or should be in some abstract sense. The definition it adopts is thus instrumental in nature: law is a system of rules to govern behaviour enforced through institutions created for that purpose.[37] This definition allows for great variability: from narrow state-centred 'black letter' definitions that restrict law to rules found in statutes and judgements, through to pluralist or decentred definitions that conceive of law as patterns of social ordering that do not derive (solely) from the state.[38] Consistent with the definitions ascribed to the book's other core concepts, the definition adopted in this book is both narrow—in the sense of being predominately state-centred—and broad—in conceiving of the law as a system and not just a collection of rules.

The law operates to govern behaviour in two primary ways: one functional, the other expressive (see Figure 1.1).[39] The functional role has three broad dimensions. First, the law shapes behaviour by permitting or encouraging some conduct, and preventing or sanctioning other conduct. Examples include criminal and tort law. Second, the law facilitates certain behaviours, including both private arrangements and government functions, as well as its own functioning and administration. Contract law, property rights and administrative law are examples of this second type. And third, the law adjudicates disputes between private entities, between private entities and governments, and between governments. Courts of common law and equity are traditional examples of this; mediation and arbitration more recent examples.

The manner with which the law performs these functions gives expression to important constitutional, democratic, ethical, moral and shared societal values. This is law's expressive role.[40] How the law protects fundamental human rights that might be infringed by regulatory action is a good example of this. Some countries have Bills or Charters of Rights that place

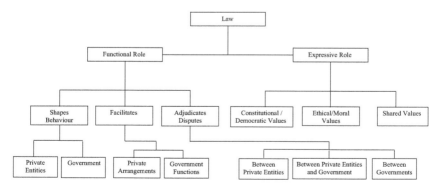

Figure 1.1 What is Law?

certain rights beyond the reach of the legislature. Other countries rely on the common law principle of legality that enables the legislature to abrogate fundamental rights provided it is explicit in doing so. While the principle of legality compels the legislature to 'squarely confront what it is doing and accept the political cost',[41] it provides only token protection in the face of a government intent on abrogating those rights—thereby delegating to the populace the role of protecting those rights through the ballot box.[42]

Administrative law principles—and the ease or difficulty with which aggrieved persons can challenge regulatory decision-making—are another example. Subjecting regulatory action to merits and judicial review guards against unfair and arbitrary government action, facilitates evidence-based policy-making and gives effect to important constitutional values and principles. These include the rule of law (equal treatment and protection before the law), constitutionalism (limited government) and accountable government (through the judiciary acting as a check and balance on the government's exercise of power).

So in summary, the law is central to both governance and regulation. The law provides the vehicles through which governments undertake their core functions of provision, (re)distribution and regulation. With respect to regulation, the law prescribes and proscribes desired standards of behaviour; establishes institutions to undertake regulatory activities; creates and shapes the regulatory tools those institutions use; furnishes the infrastructure for enforcement and dispute resolution; and establishes mechanisms through which regulatory institutions and actors are held accountable for the decisions they make and the activities they undertake. And the manner with which the law discharges these functions says a lot about that society's values and priorities—in particular, its respect for the rule of law and for individual, commercial and communal rights.

Aim and Approach of the Book

The aim of this book is to provide readers with a holistic guide to regulatory theory and practice—to demystify and make sense of the theoretical literature and to marry it with the real world of regulatory practice. This raises the question: who are my readers? Who is my intended audience? The answer is persons who find themselves working with regulation. Many of these persons have not undertaken any formal studies in the area. Their learning tends to be a combination of on-the-job training and courses taken at a post-graduate level. This creates what Pollitt refers to as the 'important overlap between the categories of "student" and "practitioner"'.[43] This book is written principally for these persons, although it also should be of assistance to both undergraduate and postgraduate students studying advanced units in governance, public policy, regulation and law, and to academics who also have not studied regulation but whose substantive area of expertise is the subject of regulation—which given regulation's prevalence today, means most (if not all) of them.

The book delivers on its aim by providing the reader with a series of frameworks (or maps) with which to explore and examine the regulatory endeavour without being overwhelmed by its complexity. Through these frameworks, the reader is introduced to important theoretical concepts and practical issues central to modern regulatory practice. Understanding these concepts and issues better equips us to diagnose and analyse regulatory issues, to construct and deconstruct regulatory regimes and to think strategically about how best to regulate complex and emerging issues.

As with all map making exercises, this book employs a number of reference points to help orientate the reader. First, the book purposively adopts a state-centred—but not state-myopic—conception of governance and regulation. The state—or more precisely, government—is central to this book's understanding of the regulatory endeavour: regulation is undertaken by government, or under its auspices. At the same time, however, regulation today is shaped and co-produced through interactions between government and non-government actors.[44] Recognising that governance, public policy and regulation are not the sole domains of government, and that the regulatory endeavour can benefit from the participation and involvement of a wide variety of private and non-government actors, creates opportunities to design innovative and flexible regulatory regimes comprising different configurations of public and private actors. Taking advantage of the opportunities which adopting this broader mindset provides is a key theme of the book.

Second, the book conceives of governing through regulation as purposive. Regulation is the result of an intentional decision of government to steer or direct society in a particular direction and manner; to address a particular issue; to produce a particular outcome. In this regard, regulation is not confined to 'problems' and 'problem solving'. This is an important point. Regulation can be as much about grasping opportunities and creating environments conducive to innovation and appropriate risk taking as it is about eliminating or minimising problems and risks. The book thus uses the term 'issue' to frame its discussion, covering both regulation to solve problems and regulation to grasp opportunities.

Third, regulation seeks to achieve its objectives by modifying the behaviour of others according to defined standards. Regulation therefore extends to all forms of intervention designed to modify or influence behaviour, whether it be by coercion, assistance, incentives, persuasion or a subtle nudge. Viewed this way, regulation can be either positive, where behaviours are encouraged, enabled or facilitated through persuasion, assistance and incentives; or negative, where behaviours are discouraged by disincentives, or restricted or prohibited through coercive measures. This broad conception of regulation opens up a world of possibilities with respect to instrument design and choice. Leveraging the opportunities this creates is another theme of this book.

Fourth, the book conceives of regulation as sustained and focused. It requires ongoing monitoring of the relevant activities, continual (re)assessment of values and trade-offs, and adjustments to changing needs and circumstances.[45] Viewed this way, regulation involves more than the passage of a law or an ad hoc operation.[46] It is an ongoing system made up of institutions, processes and procedures. Thus, the book's examination of the regulatory endeavour looks beyond a particular regulatory instrument, activity or agency to the ongoing regulatory regime that governs and coordinates them.[47]

Fifth, the book conceptualises the regulatory endeavour as both a science and an art. This duality is another fundamental theme running through the book. Regulation requires a systematic approach. This systematic approach benefits from the use of empirical or scientific methods. However, effective regulation also requires the exercise of judgement that cannot (and should not) be totally systemised. This exercise of judgement is the artful part. The book identifies and explains the elements of the regulatory endeavour aided by scientific methods, and makes transparent those elements where judgments are crucial.

At the same time, the book recognises that much regulatory decision-making also is 'political'. This is the sixth frame. Different values and interests permeate specific regulatory controversies requiring balances to be struck and trade-offs made. Different ideologies also permeate the regulatory endeavour more broadly. Levi-Faur, for example, observes that the notion of regulation is heavily contested, with the Far Right perceiving it as 'a dirty word representing the heavy hand of authoritarian governments and the creeping body of rules that constrain human or national liberties'; the Old Left as 'part of the superstructure that serves the interests of the dominant class'; and Progressive Democrats as 'a public good, a tool to control profit-hungry capitalists and to govern social and ecological risks'.[48] We do not take sides in this debate. The book does not seek to advance or prefer one set of values, interests or ideologies over another. On the contrary, the book proceeds on the basis that regulation *per se* has no political agenda. Any political agenda resides in those who employ it to achieve a particular purpose, and in how people choose to interpret its outcomes and impact. The book's goal is to be balanced in its presentation and discussion of contemporary regulatory debates and to make underlying values, interests and ideologies transparent where relevant.

Seventh, the book is written from the perspective of a democratic liberal capitalist society. Each of these is a powerful frame in its own right. 'Democratic' denotes a political system in which supreme power is vested in the people, and is exercised directly by them or by individuals whom they have elected to represent them; 'liberal' denotes a society that values individual autonomy, liberty and social equality, and recognises government's role in securing and protecting those rights; and 'capitalist' denotes an economic system in which ownership of production, distribution and wealth exchange is primarily in the hands of private individuals and organisations, and which embraces the principles of free markets, consumer sovereignty and the rule of law.

Eighth, one of the book's strengths and differentiating factors is its marriage of theory and practice. The theoretical literature is presented in the context of the practical challenges facing governments and regulators when deciding whether and how to regulate. Moreover, and importantly, the book is written by an academic with more than thirty years' experience working as a regulator of industry, and as a senior executive in heavily regulated industries in Australia, Asia and the United States. This enables the book to view regulation through the eyes of both the regulator and the regulatee, and with the assistance of the more neutral perspective of an academic. This gives the book a strong practical orientation.

Ninth, the book brings multiple and varied lenses to its examination of the regulatory endeavour. The book combines and connects concepts from across not only governance, public policy, regulation and law, but also from public administration, politics, sociology and economics where appropriate. This reflects that regulation today is an inter-disciplinary melting pot. Importantly, it also produces a richer environment from which to examine and analyse the regulation endeavour. The book also employs examples from different industry sectors. The study of regulation can often be sector specific (e.g. focused on banking, utilities, environment, etc.). However, there are generic challenges (e.g. enforcement, compliance, legitimacy, etc.) about which different sectors can learn much from each other. The goal is to elevate discussion beyond specific sectors and regulatory controversies to focus on major themes and relationships.

Tenth, the book approaches the regulatory endeavour holistically. Many discussions of regulation focus either on the processes by which governments choose which issues to regulate and how, or upon how regulators discharge regulatory functions assigned to them. Yet the two aspects of the regulatory endeavour are inextricably intertwined. It is important that those who design regulatory regimes are cognisant of the challenges faced by those charged with its implementation. And those charged with its implementation are better placed to do so well if they are cognisant of the forces that shaped the regime in the first place.

Finally, the maps and frameworks used in this book (as with all maps and frameworks) involve a degree of abstraction and simplification. In order to be able to understand and study regulatory complexity, assumptions need to be made and some simplification is required.[49] As a consequence, each element of the regulatory endeavour is unlikely to be as ordered as it appears in the frameworks employed in this book. Moreover, elements of the regulatory endeavour overlap. This means that in certain circumstances, frameworks may need to be layered one upon another to represent the complexity of the regulatory endeavour. Where this is the case, the book seeks to identify underpinning assumptions, highlight areas of overlap and explain interconnections.

It also is important to note what the book is not. It is not an exhaustive treatment of every aspect of regulatory theory and practice. This simply is not possible. The book does not, for instance, attempt to cover issues concerning global, international and transnational regulation, except to the extent they impact upon and influence national regulatory regimes. Nor is it possible to cover the intricacies and complexities of the rich body of literature that has evolved over the past forty years to describe, explain and analyse the regulatory endeavour. Our focus is on the main theories and models; or to employ the well-worn analogy—our focus is on the woods, some trees and only rarely on the leaves on the trees.

The book also does not purport to articulate a unified theory of regulation or golden thread that passes through and connects these various theories and models. No such unified theory or golden thread exists. Public policy and regulation are inherently complex and messy. Rather, we aim to draw regulatory theory and practice together, to combine and connect concepts across different disciplines and fields and to present this diverse material in a systematic and coherent manner. This is one of the book's strengths and a valuable contribution in itself. And at the risk of stretching the 'map' analogy too far, the book does not purport to prescribe one single route or approach to regulate issues. Real world regulators know that each regulatory issue is different. Rather, and consistent with one of the book's key themes that regulation is both a science and an art, we provide readers with both maps for navigating the regulatory endeavour, and advice and counsel to inform the judgments inherent in the use of those maps.

How This Book Is Structured

This book in structured into four parts. Part I is the introduction. It comprises this chapter and Chapter 2 that traces the emergence of regulation as a dominant form of governance. It begins by providing the reader with a glimpse into the historical context of modern day regulation. It then explores some of the main models employed to describe and explain the new regulatory world order, before settling on 'regulatory governance' as the best lens through which to understand the modern regulatory endeavour.

Part II provides the reader with the theories and constructs that form the backbone of the book's examination of the regulatory endeavour. It begins in Chapter 3 by introducing the reader to four sets of theories that explain why governments regulate in the form in which they regulate. They are public interest theories that provide the theoretical or technical justification for regulation; private interest theories that explain why regulation does not always advance the public interest; and institutional and ideational theories that explain the roles played by institutions and ideas in shaping the regulatory endeavour. Understanding these different theories—their strengths, weaknesses and implications—is important, as they suggest different regulatory institutional arrangements and processes. Chapter 4 next introduces two important constructs central to the book's analysis. First is regulatory space, being the environment in which the regulatory endeavour takes place.

Second is the regulatory regime through which government marshals actors and resources in the regulatory space in support of the regulatory endeavour.

In Chapter 5 the book examines a number of conceptual models that aim to explain how public policy (and regulatory policy) is made. These include Simon's bounded rationality, Lindblom's muddling through and incrementalism, Kingdon's multiple streams and stagist approaches of the type championed by Harold Laswell and Garry Brewer. From this examination, the book settles on a stagist approach—the regulatory policy cycle—as the most appropriate vehicle through which to examine the practice of regulation. The chapter then proceeds to introduce the reader to each stage of the cycle—define, design, decide, implement and evaluate—and to factors that influence the momentum and ease with which issues move through the cycle—participation, evidence, politics and capability.

Chapter 6 concludes Part II by examining what regulatory success looks like. This is done in three steps. First, the book examines regulatory failure and the lessons that can be learned from it; second it looks at better regulation reforms designed to prevent some of the main causes of regulatory failure; and third, it introduces the reader to the concept of regulatory legitimacy and the dimensions of the regulatory endeavour that give it acceptability and credibility.

In Part III of the book, each stage of the regulatory policy cycle is examined in detail. Chapter 7 examines the define stage of the cycle. It begins by examining how issues enter the cycle in the first place (known in the public policy literature as agenda-setting) before proceeding to explore the processes by which the regulatory issue's causes and attributes are diagnosed, and the desired future state—the regulatory objectives—are set. Chapter 8 then examines the design stage. This involves an examination of the various choices within each of the key regulatory design variables and the processes through which those variables can be combined to produce a set of plausible alternative regulatory options. The processes by which these alternative regulatory options are assessed and the regulatory regime to be pursued is selected is the focus of Chapter 9 (the decide stage). Chapter 10 then explores implementation and the processes and strategies by which that regulatory regime is deployed and applied. And in Chapter 11, we examine the evaluation stage: the processes by which the regulatory initiative is formally assessed with a view to making recommendations with respect to its continuation, modification or termination.

The book concludes in Part IV. Chapter 12 looks forward to what the future might hold for regulatory governance. The chapter explores likely changes in the external world and how those changes might impact how governments govern and regulate. Chapter 13 then concludes by reflecting on the main insights from our examination of the regulatory endeavour and the lessons that can be drawn from them to inform future regulatory decision-making.

Notes

1. See, e.g., Jacint Jordana, David Levi-Faur and Xavier Fernandez i Marín, 'The Global Diffusion of Regulatory Agencies: Channels of Transfer and Stages of Diffusion' (2011) 44 *Comparative Political Studies* 1343; Tara M Sinclair and Kathryn Vesey, 'Regulation, Jobs, and Economic Growth: An Empirical Analysis' (Working Paper, The George Washington University Regulatory Studies Center, March 2012); Organisation for Economic Co-Operation and Development, *Regulatory Policies in OECD Countries: From Interventionism to Regulatory Governance* (OECD Publishing, 2002).
2. Jordana, Levi-Faur and Fernandez i Marín, 'The Global Diffusion of Regulatory Agencies', above n 1.
3. See, e.g., Scott H Jacobs, 'The Golden Age of Regulation' (13 November 2000) 1<www.regulations.am/uploads/Bibliography/The_Golden_Age_of_Regulation_by_Scott_H_Jacobs.pdf>; David Levi-Faur, 'Regulatory Networks and Regulatory Agencification: Towards a Single European Regulatory Space' (2011) 18 *Journal of European Public Policy* 810, 814.
4. Eric Windholz and Graeme A Hodge, 'Conceptualising Social and Economic Regulation: Implications for Modern Regulators and Regulatory Activity' (2012) 38 *Monash University Law Review* 212, 215.
5. See, e.g., Organisation for Economic Co-Operation and Development, *Government at a Glance 2013* (OECD Publishing, 2013) ch 2, 40.
6. What we mean by these terms is explained below at 12.
7. 'Responsive' and 'smart' regulation are discussed in Chapter 10; 'better regulation' in Chapter 6; and regulatory techniques in Chapter 8.
8. Paraphrasing Richard A Posner, 'Against Constitutional Theory' (1998) 73 *New York University Law Review* 1, 4 who made a similar comment with respect to the 'academification of law school professors'.
9. The worlds of academia and policy-making have been described by some commentators as two communities separated by different values, reward systems and languages: Nathan Caplan, 'The Two-Communities Theory and Knowledge Utilization' (1979) 22 *American Behavioral Scientist* 459, 459.
10. The enforcement pyramid and the theory of responsive regulation of which it is part are discussed in detail in Chapter 10, 223–6.
11. H George Frederickson, 'Whatever Happened to Public Administration?: Governance, Governance Everywhere' in E Ferlie, L E Lynn Jr and C Pollitt (eds), *The Oxford Handbook of Public Management* (Oxford University Press, 2005) 282, 285.
12. Julia Black, 'Critical Reflections on Regulation' (2002) 27 *Australian Journal of Legal Philosophy* 1, 25.
13. Jacint Jordana and David Levi-Faur, 'The Politics of Regulation in the Age of Governance' in J Jordana and D Levi-Faur (eds), *The Politics of Regulation: Institutions and Regulatory Reforms for the Age of Governance* (Edward Elgar, 2004) 1, 5.
14. David Levi-Faur, 'From "Big Government" to "Big Governance"' in D Levi-Faur (ed), *The Oxford Handbook of Governance* (Oxford University Press, 2012) 3, 5. See also Owen Hughes, 'Does Governance Exist?' in S P Osborne (ed), *The New Public Governance? Emerging Perspectives on the Theory and Practice of Public Governance* (Routledge, 2010) 87, 88.
15. Levi-Faur, 'From "Big Government" to "Big Governance"', above n 14, 3.
16. The breadth of usages of the term is illustrated by two recent collections of essays on governance: S P Osborne (ed), *The New Public Governance? Emerging Perspectives on the Theory and Practice of Public Governance* (Routledge, 2010); David Levi-Faur (ed), *The Oxford Handbook of Governance* (Oxford University Press, 2012).

17. Hughes, 'Does Governance Exist?', above n 14, 93.
18. Ibid 90, citing S E Finer, *Comparative Government* (Penguin, 1970) 3–4.
19. Christopher Pollitt and Peter Hupe, 'Talking about Government: The Role of Magic Concepts' (2010) 13 *Public Management Review* 641, 645. Pollitt and Hupe suggest that participation forms the 'rough common core' running through various conceptions of public governance.
20. See, e.g., Lester M Salamon and Odus V Elliot, *The Tools of Government: A Guide to the New Governance* (Oxford University Press, 2002) who classify government action into direct tools (direct government provision; government corporations; economic regulation; public information; and direct loans) and indirect tools (social regulation; contracting; loan guarantees; grants; taxes, fees and charges; insurance; vouchers; tort law; and government-sponsored enterprises).
21. See, e.g., Christopher Hood, *The Tools of Government* (Chatham House, 1986) who classifies governance according to the four basic resources of government: nodality (information); authority; treasure and organisation (forming the anagram NATO).
22. Christoph Knill and Jale Tosun, *Public Policy: A New Introduction* (Palgrave Macmillan, 2012) 202–5.
23. Salamon and Elliot, *The Tools of Government*, above n 20, 11–14. Knill and Tosun observe that networked governance also has been applied to 'patterns of societal self-governance' that do not involve government at all: Knill and Jale Tosun, *Public Policy*, above n 22, 203. The book's conception of governance retains, at a minimum, a coordinating role for government, and does not extend to totally decentred conceptions of governance.
24. John Braithwaite, Cary Coglianese and David Levi-Faur, 'Can Regulation and Governance Make a Difference?' (2007) 1 *Regulation & Governance* 1, 3.
25. To this should be added a fourth 'constitutive' function of government establishing the legal and institutional framework for a society to govern itself.
26. For a selection of definitions, see Sarah Maddison and Richard Denniss, *An Introduction to Australian Public Policy: Theory and Practice* (Cambridge University Press, 2nd ed, 2013) 5.
27. Ibid 5–7.
28. For an overview of different policy typologies, see Thomas A Birkland, *An Introduction to the Policy Process: Theories, Concepts, and Models of Public Policy Making* (Routledge, 2016) ch 7.
29. Theodore J Lowi, 'Four Systems of Policy, Politics and Choice' (1972) 32 *Public Administration Review* 298. As can be seen, these categories are similar to Braithwaite, Coglianese and Levi-Faur's classification of governance functions.
30. David Levi-Faur, 'Regulation and Regulatory Governance' in D Levi-Faur (ed), *Handbook on the Politics of Regulation* (Edward Elgar, 2011) 3, 3–6.
31. Windholz and Hodge, 'Conceptualising Social and Economic Regulation', above n 4, 217. For reviews of different definitions, see Robert Baldwin, Colin Scott and Christopher Hood, *A Reader on Regulation* (Oxford University Press, 1998) 2–4; Robert Baldwin, Martin Cave and Martin Lodge, *Understanding Regulation: Theory, Strategy and Practice* (Oxford University Press, 2nd ed, 2012) 2–3; Christine Parker and John Braithwaite, 'Regulation' in P Cane and M Tushnet (eds), *The Oxford Handbook of Legal Studies* (Oxford University Press, 2003) 119; Bronwen Morgan and Karen Yeung, *An Introduction to Law and Regulation: Text and Materials* (Cambridge University Press, 2007) 4.
32. Those familiar with regulatory theory will observe this definition builds upon the earlier work of Julia Black and Philip Selznick. Black defined regulation to be 'a process involving the sustained and focussed attempt to alter the behaviour of others according to defined standards or purposes with the intention of producing a broadly identified outcome or outcomes': Black, 'Critical Reflections

on Regulation', above n 12, 26. Black's definition in turn built upon Selznick's earlier concept of regulation as 'structured and focussed control exercised by a public agency over activities that are valued by a community': Philip Selznick, 'Focusing Organisational Research on Regulation', in R G Noll (ed), *Regulatory Policy and the Social Sciences* (University of California Press, 1985) 363–4.

33. See, e.g., Neil Gunningham, 'Regulation: From Traditional to Cooperative' in S R Van Slyke, M L Benson and F T Cullen (eds), *The Oxford Handbook of White-Collar Crime* (Oxford University Press, 2016) 503; Martin Lodge and Kai Wegrich, *Managing Regulation: Regulatory Analysis, Politics and Policy* (Palgrave Macmillan, 2012) ch 5.

34. Arie Freiberg, *The Tools of Regulation* (Federation Press, 2010). For other instrumental classifications, see Salamon and Elliott, *The Tools of Government*, above n 20; Baldwin, Cave and Lodge, *Understanding Regulation*, above n 31, ch 7; Anthony I Ogus, *Regulation: Legal Form and Economic Theory* (Hart Publishing, 2004).

35. See, e.g., Ian Ayres and John Braithwaite, *Responsive Regulation: Transcending the Deregulatory Debate* (Oxford University Press, 1992); Neil Gunningham and Peter Grabosky, *Smart Regulation: Designing Environmental Policy* (Clarendon Press, 1998); Christopher Hood, Henry Rothstein and Robert Baldwin, *The Government of Risk: Understanding Risk Regulation Regimes* (Oxford University Press, 2001).

36. See, e.g., Morgan and Yeung, who suggest that broad conceptions of regulation challenge traditional legal assumptions about the centrality of rules and the role of the state by allowing for alternative regulatory techniques and government operating in non-hierarchical networks involving commercial and non-government organisations: Morgan and Yeung, *An Introduction to Law and Regulation*, above n 31, 4; and Julia Black who discusses the implications of 'rule by regulation' for the 'rule of law': Black, 'Critical Reflections on Regulation', above n 12, 29–34.

37. This definition builds on the definition of law in Geoffrey Robertson, *Crimes against Humanity: The Struggle for Global Justice* (Penguin Press, 1999) 90.

38. Black, 'Critical Reflections on Regulation', above n 12, 29–34; Christine Parker, 'The Pluralization of Regulation' (2008) 9 *Theoretical Inquiries in Law* 349.

39. This classification of the roles performed by law builds on the work of: Karl Llewellyn, 'The Normative, the Legal and the Law Jobs: The Problem of Juristic Method' (1940) 49 *Yale Law Journal* 1355; Joseph Raz, *The Authority of Law: Essays on Law and Morality* (Clarendon Press, 1979) ch 9, 163; Morgan and Yeung, *An Introduction to Law and Regulation*, above n 31, 5–7; William Twining and David Miers, *How to Do Things with Rules* (Cambridge University Press, 5th ed, 2010) 111–13.

40. Cass R Sunstein, 'On the Expressive Function of Law' (1996) 144 *University of Pennsylvania Law Review* 2021.

41. *Re Secretary of State for the Home Department; Ex parte Simms* [2000] 2 AC 115, 131 (Lord Hoffman).

42. Albert V Dicey, *An Introduction to the Study of the Law of the Constitution* (MacMillan, 1959) 83.

43. Christopher Pollitt, *Advanced Introduction to Public Management and Administration* (Edward Elgar, 2016) 2.

44. Peter Grabosky, 'Using Non-Governmental Resources to Foster Regulatory Compliance' (1995) 8 *Governance* 527; Colin Scott, 'Analysing Regulatory Space: Fragmented Resources and Institutional Design' [2001] (Summer) *Public Law* 329; Peter Grabosky, 'Beyond *Responsive Regulation*: The Expanding Role of Non-State Actors in the Regulatory Process' (2013) 7 *Regulation & Governance* 114.

45. Tony Prosser, 'Regulation and Social Solidarity' (2006) 33 *Journal of Law and Society* 364, 375; Selznick, 'Focusing Organisational Research on Regulation', above n 32, 364.
46. Levi-Faur, 'Regulation and Regulatory Governance', above n 30, 5.
47. Regulatory regimes are discussed in Chapter 4.
48. Levi-Faur, 'Regulation and Regulatory Governance', above n 30, 3.
49. Wayne Parsons, *Public Policy: An Introduction to the Theory and Practice of Policy Analysis* (Edward Elgar, 1995) 57.

2 The Rise of Regulatory Governance

How is it that regulation has become such an important feature of modern society? What can the history of regulation's rise teach us about the forces that have shaped it? And how have these forces changed the way in which societies are governed? These are the questions examined in this chapter. The chapter begins by tracing the growth and changing nature of regulation and some of the theories that have been advanced to explain its increasing prominence. The chapter then surveys three conceptual models that have been developed to describe regulation's increasingly important role within modern democratic liberal capitalist societies: the 'regulatory state', 'regulatory capitalism' and 'regulatory governance'. Of these, 'regulatory governance' is shown to be the lens that best describes the modern phenomenon of societies governed through regulation, and regulated through governance. The chapter concludes by identifying implications that flow from this choice for the book's examination of the modern regulatory endeavour.

Early History

Regulation is not a new phenomenon. It has existed for as long as monarchs, emperors and other rulers have sought to control the behaviour of the people over whom they exercise dominion. Business regulation, for example, is almost as old as trade itself. As Condliffe observes: 'In trading history, if enterprise is the theme, regulation is the counterpoint. As soon as the track begins to be beaten out, established authority intervenes to control and levy tolls upon the traders'.[1] Regulation also was a fundamental enabler of this trade: a mechanism to inject trust into transactions. Systems of standardised weights and measures, for example, have been found in ancient Egyptian, Indian, Greek and Roman civilisations. Professions also have long been the subject of regulation, with rulers keen to control any forum in which people might gather and conspire against them.[2]

Regulation also was prominent throughout the Middle Ages and Renaissance periods. Ogus, for example, observes that regulation was a feature of the Tudor and Stuart periods, with almost all areas of industry and trade subject to detailed legislative controls. However, in these earlier periods regulation was not grounded in any general theory (economic or otherwise).[3] In the main, regulation was a compromise between the needs of the populace (and the ruler's need to keep the populace tame and out of revolt) and the demands of powerful private interests such as nobles, land-owners, trade guilds and the emerging merchant class (on whose support and tax revenue the ruler depended to retain power).[4] As Williams colour-fully put it:

> '[t]he preoccupations of government mingled with the pressures of vested interest and hopeful speculation to provide a lush *bouillabaisse* of regulation that defies any attempt by the historian to subject it to precise and schematic analysis.'[5]

Regulation became more systematic in the 19th century. Industrialisation and urbanisation combined to create a plethora of new economic and social problems. At the same time, the captains of the new industrial age were able to use their wealth and influence to neuter courts as an effective vehicle for solving the problems they caused. Glaser and Schleifer, for example, refer to the 'robber barons' of the era subverting justice by intimidating and bribing judges, and using delaying tactics to postpone trials.[6] In more liberal societ-ies, governments responded to these problems by replacing litigation with regulation as the principal mechanism for controlling business. New admin-istrative structures were created to investigate the problems of industrialisa-tion and to recommend, administer and enforce solutions. This period saw new regulation designed to both facilitate the emergence of new industries such as utilities, railways and manufacturing, and to mitigate some of their worst excesses (e.g. price controls, worker safety rules and the first anti-trust laws in the United States).[7]

The Regulation Boom of the 20th Century

While regulation has always been with us, it came into its own in the 20th century. Regulation was central to government responses to the Great Depression. This was especially the case in the United States, where President Roosevelt's New Deal reforms are considered to have ushered in a new era of government regulation.[8] Regulation also was prevalent during and after World War II: during to prioritise resources and manpower for the war effort, and to control behaviours perceived to be detrimental to it; and after to rebuild countries devastated by the war, and to transition wartime economies and workforces back to civilian production.[9] Regulation also accompanied the growing national and international consumerism of the 1950s and 1960s. The early part of this period saw regulation designed to encourage production, economic development and free trade;[10] the later period the emergence of consumer protection regimes focused on issues such as product safety and the accuracy of advertising and trade descriptions.[11]

The emergence of consumer protection regulation was representative of a broader upheaval impacting Western liberal societies in the 1960s and early 1970s.[12] Sunstein refers to this period as the 'rights revolution'—a period in which people advocated for an extended concept of the 'rights' which governments should support. These included rights to welfare, employment, education, food, housing, adequate medical care, good health and safety, and security.[13] Peltzman similarly refers to 'the working of the natural progress of opulence' in which growing wealth produces growing demand for personal health and safety;[14] and Kuttner to the demands for regulation that 'flow from a recognition that society as a whole may choose to award itself certain common minima', such as clean drinking water, wholesome working environments, safer prescription drugs and food, and the like.[15]

This also was the period in which societal concerns about the risks of rapid commercialisation and technological progress became more pronounced, leading Ulrich Beck to famously employ the term 'risk society' to describe a new modernity in which there was a preoccupation (social and political) with potential and perceived risks and a systematic bias towards regulating to prevent or mitigate them.[16] Others, however, argue that this preoccupation has not led to a 'risk society', but to a 'risk averse society' in which people demand government protection from a growing array of perceived risks.[17] And others still argue that the increase in regulation is attributable not so much to the risk aversion of society as it is to the Pavlovian response of governments and regulators to over-react and over-regulate in response to public perceptions of risk.[18]

A general decrease in the public's trust in social, economic and political institutions is another reason advanced for the growth of regulation. Moran captured this idea succinctly when he said 'we audit, and we regulate, when we cease to trust'.[19] And finally, there are those who argue that the growth in regulation during this period was not the product of individual preferences or attitudes, but the result of paternalism where 'experts' or so-called 'elites' claiming to know better substituted their choices or preferences for those of the individual.[20]

Whatever the reason for the increase, what is clear is that regulation during this period became more pervasive and invasive—restricting liberties and imposing costs. It is therefore not surprising that the regulatory endeavour itself soon came under scrutiny.

The Eras of Deregulation and Better Regulation

Businesses, on which much of the direct cost of regulation falls, were the first group to voice their opposition to regulation on economic grounds, arguing it made them less competitive and innovative in an increasingly global market. These concerns were amplified by the poor economic conditions of the 1970s that saw many Western countries experience increases in both inflation and unemployment, and were given credibility by public choice and capture theories of regulation that demonised government regulation as a second-best substitute to the disciplinary forces of market economies.[21] These concerns and theories found welcoming homes in the economic rationalism, neo-liberalism and free-market ideology of newly elected conservative governments (principally those of Reagan (United States) and Thatcher (United Kingdom)). Under what came to be known as 'Reaganomics' and 'Thatcherism', governments were to steer not row; government services were to be outsourced to the private sector or exposed to competition; the private sector was to be freed from cumbersome and unnecessary government regulation and oversight; and what regulation and oversight remained was to be made more effective and efficient by adopting private sector, market-orientated approaches designed to make them more responsive and accountable.[22] Known generally as 'new public management', Ferlie et al describe it as involving the introduction into public services of the three 'M's: markets, managers and measurement.[23] Combined, these forces ushered in the deregulatory era of the 1980s, which saw governments prioritise freeing business and society from the burden of what was portrayed as ineffective and inefficient regulation.

The deregulatory era ameliorated to a degree in the 1990s with the election in the United States and United Kingdom of less ideological governments looking for more pragmatic 'third way' solutions. The 1990s also saw a number of high-profile disasters and crises impact significantly on our communal sense of safety and security. These included food safety concerns (e.g. mad cow disease and the introduction of genetically modified organisms into the food system), environmental disasters (e.g. the Exxon Valdez disaster in Prince William Sound and the Bhopal Union Carbide chemical spill) and financial market crises (e.g. the October 1987 stock market crash and the US savings and loan crises of the 1980s and 1990s). These events called into question whether the deregulation agenda had gone too far, and whether governments and regulators had the capacity and capability to deal with the increasingly complex issues confronting society. These developments combined to change the focus of the reform agenda away from deregulation and towards 'better regulation'. Championed first by the OECD and later by the European Commission,[24] 'better regulation' reforms have as their focus not less regulation, but less rigid and costly regulation.[25] Better regulation reforms encourage governments to re-examine traditional command and control regimes, to use more responsive market based regulatory tools and flexible performance based regulatory standards, and to subject regulatory proposals to cost-benefit analyses to ensure their societal net worth.[26]

The impact of deregulatory and better regulatory reforms should not be exaggerated. There has not been wide-spread deregulation. On the contrary, as Jacobs observes, 'no government activity in OECD countries has grown faster since 1980 than government regulatory functions'.[27] This is supported by a study by Gilardi, Jordana and Levi-Faur that found across thirty OECD and nineteen Latin American countries, the number of independent regulatory agencies created in the 1990s increased by two and a half times the increase over the previous three decades, and that this increase took place across both economic and social sectors.[28] And nor has the better regulation agenda significantly slowed the growth of regulation. While many governments claim to have reduced the administrative burden regulation imposes on businesses and others, the evidence in support of their claims is scant and selective. As May observes, the new reforms have not 'wholly or even widely supplemented traditional forms of regulation'.[29] Nor have regulatory expectations of business reduced dramatically. Rather, what we have seen is a change in the manner in which regulation is framed and imposed, with a decrease in the use of prescriptive standards and coercive tools and a corresponding increase in the use of performance-based standards and tools that seek to incentivise, persuade and assist compliance.[30] This change might best be described as 'regulatory reconfiguration' rather than reform in some fundamental sense.[31]

So how did the regulatory capacities of the state expand in an era dominated by deregulatory rhetoric? The answer to this question is that the neo-liberalism and free market ideology of the 1980s led to a change in the style of governance, not a change in the level of governance; and that this change in style saw regulation emerge (somewhat paradoxically) as the dominant form of governance. As Majone observed some twenty years ago, modern Western governments moved from a positive state— in which governments intervened directly in order to achieve a range of social and economic goals—to a regulatory state—in which direct service delivery was increasingly outsourced or privatised to third parties which governments sought to control and influence through a mix of contractual arrangements, rules and regulations.[32] The era of privatisation also saw governments change their role from owner to overseer and, with that, the creation of new regulatory agencies to ensure the efficiency, effectiveness and social responsibility of the private sector organisations to which governments delegated their functions.[33] This has seen a reciprocal and mutually reinforcing relationship develop between capitalism and regulation,[34] a relationship that is particularly evident in the area of trade liberalisation which, despite its name, is built on thousands of pages of complex regulations designed to facilitate the free movement of goods, services and capital—a phenomenon Vogel describes as 'Freer Markets; More Rules'.[35]

A New Regulatory World

While the effects of the deregulation and better regulation reforms will continue to be debated, what cannot be denied is that over the past forty years there has been a fundamental change in how modern societies are governed. Regulation has emerged as a distinct and increasingly important mode of governance. As Talesh observes, '[s]ince the 1980s, governance through regulation has been the central reform across the United States, the European Union, Latin America, East Asia and developing countries'.[36] To this can be added Australia and New Zealand.[37] A number of commentators have sought to develop conceptual models to describe this new regulatory world. It is to three of the more prominent of these models that the book now turns.[38]

Regulatory State

We have already observed that Majone employed the phrase 'regulatory state' to describe the parallel changes of increased reliance by the state on markets and private providers to deliver traditional government services, and the accompanying increase in the use by the state of regulatory techniques to control and influence that service delivery.[39] Majone's use of the 'regulatory state' quickly became a popular label for describing the increased use by the state of regulation as a mode of governance, and one upon which other commentators were quick to build.[40]

Three features characterise Majone's regulatory state. First is the separation of policy-making functions (which are retained within the government bureaucracy) from service provision functions (which increasingly are outsourced to private providers) from regulatory functions (which increasingly are undertaken by independent, specialist regulatory agencies). Second is the increased reliance on formal rules, regulations and contracts to govern the relationships created by the separation of these once combined functions. Government departments utilise contracts, and regulatory agencies employ rules, to set, monitor and enforce standards upon third party service providers; and integrity regulation and new public management tools are employed to ensure the now separated state functions exercise their roles effectively, efficiently and in the public interest. And third, and as a result of the first two features, regulation (and the 'regulocracy') emerges as a distinct and prominent government function.[41]

Part of the regulatory state's appeal is that it serves as a convenient juxtaposition to the traditionally conceived of 'welfare' or 'provider' state.[42] However, use of 'regulatory state' in this way is potentially misleading. As Levi-Faur points out, the regulatory state and welfare state are not mutually exclusive. Not only can both coexist (no one label being capable of capturing the 'essence' of a state), but regulation also has a 'purpose', and one of those purposes can be to advance welfare related goals.[43] Moreover, the 'regulatory state' label risks unduly narrowing our focus. As Black points out, it adopts 'a state-centric, hierarchical model of government and regulation' that de-emphasises the prominent role played by non-state actors in the regulatory endeavour, and does not directly allow for multiple and overlapping state, non-state and even inter-state sites of governance.[44]

Regulatory Capitalism

The notion of regulation moving beyond formal state-centred rule-making and even national boundaries (and thus the regulatory state) was captured by Levi-Faur in the concept of 'regulatory capitalism'.[45] Regulatory capitalism reflects a new division of labour between state and society, not only through outsourcing and privatisation, but also through the increased delegation of regulatory responsibilities to autonomous expert regulatory agencies, civil society, business and the professions. It is a world in which these actors cooperate and combine to produce hybrid forms of regulation employing new regulatory technologies: in which 'statist regulation co-evolves with civil regulation; national regulation expands with international and global regulation; private regulation co-evolves and expands with public regulation; voluntary regulations expand with coercive ones; and the market itself is used or mobilized as a regulatory mechanism'.[46] It also is a world in which the development and spread of these new regulatory technologies are increasingly influenced by international networks of experts.

'Regulatory capitalism', like the regulatory state before it, quickly gained a strong foothold among regulatory scholars. For Brathwaite, 'regulatory capitalism' captured what was being seen at the time—'more capitalism; more regulation'[47]—a world in which 'capitalist markets had become more vibrant at the same time as regulation of markets had become more earnest'.[48] However, regulatory capitalism as a label or concept too has its limitations. The term implies a capitalist-centric view of the world. Its use is frequently associated with belief in markets as the best mechanism for maximising the public good. Yet much regulation today is based on a distrust of markets and capitalism: that regulation sometimes is required to adjust for their morally arbitrary (and undemocratic) outcomes.[49]

What is needed is a broader and more inclusive concept: one that does not marginalise the important roles played by non-state actors (as does the regulatory state) and does not confer too exulted a position on economic values and the market (as does regulatory capitalism). Such a concept can be found in the coupling of the regulatory and governance agendas.

Regulatory Governance

'Regulatory governance' eloquently captures both the growth and changing nature of regulation.[50] The marriage of regulation and governance reflects that regulation is the expanding part of governance,[51] and the policy preference of government in many areas of state activity.[52] Governments increasingly rely on regulation not only to oversee the provision of services by those actors to whom it has outsourced its responsibilities, but more broadly to steer and direct society through its more complex economic and social challenges.

Regulatory governance reflects that as regulation has grown in importance, it also has changed. Regulatory governance recognises that top-down 'command and control' regulatory models are too narrow and limited to deal with increasingly complex social and economic issues about which different audiences have different values, interests and perspectives. It recognises that for new and complex issues to be addressed effectively, the collaboration of a range of non-state actors (be they experts, public interest groups, professional and business organisations, or international organisations) is required.[53] It also recognises that while regulation is undertaken by or under the auspices of government, government is not the sole locus of regulatory activity. As Black observes, 'the "governance turn" . . . reveals a plethora of non-governmental actors at the national, supranational and global levels who are performing what had been traditionally seen as core "governmental" functions—welfare and regulation'.[54] Illustrative of this change has been the increase in hybrid, networked and polycentric regulatory regimes.[55]

Regulatory governance recognises that regulation today is both more diverse and increasingly complex, with regulatory functions being undertaken by a variety of different actors (public and private; state and non-state) across multiple sites (local, national and international) through a variety of different mechanisms (rule based and non-rule based). Regulatory governance is the most holistic and inclusive of the conceptual models advanced to capture the new regulatory world order, capturing the important roles played both by state and non-state actors, and by economic, social and democratic values. Regulatory governance is the lens through which this book views the regulatory endeavour.

Concluding Insights and Implications

This chapter began by tracing the rise of regulation as a distinct and increasingly important form of governance. The chapter observed that regulation's rise continued through an era dominated by deregulation rhetoric and, somewhat paradoxically, may have been accelerated by the neo-liberalism that accompanied it. Indeed, regulation emerged from the era of deregulation as strong as ever, albeit with a focus on doing it better. The golden age of regulation is not over; just maybe a little tarnished.

This chapter's historical journey revealed that from its earliest manifestations, regulation has been shaped by its economic, social and political environment. This has not changed. Regulation takes place in a complex and sometimes confused and contradictory world in which people simultaneously want freedom from government and protection of government; innovation and protection from innovation; rights without risks. It is no wonder modern governments find themselves 'constantly dangling in an uneasy equilibrium between competing values'.[56] How governments can achieve this equilibrium in a manner that is both effective and legitimate (credible and acceptable) is a focus of this book.

This chapter next surveyed the main conceptual models developed to describe the place of regulation within modern democratic liberal capitalist societies: regulatory state, regulatory capitalism and regulatory governance. Each model captures an important feature of the modern regulatory endeavour. The regulatory state encapsulates the emergence of regulation as a distinct and prominent government function; regulatory capitalism, the emergence of complex hybrid regulatory regimes and new regulatory techniques to govern the increasing dependence of capitalism and markets on regulation; and regulatory governance that societies increasingly are being governed through regulation and regulated through governance. Of these, regulatory governance was shown to best capture the essence of the modern regulatory endeavour—one in which governments do not only regulate top-down and hierarchically, but increasingly regulate cooperatively through networks of actors whom they engage and enlist in support of the regulatory endeavour.

Viewing the world through the lens of regulatory governance involves a shift in thinking: from regulation being state-based to being state-led; in which hierarchical state command and control regulation is not abandoned but operates as part of a broader suite of regulatory techniques undertaken by a more diverse set of regulatory actors.[57] Regulatory governance invites us to take a wide angle lens to our analysis of the regulatory endeavour—to examine it within the larger governance and public policy processes in which it is embedded and the broader economic, social, cultural and political context in which it takes place. It also invites us to think laterally about the actors, tools and institutional settings in and through which regulation can take place, and the possibilities this creates. This book takes up this invitation.

Notes

1. J B Condliffe, *The Commerce of Nations* (W W Norton, 1950) 27.
2. See generally, John Braithwaite and Peter Drahos, *Global Business Regulation* (Cambridge University Press, 2000).
3. Anthony I Ogus, *Regulation: Legal Form and Economic Theory* (Hart Publishing, 2004) 6.
4. Ibid 6–12; Anthony I Ogus, 'Regulatory Law: Some Lessons from the Past' (1992) 12 *Legal Studies* 1.
5. Penry Williams, *The Tudor Regime* (Oxford University Press, 1979) 144, cited in Ogus, 'Regulatory Law', above n 4, 4.
6. Edward L Glaeser and Andrei Shleifer, 'The Rise of the Regulatory State' (2003) 41 *Journal of Economic Literature* 401, 402.
7. Ogus, 'Regulatory Law', above n 4, 7–8; see also Marc T Law and Sukkoo Kim, 'The Rise of the American Regulatory State: A View from the Progressive Era' in D Levi-Faur (ed), *Handbook on the Politics of Regulation* (Edward Elgar, 2011) 113.
8. Cass R Sunstein, *After the Rights Revolution: Reconceiving the Regulatory State* (Harvard University Press, 1990) 18–24.
9. J Bradford De Long and Barry Eichengreen, 'The Marshall Plan: History's Most Successful Structural Adjustment Program' (Working Paper No 3899, National Bureau of Economic Research, November 1991).
10. Emblematic of this period was the creation in 1951 of the European Coal and Steel Community, which became the European Economic Community in 1958,

and the development in 1947 and subsequent expansion of the General Agreement on Tariffs and Trade.

11. Matthew Hilton, 'Consumers and the State since the Second World War' (2007) 661 *Annals of the American Academy of Political and Social Science 66.*

12. See Eric Windholz and Graeme A Hodge, 'Conceptualising Social and Economic Regulation: Implication for Modern Regulators and Regulatory Activity' (2012) 38 *Monash University Law Review* 212, on which this section draws.

13. Sunstein, *After the Rights Revolution,* above n 8.

14. Sam Peltzman, *Regulation and the Natural Progress of Opulence* (AEI-Brookings Joint Center for Regulatory Studies, 2005) 5. See also Ogus, *Regulation,* above n 3, 54.

15. Robert Kuttner, *Everything for Sale: The Virtues and Limits of Markets* (Alfred A Knopf, 1997) 282. See also: W Kip Viscusi and Ted Gayer, 'Safety at Any Price?' (2002) 25(3) *Regulation 54,* 59.

16. Ulrich Beck, *Risk Society: Towards New Modernity* (Sage Publications, 1992). See also: Anthony Giddens, 'Risk and Responsibility' (1999) 62 *Modern Law Review* 1.

17. Tony Blair, 'Compensation Culture' (Speech delivered at the Institute for Public Policy Research, University College London, 26 May 2005)<www.guardian. co.uk/politics/2005/may/26/speeches.media>; Regulation Taskforce, Parliament of Australia, *Rethinking Regulation: Report of the Taskforce on Reducing Regulatory Burdens on Business* (2006).

18. Christopher Hood and Martin Lodge, 'Pavlovian Innovation, Pet Solutions and Economizing on Rationality? Politicians and Dangerous Dogs' in J Black, M Lodge and M Thatcher (eds), *Regulatory Innovation: A Comparative Analysis* (Edward Elgar, 2005) 138; Christopher Hood, Henry Rothstein and Robert Baldwin, *The Government of Risk: Understanding Risk Regulation Regimes* (Oxford University Press, 2001) 4–5; James Q Wilson, 'The Politics of Regulation' in J Q Wilson (ed), *The Politics of Regulation* (Basic Books, 1980) 357, 376; Fiona Haines, Adam Sutton and Chris Platania-Phung, 'It's All about Risk, Isn't It? Science, Politics, Public Opinion and Regulatory Reform' (2007–2008) 10 *Flinders Journal of Law Reform* 435.

19. Michael Moran, 'The Frank Stacey Memorial Lecture: From Command State to Regulatory State?' (2000) 15(4) *Public Policy and Administration* 1, 10. See also: Jacint Jordana and David Levi-Faur, 'The Politics of Regulation in the Age of Governance' in J Jordana and D Levi-Faur (eds), *The Politics of Regulation: Institutions and Regulatory Reforms for the Age of Governance* (Edward Elgar, 2004) 1, 12–15.

20. Gerald Dworkin, 'Paternalism' in R A Wasserstrom (ed), *Morality and the Law* (Wadsworth, 1971) 107.

21. These theories are discussed under 'Private Interest Theories' in Chapter 3.

22. David Osborne and Ted Gaebler, *Reinventing Government: How the Entrepreneurial Spirit Is Transforming the Public Sector* (Plume, 1993).

23. Ewan Ferlie et al, *The New Public Management in Action* (Oxford University Press, 1996). See also: Eran Vigoda, 'New Public Management' in E M Berman (ed), *Encyclopedia of Public Administration and Public Policy* (CRC Press, 2nd ed, 2007) 1321.

24. Organisation for Economic Co-Operation and Development, *Recommendations of the Council on Improving the Quality of Government Regulation* (OECD, 9 March 1995); Mandelkern Group on Better Regulation, *Final Report* (European Commission, 13 November 2001).

25. The mindset that better regulation is less regulation continues to permeate the reform agenda, however, and is sometimes given expression, such as in the

United Kingdom's Better Regulation Task Force's (BRTF) 2005 report entitled *Regulation—Less Is More: Reducing Burdens, Improving Outcomes: A BRTF Report to the Prime Minister* (BRTF, March 2005).

26. Better regulation reforms are discussed in more detail in Chapter 6.
27. Scott H Jacobs, 'The Golden Age of Regulation' (13 November 2000) 1<www. regulations.am/uploads/Bibliography/The_Golden_Age_of_Regulation_by_ Scott_H_Jacobs.pdf>.
28. Jacint Jordana, David Levi-Faur and Xavier Fernandez i Marín, 'The Global Diffusion of Regulatory Agencies: Channels of Transfer and Stages of Diffusion' (2011) 44 *Comparative Political Studies* 1343.
29. Peter J May, 'Regulatory Regimes and Accountability' (2007) 1 *Regulation & Governance* 8, 8.
30. Shauhin Talesh, 'Public Law and Regulatory Theory' in C Ansell and J Torfing (eds), *Handbook on Theories of Governance* (Edward Elgar, 2016) 102, 104.
31. Neil Gunningham, 'Reconfiguring Environmental Regulation' in P Eliadis, M M Hill and M Howlett (eds), *Designing Government: From Instruments to Governance* (McGill-Queen's University Press, 2005) 333; Arie Freiberg, *The Tools of Regulation* (Federation Press, 2010) 23.
32. Giandomenico Majone, 'The Rise of the Regulatory State in Europe' (1994) 17 *West European Politics* 77; Giandomenico Majone, 'From the Positive to the Regulatory State: Causes and Consequences of Changes in Modes of Governance' (1997) 17 *Journal of Public Policy* 139.
33. David Levi-Faur, 'The Global Diffusion of Regulatory Capitalism' (2005) 598 *Annals of the American Academy of Political and Social Science* 12.
34. John Braithwaite, *Regulatory Capitalism: How It Works, Ideas for Making It Work Better* (Edward Elgar, 2008).
35. Steven Kent Vogel, *Freer Markets, More Rules: Regulatory Reform in Advanced Industrial Countries* (Cornell University Press, 1996). For example, each of the European Union's Single Market, the General Agreement on Tariffs and Trade and the Agreement on Trade-Related Aspects of Intellectual Property Rights is underpinned by literally thousands of pages of regulations, directives, technical standards and notification procedures.
36. Talesh, 'Public Law and Regulatory Theory', above n 30, 105 (references omitted).
37. Graeme Hodge, 'Revisiting State and Market through Regulatory Governance: Observations of Privatisations, Partnerships, Politics and Performance' (2012) 18 *New Zealand Business Law Quarterly* 251, 263.
38. For a fuller list of some of these different theories, see Talesh, 'Public Law and Regulatory Theory', above n 30. The three chosen for discussion in this chapter are those that have garnered the most currency in the academic literature and which have clear theoretical differences.
39. Majone was not the first person to employ the term 'regulatory state'. It has long been used as a label for the growth of administrative forms of regulation, especially in the United States: see e.g., James E Anderson, *The Emergence of the Modern Regulatory State* (Public Affairs Press, 1962). Majone was, however, the first person to employ the term to describe this phenomenon: David Levi-Faur, 'The Odyssey of the Regulatory State: From a "Thin" Monomorphic Concept to a "Thick" and Polymorphic Concept' (2013) 35 *Law & Policy* 29, 31–6.
40. See, e.g., Moran, 'The Frank Stacey Memorial Lecture', above n 19; Glaeser and Shleifer, 'The Rise of the Regulatory State', above n 6; Ian Bartle and Peter Vass, 'Self-Regulation within the Regulatory State: Towards a New Regulatory Paradigm?' (2007) 85 *Public Administration* 885; Levi-Faur, 'The Odyssey of the Regulatory State', above n 39.

41. Levi-Faur, 'The Odyssey of the Regulatory State', above n 39, 37.
42. Majone, 'From the Positive to the Regulatory State', above n 33; Julia Black, 'Critical Reflections on Regulation' (2002) 27 *Australian Journal of Legal Philosophy* 1, 14.
43. Levi-Faur, 'The Odyssey of the Regulatory State', above n 39, 41–6. See also Deborah Mabbett, 'The Regulatory Rescue of the Welfare State' in D Levi-Faur (ed), *Handbook on the Politics of Regulation* (Edward Elgar, 2011) 215.
44. Julia Black, 'Tensions in the Regulatory State' (2007) *Public Law* 58, 58. See also Hodge, 'Revisiting State and Market through Regulatory Governance', above n 37, 266.
45. Levi-Faur, 'The Global Diffusion of Regulatory Capitalism', above n 33.
46. David Levi-Faur, 'Regulation & Regulatory Governance' (Jerusalem Papers in Regulation & Governance Working Paper No 1, February 2010) 24.
47. Braithwaite, *Regulatory Capitalism*, above n 34, 11.
48. Ibid xi.
49. Windholz and Hodge, 'Conceptualising Social and Economic Regulation', above n 12, 223–4.
50. See generally: Martin Minogue and Ledivinia V Carino, *Regulatory Governance in Developing Countries* (Edward Elgar, 2006).
51. John Braithwaite, Cary Coglianese and David Levi-Faur, 'Can Regulation and Governance Make a Difference?' (2007) 1 *Regulation & Governance* 1, 1.
52. David Levi-Faur, 'Regulation and Regulatory Governance' in D Levi-Faur (ed), *Handbook on the Politics of Regulation* (Edward Elgar, 2011) 3, 16; Hodge, 'Revisiting State and Market through Regulatory Governance', above n 37, 263.
53. Braithwaite, Coglianese and Levi-Faur, 'Can Regulation and Governance Make a Difference?', above n 51. See also Talesh, 'Public Law and Regulatory Theory', above n 30.
54. Julia Black, 'Constructing and Contesting Legitimacy and Accountability in Polycentric Regulatory Regimes' (2008) 2 *Regulation & Governance* 137, 141.
55. See, e.g., Julia Black, 'Decentring Regulation: Understanding the Role of Regulation and Self-Regulation in a "Post-Regulatory" World' (2001) 54 *Current Legal Problems* 103; Black, 'Critical Reflections on Regulation', above n 42; Christine Parker, 'The Pluralization of Regulation' (2008) 9 *Theoretical Inquiries in Law* 349.
56. Steve Van de Walle, 'International Comparisons of Public Sector Performance' (2009) 11 *Public Management Review* 39, 45.
57. John Yasuda, 'Regulatory Governance' in C Ansell and J Torfing (eds), *Handbook on Theories of Governance* (Edward Elgar, 2016) 428, 428–9.

Part II

Regulatory Theory, Concepts and Constructs

3 Theories of Regulation

As regulation has emerged as a distinct and increasingly prominent form of governance, so too have the theories that purport to justify and explain it. These theories range from technical justifications for government intervention to explanations of motivating forces; from statements of the ideal to statements of realpolitik; from those that focus on the preferences and interests of regulatory actors to those that focus on the nature and impact of the institutions through which they act; and from those that view the regulatory process positively and operating in the public interest to those that view it more darkly and operating for the benefit of vested interests. Understanding these theories is important. They help us to understand how regulation has evolved until now, and how it might evolve in the future. Understanding different theories also gives us the capacity to question our own beliefs and perceptions, and to think more broadly and laterally. This chapter categorises these theories into four sets: public interest theories, private interest theories, institutional theories and ideational theories.[1] Each set of theories is considered in turn, after which the chapter concludes by examining how the different theories might be combined to produce a framework through which to better understand the regulatory world around us.

Public Interest Theories

Public interest theories emanate from the basic proposition that the fundamental task of government is to act in the 'public interest'. But what is the 'public interest' and how is it defined? At one level, it is tempting to dismiss the term as nothing more than a rhetorical device used by governments to clothe their decisions in legitimacy, and by non-government actors to mask their self-interest. As Shafritz and Russell observe, no one would advocate for public policy that was not in the public interest.[2] However, to so easily place the term in the realm of grand rhetoric is to suggest that it is devoid of significant content. This is not the case. The public interest is central to the regulatory endeavor. 'It goes to the heart of why governments regulate, what they regulate, and the manner with which they regulate'.[3] Yet for such an important term, the public interest is more often invoked than described; its meaning assumed rather than defined.[4] Having said that, however, a review of the literature reveals three broad approaches to conceptualising the public interest: (a) an economic (or market-orientated) approach; (b) a social (or value-orientated) approach; and (c) a risk control approach. Each of these approaches is discussed below.

Economic (or Market-Orientated) Approach

The economic (or market-orientated) approach to conceptualising the 'public interest' adopts a utilitarian approach and assumes that what is good for society is the aggregation of individual preferences given expression through market behaviour.[5] This approach views the market as the most legitimate mechanism for the effective production of goods and services, and for their efficient allocation between members of society. According to economic conceptions of the public interest, regulation is a second-best alternative to market-based solutions—a 'regrettable means of correcting market failures'—something to be minimised.[6]

Market failures or imperfections with respect to which regulation may be an appropriate remedy can be categorised into three broad groups.[7] First, there are those that reduce competition or economic efficiency within a specific market. There are numerous types of these failures and imperfections. In this section, we consider five of the more common imperfections. The first type are monopolies and oligopolies, where one or a few suppliers dominate a market, enabling them to maximise profits by charging prices higher than would be the case in a competitive market. Monopolies can be the result of competitive excellence (think IBM and Microsoft), or can be 'natural' in the sense that the costs of duplicating their infrastructure are prohibitive (think water pipes and electricity transmission wires). There are a number of ways government can respond to monopolies. They can apply competition or anti-trust laws to break them up or to prohibit the misuse of their market power. They can impose price controls that prevent them charging more than would be the case in a competitive market, and they can require them to make their infrastructure available to competitors. All of these measures have been used to varying degrees in different markets. For example, telecommunication monopolies have been broken up, computer hardware and software providers forced to make their platforms available to competitors, and utilities such as electricity and water often operate under regimes where price increases need to be justified and approved.[8]

Another common form of market failure are information asymmetries. These exist where one party to a transaction does not have adequate information with which to make a fully informed decision. These information mis-matches commonly exist between consumers and manufacturers, and investors and companies. Product labelling laws and mandatory and continuous disclosure obligations imposed on listed companies are examples of regulatory mechanisms employed to correct for this type of failure.[9]

However, even in situations where parties are possessed of all the information needed to make an informed decision, some are nevertheless unable to do so. This can be the case because of unequal bargaining power (as might exist between some manufacturers and consumers, and management and workers), vulnerability (as might exist with people who are financially desperate) or incompetence (as might exist with minors and the mentally ill). Regulation that imposes minimum terms into consumer and employment contracts and that prohibits people entering into contracts without independent legal and financial advice are examples of regulation designed to correct for these failures.[10]

Other efficiency reducing market imperfections include coordination and rationalisation problems where individual behaviour, left unregulated, would cause chaos or lead to a depletion of finite natural resources. Road and air traffic rules and fishing and logging quotas are examples of regulation designed to address these failures. Another common efficiency reducing imperfection are moral hazard problems. Moral hazards arise where persons choose to take more risks in the knowledge that someone else will bear the costs of those risks. The concept of 'moral hazard' initially arose in the insurance industry to describe the tendency of insured persons to engage in risky behaviours comforted by the knowledge that they are insured for, and therefore shielded from, the costs of those behaviours.[11] More recently it has been used to describe the marketing of subprime loans by lending institutions that considered themselves too big for governments to let fail.[12] Moral hazards can be corrected for by adjusting insurance premiums for past behaviours and having significant excesses, and by requiring persons wishing to engage in high-risk activities to be licensed or to otherwise obtain the permission of the state.[13]

Next, there are market failures or imperfections that reduce economic efficiency by conferring benefits or imposing costs on persons not involved in the transaction that gave rise to them. Economists refer to these as externalities (because they impact persons external to the transaction). Externalities can be positive or negative. An example of a positive externality is vaccinations. Vaccinations protect both those vaccinated and those with whom vaccinated persons interact against contagious diseases. However, in circumstances where the persons to be vaccinated are solely responsible for the costs of being vaccinated, and the wider community makes no contribution to those costs, fewer people are likely to be able to afford to be vaccinated, thus undermining public health. Vaccinations also are sometimes referred to as a merit good. Merit goods are goods that society decides people should have on the basis of need, rather than an ability and willingness to pay. Education is another example of a merit good. Governments generally encourage the consumption of these goods by both subsidising and compelling their use.[14]

An example of a negative externality, on the other hand, is pollution. Pollution has a negative impact on the environment and neighbouring communities. The costs of these negative impacts often are not factored into the costs of production, however, resulting in more polluting activity taking place than would be the case if fully costed. Pollution taxes and emissions trading schemes that compel businesses to internalise the costs of polluting activities are examples of regulation to correct for these failures.[15]

The third group of market failures prevent a market from forming in the first place. 'Public goods' are an example of this. Public goods are goods that once produced, people cannot be prevented from consuming. Examples include defence, police and other emergency services. The inability to prevent people who did not pay for the good from consuming it ('free riding') means it is unlikely these goods will be produced by private markets, thus necessitating government intervention. This intervention generally takes the form of government providing these goods itself, or outsourcing their provision to the private sector, which it then regulates to ensure their provision aligns with the public interest.[16]

Market failure is a necessary but insufficient basis for regulation. Two other conditions also need to be satisfied for regulation to be justified under an economic (or market-orientated) approach. First, private forms of market failure correction (e.g. private law remedies) must be more costly or less effective than regulatory intervention. That is, the market must be unable to heal itself before government intervention is warranted. In this regard, private law remedies themselves are provided through a market (for legal services) that itself can fail or have imperfections. The high cost of access to the justice system, and the slowness with which its wheels can turn, are two oft cited imperfections that commentators rightfully argue make it unable to correct for failures or imperfections in other markets efficiently and effectively.[17] Second, the costs and risks of regulatory intervention must be less than the costs and risks of the market failure. In this regard, market failure theories need to be tempered by considerations of regulatory failure. In deciding whether government regulation is appropriate, it is not sufficient simply to demonstrate that the market is operating imperfectly. What also needs to be demonstrated is that regulation will be effective in addressing the market imperfections and will not produce costs and unintended consequences that outweigh its intended benefits.[18]

An economic (or market-orientated) approach treats regulation as a technical issue to be undertaken by technical experts employing technical calculation methods such as cost-benefit analyses. However, treating regulation as a mere technical process risks masking important social considerations.[19] Markets do not operate in a vacuum insulated from broader societal values. Decisions to set wealth maximisation as a societal priority, to rely upon markets as the vehicle for maximising that wealth and to correct for an externality are all value judgements.[20] Moreover, there can be compelling social reasons for government intervention, even in a perfectly operating market. This leads us to the next approach of conceptualising the 'public interest'.

Social (or Value-Orientated) Approach

The second approach to conceptualising the 'public interest' defines it in terms of attaining socially desirable outcomes different to and better than those produced by an efficiently operating market economy.[21] These socially desirable outcomes might be based on human rights and democratic principles;[22] or broader societal values such as justice, equity and fairness,[23] social cohesion and solidarity,[24] or enhancing trust.[25] Examples of social regulation include equal opportunity and anti-discrimination regulation (advancing human rights), political donation and advertising regulation (advancing democratic principles), and regulation designed to correct for the negative effects of economic activity such as pollution, dangerous products and unsafe working conditions (advancing broader societal values).

This approach views regulation positively: as a first choice in ordering society—not a second preference to efficiently operating markets. Pollution, for example, is to be addressed, not because it is an economic negative externality, but because as a society, we desire clean air, clean water and clean land. Under this approach, markets are no longer the ideal. Rather, they are simply one mechanism that governments can choose to employ (with or without modification) to serve society's broader interests.[26] Implicit in this approach is that markets cannot always be relied upon or trusted to produce socially desirable outcomes.[27] Indeed, this approach views the term 'market failure' somewhat as a misnomer—that some problems are caused not because the market has 'failed' but because it is operating exactly as expected to maximise each individual's utility (wealth).[28] As Braithwaite observed: 'Markets do not make moral judgements. If they work more efficiently, they will more efficiently produce bads as well as goods'.[29]

Unlike the economic or market-orientated approach that is traditionally characterised as a technical process undertaken by technical experts employing technical calculation methods, a social or value-orientated approach to determining the public interest is an inherently political judgement. While technical calculation methods can (and in many cases should) inform that judgment,[30] it ultimately is made employing political calculation methods such as consultation, deliberation and negotiation to balance and, if necessary, trade-off sometimes conflicting societal values.[31]

Risk Control Approach

Our third way of conceiving of the public interest is risk control. Risk control increasingly is the language with which regulatory decisions are explained and justified,[32] with some commentators going so far as to argue 'that stability is the state's primary purpose and risk management its distinctive feature'.[33]

Haines points out that risk has three dimensions—actuarial, socio-cultural and political.[34] The actuarial dimension is the one most commonly associated with risk-based regulation. Actuarial definitions of 'risk' centre on the possibility of adverse events and the loss and injury that flow from them, and are often presented as a mathematical formula. The following is typical:

> Risk = Probability an event will occur × Magnitude   (Equation 3.1)
> (severity) of harm should the event occur

The two variables in the formula reflect the two foci of risk-based regulation: (1) eliminating or reducing the likelihood or probability of the event occurring; and (2) lessening the severity of harm should the event occur. Risk-based frameworks are today central to the regulation of numerous sectors including the environment, food safety, financial markets and workplace health and safety, to name but a few.[35]

This actuarial conception of risk (and of risk-based regulation) implies that it is something capable of measurement, or at least estimation (quantitatively and/or qualitatively) using scientific methods. However, measuring risk is not as scientific as it first appears. First, measuring risk is an estimation process heavily dependent upon its methodology. In some cases, small changes in assumptions and parameters can lead to significant variations in risk estimates. Viscusi and Gayer, for example, argue that the principle of 'conservatism' leads governments to operate on the basis of the 'worst case scenario' when faced with uncertainty and to choose assumptions that lead to higher assessments of risk, overestimation of the benefits of regulation and a misallocation of resources.[36]

Second, 'the concept of risk is strongly shaped by human minds and cultures'.[37] These are its socio-cultural dimensions. Perceptions of risk have an emotional as well as an intellectual logic.[38] People have a heightened sensitivity to risks that threaten social cohesion and their individual sense of security and belonging (a sensitivity that increases with their sense of vulnerability).[39] People also tend to overestimate risks with small probabilities that impact them directly, or that receive significant media attention.[40] This can lead to individuals holding beliefs about risk that differ (sometimes substantially) from empirical evidence and expert determinations. While to the expert these differing beliefs may appear irrational, they nevertheless can be strongly held and call for reassurance from government.

This leads to risk's third and political dimension. Political parties seek election; governments re-election. A government's prospects of re-election are dependent in part on its ability to manage the economy, maintain social cohesion and make people feel safe and secure. Events and occurrences with the potential to jeopardize a government's ability to discharge these functions—or perceptions of its ability to discharge these functions— constitute a political risk to that government's re-election, and potentially to the legitimacy of the system of government a whole. The need to manage this political risk can lead governments to regulate in response to sometimes irrational perceptions of risk.[41] The OECD refers to government action in response to perceived risks as 'symbolic public action'.[42] However, while arguably symbolic, it is not necessarily irrational. Governments can rationally regulate in response to irrational assessments of risk, especially when the public respond to their fears by avoiding welfare-enhancing activities.[43] A case on point is the 1989 European Commission ban on the importation of beef from cattle that had received growth hormones. The Commission maintained the ban in defiance of a World Trade Organisation ruling that it was not supported by scientific risk assessments, arguing the ban was justified to address consumer anxiety that was undermining confidence in the food safety regulatory system and leading consumers to avoid all beef products.[44] Other examples include government responses to terrorism and attacks by dangerous dogs.[45]

While much of the literature focuses on actuarial risk, the above makes clear that all three risk dimensions play an important role in determining the nature and shape of risk-based regulation. Indeed, Haines makes the point that socio-cultural and political dimensions of risk determine which issues are addressed consistent with the actuarial risk—with socio-cultural and political risk assessments sometimes resulting in either too hard or too soft a treatment compared to expert assessments of the actuarial risk.[46]

Summing up Public Interest Theories

The simple question with which this section began—what is the 'public interest'—has no simple answer. Our examination of public interest theories reveals there are varied and conflicting conceptions of when regulation is justified in the public interest. These are summarised in Table 3.1.

Within each approach there is ample room for different views and perspectives. Proponents of market-orientated approaches can differ about the existence and nature of market failures and imperfections; proponents of value-orientated approaches can disagree about the priority to be given to different values; and with respect to risk-based regulation, people's assessments of, and appetite for, risk can (and do) differ. All of this means that regulation in the public interest is more complicated than suggested by its simple yet positive label. Baldwin, Cave and Lodge were correct when they observed that 'regulation generally takes place amidst a clashing of images of the public interest'.[47] Different groups with different interests will hold and promote different conceptions of the public interest. Yet public interest theories tend to ignore the role played by these competing interests and assume a highly benevolent (some say naïve) view of the regulatory policy process.[48] Public interest theories assume that proponents of regulation advocate for the public interest and not their own private interests; that politicians act altruistically in the public interest on the basis of evidence dispassionately and objectively assessed; and that the public servants

Table 3.1 Public Interest Theories

Theory	Justification	Examples
Economic (market-orientated)	**Regulation to correct for market failures or imperfections**	
Monopolies (oligopolies)	To ensure persons with market power do not misuse that power to charge excessive prices and/or to prevent competition	Competition (anti-trust) regulation of telecommunications; computer hardware and software providers Pricing regulation of utilities
Information asymmetries	To ensure parties to transactions have adequate information with which to make an informed decision	Product labelling laws Company disclosure requirements
Unequal bargaining power, vulnerability incompetence	To ensure weaker parties to a transaction are protected against unscrupulous or unconscionable conduct	Minimum contractual terms Third party advice requirements
Coordination/rationalisation problems	To ensure efficient use of public and/or scarce resources	Road rules Fishing quotas
Moral hazard problems	To guard against people engaging in risky activities because they do not incur the full costs of their actions	Risk-rated insurance Licensing/permissioning schemes
Positive externalities (merit goods)	To ensure goods with societal benefits are supplied and consumed in appropriate quantities	Subsidised and compelled vaccinations and education
Negative externalities	To minimise the damaging effect of industrial activity by ensuring the full costs of those effects are factored into the costs of production	Pollution taxes Emission trading schemes
Public goods	To provide (or regulate the provision of) goods that the market will not provide (or not provide in a manner consistent with the public interest)	Defence Emergency services
Social (or value-orientated)	**Regulation to attain socially desirable outcomes**	
Human rights	To secure and protect individual human rights	Equal opportunity/anti-discrimination regulation
Democratic principles	To ensure 'equality of citizenship'	Political donations and advertising regulation
Broader social values	To ensure a just, equal, fair, socially cohesive and trusting community	Health and safety, environment and product safety regulation

Risk control	Regulation to address risks to the economy, social cohesion or safety and security	
Actuarial	To reduce the likelihood or probability of an adverse event occurring and/or the severity of harm should the event occur	Food safety, environment and workplace health and safety regulation
Socio-cultural & Political	To address risks to the government's (and system of government's) legitimacy by reducing perceptions of risk that threaten social cohesion and an individual's sense of security, safety and belonging	Bans on hormone treated beef Terrorism laws Dangerous dogs regulation

and experts who advise them, and the regulators who implement their decisions, are trustworthy, independent, appropriately skilled and motivated by the public good unaffected by their own beliefs, values, interests and ideologies. However, doubts exist as to whether these conditions hold true, with people able to point to many instances where regulation appears to have operated for the benefit of private interests, and not the public interest. The impact of private interests on the regulatory endeavour is the focus of the next section.

Private Interest Theories

Private interest theories posit that regulation emerges, not from a benevolent pursuit of the 'public interest', but from the actions of individuals and groups motivated to maximise their (private) self-interest.[49] Over time, a number of different private interest theories have evolved, each with its own emphasis and focus. Two of the more extreme theories are capture theory and public choice theory. Combined, they paint a dark picture of the regulatory endeavour. A less dark and arguably more realistic version is interest group theory. Each of these theories is discussed below.

Capture Theory

Capture theories analogise regulatory decision-making to market decision-making: they treat legislative and regulatory institutions as an economy in which regulation is a 'good' which is 'demanded' and 'supplied' according to the same basic principles governing the demand and supply of ordinary economic goods. Posner described the approach best when he said 'regulation [is] a product allocated in accordance with basic principles of supply and demand . . . [and] other things being equal, we can expect a product to be supplied to those who value it the most'.[50] Initial capture theories posited that regulation is supplied to—captured by—businesses to advance their commercial interests. However, there is no reason why regulation cannot be captured by other interest groups and operate primarily for the benefit of the causes they advocate.[51] In fact, during the deregulation era of the Reagan and Thatcher governments, regulation often was portrayed as the product of capture by trade unions and other special interest groups.[52]

There are two broad types of capture theories—point of origin theories and over time theories. Stigler's 'theory of economic regulation' is a classic example of the former. Stigler argues that 'as a rule, regulation is acquired by industry and is designed and operated primarily for its benefit'.[53] According to Stigler, regulation offers industry a mechanism through which to erect barriers to control the entry and growth of new rivals, thereby securing and protecting oligopolistic profits and windfall gains against competition (what economists call 'regulatory rents'). This theory has been applied to explain industry's support of entry controls and price regulation in a variety of industries, including transportation (airlines, railways, ocean shipping and taxi services); insurance, banking and stockbroking; broadcasting; utilities; and the legal and medical professions.[54] Capture theory also has been applied to deregulation (as well as regulation). Peltzman, for example, argues there is a point at which initially sought after regulation becomes a constraint on industry (especially when the industry is facing declining demand or exogenous challenges such as rapidly changing technology), leading it to advocate for (and capture) a return to its pre-regulation environment.[55]

Over time theories, on the other hand, allow for regulation initially being produced in the public interest, but posit that the regulator is eventually captured over time (and sometimes, in a very short time). Three broad causative mechanisms are advanced to explain over time capture. First there is direct capture, where the regulator knowingly and intentionally acts in the regulated industry's best interests, either because of bribery or corruption, or because they believe doing so is the best way to curry favour (or avoid conflict) with the government of the day.[56] Next there is cognitive or cultural capture, where the regulator unknowingly and unintentionally thinks and acts like the regulated industry.[57] This often is the result of a comparative lack of industry and technical expertise that makes governments and regulators reliant on the regulated industry's know-how and worldview with respect to both the design of the regulatory regime and its effective implementation. And third there are capture theories that focus on regulators losing their regulatory zeal as they age. The most prominent of these is Bernstein's 'life-cycle' regulatory theory.[58] According to Bernstein, as regulators age, the political and community support that gave birth to the regulator dissipates, lethargy sets in and the regulator loses its initial zeal and enthusiasm. Stability and predictability become more valued, there is increasing reliance on precedents and procedures, and little innovation, leading the regulator to give greater weight to the needs and interests of, and eventually to be captured by, the industry it is designed to regulate.[59] Over time capture theories have been applied to explain a number of recent regulatory failures, including the BP Deepwater Horizon oil spill in the Gulf of Mexico and the global financial crisis.[60]

Capture theories (or maybe more correctly, the proponents of capture theories) have been criticised for being too 'quick to see capture as the explanation for almost any regulatory problem'.[61] There is some truth to this: capture rarely is the only factor explaining regulatory failure, and focusing on it can mask other more significant causes. At the same time, however, capture is real and a threat to regulation in the public interest. Capture theories also have been criticised for focusing almost exclusively on the intent and actions of the regulated industry, and failing to attach appropriate weight to the interests and motivations of regulators and other interested groups. These criticisms are addressed by the other private interest theories considered in this chapter: public choice theory and interest group theory.

Public Choice Theory

Public choice theory starts from the assumption that individuals are self-interested utility maximisers. The theory then applies that assumption with equal force to politicians, public servants and regulators, as it does to private actors. Thus, according to public choice theory, politicians, public servants and regulators seek to advance their own private interest, and not the public interest.

In the case of politicians, public choice theory posits they are primarily motivated by a desire to be elected (and then re-elected). They are therefore interested in obtaining the resources to ensure this happens, being votes from the electorate and campaign donations from private individuals and groups. This, it is argued, leaves them susceptible to being bought or unduly influenced by private interests able to provide them with these resources.[62] Political public choice theories come in a variety of shades, from very dark versions pursuant to which politicians act exclusively for the benefit of vested interests, through to lighter (more grey) versions that allow for some (albeit marginal) public interest element. Peltzman, for example, acknowledges that as long as consumers can offer some votes, satisfaction of business interests to the exclusion of others will not, in general, be the dominant political strategy.[63] Public choice theory has been used to explain trade policies that protect the interests of pharmaceutical companies, as well as perceived lenient policies towards gambling, for example.[64]

In the case of public servants and regulators, public choice theory posits that they are interested in securing influence and prominence—both individually and organisationally. At an individual level, this is measured principally in terms of personal power, prestige and career progression.[65] Downs, for example, differentiates between two groups and five types of public servants by their susceptibility to engage in 'public choice' behaviour.

The first group comprises 'purely self-interested officials'. Within this group there are two types of officials: 'climbers' who seek to acquire and maximise their personal power, income and prestige; and 'conservers' whose focus is on retaining and protecting the power, income and prestige they already have. The second group are 'mixed-motive officials'. These officials combine self-interest and loyalty to larger values. Within this group are three types of officials: 'zealots' who are loyal to their own perspective of the organisation's goals, and who seek power to give effect to that perspective; 'advocates' who are devoted to the organisation's goals, and who seek power to influence the manner with which those goals are given effect; and 'statesmen' who are loyal to society as a whole, and desire power to influence national policies and actions.[66]

At an organisational level, public servant and regulator influence and prominence is measured primarily in terms of budget size or bureau shape. Niskansen, for example, argues that bureaucrats try to maximise their budgets to increase their prestige (and own salaries). This, Niskansen argues, leads them to maximise the quantity of functions they provide—the greater the size of the functions they provide, the greater their budget.[67] The crudeness of this theory (that big is always better) led others to develop more refined theories. Dunleavy, for example, argues that senior government officials focus not on budget maximisation, but on bureau-shaping. According to Dunleavy, bureaucrats seek to maximise their status through the quality of their work. This leads them to reshape their bureaus to focus on the work that their superiors (and they) value the most, and to transfer to other agencies functions that are inconsistent with, or ancillary to, the ideal shaped bureau.[68]

Other public choice theorists explain public servant and regulator self-interest by reference to the 'revolving door' that sees individuals move between government and industry, and back again. These 'revolving door' theories postulate that individuals who have moved from industry to government are likely to be friendly to industry because they have been socialised in, and adopted, the industry's worldview.[69] The position is more complicated in the case of individuals moving from government to industry, however. One view is that these individuals will deal with industry leniently in order to build relationships with prospective employers;[70] whereas others argue that the prospect of a post-government industry job could, in certain circumstances, incentivise regulators to be more aggressive, as a mechanism to demonstrate competence and create demand for their services.[71]

Other commentators argue that some public servants and regulators 'are more risk averse than imperialistic', and that they prioritise autonomy, stability and security over influence and prominence.[72] This risk aversion can manifest itself in two ways. First, risk aversion can make public servants and regulators reluctant to enter new fields that are complex or in respect of which their presence is contentious and contested. Perez, for example, recently wrote of how the three main social systems through which *ex post* judgments of regulatory decisions are made—law (with its focus on outcomes, and less so on intentions and conduct), politics (with its blame and buck-passing culture) and the mass media (with its focus on villains and victims, and avoidance of complexity)—can combine to create an environment that encourages passivity, over-cautiousness and defensive tactics on the part of regulators.[73] On the other hand, once a public servant or regulator enters a field, risk aversion can see it respond to risk with a proliferation of rules and activity to protect it from being accused of having done nothing. Wilson calls this 'covering your flanks';[74] Bardach and Kagan call it 'covering your arse'.[75] The ongoing risk of a crisis or disaster then makes it difficult to remove protective regulation once made, lest it be perceived by some as a decision by government to expose citizens to risk, or because of the consequences (real and political) should a deregulated risk materialise injuring people or causing damage. Bardach states that '[i]t is as though protective regulation were governed by a ratchet mechanism that allows it to move upward but never, or at least infrequently and only by small degrees, downward'.[76]

Public choice theories have been criticised for their lack of supporting empirical evidence. Christensen, for example, recently observed that while the underpinning logic of these theories is plausible, they are unsupported by rigorous empirical tests of their theoretical claims,[77] echoing the comments of Dunsire et al some twenty years earlier that 'public choice theory is strong on a priori reasoning but short on empiricism'.[78] Notwithstanding this, public choice theories remain popular and continue to underpin deregulatory and better regulatory agendas. They also frame how a number of commentators see politicians, public servants and regulators responding to pressure from different interest groups—which brings us to the third (and last) private interest theory considered in this chapter.

Interest Group Theory

Interest group theories posit that regulation is the product of competition between different self-interested groups. An early proponent of this view was Becker, who built on Stigler's and Peltzman's theory of economic regulation to demonstrate how private interests organise themselves into groups to exert pressure on the political process to grant themselves benefits, including favourable regulation.[79] According to Becker, a group's influence is a product of its size (the number of votes it can represent) and its ability to mobilise those votes. The latter, in turn, is influenced by the value and importance members of the group attach to the issue and their homogeneity (the confidence that members of the group will act as one and in a manner consistent with that group's cause). Thus, according to Becker, compact well-organised groups are better placed than broad diffuse groups to influence politicians and regulators to design and implement regulations consistent with their interests.

Interest group theory is most commonly thought of as a competition for political and regulatory influence between sectional interests (e.g. industry and professional associations) and those representing 'causes' or ideologies (e.g. environmentalists and consumer rights groups). In this regard, and consistent with Becker's theory, early studies suggested that well-organised business groups prevailed over less organised and more diffuse consumer and environmentalist groups. However, more recent studies show that with the formation of well-organised and well-funded special interest groups (and, in some cases, coalitions of special interest groups) representing consumers and environmentalists, some balance has been restored.[80]

Over time, a number of different models or typographies have been put forward to explain and describe the different patterns of interest group conflict associated with policy-making. Of these, Wilson's typology that classifies policies according to the manner with which their benefits and costs are distributed is particularly instructive.[81] Wilson observed that both the benefits and costs of a policy can be either diffuse (widely distributed) or concentrated (tightly held). From this, Wilson identified four types of politics, his thesis being that 'policies determine politics'. Wilson's first type is *client politics*. Client politics occurs where the benefits of a policy are concentrated in the hands of a comparatively small homogenous group (e.g. industry; profession) and the costs are dispersed across a large heterogeneous group (e.g. consumers; taxpayers). In this situation, the beneficiaries of the policy have an incentive to organise themselves to advocate for the policy (be it more or less regulation), whereas those on whom the cost is borne (which on a per capita basis is low) have no incentive to organise themselves to oppose the policy. The result is that the interest group in favour of the policy dominates debate on it. Wilson describes the creation of the US Federal Communications Commission as an example of client politics. It enabled radio and television stations to secure property rights over broadcast frequencies at the expense of consumers.

The opposite of client politics is *entrepreneurial politics*. Here, the costs of the policy are concentrated and the benefits diffuse. The result is that debate is dominated by an interest group hostile to the policy goals. Policy change in this situation requires a skilled and strong 'political entrepreneur' either to galvanise the diffuse beneficiaries, or to obtain change for their benefit in the face of opposition from the dominant interest group. Wilson gives as an example of this Ralph Nader's championing of new vehicle safety standards in the face of opposition from US automotive manufacturers.

Wilson's third type of politics is *interest group politics*, where both the benefits and costs of the policy are concentrated, leading to the creation of two rival interest groups. In this situation, the policy outcome is impacted strongly by the comparative strength and resources of the competing groups. The struggle between unions and management over workplace health and safety is an example of interest group politics. Wilson's final type is *majoritarian politics*, where both benefits and costs are diffuse, no important interest groups form and the policy outcome generally follows voter preferences. Wilson recently cited marriage equality as an example of majoritarian politics.[82]

The extent to which these patterns of conflict are applicable to regulatory policy is debatable. Levi-Faur, for example, argues that the patterns of political conflict associated with regulatory policy differ from those espoused by Wilson because the benefits and, in particular, the costs of regulation, are less visible and more opaque.[83] To the extent this is true, however, the lack of transparency arguably has the same effect as if that benefit or cost was diffuse, namely it is less likely that an interest group will form to act in response.

What is important from this discussion, however, is the broader observation that regulatory policies entail political conflict, and that regulatory decision-making is inherently political. This makes the role played by politicians, public servants and regulators mediating competition between different interest groups especially critical. Early proponents of interest group theories assigned to politicians, public servants and regulators a largely benign role. They viewed them primarily as neutral conduits and mechanical aggregators of the preferences and demands of private interest groups, seeking 'to accommodate—to the extent possible—the varying demands placed upon government by competing groups'.[84] Others, however, merge interest group theory with public choice theory and are less generous. According to these versions, politicians, public servants and regulators are entrepreneurs who broker compromises and form coalitions to advance their own interests, using regulation to accommodate some interests and to appease others.[85]

Summing up Private Interest Theories

In this section we have explored three versions of private interest theory: capture theory, public choice theory and interest group theory. These are summarized in Table 3.2.

Each of the private interest theories is premised on the assumption that people are essentially self-interested utility maximisers: that businesses act to maximise profits; politicians act to maximise electoral votes; and public servants and regulators act to maximise or protect their influence. The extent to which this assumption holds true is a matter of significant debate. While self-interest does have an influence (and arguably a strong influence) on human behaviour, it is an over-simplification to posit it as the only or main motivation. Individuals are not simply economic beings. As Boston reminds us, they also are 'political, cultural and moral beings who inhabit an economic system which is profoundly influenced by, and in a sense dependent upon, the attitudes, habits, beliefs, aspirations, ideals, and ethical standards of its members'.[86] Businesses today increasingly are cognisant that their ability to make profits over the long term is dependent upon their ability to maintain the trust of the communities in which they operate, and that their social licence to operate can be just as important as any regulatory licence.[87]

Table 3.2 Private Interest Theories

Theory	Explanation	Examples
Capture	**Regulation (and regulators) are captured by—and operate primarily for the benefit of— those who value it the most**	
Point of origin	Regulation is acquired, designed and operated by industry to create barriers to entry and competition	Transportation Banking Legal and medical professions
Over-time	Regulation is captured over-time, as a result of corruption, over-familiarization or regulator lethargy	Banking & finance (global financial crisis) Mining (Deepwater Horizon oil spill)
Public choice	**Regulation operates for the benefit of politicians, public servants and regulators to advance their private interests**	
Electoral resources	Regulation is supplied to interests that can provide politicians with the resources required for re-election (votes/money)	Trade policy (pharmaceuticals) Gambling regulation
Influence and prominence	Regulation is operated by public servants in a manner designed to secure them influence and prominence (personally or organisationally)	Maximising departmental budgets Optimising departmental shape
Revolving door	Regulatory enforcement reflects relationships built/sought through the revolving door that exists between industry and government	SEC officials' regulatory decisions reflect previous industry employer's world view SEC officials regulate to demonstrate credentials to prospective employers
Risk aversion	Regulation is operated in a manner designed to minimise risk to the regulator	Reluctance of workplace health and safety regulators to regulate professional sport FDA risk-averse drug trials in response to criticism by Congress and media
Interest Group	**Regulation is the product of competition between different self-interested groups**	
Client politics	Regulation is shaped by interests of small well-organised groups over interests of larger but diffuse groups	Television and radio regulation

Entrepreneurial politics	Regulation is shaped by the efforts of skilled entrepreneurs who prevail over larger well-organised groups	Consumer advocates over car manufacturers
Interest group politics	Regulation is shaped by the comparative strengths and resources of competing groups	Workplace health and safety (management vs unions) Environmental regulation (industry vs public interest groups)
Majoritarian politics	Regulation that follows voter preferences	Marriage equality

Politicians too exist on a social licence (granted through the ballot box), and while some may be motivated to varying degrees by the allure of power, high office, party loyalty and ideology, they also are motivated to act in the public interest, at least as assessed by a majority of voters in their electorate. And as for public servants and regulators, they are, as Hodge observes, 'as much concerned with notions of public interest, personal integrity, pride in their work, professional standards, and simply doing a good job, as in their own self-interest'.[88] Put simply, people are, in varying degrees, altruistic as well as selfish, and community minded as well as self-interested, and '[a]ny theory which ignores these broader contextual factors, social relations and normative commitments, is at best incomplete, and at worst misleading and damaging'.[89]

It is therefore difficult to argue for a strict version of any of the private interest theories. Capture theories are real, but arguably overstated; and public choice theories tend to be as one-dimensional as the public interest theories they criticise. Interest group theories on the other hand appear more balanced. However, they too do not give adequate weight to the public interest. Nor do they (or any of the public or private theories considered thus far) give adequate consideration to the role institutions play in shaping the regulatory endeavour—which brings us to our next set of regulatory theories.

Institutional Theories

Institutional theories are the most amorphous and variable of the theoretical groupings considered in this chapter. Baldwin, Cave and Lodge refer to them as a 'broad church';[90] Morgan and Yeung as a '"grab bag", grouping [of] otherwise very different theories'.[91] Common to all institutional theories is one basic premise: institutions matter. That 'institutions matter' can be seen at the highest level. How the public policy and legislative agenda is set, and the manner with which public policy and regulation is made and deployed, is shaped by: the nature of government (whether presidential or parliamentary; unitary, federal or confederal); how power is divided up within governments (between legislature, executive and judiciary; centralised or decentralised); the strictness of that division (US Presidential vs Westminster Parliamentary; coordinate or concurrent); and the manner with which courts discharge their role as constitutional umpires (interventionist or conservative; purposive or literal).[92]

In this section, we focus on three broad schools of institutional thought: rational choice, sociological and historical.[93] Each of these theories seeks to explain the role institutions play, first in determining the initial formation and shape of regulatory agencies; and second, in how regulatory agencies evolve in response to changing circumstances. According to these theories, institutions and institutional variables are not passive entities, but 'political actors in their own right'.[94]

Rational Choice Institutionalism

Rational choice institutionalism focuses on how institutional rules shape the behaviour of regulatory actors. Rational choice institutionalism starts from the assumption that regulatory actors act rationally in pursuit of their goals. This rationality manifests itself in strategic decisions taken after careful consideration of the benefits and costs of different courses of action. Rational choice institutionalism then posits that institutions operate to affect these calculations in two ways. First, how existing institutions are structured and arranged can affect the range of choices available to regulatory actors or, more precisely, the comparative costs of pursuing different courses of action—the greater the degree of change required from existing institutional arrangements, the greater the cost to change them. The establishment of an independent regulatory agency, for example, is said to communicate a 'credible commitment' that the agency (and the policy it reflects) is better placed than a centralised government department to withstand a change of government. This, it is argued, enables persons subject to, or impacted by, the policy and agency to plan with a greater degree of certainty.[95]

Second, institutions impact each regulatory actor's expectations about the actions other regulatory actors are likely to take in response to or simultaneously with its own actions. Institutions do this by providing information about the behaviours of other actors and enforcement mechanisms that reduce the prospects of irrational, perverse or otherwise non-complimentary responses. This, it is argued, enables regulatory actors to enter into exchanges with one another with confidence, thereby enabling each actor to attain its preferences and, collectively, to maximise societal benefits.[96] Regulatory regimes that impose and sanction breaches of duties of care, skill and diligence and continuous disclosure obligations (e.g. workplace health and safety, and corporations regulation) are examples of regimes that create behavioural expectations and reduce the prospects of perverse or irrational responses.

It follows from this that rational choice institutionalists see the creation and evolution of regulatory institutions as the product of a rational process to design structures that will perform their public function effectively and efficiently, with efficiency measured principally in terms of minimising regulatory actors' transaction, production and influencing costs.[97] Rational choice institutionalists further argue that once created, institutions that provide certainty and confidence to regulatory exchanges become self-reinforcing—the more an institution contributes to the resolution of past conflicts in a manner that enables each actor to gain from their exchanges, then the more robust will be the institution—any disruption of the status quo risking losses to one or more of the actors. Moreover, the stability of these regimes incentivises actors to 'adapt their strategies in ways that reflect but also reinforce the "logic" of the system'.[98] This further increases the costs of changing those patterns, thus reinforcing or 'locking-in' existing institutional arrangements.

Rational choice institutionalism's parallels with economic or market-orientated approaches to conceptualising the public interest are obvious. Rational choice institutionalism views institutions as coordinating mechanisms that aggregate individual preferences, control (or at least constrain) self-interest and mediate between public and private interests in a manner that generates more stable collective benefits.[99] However, like its public interest theory counterpart, rational choice institutionalism has it weaknesses. First, it ignores or discounts the extent to which non-economic factors can influence an individual's preferences and choices; and second, it tends to view exchanges between rival interest groups as a quasi-contractual process between relatively equal actors, thereby downplaying the role of politics and power.[100] These weaknesses are addressed in the next two schools of institutionalism.

Sociological Institutionalism

Sociological institutionalism views the creation of regulatory agencies not simply in terms of efficiency, but also in terms of legitimacy.[101] Sociological institutionalists see institutions as more than a collection of formal rules, procedures and norms; they also are an expression of the way the world works, embodying and embedding shared cultural understandings of what is socially acceptable and legitimate. Viewed this way, institutions operate as cognitive templates that guide human action, and in doing so, shape the regulatory endeavour in two principal ways.[102] First, the world view and values embodied by the institution shape the preferences and actions of individuals within the institution, such that those individuals are more likely to share common values and to form a more coherent community. Influencing (steering and directing) this community in a common direction and for a common purpose therefore should be easier.[103] An example of this is the manner with which people who have committed themselves to a mega-project (regulatory or otherwise) 'become the project', and when faced with a choice between continuing with the project's direction and an alternative, choose (consciously or subconsciously) to continue with the existing direction.[104]

Second, these socially acceptable and legitimate institutions operate as templates for future decision-making. Thelen explained this reproductive dynamic well when she said:

> Specific organisations come and go, but emergent institutional forms will be 'isomorphic' with (i.e. compatible with, resembling, and similar in logic to) existing ones because political actors extract causal designations from the world around them and these cause-and-effect understandings inform their approaches to new problems. This means that even when policy makers set out to redesign institutions, they are constrained in what they can conceive of by these embedded, cultural constraints.[105]

The cross-sectoral and global diffusion of independent regulatory agencies discussed in Chapter 2 is an excellent example of this.[106] Today, independent regulatory agencies are seen as a successful model and the most logical and obvious choice for regulators. This both shapes and constrains future regulatory design decisions. Their strong credibility and acceptability makes their adoption in new settings easier to explain and execute, and departures from the template more difficult to justify.[107] Gilardi goes so far as to argue that their symbolism and the reassurance they provide matters more than the functions they perform.[108]

Sociological institutionalists argue that cultural-cognitive dimensions of decision-making are just as important (if not more important) as rational-economic dimensions, and that cultural understandings embedded in existing institutions serve as cognitive templates that shape the manner with which regulatory institutions emerge, evolve and are then diffused across sectors and systems. These are important insights. However, like rational choice institutionalism, sociological institutionalism does not directly address notions of power and conflict. This is where historical institutionalism makes a valuable contribution.

Historical Institutionalism

Historical institutionalism focuses on how past decisions with respect to institutional creation and design shape and constrain current and future decisions.[109] There are two broad ways in which institutions do this. First, 'institutions create historically rooted trajectories of growth'.[110] Each nation's historical course has seen it develop a political economy with a distinctive institutional structure, and that distinctive institutional structure 'induces particular kinds of corporate and government behavior by constraining and by laying out a logic to the market and policy-making process that is particular to that political economy'.[111] In this regard, historical institutionalism shares similarities with rational choice institutionalism, arguing that once a particular institutional path is chosen, actors adapt to that path in ways that push them further along that trajectory.[112] An excellent example of this is Vogel's study of regulatory reform in advanced industrial countries in which he found that each nation's response to the pressures of globalisation, privatisation and deregulation followed distinct national trajectories in which 'political-economic institutions shape policy choices and ... these choices in turn reshape the institutions'.[113]

Second, and this time unlike rational choice institutionalism, historical institutionalism emphasises that 'institutions are not neutral coordinating mechanisms but in fact reflect, and also reproduce and magnify, particular patterns of power distribution in politics'.[114] Institutions do this by providing one set of interest groups greater access to decision-making processes and decision-makers than other interest groups, thereby creating or entrenching asymmetries of power amongst these groups with respect to the formation or operation of the regulatory institution. These power imbalances then become self-reinforcing, as empowered groups exert their influence to advance their interests (and further marginalise the disempowered groups), thereby entrenching historical political patterns and policy outcomes.[115]

The strength of an institution's historically rooted trajectory has important implications for how that institution evolves and adapts to changes in its environment. First, institutions are said to be 'path dependent', such that they will continue along their established (historical) path until forced to change by a significant external shock that causes the fundamental underpinnings of the prevailing paradigm to be reassessed (what Baumgartner and Jones refer to as an equilibrium puncturing event).[116] Second, absent such an external shock, regulatory change will be gradual and incremental. Historical institutionalists refer to this as 'layering', whereby regulatory change is evolutionary not revolutionary, and is achieved through a process in which additions and extensions are attached to—layered upon—existing institutions.[117]

Summing up Institutional Theories

The institutional theories considered in this section are summarized in Table 3.3.

Each institutional theory is useful for the insights it brings to the impact institutions can have on human behaviour: rational choice institutionalism that institutions coordinate and stabilise each actor's expectations about other actors; sociological institutionalism that institutions establish norms of what is acceptable, legitimate and appropriate; and historical institutionalism that institutions create historical pathways that constrain, shape and drive particular patterns of behaviour. At the same time, however, each theory provides only a partial account of the forces at work in a given situation.[118] Rational choice institutionalist theories do not allow for non-economic factors influencing regulatory actors; sociological institutional theories ignore or discount the role of power and politics; and historical

Table 3.3 Institutional Theories

Theory/Rationale	Justification	Example
Rational-Choice	(a) Institutional arrangements affect the comparative costs of pursuing different courses of action	(a) Credible commitment of independent regulatory agencies
	(b) Institutional enforcement mechanisms reduce prospects of irrational, perverse or non-complimentary responses	(b) Workplace health and safety regulation; corporations regulation
Sociological	(a) Institution shapes views and preferences of individuals within it	(a) People working on major regulatory projects 'becoming the project'
	(b) Institution operates as a template of what is socially acceptable	(b) Global diffusion of independent regulatory agencies
Historical	(a) Institutions create historically rooted trajectories	(a) Different nations' governmental institutions shape each particular nation's responses to risks to health, safety and the environment
	(b) Institutions reflect, reproduce and magnify established patterns of power distribution	(b) Political and economic institutions in oil dependent nations actively reinforce the economy's dependence on oil

institutional accounts have been criticised for not readily translating into systemic theories about institutional creation and reform.[119] Common to all the theories though is that institutions operate to both shape and stabilise the regulatory endeavour. With this, however, comes a significant risk, namely that institutions can entrench the habitual use of regulatory techniques and instruments that can blind governments to the existence of more effective forms of regulatory interventions.[120] Often it takes the power of a new idea to remove the blinkers and to chart a new path. This brings us to our final set of regulatory theories.

Ideational Theories

Common to ideational theories is that ideas are powerful regulatory forces in their own right capable of playing a significant role in shaping the regulatory endeavour. Ideational theories recognise that public policy and regulation are impacted by the prevailing ideological, social and political climate, the intellectual storms within it, and the relative strength, prominence and influence of the professionals and intellectuals that engage with it.

As explained in the Introduction, this book is written from the perspective of a democratic liberal capitalist society.[121] Each of these words represents a powerful idea, and each of these ideas influences how regulatory actors respond to new pressures and changed circumstances. Vogel's study of regulatory reform in advanced industrial countries found each nation's response to globalisation, privatisation and deregulation (also powerful ideas in their own right) was influenced not only by that nation's political and economic institutions, but also by different ideas 'about the proper scope, goals and methods of government intervention in the economy'.[122] As Vogel observed:

> In regulatory reform . . . ideas influence how officials interpret market trends, apply lessons from abroad, and determine how new regulations should be put into practice. Ideas are important analytically because they structure state actors' preferences and thereby eliminate one of the greatest potential weaknesses of a state-centered model: that it tells you that state actors lead without telling you where they are likely to go. Without this element, a state-centered model can leave the state as a black box, powerful yet devoid of content.[123]

There is no shortage of examples of the power of ideas influencing the regulatory agenda: of a new way of doing things (or a new way of explaining an old way of doing things) capturing the imagination of one or more disciplines interested in the regulatory endeavour and, in time, becoming a *tour de force* sweeping through regulatory practice on a global scale. An excellent example of this is the manner with which the Chicago School of Economics and the capture and public choice theories they propagated ignited the deregulatory reforms of the Thatcher and Reagan eras.[124] Other examples include the global application of responsive regulation and its enforcement pyramid,[125] the global diffusion of regulatory capitalism and independent regulatory agencies[126] and the rebirth of behavioural economics and the nudge techniques it has spawned.[127]

The power of ideas also grants high status to those who promulgate and propagate them. Braithwaite in his history of the evolution of regulatory capitalism refers in several places to the influence of economic missionaries such as the 'Chicago boys' and the International Monetary Fund in spreading the economic regulatory theory of the day.[128] Parker similarly refers to Ayres' and Braithwaite's *Responsive Regulation* becoming 'one of those "canonical" texts that helped constitute the very field of which it is part';[129] Gilardi, Jordana and Levi-Faur refer to the central role played by national and international networks of professionals and experts in the diffusion of independent regulatory agencies;[130] and Kosters and Van der Heijden to the role played by Sunstein and Thaler in making behavioural economics the regulatory strategy *du jour*.[131]

'Power of ideas' theories have intuitive appeal. That ideas have force is clear. What is less clear, however, is how ideas are generated and communicated, why some ideas take root and others do not and how the power of an idea is harnessed by strategic actors to advance their cause. Progress in this area is being made, however. Parsons, for example, identifies four ways ideas gain power: because they are adopted by already powerful actors; because they empower actors on the road to power; because they provide a platform for creating new coalitions of actors and because they inform the reform of important institutions.[132] Other commentators emphasise the role of political discourse and democratic consensus building in conferring legitimacy on certain ideas.[133]

The power of ideas also means that regulation can be impacted by 'fads and fashions' with different flavours of the month (or year(s)) periodically dominating regulatory thinking, and by 'herd behaviour' in which a particular regulatory idea is diffused across countries in a less than rational manner.[134] Ideas should not be adopted uncritically as articles of faith, and their proponents not feted as deliverers of messianic truths. Ideas should be starting points, not end points. The applicability of a particular idea to a particular situation should be carefully considered. This behoves all involved with regulation to focus on the core principles and processes of effective regulatory design and implementation, and to avoid tempting short-cuts. It is on these principles and processes that much of the rest of this book focuses.

Concluding Insights and Implications

This chapter's exploration of different regulatory theories commenced by observing that the fundamental task of government is to act in the 'public interest'. The chapter then went on to examine three theoretical conceptions of the public interest: economic, social and risk-based. That examination revealed there are different and sometimes conflicting conceptions of the 'public interest', and that regulation in the public interest can require balances to be struck, and trade-offs to be made, between these different understandings.

The chapter next examined private interest, institutional and ideational theories. Private interest theories cast doubt over whether regulation can meet the ideals of public interest theories given the plethora of interested parties that seek to influence its shape for their own benefit. Similar doubts also arise from the sometimes entrenched nature of the institutions through which regulation is made, and the less than rational way some ideas can be adopted.

Each regulatory theory is analytically useful and instructive. Studying them enables us to better understand the regulatory world around us. However, as we have already seen, each also suffers from a number of conceptual or empirical shortcomings. Moreover, none of the theories (on their own) conveys a complete picture of what occurs in practice. The reality of modern regulation making is that most regulation involves a mix of different values, interests and forces, and that the stability and legitimacy of modern regulatory regimes are increasingly dependent upon the ability of governments and regulators to bring these sometimes competing values, interests and forces into alignment—to balance economic values with social values; risk control with the benefits of risk taking; the public interest with appropriate private interests; and proven institutions and processes with new ideas for how regulation can be done better.[135] This is consistent with the political view of regulation as the product of compromise and accommodation, rather than the consistent application of coherent theory.[136]

At best, each regulatory theory provides only a partial and limited explanation of the regulatory endeavour. Yet at the same time, they combine to produce a framework for examining why governments regulate in the form in which they regulate, although more so with the benefit of hindsight than with predictive force. Public interest theories supply the technical or theoretical justifications for why governments regulate—the stated objectives it seeks to achieve; the values it seeks to advance. Private interest theories cast light on the darker motivations of actors involved in the regulatory process, providing what Morgan and Yeung refer to as 'a necessary corrective to the excessive optimism or even naïveté of public interest theories'.[137] Institutional and ideational theories focus on the broader environment in which regulation takes place and how existing institutional arrangements, prevailing ways of seeing the world and ideational currents can variably empower, constrain or otherwise affect the distribution of power and influence among regulatory actors and the choices they make, at times pushing them along existing path trajectories and at other times setting a new path.

The interplay of the various theories highlights the complexity of the regulatory endeavour, and the importance of understanding the environment—the actors, the institutional and contextual parameters and the ideational currents—within which it takes place. In the regulatory literature, this environment frequently is referred to as the 'regulatory space' and is the focus of the next chapter (Chapter 4).

The complexity of the regulatory endeavour also gives rise to risks of failure: of regulation that fails to advance the public interest or succumbs to private interests; of regulation continuing down path trajectories rendered sub-optimal by changes in the economic, social or political environment; and of regulation that transplants an idea ill-suited to the task at hand. These risks are real and significant and are discussed in more detail in Chapter 6. Importantly, the theoretical literature also suggests different regulatory institutions and processes to guard against these risks. These include: robust issue diagnosis to carefully scrutinise claims made in the name of the public interest; structuring regulatory agencies to immunise them from being captured or manipulated by private interests or political and bureaucratic self-interest; open and inclusive participatory processes that provide all affected parties with an equal opportunity to be heard and create a fair forum for the competition of ideas; the use of scientific, evidence based methods of analysis and decision-making; and appropriate accountability and control mechanisms. These and other institutional design variables are the focus of Part II of this book.

Notes

1. These categories are similar to those employed by Bronwen Morgan and Karen Yeung, *An Introduction to Law and Regulation: Text and Materials* (Cambridge University Press, 2007); Robert Baldwin, Martin Cave and Martin Lodge, *Understanding Regulation: Theory, Strategy, and Practice* (Oxford University Press, 2nd ed, 2012).
2. Jay M Shafritz and E W Russell, *Introducing Public Administration* (Pearson Longman, 4th ed, 2005) 9–11.
3. Eric Windholz, 'The Harmonisation of Australia's Occupational Health and Safety Laws: Much Ado about Nothing?' (2013) 26 *Australian Journal of Labour Law* 185, 187–8.
4. Mike Feintuck, 'The Holy Grail or Just Another Empty Vessel? "The Public Interest" in Regulation' (Speech delivered at the Middleton Hall, University of Hull, 21 February 2005) 1.
5. Eric Windholz and Graeme A Hodge, 'Conceptualising Social and Economic Regulation: Implications for Modern Regulators and Regulatory Activity' (2012) 38 *Monash University Law Review* 212, 220–3. See also Organisation for Economic Co-Operation and Development, *Regulatory Policies in OECD Countries: From Interventionism to Regulatory Governance* (OECD Publishing, 2002) 20–5.
6. Tony Prosser, *The Regulatory Enterprise: Government, Regulation, and Legitimacy* (Oxford University Press, 2010) 1.
7. For a more detailed explanation of the different types of market failures, imperfections and regulatory responses, see Anthony I Ogus, *Regulation: Legal Form and Economic Theory* (Hart Publishing, 2004) 29–46; Baldwin, Cave and Lodge, *Understanding Regulation*, above n 1, ch 2.
8. See, e.g., Robert W Crandall, *After the Breakup: US Telecommunications in a More Competitive Era* (Brookings Institution Press, 1991); Robert J Levinson, R Craig Romaine and Steven C Salop, 'The Flawed Fragmentation Critique of Structural Remedies in the *Microsoft* Case' (2001) 46 *Antitrust Bulletin* 135; Paul Simshauser, 'When Does Electricity Price Cap Regulation Become Distortionary?' (2014) 47 *Australian Economic Review* 304.
9. See, e.g., Janice Albert (ed), *Innovations in Food Labelling* (Woodhead Publishing, 2010); Gill North, 'Timely Public Disclosure of Company Information: A Likely Precondition for Optimal Long-Term Corporate and National Outcomes' (2014) 32 *Company and Securities Law Journal* 560.
10. See, e.g., Mary Keyes and Kylie Burns, 'Contract and the Family: Whither Intention' (2002) 26 *Melbourne University Law Review* 577, 593, which notes that in Australia prenuptial agreements are only binding if each party receives independent legal advice.
11. Allard E Dembe and Leslie I Boden, 'Moral Hazard: A Question of Morality' (2000) 10 *New Solutions* 257.
12. Andrew R Sorkin, *Too Big to Fail* (Viking Penguin, 2009); Aseem Prakash and Matthew Potoski, 'Dysfunctional Institutions? Towards a New Agenda in Governance Studies' (2016) 10 *Regulation & Governance* 115.
13. See, e.g., Tom Baker, 'On the Geneology of Moral Hazard' (1996) 75 *Texas Law Review* 237.
14. See, e.g., Charles Helms et al, 'Implementation of Mandatory Immunisation of Healthcare Workers: Observations from New South Wales, Australia' (2011) 29 *Vaccine* 2895; Jenna Zerylnik, 'The Evolution of Colorado's School Attendance Laws: Moving towards Prevention and Restoration' (2014) 43(7) *Colorado Lawyer* 63.

15. See, e.g., Organisation for Economic Co-Operation and Development, 'Environmentally Related Taxes in OECD Countries: Issues and Strategies' (OECD, 2001); Baldwin, Cave and Lodge, *Understanding Regulation*, above n 1, ch 10 (Emissions Trading).

16. See, e.g., Peter Drahos, 'The Regulation of Public Goods' (2004) 7 *Journal of International Economic Law* 321.

17. Eugene Bardach, 'Social Regulation as a Generic Policy Instrument' in L M Salamon (ed), *Beyond Privitization: The Tools of Goverment Action* (The Urban Institute Press, 1989) 197, 198. See also Eugene Bardach and Robert A Kagan, 'Introduction' in E Bardach and R A Kagan (eds), *Social Regulation: Strategies for Reform* (Institute for Contemporary Studies, 1982) 3; Anthony Ogus, 'W(h)ither the Economic Theory of Regulation? What Economic Theory of Regulation?' in J Jordana and D Levi-Faur (eds), *The Politics of Regulation: Institutions and Regulatory Reforms for the Age of Governance* (Edward Elgar, 2004) 31. Some of these commentators also argue that market-orientated regulation can correct for imperfections in the legal system (especially liability and tort law), which would then enable private law remedies adequately to correct for imperfections in other market systems.

18. Regulatory failure is discussed in Chapter 6.

19. Windholz and Hodge, 'Conceptualising Social and Economic Regulation', above n 5, 225–6. See also Tony Prosser, 'Regulation and Social Solidarity' (2006) 33 *Journal of Law and Society* 364, 373–5. See also Peter J May, 'Social Regulation' in Lester M Salamon (ed), *The Tools of Government: A Guide to the New Governance* (Oxford University Press, 2002) 156, 171; Julia Black, 'Critical Reflections on Regulation' (2002) 27 *Australian Journal of Legal Philosophy* 1, 9.

20. Sunstein makes the point that what constitutes an externality justifying regulation is, in the first place, an inherently moral and political decision. It requires one to determine who has caused the external effect, and to choose which of the many activities that impose costs on third parties ought to be regulated: Cass R Sunstein, *After the Rights Revolution: Reconceiving the Regulatory State* (Harvard University Press, 1990) 54–5.

21. Sunstein, *After the Rights Revolution*, above n 20, 57–60; Prosser, 'Regulation and Social Solidarity', above n 19, 375; Windholz and Hodge, 'Conceptualising Social and Economic Regulation', above n 5, 223–4.

22. Mike Feintuck, *'The Public Interest' in Regulation* (Oxford University Press, 2004), for example, argues it is based on the 'equality of citizenship'.

23. John Rawls, *A Theory of Justice* (Oxford University Press, 1971) 15; Arthur M Okun, *Equality and Efficiency: The Big Tradeoff* (Brookings Institution Press, 1975); Ogus, *Regulation*, above n 7, 46–54; Steven Breyer, *Regulation and Its Reform* (Harvard University Press, 1982) 20, 22.

24. Prosser, 'Regulation and Social Solidarity', above n 19.

25. Michael Moran, 'The Frank Stacey Memorial Lecture: From Command State to Regulatory State?' (2000) 15(4) *Public Policy and Administration* 1, 10; Arie Freiberg, *The Tools of Regulation* (Federation Press, 2010) 13–16.

26. Windholz and Hodge, 'Conceptualising Social and Economic Regulation', above n 5, 223–4.

27. Sunstein, *After the Rights Revolution*, above n 20, 39; Robert Kuttner, *Everything for Sale: The Virtues and Limits of Markets* (Alfred A Knopf, 1997) 281–2; Neil Gunningham, *Safeguarding the Worker: Job Hazards and the Role of the Law* (Law Book, 1984) 293.

28. Robert Baldwin, Colin Scott and Christopher Hood, *A Reader on Regulation* (Oxford University Press, 1998) 41; Kuttner, *Everything for Sale*, above n 27,

281; Windholz and Hodge, 'Conceptualising Social and Economic Regulation', above n 5, 223–4.

29. John Braithwaite, *Regulatory Capitalism: How It Works, Ideas for Making It Work Better* (Edward Elgar, 2008) 198.

30. 'When policies involve issues suffused with the complex scientific and technical questions posed by social regulation, it is impossible to exclude experts entirely from a role in the policy process': Bruce A Williams and Albert R Matheny, *Democracy, Dialogue, and Environmental Disputes: The Contested Languages of Social Regulation* (Yale University Press, 1995) 46.

31. Richard Mulgan, 'Perspectives on "The Public Interest"' (2000) 95 *Canberra Bulletin of Public Administration* 5; Richard Mulgan, 'Public Servants and the Public Interest' (2000) 97 *Canberra Bulletin of Public Administration* 1.

32. See: Christopher Hood, Henry Rothstein and Robert Baldwin, *The Government of Risk: Understanding Risk Regulation Regimes* (Oxford University Press, 2001); Ulrich Beck, *Risk Society: Towards a New Modernity* (Sage Publications, 1992); Martin Lodge, 'The Public Management of Risk: The Case for Deliberating among Worldviews' (2009) 26 *Review of Policy Research* 395; Julia Black, 'Risk-Based Regulation: Choices, Practices and Lessons Being Learnt' in Organisation for Economic Co-Operation and Development (ed), *Risk and Regulatory Policy: Improving the Governance of Risk* (OECD Publishing, 9 April 2010) 185; Cass Sunstein, *Risk and Reason: Safety, Law and the Environment* (Cambridge University Press, 2002).

33. Fred Thompson and Polly Rizova, 'Understanding and Creating Public Value: Business Is the Engine, Government the Flywheel (and Also the Regulator)' (2015) 17 *Public Management Review* 565, 570.

34. Fiona Haines, *The Paradox of Regulation: What Regulation Can Achieve and What It Cannot* (Edward Elgar, 2011).

35. Black, 'Risk-Based Regulation', above n 32, 185. Risk-based regulation is discussed in more detail in Chapter 10, 239–49.

36. W Kip Viscusi and Ted Gayer, 'Safety at Any Price?' (2002) 25(3) *Regulation* 54.

37. Carol Harlow and Richard Rawlings, *Law and Administration* (Cambridge University Press, 3rd ed, 2009) 270.

38. Haines, *The Paradox of Regulation*, above n 34, 44.

39. Ibid 43–8.

40. See, e.g.: Paul Slovic, Baruch Fischhoff and Sarah Lichtenstein, 'Facts versus Fears: Understanding Perceived Risk' in D Kahneman, P Slovic and A Tversky (eds), *Judgement under Uncertainty: Heuristics and Biases* (Cambridge University Press, 1982) ch 33; Paul Slovic, *The Perception of Risk* (Earthscan Publisher, 2000).

41. Haines, *The Paradox of Regulation*, above n 34, 48–52.

42. Organisation for Economic Co-Operation and Development, *Regulatory Policies in OECD Countries*, above n 5, 21.

43. Cass R Sunstein, 'Probability Neglect: Emotions, Worst Cases, and Law' (2002) 112 *Yale Law Journal* 61, 103–4; Frank Fischer, 'Citizen Participation and the Democratization of Policy Expertise: From Theoretical Inquiry to Practical Cases' (1993) 26 *Democracy and the Policy Sciences* 165.

44. Robert Howse, 'Democracy, Science, and Free Trade: Risk Regulation on Trial at the World Trade Organization' (2000) (7) *Michigan Law Review* 2329; Howard F Chang, 'Risk Regulation, Endogenous Public Concerns, and the Hormones Dispute: Nothing to Fear But Fear Itself' (2004) 77 *Southern California Law Review* 743; François Salanié and Nicholas Treich, 'Regulation in Happyville' (2009) 119 *The Economic Journal* 665, 673.

45. See e.g.: Haines, *The Paradox of Regulation*, above n 34; Christopher Hood and Martin Lodge, 'Pavlovian Innovation, Pet Solutions and Economizing on Rationality? Politicians and Dangerous Dogs' in J Black, M Lodge and M Thatcher (eds), *Regulatory Innovation: A Comparative Analysis* (Edward Elgar, 2005) 138.

46. Haines, *The Paradox of Regulation*, above n 34; Fiona Haines, Adam Sutton and Chris Platania-Phung, 'It's All about Risk, Isn't It? Science, Politics, Public Opinion and Regulatory Reform' (2007–2008) 10 *Flinders Journal of Law Reform* 435.

47. Baldwin, Cave and Lodge, *Understanding Regulation*, above n 1, 42.

48. See, e.g.: Morgan and Yeung, *An Introduction to Law and Regulation*, above n 1, 52; Jørgen Grønnegård Christensen, 'Competing Theories of Regulatory Governance: Reconsidering Public Interest Theory of Regulation' in D Levi-Faur (ed), *Handbook on the Politics of Regulation* (Edward Elgar, 2011) 96.

49. These theories were given prominence by the 'economic theory of regulation' championed by the Chicago School of Economics in the 1970s. See, e.g.: George J Stigler, 'The Theory of Economic Regulation' (1971) 2 *Bell Journal of Economics and Management Science* 3; Richard A Posner, 'Theories of Economic Regulation' (1974) 5 *Bell Journal of Economics and Management Science* 335; Sam Peltzman, 'Towards a More General Theory of Regulation' (1976) 19 *Journal of Law and Economics* 211.

50. Posner, 'Theories of Economic Regulation', above n 49, 344.

51. Levi-Faur has suggested that regulation also can be captured by economists and other professional experts, a result of regulation's increasing reliance on analytical techniques such as regulatory impact assessments and risk-based regulation: David Levi-Faur, 'Regulatory Excellence via Multiple Forms of Expertise' in C Coglianese (ed), *Achieving Regulatory Excellence* (Brookings Institutions Press, 2017) 225.

52. Ogus, *Regulation*, above n 7, 11.

53. Stigler, 'The Theory of Economic Regulation', above n 49, 3.

54. Posner, 'Theories of Economic Regulation', above n 49.

55. Sam Peltzman, 'The Economic Theory of Regulation after a Decade of Deregulation' (1989) *Brookings Papers on Economic Activity* 1.

56. Gene M Grossman and Elhanan Helpman, 'Protection for Sale' (1994) 84 *American Economic Review* 833; Ernesto Dal Bó and Rafael Di Tella, 'Capture by Threat' (2003) 111 *Journal of Political Economy* 1123; Sanford C Gordon and Catherine Hafer, 'Flexing Muscle: Corporate Political Expenditure as Signals to the Bureaucracy' (2005) 99 *American Political Science Review* 246.

57. James Kwak, 'Cultural Capture and the Financial Crisis' in D Carpenter and D A Moss (eds), *Preventing Regulatory Capture: Special Interest Influence and How to Limit It* (Cambridge University Press, 2014) 71.

58. Marver H Bernstein, *Regulating Business by Independent Commission* (New York, 1955). Bernstein's life-cycle describes four genealogical phases: gestation, youth, maturity and old-age. Howlett and Newman recently built on Bernstein's work evolving it to six phases: gestation, infancy, childhood, youth, maturity and old-age: Michael Howlett and Joshua Newman, 'After "The Regulatory Moment" in Comparative Regulatory Studies: Modelling the Early Stages of Regulatory Life Cycles' (2013) 15(2) *Journal of Comparative Policy Analysis* 107.

59. See also Anthony Downs, *Inside Bureaucracy* (Little, Brown, 1967), who describes how organisations reaching maturity lose 'zealots' and 'climbers' and become 'conservative'. Prosser suggest this is not so much a capture theory as it is a 'lack of responsiveness' theory, which Prosser argues generally is a greater danger than capture: Prosser, *The Regulatory Enterprise*, above n 6, 6.

60. See, e.g.: N Adam Dietrich II, 'BP's Deepwater Horizon: "The Goldman Sachs of the Sea"' (2012) 13 *Transactions: The Tennessee Journal of Business Law* 315; Kwak, 'Cultural Capture and the Financial Crisis', above n 57, 71; Christopher Carrigan, 'Captured by Disaster? Reinterpreting Regulatory Behaviour in the Shadow of the Gulf Oil Spill' in D Carpenter and D A Moss (eds), *Preventing Regulatory Capture: Special Interest Influence and How to Limit It* (Cambridge University Press, 2014) 239.

61. Daniel Carpenter and David A Moss, 'Introduction' in D Carpenter and D A Moss (eds), *Preventing Regulatory Capture: Special Interest Influence and How to Limit It* (Cambridge University Press, 2014) 1, 3.

62. See, e.g.: Gene M Grossman and Elhanen Helpman, 'Protection for Sale', above n 56; Dal Bo and Di Tella, 'Capture by Threat', above n 56.

63. Peltzman, 'Towards a More General Theory of Regulation', above n 49.

64. See, e.g.: Ruth Lopert and Deborah Gleeson, 'The High Price of "Free" Trade: US Trade Agreements and Access to Medicines' (2013) 41 *Journal of Law, Medicine & Ethics* 199; Jan McMillen and John S Wright, 'Re-Regulating the Gambling Industry: Regulatory Reform in Victoria and New South Wales, 1999–2006' (2008) 43 *Australian Journal of Political Science* 277.

65. See, e.g.: William A Niskanen Jr, *Bureaucracy and Public Economics* (Edward Elgar, 1994); Patrick Dunleavy, *Democracy, Bureaucracy and Public Choice: Economic Explanations in Political Science* (Harvester Wheatsheaf, 1991) 202.

66. Downs, *Inside Bureaucracy*, above n 59.

67. William A Niskansen, *Bureaucracy and Representative Government* (Aldine-Atherton, 1971).

68. Dunleavy, *Democracy, Bureaucracy and Public Choice*, above n 65, 200–5. See also David Marsh, M J Smith and D Richards, 'Bureaucrats, Politicians and Reform in Whitehall: Analysing the Bureau-Shaping Model' (2000) 30 *British Journal of Political Science* 461. The recent restructuring of the Environment Protection Authority of Victoria, Australia, is a good example of this. See Eric Windholz, 'The Evolution of a Modern (and More Legitimate) Regulator: A Case Study of the Victorian Environment Protection Authority' (2016) 3 *Australian Journal of Environmental Law* 17.

69. See Stavros Gadinis, 'The SEC and the Financial Industry: Evidence from Enforcement against Broker-Dealers' (2012) 67 *Business Lawyer* 679, 725–6, who notes concern in the literature that US Securities and Exchange Commission (SEC) officials may show favouritism towards certain broker dealers because either they share the industry's perspective. See also Per J Agrell and Axel Gautier, 'Rethinking Regulatory Capture' in J E Harrington Jr and Y Katsoulacos (eds), *Recent Advances in the Analysis of Competition Policy and Regulation* (Edward Elgar, 2012) 286, 291.

70. See Wentong Zheng, 'The Revolving Door' (2015) 90 *Notre Dame Law Review* 1265, 1275, who notes a study in which regulators who accepted jobs in the insurance industry after leaving office were found to have allowed higher insurance prices when in office. See also George J Stigler, 'Supplemental Note on Economic Theories of Regulation' in G J Stigler (ed), *The Citizen and the State: Essays in Regulation* (University of Chicago Press, 1975) 165; Ernestó Dal Bo, 'Regulatory Capture: A Review' (2006) 22 *Oxford Review of Economic Policy* 203, 214; Agrell and Gautier, 'Rethinking Regulatory Capture', above n 69, 292.

71. See Zheng, 'The Revolving Door', above n 70, 1268, who notes a study in which it was found that SEC lawyers were more aggressive before leaving to join defendant law firms. See also Paul J Quirk, *Industry Influence in Federal Regulatory Agencies* (Princeton University Press, 1981) 170–1; Jeffrey E Cohen, 'The Dynamics of the "Revolving Door" on the FCC' (1986) 10

American Journal of Political Science 689, 695; Yeon-Koo Che, 'Revolving Doors and the Optimal Tolerance for Agency Collusion' (1995) 26 *Rand Journal of Economics* 378, 379–80.

72. James Q Wilson, 'The Politics of Regulation' in J Q Wilson (ed), *The Politics of Regulation* (Basic Books, 1980) 357, 376.

73. Oren Perez, 'Courage, Regulatory Responsibility, and the Challenge of Higher-Order Reflexivity' (2013) 8 *Regulation & Governance* 203, 213–16. See also: Eric Windholz, 'Professional Sport, Work Health and Safety Law and Reluctant Regulators' (2015) *Sports Law eJournal* 7 <http://epublications.bond.edu.au/slej/28/> who describes the reluctance of work, health and safety regulators to regulate professional sports.

74. Wilson, 'The Politics of Regulation', above n 72, 377.

75. Bardach and Kagan, 'Introduction', above n 17, 16. See, e.g., Henry I Miller and David R Henderson, 'The FDA's Risky Risk-Aversion' (2007) 27 *Genetic Engineering and Biotechnology News* 6 who argues that the US Food and Drug Administration has become increasingly risk averse in its clinical testing of new drugs as a result of criticism from Congress and the media regarding drug safety.

76. Bardach, 'Social Regulation as a Generic Policy Instrument', above n 17, 224. See, e.g., Cynthia Estlund, 'Rebuilding the Law of the Workplace in an Era of Self-Regulation' (2005) 105 *Columbia Law Review* 319, 333–4, who suggests workplace anti-discrimination law is an example of this.

77. Christensen, 'Competing Theories of Regulatory Governance', above n 48, 103. See also: Ogus, *Regulation*, above n 7, 74–5.

78. Andrew Dunsire et al, 'Organizational Status and Performance: A Conceptual Framework for Testing Public Choice Theories' (1988) 66 *Public Administration* 363, 365.

79. Gary S Becker, 'A Theory of Competition among Pressure Groups for Political Influence' (1983) 98 *Quarterly Journal of Economics* 371.

80. Ogus, *Regulation*, above n 7, 70–5.

81. James Q Wilson, *Bureaucracy: What Government Agencies Do and Why They Do It* (Basic Books, 1989) 76–8. For an alternative classification, see Theodore J Lowi, 'Four Systems of Policy, Politics, and Choice' (1972) 32 *Public Administration Review* 298, who classifies policies according to whether government seeks to control individual conduct or the environment in which the conduct takes place, and whether government acts immediately upon the individual or via more indirect and remote means.

82. James Q Wilson et al, *American Government: Institutions & Policies* (Cengage Learning, 15th ed, 2017) 146.

83. David Levi-Faur, 'Regulation and Regulatory Governance' in D Levi-Faur (ed), *Handbook on the Politics of Regulation* (Edward Elgar, 2011) 3, 4.

84. Robert B Reich, 'Public Administration and Public Deliberation: An Interpretative Essay' (1985) 94 *Yale Law Journal* 1617, 1620. See also Becker, 'A Theory of Competition among Pressure Groups for Political Influence', above n 79.

85. Steven P Croley, 'Theories of Regulation: Incorporating the Administrative Process' (1998) 98 *Columbia Law Review* 1, 58–9; P N Grabosky, 'Counterproductive Regulation' (1995) 23 *International Journal of the Sociology of Law* 347, 356.

86. Jonathan Boston, 'The Theoretical Underpinnings of Public Sector Restructuring in New Zealand' in J Boston et al (eds), *Reshaping the State: New Zealand's Bureaucratic Revolution* (Oxford University Press, 1991) 13.

87. See, e.g.: John Morrison, *The Social License: How to Keep Your Organization Legitimate* (Palgrave, 2014); Brian F Yates and Celesa L Horvath, *Social*

Licence to Operate: How to Get It and How to Keep It (Working Paper, Pacific Energy Summit, 2013).

88. Graeme Hodge, *Privatization: An International Review of Performance* (Westview Press, 2000) 37. See also Ogus, *Regulation*, above n 7, 73.
89. Boston, 'The Theoretical Underpinnings of Public Sector Restructuring in New Zealand', above n 86, 13. See also: Neil Gunningham and Peter Grabosky, *Smart Regulation: Designing Environmental Policy* (Clarendon Press, 1998) 24; Graeme Hodge, 'Revisiting State and Market through Regulatory Governance: Observations of Privatisations, Partnerships, Politics and Performance' (2012) 18 *New Zealand Business Law Quarterly* 251, 274.
90. Baldwin, Cave and Lodge, *Understanding Regulation*, above n 1, 53.
91. Morgan and Yeung, *An Introduction to Law and Regulation*, above n 1, 53.
92. See, e.g.: Bjorn E Rasch and George Tseblis (eds), *The Role of Government in Legislative Agenda-Setting* (Routledge, 2010); Thomas H Hammond and Jack H Knott, 'Who Controls the Bureaucracy?: Presidential Power, Congressional Dominance, Legal Constraints, Bureaucratic Autonomy in a Model of Multi-Institutional Policy Making' (1996) 12 *Journal of Law, Economics, and Organization* 119.
93. These schools are far from being distinct categories. Nor are they universally agreed. As Thelen observes: each school 'represents a sprawling literature characterized by tremendous internal diversity, and it is often difficult to draw hard and fast lines between them'; Kathleen Thelen, 'Historical Institutionalism in Comparative Politics' (1999) 2 *Annual Review of Political Science* 369, 370.
94. James G March and Johan P Olsen, 'The New Institutionalism: Organizational Factors in Political Life' (1984) 78 *American Political Science Review* 734, 738.
95. Giandomenico Majone, 'Temporal Consistency and Policy Credibility: Why Democracies Need Non-Majoritarian Institutions' (Working Paper No 96/57, European University Institute, 1996); Fabrizio Gilardi, 'Policy Credibility and Delegation to Independent Regulatory Agencies: A Comparative Empirical Analysis' (2002) 9 *Journal of European Public Policy* 873. Credible commitment and independent regulatory agencies also are discussed in Chapter 8, 185.
96. Peter A Hall and Rosemary C R Taylor, 'Political Science and the Three New Institutionalisms' (1996) 44 *Political Studies* 936, 942–6.
97. Ibid 946.
98. Thelen, 'Historical Institutionalism in Comparative Politics', above n 93, 392.
99. B Guy Peters, 'Institutional Theory' in C K Ansell and J Torfing (eds), *Handbook on Theories of Governance* (Edward Elgar, 2016) 308, 311; Kenneth A Shepsle, 'Rational Choice Institutionalism' in R A W Rhodes, S A Binder and B A Rockman (eds), *The Oxford Handbook of Political Institutions* (Oxford University Press, 2008) 23.
100. Hall and Taylor, 'Political Science and the Three New Institutionalisms', above n 96, 952.
101. Regulatory legitimacy is examined in Chapter 6.
102. Hall and Taylor, 'Political Science and the Three New Institutionalisms', above n 96, 946–50.
103. Peters, 'Institutional Theory', above n 99, 310.
104. See, e.g.: Sophie Sturup, 'A Foucault-Perspective on Public-Private Partnership Mega-Projects' in C Greves and G Hodge (eds), *Rethinking Public-Private Partnerships: Strategies for Turbulent Times* (Routledge, 2013) 132.
105. Thelen, 'Historical Institutionalism in Comparative Politics', above n 93, 386.
106. See Chapter 2, 23–4.
107. Fabrio Gilardi, 'The Institutional Foundations of Regulatory Capitalism: The Diffusion of Independent Regulatory Agencies in Western Europe' (2005) 598 *Annals of the American Academy of Political and Social Sciences* 84, 90.

108. Ibid.
109. Hall and Taylor, 'Political Science and the Three New Institutionalisms', above n 96, 937–42.
110. John Zysman, 'How Institutions Create Historically Rooted Trajectories of Growth' (1994) 3 *Industrial and Corporate Change* 243, 243.
111. Ibid.
112. Thelen, 'Historical Institutionalism in Comparative Politics', above n 93, 384–6.
113. Steven K Vogel, *Freer Markets, More Rules: Regulatory Reform in Advanced Industrial Countries* (Cornell University Press, 1996) 9. See also David Vogel, *The Politics of Precaution: Regulating Health, Safety and Environmental Risks in Europe and the United States* (Princeton University Press, 2012) who argues the United States' more permissive attitude to risk and Europe's more risk averse attitude reflects their different government, administrative and legal traditions and institutions.
114. Thelen, 'Historical Institutionalism in Comparative Politics', above n 93, 394.
115. Ibid 384. Zysman gives as an example how the political and economic institutions in oil dependent nations actively reinforce the economy's dependence on oil: Zysman, 'How Institutions Create Historically Rooted Trajectories of Growth', above n 110.
116. F R Baumgartner and B D Jones, *Agendas and Instability in American Politics* (University of Chicago Press, 1993).
117. James Mahoney and Kathleen Thelen, 'A Theory of Gradual Institutional Change' in J Mahoney and K Thelen (eds), *Explaining Institutional Change: Ambiguity, Agency, and Power* (Cambridge University Press, 2010) 1.
118. Hall and Taylor, 'Political Science and the Three New Institutionalisms', above n 96, 955.
119. Ibid 954–5; Jeroen Van der Heijden, 'Through Thelen's Lens: Layering, Conversion, Drift, Displacement and Exhaustion in the Development of Dutch Construction Regulation' (Research Paper No 2014/46, Regulatory Institutions Network Australian National University, 2014) 25.
120. Organisation for Economic Co-Operation and Development, *Reducing the Risk of Policy Failure: Challenges for Regulatory Compliance* (OECD Publishing, 2000) 21.
121. See Chapter 1, 12.
122. Vogel, *Freer Markets, More Rules*, above n 113, 20.
123. Ibid 21.
124. See, e.g.: Martha Dethrick and Paul J Quirk, *The Politics of Deregulation* (Brookings Institution Press, 1985) 13 who ask: 'Why did deregulation occur? How did a diffuse public interest, articulated by a "few lonely economists", get embodied in law'. See also Christopher Hood, *Explaining Economic Policy Reversal* (Open University Press, 1994) 28. Capture and public choice theory are discussed under Private Interest Theories above; the deregulation era in Chapter 2.
125. Christine Parker, 'Twenty Years of Responsive Regulation: An Appreciation and Appraisal' (2013) 7 *Regulation & Governance* 2. Responsive regulation is discussed in Chapter 10.
126. David Levi-Faur, 'The Global Diffusion of Regulatory Capitalism' (2005) 598 *Annals of the American Academy of Political and Social Science* 12. Regulatory capitalism is discussed in Chapter 2.
127. Mark Kosters and Jeroen Van der Heijden, 'From Mechanism to Virtue: Evaluating Nudge Theory' (2015) 21 *Evaluation* 276, 277. Nudge techniques are discussed in Chapter 8.
128. Braithwaite, *Regulatory Capitalism*, above n 29, 4–28.
129. Parker, 'Twenty Years of Responsive Regulation', above n 125.

130. Fabrizio Gilardi, Jacint Jordana and David Levi-Faur, 'Regulation in the Age of Globalization: The Diffusion of Regulatory Agencies across Europe and Latin America' in G A Hodge (ed), *Privitization and Market Development: Global Movements in Public Policy Ideas* (Edward Elgar, 2006) 127, 139–41. See also: Peter M Hass, 'Introduction: Epistemic Communities and International Policy Coordination' (1992) 46 *International Organization* 1, who notes the important role played by epistemic communities (networks of professionals with recognised expertise in the policy area) in coordinating policy internationally.

131. Kosters and Van der Heijden, 'From Mechanism to Virtue', above n 127, 277.

132. Craig Parsons, 'Ideas and Power: Four Intersections and How to Show Them' (2016) 23 *Journal of European Public Policy* 446–63.

133. Vivien A Schmidt, 'Taking Ideas and Discourse Seriously: Explaining Change through Discursive Institutionalism as the Fourth "New Institutionalism"' (2010) 2 *European Political Science Review* 1; Martin B Carstensen and Vivien A Schmidt, 'Power through, over and in Ideas: Conceptualizing Ideational Power in Discursive Institutionalism' (2016) 23 *Journal of European Public Policy* 318.

134. Covadonga Meseguer, 'Policy Learning, Policy Diffusion, and the Making of a New Order' (2005) 598 *Annals of the American Academy of Political and Social Science* 67; Christopher Pollitt et al, 'Agency Fever: Analysis of an International Policy Fashion' (2001) 3 *Journal of Contemporary Policy Analysis* 271.

135. Windholz and Hodge, 'Conceptualising Social and Economic Regulation', above n 5, 225–8, 235.

136. See, e.g.: Levi-Faur, 'Regulation and Regulatory Governance', above n 83, 14–16. See also Graeme A Hodge, 'Reviewing Public-Private Partnerships: Some Thoughts on Evaluation' in G A Hodge, C Greve and A E Boardman (eds), *International Handbook on Public-Private Partnerships* (Edward Elgar, 2010) 81.

137. Morgan and Yeung, *An Introduction to Law and Regulation*, above n 1, 52.

4 Regulatory Space and Regulatory Regimes

In this chapter, we introduce two constructs critical to understanding the regulatory endeavour: regulatory space and regulatory regimes. Regulatory space is the environment governments enter when choosing to regulate.[1] Regulatory space can be complex, crowded and contested. The terrain can be unfamiliar and treacherous, and its occupants supportive and hostile to the regulatory objective in equal measure. A regulatory regime is government's attempt to impose order on that space: to harness, steer and direct actors occupying the space in support of the regulatory endeavour. In this chapter, we examine the constructs of regulatory space and regulatory regimes using tobacco control as an example. The implications of these constructs for the regulatory endeavour are then discussed.

Regulatory Space

'Regulatory space' is an analytical construct employed to describe and examine the environment within which regulation takes place. Hancher and Moran (who generally are acknowledged as having coined the term) explain that regulatory space has a number of attributes in common with all geographic spaces: it has boundaries, climate and contours, and is available for occupation.[2] Each of these attributes is discussed below.

The boundaries of regulatory space are fluid, and are defined by reference to the range and scope of issues within it. Thus, regulatory space can be defined broadly as might be the case were it to include all issues impacting public health; or narrowly if it were defined to include only the impacts from tobacco consumption. Similarly, the issue of tobacco consumption itself can be defined broadly to include all economic, social and cultural dimensions of the issue; or narrowly to include only its economic or health aspects. How the boundaries are defined is important because it determines which interest groups are inside the space and have the power and influence that comes from participation in its political and regulatory processes, and which interest groups are excluded from it and have no or less power and influence. This makes the boundaries of regulatory space contestable. Different interest groups will conceive of the space differently, and will seek to expand or contract its boundaries to suit their interests. Narrowing the space can entrench existing interests and exclude issues unamicable to those interests; whereas expanding the space can dilute the power held by existing interests, create new centres of power and influence and expand the issues subject of debate.

Extending the geographic analogy, regulatory space also has climate and contours. These are defined by its economic, socio-cultural, political, legal and constitutional systems, customs and conventions. Consistent with institutional and ideational theories, regulatory space emphasises that regulatory issues and actors are embedded in existing systems, institutional dynamics and ideational constructs that influence how issues are identified and defined, impact the allocation of power and influence within the regulatory space and determine the manner with which actors within the space interact with the issue, each other and government.[3] Moreover, these systems generally are interconnected and interdependent. Efforts to influence one variable in one system are likely to influence other variables in other systems, often in ways that are difficult to predict and plan.[4] Each system also has its own language, rationales and ways of working. An intervention in one system may not readily translate to other systems, or at least not in the manner intended by those who initiated it. The law in particular is seen as vulnerable in this regard. A number of commentators attribute this to the law's inability effectively to interact with other systems, with the result that the 'law is more marginal to actions within the regulatory space than lawyers might assume'.[5] Teubner takes this further, suggesting that not only may the law be irrelevant to other systems (what he refers to as 'incongruence'), but that it also may inhibit other systems ('over-legalisation') or itself be inhibited by those systems ('over-socialisation'). Teubner refers to this as a 'regulatory trilemma'.[6]

The final attribute of regulatory space arguably is its most important, namely, that 'because it is a space it is available for occupation'.[7] Other commentators have expanded upon this point to observe that regulatory space is never completely empty and that '[p]ublic agencies that seek to regulate members of society never issue their regulation onto a blank slate'.[8] Regulatory space invariably is occupied by a variety of state and non-state actors, and by a variety of existing formal and informal legal, economic and social controls. These could include pre-existing regulation, market forces, contractual arrangements and societal and business norms. A number of important consequences flow from this. First, the actors occupying the regulatory space possess resources relevant to government's exercise of regulatory power. These include information, institutional credibility and political influence, people and money, and organisational capacities and networks.[9] Employed constructively these resources can support and enhance the regulatory endeavour. However, if not engaged constructively, they can be employed to hinder or derail it. In this regard, government and regulators can be thought of as competing with these other actors for influence within the space.[10] Second, these resources—and the power and influence that attach to them—generally are divided unevenly between actors within the space. Some actors are major participants; some are minor participants. Minor participants often seek to expand their power and influence to become major participants; and major participants act to entrench their power and influence from being usurped by others.[11] As such, regulatory space has the attributes of an arena in which various actors are involved in a struggle for advantage, and in which different interests and values compete for supremacy.[12] And third, recognition that resources relevant to the exercise of regulatory power are dispersed among both state and non-state actors means that governments and regulators do not have a monopoly over authority within the regulatory space, and that the formal authority they do possess 'may be significantly tempered by the informal authority possessed by other actors'.[13] Power and influence within the regulatory space is not solely exercised hierarchically, regulator over regulatee, but also can be exercised horizontally and vertically by non-state actors seeking to modify the behaviour of (that is, regulate) each other and government, creating 'a reflexive process of influence and change within [the] regulatory space'.[14]

The Tobacco Control Regulatory Space

To illustrate the concept of regulatory space and its attributes, in this section we examine the regulatory space within which tobacco is regulated. To simplify the example, we will look at one country only, Australia.[15]

Looking first at government bodies (see Figure 4.1), Australia has three levels of government—a national government and two levels of sub-national

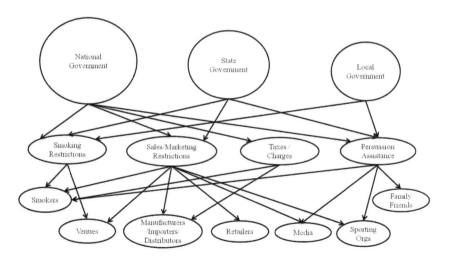

Figure 4.1 Government Regulation Within the Tobacco Control Regulatory Space

government (state and local). All three levels of government have implemented policies designed to reduce the number of people smoking. Laws have been passed restricting tobacco consumption (smoking) in public places such as airports, restaurants, hotels, shopping centres, playgrounds, parks and beaches. These laws operate upon both the consumer (smoker) and the venues at which they might otherwise smoke. National and state governments also strictly regulate the marketing and sale of tobacco products by, for example, requiring tobacco products to be sold in plain packaging, prohibiting tobacco advertising and sponsorship and restricting the places at which tobacco products may lawfully be sold. These laws operate upon manufacturers, importers, distributors and retailers of tobacco products, as well as on entities that might otherwise carry tobacco advertising such as media outlets and sporting organisations. The national government also taxes manufacturers of tobacco products. These taxes increase the price of tobacco products to incentivise smokers to cease smoking or to smoke less. They also raise revenue to cover the costs of treating tobacco related diseases and to fund anti-tobacco activities. Finally, national, state and local governments also seek to assist and persuade people to stop smoking and potential smokers not to commence. This is done through providing or subsidising smoking cessation services and devices as well as through public information campaigns. Some of these campaigns target smokers directly; others seek to enlist their family and friends as messengers.

Governments are not the only actors regulating (modifying behaviours with respect to) tobacco use in Australia. A number of non-government actors also regulate tobacco use. Some of these actors are commercial for profit entities, such as pharmaceutical companies that manufacture smoking cessation devices, medical professionals that counsel and assist smokers to stop and insurance companies that vary premiums according to whether the insured is a smoker or non-smoker. Others are not for profit organisations such as health promotion foundations and anti-smoking groups. These organisations also provide smoking cessations services and conduct research and public information campaigns to persuade and assist smokers to stop and non-smokers not to commence.

These and other actors within the space also seek to influence (regulate) government to implement policies consistent with their values and interests. The two main protagonists are, on the one side, health promotion foundations, anti-smoking groups and public health and medical professionals that advocate for tougher restrictions on tobacco use and, on the other side, businesses impacted by those restrictions that advocate for less or lighter regulation that respects individual autonomy and commercial property rights. Other influencers in the space include insurance companies, plaintiff lawyers, unions representing workers in the tobacco industry and those potentially put at risk by the use of tobacco products, and organisations that represent welfare service providers (tobacco being a product consumed disproportionally by lower socio-economic groups). There also are transnational bodies that seek to influence government policies, such as the World Health Organisation (WHO) that monitors compliance with its Framework

Convention on Tobacco Control, the International Labour Organisation (ILO) that, for example, requires tobacco products to be included in consumer price indices, and the World Trade Organisation (WTO) and other international trade organisations that advocate for free trade agreements. These non-government actors are shown in Figure 4.2, and their influence relationships are shown in Figure 4.3 (by way of illustration only).

Figure 4.3 illustrates the complex, crowded and contested nature of regulatory space. It reveals the complex interactions and interdependencies in the regulatory process,[16] as actors occupying the space seek to enlist and

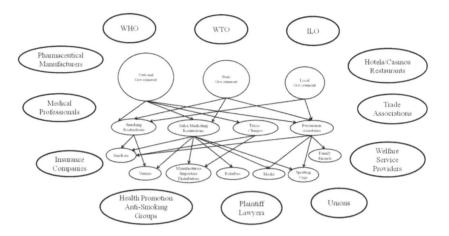

Figure 4.2 State and Non-State Actors Occupying the Tobacco Control Regulatory Space

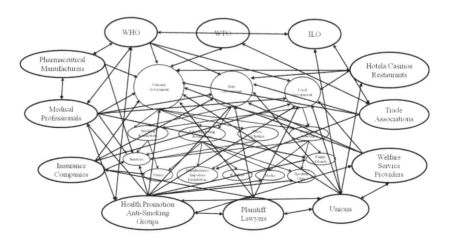

Figure 4.3 Influence Relationships Within the Tobacco Control Regulatory Space

enrol each other in support of their mission and objectives—a process Black refers to as 'mutual enrolment'.[17] It also reveals that governments seeking to implement measures to change smoker behaviour must compete with other actors occupying the regulatory space with it. This can see governments buffeted by the norms and standards espoused by business, unions, professional bodies, public interest groups, transnational bodies and the like, all seeking to modify government behaviour and policy consistent with their interests and values.[18] Viewed this way, government both regulates (in the sense of trying to change other people's behaviour) and is regulated (in the sense of others trying to change its behaviour).

It also is clear from this discussion that regulation cannot be conceptualised in a simple linear fashion as a set of cause and effect relationships emanating solely from the actions of the state. Rather, regulation originates from a variety of state and non-state sources. Some commentators have described these sources forming a regulatory web operating upon the regulatee: the more complex the issue, the greater the number of webs layered over each other (illustrated well in Figure 4.3).[19] Other commentators emphasise the fragmented and dispersed nature of power and authority within regulatory space and observe that regulation increasingly is polycentric and decentred, taking place across multiple and overlapping sites of governance within which government is but one influential player.[20] This book's interest in regulatory space resides primarily in the opportunities it provides to harness and coordinate its various actors and their resources in support of the regulatory endeavour. This brings us to the concept of the 'regulatory regime'.

Regulatory Regimes

A regulatory regime refers to the network of actors involved in regulating an issue, the aggregate activities undertaken by them to modify the behaviour of the target audience and the norms, principles, rules and decision-making processes according to which, and through which, those activities are coordinated.[21] The central idea behind a regulatory regime is that it is coordinated—steered and directed (to employ governance parlance). And consistent with this book's approach that adopts a state-centric conception of governance and regulation, the regulatory regimes with which we are concerned are coordinated (steered and directed) by government. This coordination rarely is achieved through the exercise of coercive power alone, however. More often, it is achieved through participatory processes that seek to enlist and co-opt actors and resources likely to support the regulatory policy's objectives, and to quieten and neutralise those actors and resources prejudicial to them.[22]

'Regulatory space' and 'regulatory regimes' are parallel concepts.[23] Like regulatory space, regulatory regimes have boundaries, contours, occupants and climate. A regime's boundaries are defined by the size of the issues assigned to it and the scope of its outcomes, goals and objectives. Like regulatory space, it too can be defined broadly or narrowly. Its contours can be thought of as its structure. This includes the institutional arrangements and processes through which the regulator steers and coordinates the actors occupying the space, and the resources and tools at its disposal. And, of course, those actors are the regime's occupants. And finally, a regime's climate will reflect the style of the regulator and the nature of the relationships it develops with the regime occupants.[24] Importantly, governments determine a regulatory regime's size, scope and structure, and regulators its style. This gives governments and regulators the capability to bring some order to the regulatory space within which an issue is debated; to centre what was previously decentred; to coordinate what was previously uncoordinated and to admit or exclude actors that were previously excluded or admitted (as the case may be).

The Tobacco Control Regulatory Regime

Earlier we observed that the Australian tobacco control regulatory space is complex, crowded and contested. This made it an excellent candidate for a regime approach. Coordination of the actors and resources within the Australian tobacco control regulatory space is achieved through the National Tobacco Strategy 2012–2018.[25] Developed by the Intergovernmental Committee on Drugs, the Strategy was developed with input from a range of stakeholders, including governments, health groups, community-based organisations, industry organisations and the public.[26] The strategy includes a comprehensive range of policies designed to reduce tobacco consumption, including mass media campaigns, cessation services, prohibitions on tobacco advertising, price increases and controls on second-hand smoke and access to tobacco. The strategy states that these policies are to be delivered through partnerships between governments, non-government organisations and community groups. The Strategy also states that Australia will engage in international partnerships to maximise the effectiveness of global tobacco control efforts, and to learn and share best practice approaches. Interestingly, the Strategy's focus on partnering with actors supportive of its policy objectives is matched by a focus on protecting those policy objectives from interference by actors in the space hostile to them, namely the tobacco industry.[27]

Concluding Insights and Implications

This chapter examined two constructs central to our understanding of the regulatory endeavour: regulatory space, the initial environment a government encounters when choosing to regulate; and regulatory regimes, a government's attempt to impose order upon that space to achieve the regulatory objective.

Thinking in terms of regulatory space reminds us that the regulatory environment often is crowded, complex and contested. It encourages us to think about who occupies the space; who has power and who does not; and their interests, values and perspectives. It also encourages us to think about the existing systems, customs, norms and controls that shape their attitudes and behaviours. Thinking in terms of regulatory space also highlights the contested nature of the regulatory endeavour: that it is an arena in which many interests and actors compete for supremacy, and with whom governments must compete for influence. This makes understanding regulatory space an essential component of issue diagnosis (Chapter 7).

Regulatory space challenges traditional assumptions that regulatory outcomes can be achieved by the state solely through the direct and hierarchical application of its coercive powers.[28] Rather, regulatory space encourages us to think in terms of regulatory regimes that harness its various actors and resources in support of the regulatory objective.[29] Regulatory regimes, in turn, encourage us to think of regulatory design not in terms of single regulators and regulatory instruments, but in terms of the overall configuration of actors and resources, and the institutional arrangements, rules and processes by which they are coordinated and steered. Under a regime approach, regulation is a collaborative effort led by government and undertaken in partnership with non-government actors occupying the regulatory space.[30] Regulatory space also encourages us to think broadly and laterally as to who those partners might be. Doing so expands design possibilities and offers the promise of creative and innovative ways to address regulatory issues.

However, taking advantage of this promise is not without its challenges. First are what Black describes as democratic challenges—deciding who should be included in the regime's decision-making processes, when and how.[31] There also are functional and accountability challenges. How do you coordinate actors with different values, interests and conceptions of the public interest? How do you ensure their activities are consistent with the regime's objectives, and with each other? And to what extent can they be held accountable if they fail to deliver in accordance with a collaborative plan or strategy? Grasping the opportunities presented by regime thinking while meeting these challenges is an important focus of this book.

Notes

1. In public policy circles, this space is called the public policy arena.
2. Leigh Hancher and Michael Moran, 'Organizing Regulatory Space', in L Hancher and M Moran (eds), *Capitalism, Culture and Economic Regulation* (Oxford University Press, 1989) 271.
3. Ibid 291–3; Bronwen Morgan and Karen Yeung, *An Introduction to Law and Regulation* (Cambridge University Press, 2007) 59.
4. P N Grabosky, 'Counterproductive Regulation' (1995) 23 *International Journal of the Sociology of Law* 347, 357; Volker Schneider, 'Governance and Complexity' in D Levi-Faur (ed), *Oxford Handbook of Governance* (Oxford University Press, 2012) 129.
5. Colin Scott, 'Analysing Regulatory Space: Fragmented Resources and Institutional Design' [2001] (Summer) *Public Law* 329, 334. See also Julia Black,

'Critical Reflections on Regulation' (2002) 27 *Australian Journal of Legal Philosophy* 1, 29–34; Morgan and Yeung, *An Introduction to Law and Regulation*, above n 3, 4.

6. Gunther Teubner, *Dilemmas of Law in the Welfare State* (Walter de Gruyter, 1986) 309.

7. Hancher and Moran, 'Organizing Regulatory Space', above n 2, 277.

8. Christine Parker, 'Reinventing Regulation within the Corporation' (2000) 32 *Administration and Society* 529, 532; Scott, 'Analysing Regulatory Space', above n 5.

9. These match Hood's NATO classification of government resources (see Chapter 1, p. 17 n 21). Of these, information arguably is the most important and difficult for government to replicate. Regulated firms and other actors within the regulatory space typically have more information about the regulated activity than government regulators. This 'information asymmetry' is one of the greatest challenges faced by government and regulators.

10. Parker, 'Reinventing Regulation within the Corporation', above n 8, 532.

11. Hancher and Moran, 'Organizing Regulatory Space', above n 2, 277.

12. Ibid. See also Mark H Moore, *Creating Public Value: Strategic Management in Government* (Harvard University Press, 1995) 118–32. Regulatory space has parallels with Moore's concept of the 'authorising environment', the support of which, according to Moore, is necessary for public managers to create value. Moore's authorising environment also is crowded, comprising political superiors, legislative overseers, department heads, other regulators, the media, interest groups and the courts.

13. Scott, 'Analysing Regulatory Space', above n 5, 336. Parker, Scott, Lacey and Braithwaite similarly observe that conflicting non-legal norms can limit the effectiveness of legislated rules: Christine Parker et al, 'Introduction' in C Parker et al (eds), *Regulating Law* (Oxford University Press, 2004) 1, 6–7.

14. Morgan and Yeung, *An Introduction to Law and Regulation*, above n 3, 76.

15. For an overview of tobacco control in Australia, see M M Scollo and M H Winstanely, *Tobacco in Australia: Facts and Issues* (Cancer Council Victoria, 2015).

16. Julia Black, 'Decentring Regulation: Understanding the Role of Regulation and Self-Regulation in a "Post-Regulatory" World' (2001) 54 *Current Legal Problems* 103, 109.

17. Julia Black, 'Legitimacy and the Competition for Regulatory Share' (LSE Law, Society and Economy Working Paper 14/2009, London School of Economics and Political Science, Law Department, 2009) 7.

18. Colin Scott, 'Private Regulation of the Public Sector: A Neglected Facet of Contemporary Governance' (2002) 29 *Journal of Law and Society* 56.

19. John Braithwaite and Peter Drahos, *Global Business Regulation* (Cambridge University Press, 2000) ch 23; P N Grabosky, 'Using Non-Governmental Resources to Foster Regulatory Compliance' (1995) 8 *Governance* 527, 529 suggests '[i]t is perhaps more useful nowadays to regard a regulatory system as consisting of layered webs of regulatory influence, of which conventional activities of public regulatory agencies constitute but a few strands'.

20. Black, 'Decentring Regulation', above n 16; Julia Black, 'Constructing and Contesting Legitimacy and Accountability in Polycentric Regulatory Regimes' (2008) 2 *Regulation & Governance* 137; Christine Parker, 'The Pluralization of Regulation' (2008) 9 *Theoretical Inquiries in Law* 349.

21. For variations on this theme, see: David Levi-Faur, 'Regulation and Regulatory Governance' in D Levi-Faur (ed), *Handbook on the Politics of Regulation* (Edward Elgar, 2011) 3, 13; Christopher Hood, Henry Rothstein and Robert Baldwin, *The Government of Risk: Understanding Risk Regulation Regimes*

(Oxford University Press, 2001) 9; Colin Scott, 'Regulating Everything' (Discussion Paper No 24/2008, UCD Geary Institute, 26 February 2008) 7.

22. Hancher and Moran, 'Organizing Regulatory Space', above n 2, 271, 275; Scott, 'Analysing Regulatory Space', above n 5, 330. Participatory processes are discussed in Chapter 5.

23. David Levi-Faur, 'Regulation and Regulatory Governance', above n 21, 13.

24. This mirrors the three elements of a risk regulation regime (size; structure; style) identified by Hood, Rothstein and Baldwin, *The Government of Risk*, above n 21, 9–14.

25. Intergovernmental Committee on Drugs, Parliament of Australia, *National Tobacco Strategy 2012–2018* (2012).

26. The Intergovernmental Committee on Drugs comprises senior national and state government officials representing government portfolios involved in tobacco control. The Committee reports to the Council of Australian Governments Health Council that is made up of national and state health ministers.

27. The Strategy's first priority action area is: 'Protect public health policy, including tobacco control policies, from tobacco industry interference'.

28. Scott, 'Analysing Regulatory Space', above n 5, 330, 346–7.

29. Neil Gunningham and Peter Grabosky, *Smart Regulation: Designing Environmental Policy* (Clarendon Press, 1988) 93.

30. Tony Prosser, *The Regulatory Enterprise: Government, Regulation, and Legitimacy* (Oxford University Press, 2010) 29.

31. Julia Black, 'Constructing and Contesting Legitimacy and Accountability', above n 20.

5 Policy Processes and the Regulatory Policy Cycle

This chapter introduces the regulatory policy cycle through which the various components of the regulatory endeavour will be examined in Part III. The regulatory policy cycle is a specific application of the policy cycle tailored to the regulatory endeavour. The policy cycle, in turn, is one of several models that purport to explain the public policy process more generally. Two schools of thought dominate discussions about the public policy process: the normative school for whom policy-making should be rational, analytical and orderly; and the positivist or empirical school, who observe that policy-making, far from being rational and orderly, is characterised by ambiguity, chance, expediency, power, influence and self-interest. The regulatory policy cycle falls within the normative, rational school. It provides a comparatively simple, logical and easy-to-understand framework through which to study and examine the regulatory endeavour. The cycle's simplicity has been criticised, however, for ignoring the real world of policy-making. There is merit to this criticism. It is therefore important that its application is tempered by a recognition of the role and influence exerted on the process by private and other non-governmental interests, political and bureaucratic self-interest, the institutions through which the process plays out, and prevailing ideational currents. The chapter begins by exploring a number of the more influential theories that have shaped how we understand the regulatory policy process,[1] after which the regulatory policy cycle is introduced, its component stages are overviewed and factors that influence the momentum with which issues move through those stages are explored. The chapter concludes by discussing some of the implications that flow from the book's use of the regulatory policy cycle to frame its examination of the regulatory endeavour.

Theories of the Policy Process

Bounded Rationality

Our starting point is Professor Herbert A Simon. Simon's interest was understanding decision-making behaviour in real organisations, rather than ideal ones. His 1947 book, *Administrative Behavior*, introduced two powerful concepts that have exerted significant influence across a number of disciplines, including public policy, public administration, economics and political science.[2] First, Simon proposed a rational and sequential process of policy-making through his three stage model of: 'intelligence gathering' (identifying the issue and gathering data about it), 'design' (generating solutions to the issue) and 'choice' (selecting the 'best' solution from amongst the alternatives). We return to stagist approaches to policy-making later in this chapter.

Second, Simon recognised that decision-making within this rational process is bounded by our psychological and organisational environments— that is, we have 'bounded rationality'.[3]

Simon observed that the social sciences suffer an 'acute case of schizophrenia' when thinking about rationality. At one extreme are economists who assume people have 'preposterously omniscient rationality' (i.e. perfect knowledge and infinite processing capacity with which to compare alternative courses of action and to select from them the one that provides the highest return), and at the other extreme are psychologists who believe people are primarily driven by passions, emotions and subconscious feelings and anxieties (tracing back to Freud).[4] Simon argued that real world decision-making occupied a middle ground. Human behaviour was neither completely 'rational' nor completely 'irrational'. Rather, Simon argued that while persons within organisations intended to act rationally, that rationality is bounded by several factors, including: the incomplete or fragmented nature of knowledge, in particular about the future; cognitive limitations on an individual's capacity (intellectual, memory and attention) to process multiple complex issues simultaneously; and institutional limitations (budgetary, time and technological) on an organisation's capacity to gather and process the information necessary to rank and choose the best or optimal solution from among competing policy options. According to Simon, these factors lead decision-makers to adopt a simplified model of the world, to focus only on those factors they consider most relevant and important to the decision at hand, and to rely on a series of social, psychological, technological and environmental 'givens' to frame and set boundaries around the choices to be made. Simon expressed it well when he said:

> The capacity of the human mind for formulating and solving complex problems is very small compared with the size of the problems whose solution is required for objectively rational behaviour in the real world— or even for a reasonable approximation to such objective rationality.[5]

Simon concluded that whilst economic man maximises utility (in theory anyway), 'administrative man' 'satisfies' (in reality) and adopts the course of action that is 'good enough' from the limited options available.

Having accepted that decision-makers' rationality is bounded, Simon nevertheless argued that organisations should be designed in a manner that enables them to operate as rationally as possible and, in his 1960 book, *The New Science of Management Decisions*, advocated for the use of training, technology and rational management techniques to improve administrative decision-making.[6] In some ways, these techniques, and his rational and sequential process of policy-making, can be seen as the forebears of better regulation reforms, and the processes and techniques explored in Part III of the book.

Simon's concept of bounded rationality was accepted well in academic and policy circles, and his observation that the fallibilities of human cognition undermine many of the basic assumptions of economic rationalism continues to exert significant influence.[7] His rational and sequential process of policy-making, however, was met with criticism by those who observe that some policy-making appears to operate to a different (and less rational) logic. It is to two of the more influential and prominent of these alternative logics that the chapter now turns.

Muddling Through and Incrementalism

One of the first people to challenge the rational and sequential blueprint of policy-making was Charles Lindblom. Lindblom agreed with Simon that our decision-making ability is bounded by limited information, cognitive restrictions and time and budgetary constraints. However, Lindblom was hostile to the prominence given by Simon to the use of rational analytical techniques, which Lindblom argued could not replace the need for political agreement and consensus. According to Lindblom, policy decision-making does not conform to a neat set of sequential steps that commence with goal definition and end with option selection. Rather, Lindblom argued that policy-making is more about 'muddling through'—an iterative process of trial and error, and mutual adjustment and negotiation; where the ends being pursued and the means for pursuing them often are not clear or clearly delineated, with both shifting as more is learned about the issue.[8]

Notwithstanding its name, Lindblom considered 'muddling through' to be a policy science whereby policy analysis is limited to policy options that differ only slightly from policies already in effect. Lindblom referred to this method as 'successive limited comparison'. Limiting the analysis to similar existing policies has three important consequences: first, other options are excluded, not rationally and systematically, but by accident and neglect—a consequence of the decision-maker not looking beyond the immediate and present; second, limiting the analysis to a small number of similar options means that policy evolves through a succession of incremental changes (thus the name incrementalism); and three, the narrow focus of the analysis means that significant and lasting reforms often are not produced.

While muddling through is reflective of the conditions of bounded rationality, Lindblom's opposition to the use of rational analytical decision-making techniques to assist the policy process seemed somewhat incongruous. Criticisms of this stance led Lindblom to soften his position in his later years, during which he advocated for 'analytical incrementalism' and the 'informed and thoughtful' use of strategic analytical techniques that provide 'new and improved' ways of muddling through.[9] What did not change, however, was Lindblom's hostility to the idea that these techniques could somehow supplant the need for political agreement and consensus, which for Lindblom remained the main game.

One feature of Lindblom's model that continues to attract criticism is incrementalism's failure to adequately explain comprehensive (non-incremental) policy shifts. As Rajagopalan and Rasheed observe, Lindblom paints a picture of 'policy making [that] is serial and remedial in that it focuses heavily on remedial measures that happen to be at hand rather than addressing itself to a more comprehensive set of goals and alternative policies'.[10] It is to a model that explains non-incremental change that the chapter now turns.

Multiple Streams and Windows of Opportunity

A model of policy-making that both accommodates non-incremental policy change and challenges systematic and sequential policy-making models is John Kingdon's 'multiple streams' model of policy development.[11] Kingdon theorised that three 'streams' exist. First, there is the problem stream, being those issues that society has chosen to define as problems. Second is the policy stream that Kingdon conceptualises as a 'primeval soup' in which policy ideas float about, being discussed, revised and discussed again. And third is the political stream—the prevailing political processes, forces and climate. Kingdon then theorised that policy change takes place when the three streams are 'coupled', to use Kingdon's terminology. Coupling occurs when changes in the problem or political streams (i.e. how an issue is defined and perceived) trigger dissatisfaction with the status quo and create an environment conducive to policy action. Kingdon refers to these critical junctures opening a 'window of opportunity' for 'policy entrepreneurs' to push attention towards their preferred policy solution (which resides in the policy stream). As Kingdon explains, entrepreneurs 'lie in wait in and around government with their solutions in hand, waiting for problems to float by to which they can attach their solutions, waiting for a development in the political stream they can use to their advantage'.[12] Policy entrepreneurs are individuals willing to invest 'time, energy, reputation, money—to promote a position for anticipated future gain'.[13] They range from the genuinely community minded to the self-interested, and can include politicians, bureaucrats, academics, lobbyists and even journalists. The importance the model attaches to the policy entrepreneur recognises both the power of ideas and the role played by power and influence, themes on which we have already touched. Ideas (and ideologies) help policy entrepreneurs frame issues and define problems; and entrepreneurs with more power, influence and resources are better placed to advance their preferred policy solution.

Policy-making under the multiple streams model does not commence with a problem, and does not proceed in a rational and orderly manner to a solution. Rather, policy-making has a certain opportunistic quality about it: issues lay dormant or underappreciated until awoken (either by a change in the nature of the issue or in how the issue is perceived politically); solutions float around waiting for problems to which they might be the answer (thus the phrase 'a solution looking for a problem'); and entrepreneurs look for political changes that open a window of opportunity for them to couple problems and solutions in a manner aligned to the political zeitgeist of the day. As such, the multiple stream model can be thought of as the antithesis of rational, sequential models to which the chapter now turns.

Stagist Approaches

Our exploration of policy-making theories commenced with Simon's three-stage rational decision-making sequence: intelligence, design and choice. This is an early example of what has become known as a stagist approach—one that breaks the policy process down into discrete and separate stages or steps. Another early proponent of the stagist approach was Harold Laswell. Laswell divided the policy process into seven stages: intelligence gathering, promotion, prescription, invocation, application, termination and appraisal. According to Laswell, these stages not only described how policy was made, but also how it should be made.[14] Numerous stagist approaches have since been built on the foundations laid by Simon and Laswell. Amongst these, arguably the most significant advance was to move from a linear sequence to a cycle. Brewer, for example, proposed a six stage cyclical model of: invention/initiation, estimation, selection, implementation, evaluation, with the evaluation results either leading to termination of the policy program (the sixth stage), or to further invention and the cycle repeating itself.[15] Presenting the stages as an ongoing cycle recognises the trial and error nature of policy-making and that most issues and policies do not have a finite life-cycle: that issues evolve in response to changing circumstances (including the policy itself); and policies evolve in response to changes in the issue.

Stagist approaches have a number of important strengths. First, they enable us to examine the regulatory endeavour without being overwhelmed by its complexity. We already have observed that as individuals, our rationality is bounded and our ability to deal with complexity limited. Stagist approaches are comparatively simple (compared to other models and theories), logical and easy to understand and apply. By breaking the policy process into a series of discrete and smaller stages or steps, stagist approaches simplify the complexity of the real world, thereby enabling us to more easily conceptualise, explain and understand the policy process. Stagist approaches allow each of the stages to be separately studied, as well as their inter-relationship with each other, and the whole they form. Second, stagist approaches have great normative appeal, and are part of the prescription for better regulation. Employing a systematic approach and stepping sequentially through each of the key stages from problem definition through to evaluation should produce better outcomes or, put another way, prevent obvious (and not so obvious) mistakes that may cause regulatory failure.[16] And third, from a practitioner perspective, stagist models provide much needed structure and functional guidance for the policy-maker that alternative frameworks do not provide. As Sparrow observes:

> . . . problem-solving teams, given tasks they really care about and want to succeed in, come back time and time again asking for procedural guidance. Without some discernible structure to the process and a sense of orderly transition from phase to phase, they feel totally at sea, and their meetings tend to dissolve into confusion.[17]

Stagist approaches also have their weaknesses, however. The source of a stagist approach's strengths—its simplicity—also makes it deceptively inaccurate. Real world policy-making is far more complex, interactive and dynamic than a stagist approach admits. Many policy issues do not proceed through distinct and separate stages; others miss, compress and, in some cases, reverse stages;[18] and others still suffer from policy reflux, moving forwards and backwards to revisit and repeat stages previously completed. The process also can be ad hoc and idiosyncratic:[19] 'policies bubble and coalesce within complex, iterative processes and communities' and policy-making 'occurs in all manner of ways, emerging from all manner of sources and settling in all manner of forms'.[20]

Critics also point out that stagist approaches ignore the interrelationship between issues, that issues can advance along multiple pathways (some, for example, advance simultaneously though government policy processes, the courts and political machinery), and that for many issues, proceeding sequentially through the various stages would span decades or more, a period over which any systematic and orderly process would most likely break down. Stagist approaches also fail as causal theories as they do not explain how issues move from one stage to the next. The implicit assumption underpinning stagist approaches is that issues move at the discretion and direction of a centrally located government official. However, assuming a top-down centrally coordinated process fails to give adequate weight to the role played by other actors.[21]

Notwithstanding these weaknesses and criticisms, this book adopts a stagist approach (in the form of the regulatory policy cycle) to examine the regulatory endeavour—the conclusion being that its strengths outweigh its weaknesses.[22] However, to choose to employ a stagist approach is not to ignore its weaknesses and the merit in the criticisms that have been made. Rather, it requires us to be clear about the purposes for which the stagist approach is being used and the manner in which it is being used.[23] The stagist model employed in this book—the regulatory policy cycle discussed below— is being used as an analytical device to simplify the complexity of the real world to enable us to better understand the regulatory endeavour: to deconstruct and examine past and present regulatory initiatives and to construct better future ones. Having said that, the regulatory policy cycle is employed in this book cognisant that actors pursuing their self-interest, institutional dynamics, and ideas, values and beliefs, all play a role in regulatory policy-making. These real-world complexities are factored into the discussion of each of the cycle's stages, and are reflected within the cycle itself as gears that influence the momentum with which issues move through the cycle's various stages.

The Regulatory Policy Cycle

The regulatory policy cycle employed in this book is shown in Figure 5.1. As can be seen, it is made up of five stages and has four gears.

Stages of the Cycle

The regulatory policy cycle's five stages are define, design, decide, implement and evaluate.[24] Each stage, in turn, is made up of a series of sub-stages or processes. The *define* stage begins with an issue entering the policy cycle though a process known as agenda-setting. The stage then comprises the processes by which that issue is defined, its causes diagnosed and regulatory objectives set; the *design* stage refers to the processes by which a plausible set of regulatory options capable of achieving the regulatory objective are formulated; the *decide* stage refers to the processes through which those regulatory options are assessed and compared and

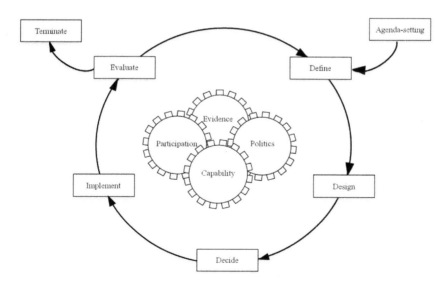

Figure 5.1 The Regulatory Policy Cycle

the regulatory initiative to be pursued chosen; the *implement* stage refers to the processes by which the chosen regulatory initiative is deployed and administered; and the *evaluate* stage refers to the processes by which the regulatory initiative is formally assessed. Evaluation findings can lead either to termination of the regulatory initiative (assuming it has achieved its objectives) or the cycle repeating itself (in cases where the evaluation findings require a fundamental reassessment of the issue definition, the regulatory objectives, the regime design or the manner in which it is being implemented). Each of these stages is discussed in detail in Part III.

Gears of the Cycle

In the centre of the cycle are factors that influence the momentum with which issues move through its various stages. These factors are participation, evidence, politics and capability. The factors are shown as gears. This is an apt metaphor. Gears on a motorcycle take power from the engine and convert it into momentum (strength and force). Each gear plays a role in converting energy into momentum, but no gear on its own is determinative. Similarly, each of participation, evidence, politics and capability play a role in converting pressure (energy) for an issue to be regulated or regulated differently into momentum (strength and force) through the regulatory policy cycle. Each factor is important but not determinative. The more they are aligned, the greater the speed and ease with which an issue is likely to move through the stages of the cycle. However, if not aligned, they can act as a brake on the process. Each factor (gear) is discussed below.

Participation

Our examination of the regulatory endeavour has revealed that regulation rarely is a top-down hierarchical exercise undertaken by government alone, but generally is a collaborative effort coordinated by government and undertaken with the support and assistance of a variety of state and non-state actors. The effective participation of these actors therefore is an essential part of the regulatory endeavour.[25]

Many of the benefits of participation have been touched on already and need only be summarised here.[26] First, effective participation leads to better issue diagnosis and better designed regulatory regimes. Governments and regulators, no matter how expert, do not have all the information and knowledge with which to diagnose issues and to identify, assess and compare all design options. Including other actors in regulatory decision-making processes enables their 'dispersed knowledge'—their experience, perspectives, ideas and information—to inform decision-making processes.[27] Second, effective participation leads to better implementation. We already have observed that governments do not have a monopoly on the power, influence and resources required to effect behavioural change, and that these also are held by non-state actors that occupy the regulatory space with it.[28] Participation enables these 'dispersed resources' to be brought to bear in support of the regulatory endeavour. Effective participation also operates as an educative process. Participatory processes enable regime participants, and those subject to the regime, to reach a shared understanding of how rules should be interpreted, applied and enforced in particular circumstances.[29] This, in turn, can lead to enhanced voluntary compliance. As Gunningham and Grabosky observe, 'policies are usually more easily implemented when people understand the reasons behind them'.[30] And third, effective participation enhances regulatory legitimacy.[31] Regulation, regulators and regulatory regimes appear more legitimate to people if they have participated in their development, implementation and evaluation.[32] Inclusive, fair and transparent decision-making processes increase trust and confidence, reduce suspicion and alienation and add to the legitimacy of both the process and its outputs.[33]

Participation is not risk free, however.[34] First, no matter how well designed and executed, participatory processes require governments and those participating to invest time, effort and resources into the process. The more inclusive and transparent the process, the more costly and time-consuming it is to administer. Participatory processes therefore involve trade-offs with other important regulatory values and principles, in particular decision timeliness, decisiveness and efficiency.[35] Second, if not well designed and executed, participatory processes can lead to poor decision-making (e.g. by giving one set of views or perspectives more or less prominence than they deserve);[36] to less effective implementation (e.g. by creating confusion and ambiguity around regime objectives and standards); and diminish regulatory legitimacy (e.g. if conducted in an unequal or unfair manner, or in a manner which leads some participants to believe information provided by them in good faith was ignored).[37] And third, participatory processes themselves can become a conflict zone. Deciding who is allowed to participate in the regulatory process and to have their views heard (and who is not) is an inherently political decision, providing those included with influence denied to those not included. And amongst those included, participants whose interests and values are likely to be advanced by the regulatory process will act to accelerate the issue's progress through the stages of the cycle, and those whose interests and values are likely to be adversely affected will act to slow and possibly derail the process. Common tactics to slow the process include challenging its nature and rules, overloading and overwhelming it with data and information and seeking to reopen and re-litigate decisions previously made.[38]

All of this can make participation a complex and sometimes contested process. The challenge for governments and regulators is to design and implement participatory processes that maximise the benefits of participation and mitigate its risks. Designing effective participatory processes involves answering two interrelated sets of questions: why and when; and who and how.[39] Why and when to invite people to participate in the process has already been discussed. Effective participation has the potential to improve each stage of the regulatory policy process. It is nevertheless important for policy-makers and regulators to turn their mind to the exact nature of the benefits (inputs) they seek to obtain from participation at a particular stage of the cycle because the answers to these questions inform who should be invited to participate and how. For example, during the define and design stages of the cycle, when the nature and causes of the issue, regulatory objectives and potential solutions are being discussed and canvassed, broad stakeholder participation is most valuable, and inclusive and dialogical models of participation are warranted; whereas at the individual enforcement level when regulator and regulatee are negotiating the consequences of non-compliance, third parties are less likely to have meaningful contributions to make, leading those processes to be less inclusive and less transparent.[40]

These examples illustrate that answers to the 'who' question exist on a continuum. At one end of the continuum are pluralist systems that engage a broad range of different interest groups. Pluralist systems have the advantages of maximising the amount and diversity of views and information available to the decision-maker. Their disadvantages relate to the cost and time involved in administering the process, the risk of the volume of information becoming unmanageable and the difficulty of identifying common ground. At the other end of the continuum are (neo-)corporatist systems that limit participation to established representative groups (e.g. peak employer associations, peak union bodies, peak environmental groups). Corporatist systems are more manageable than pluralist systems, both because of the smaller number of actors who participate, and because those actors usually are resourced and skilled in government politics and processes. Limiting participation to established groups, however, also limits the range of views, perspectives, ideas and information to which decision-makers are exposed. They also can be perceived as a grant of monopoly to select groups to which attaches the risk of capture.

The answers to the 'how' question also sit on a continuum. At one end of the continuum are formal processes such as legislated notice and comment periods, statutory advisory committees and rights of review; at the other end are the informal phone calls, discussions and myriad other ways government and regulatory officials interact with regulatees and other regulatory actors on a near daily basis; and in-between, a range of participatory mechanisms of varying formality, including stakeholder and community forums and joint working groups.[41] Formal processes tend to be more transparent and consistent with the principles of due process and procedural fairness, but can be costly and time consuming to administer and less interactive than informal processes. Less formal processes, on the other hand, while inexpensive to administer, are not transparent and tend to favour better resourced and organised groups.

Participatory processes also are mechanisms by which power is shared between government and those that are governed. This arguably is their most important feature. Numerous models have been developed that purport to capture this dimension. Arnstein, for example, conceptualised a 'ladder of participation' beginning with manipulation and empty rhetoric at the bottom, climbing through information provision and consultation (which she described as 'tokenism'), with power sharing and citizen control at the top.[42] Other models differentiate between thin and thick participation.[43] Thin versions are concerned primarily with information gathering and the striking of bargains and compromises. Under thin participation models, there is minimal discourse between parties whose preferences remain largely unchanged. Thick versions of participation, on the other hand, encourage dialogue amongst regulatory actors about each other's perspectives and preferences, and through this 'mutual learning', a shared understanding of the issue, the regulation's goals and objectives, and how regulatory rules should be interpreted, applied and enforced in particular circumstances.[44] And others still seek to match participation processes to the participation goal, and to the nature, importance and politics of the issue. For example, Bishop and Davis developed a map of participatory approaches beginning with two-way information provision, through varying processes that allow third parties a degree of influence over the policy process, and ending with handing control of the issue to the electorate through referenda and the like.[45]

These participation approaches, their purpose, key techniques and the stages of the regulatory policy cycle to which they are best suited are summarised below in Table 5.1.[46]

This discussion of participation has highlighted its importance to the regulatory endeavour and to how issues move within and between stages of the regulatory policy cycle. It also has highlighted that there is no one-size-fits-all approach to participation. Several participatory approaches exist from which government and regulators can choose. The choice of approach is an exercise of judgement. There are a number of principles that should guide that judgement. First, governments and regulators should be purpose orientated: who is invited to participate, through which technique and at which stages should be tailored to the government's or regulator's purpose in seeking to enlist their input or support. Not all issues require extensive participation at all stages. Second, governments and regulators should manage expectations: they should be clear with participants about the purpose, nature and process of participation at each stage. Third, governments and regulators should act consistently with those expectations: they should do what they said they would do, when they said they would do it. Failure to do so can raise concerns about due process and the integrity of the regulatory endeavour.[47] And fourth, governments and regulators should approach every engagement as an

Table 5.1 Participation Approaches

Type	Purpose	Key Techniques	Stages
Consultation	• Gather perspectives, ideas, information to inform regulatory decision-making • Gauge reaction to/stress test proposals	• Informal discussions • Meetings with interest groups • Discussion papers • Notice and comment periods • Hearings/inquiries/ community forums	• All stages
Dialogue	• Learn about perspectives/ preferences of other regulatory actors • Shape/change perceptions of issue; behaviour of participants	• Stakeholder committees • Joint working groups • Mediated discussions • Open deliberative models	• All stages
Partnership	• Involve affected and interested parties in aspects of regulatory decision-making and implementation	• Joint working groups • Representative inquiries • Advisory committees • Enforcement powers • Prosecutorial powers	• All stages
Standing	• Allow affected and interested parties to challenge aspects of regulatory decision-making	• Merits review • Judicial review • Commissions/ inquiries	• Decide • Implement • Evaluate
Control	• Empower affected and interested parties to make regulatory decisions	• Regulators with representative boards/ commissioners • Referenda • Community/citizen juries	• Diagnose • Design • Decide • Evaluate

opportunity to enhance legitimacy: they should treat participants impartially and with respect, politeness and dignity. Participants' perceptions of how they have been treated can be just as influential in shaping their attitudes towards the regulatory endeavour as their substantive positions on the issue.[48]

Evidence

The second gear that drives the regulatory policy cycle is evidence. Strong and consistent evidence, first of the problem, opportunity or risk, and second of feasible initiatives to solve that problem, grasp that opportunity or address that risk, helps to build momentum through the cycle. Weak or equivocal evidence that questions the existence or nature of the issue or government's ability to deal with it can slow the cycle. This is not to say, however, that policy cannot be made in the absence of good evidence. As Birkland observes, relatively little evidence may be all that is required if it is possible to frame the issue in a manner that appeals to societal fears, popular prejudices and common misconceptions.[49]

What constitutes 'evidence' and, more particularly, 'good' evidence? 'Evidence' is another term that defies precise definition. Watts observes that it is common in the evidence-based policy literature for the term to be left undefined, the assumption being that its meaning is so commonplace as not to warrant elucidation.[50] Watts also observes that among those authors who choose to define it, some employ legalistic definitions (evidence is information that tends to establish a fact); some employ definitions that limit evidence to scientific knowledge (data produced by scientific analytical methods); and others employ pluralistic definitions that include, in addition to information and data, opinions, inferences and beliefs. This book argues for a pluralistic approach to evidence-based policy-making. Evidence should come from a variety of different perspectives and viewpoints.[51] As the European Commission's principles and guidelines on the use of expertise state:

> Wherever possible, a diversity of viewpoints should be assembled. This diversity may result from differences in scientific approach, different types of expertise, different institutional affiliations, or contrasting opinions over the fundamental assumptions underpinning the issue.
>
> Depending on the issue and the stage in the policy cycle, pluralism also entails taking account of multi-disciplinary and multi-sectoral expertise, minority and non-conformist views. Other factors may also be important, such as geographical, cultural and gender perspectives.[52]

Three common ways of characterising evidence are: direct and circumstantial, scientific and non-scientific and expert and non-expert. Direct evidence establishes the truth of an assertion without the need for any additional evidence or inferences to be drawn (e.g. witnessing fish flounder in waters muddied by channel dredging is direct evidence that dredging killed the fish). Circumstantial evidence relies on other evidence or an inference to connect it to a conclusion of fact (e.g. seeing dead fish after channel dredging is circumstantial evidence that the dredging killed the fish). Direct evidence is stronger than circumstantial evidence, but even direct evidence can suffer from incorrect recollections and interpretations, the result of the interpretive and cognitive biases of the person observing it.

The above examples are of non-scientific evidence. They are anecdotal and have not been collected in accordance with an accepted scientific method. Scientific evidence, on the other hand, is knowledge derived from data collected and interpreted in accordance with the standards of an accepted field of scientific inquiry. 'Science' is used here broadly to include both the physical and social sciences. Scientific evidence can come from laboratory experiments on the chemical properties of a pollutant and epidemiological studies of the pollutant's health effects on a population. Evidence also can come from econometric or statistical studies that estimate the financial costs to the health system of treating persons affected by the pollutant, and from psychological or cognitive studies on how persons are likely to respond to information about the pollutant's health effects. Each scientific field has standards for ensuring scientific research is reliable, robust and produced in a manner designed to ensure accuracy and eliminate error. Generally, this includes publishing the data and processes employed to enable third parties to verify and reproduce the results.

Scientific evidence generally comes from experts. An expert is a person who has special skill or knowledge in a particular area. This knowledge or skill normally is associated with academic training. However, it also can be obtained through practical experience. Persons who have worked for many years in a particular industry or with a particular cause can become experts in that industry or cause even if they have no formal training in that area. Experts generally are accepted as being better placed than non-experts in interpreting and drawing inferences and conclusions from other forms of evidence. Persons trained in investigation techniques are generally better at drawing inferences from circumstantial evidence, and scientists are better placed to interpret and draw conclusions from scientific studies conducted within their field of expertise. However, expert scientific evidence is not infallible. It can be subject to data or process limitations, and the experts who interpret and draw inferences and conclusions from the results also can be subject to cognitive biases and ideological and political influences.[53]

Evidence does not have to be scientifically produced or to have come from an expert to be useful. Evidence also can come from non-experts—after all, this is one of the main purposes of broad, inclusive participatory processes. We have observed that regulation frequently involves prioritising, balancing and sometimes trading-off different interests and values. The opinions of persons who hold those interests and values are important evidence informing the striking of those balances and the making of those trade-offs. Even biased and ill-informed opinions from these persons are valuable if only to identify attitudes and behaviours that may need to be changed or neutralised for the regulatory intervention to succeed.

The rational expectation is that good (direct, scientific and expert) evidence will build momentum through the regulatory policy cycle and, ultimately, lead to better decisions and better outcomes. However, this expectation must be tempered by the real world of political decision-making. Not all decisions are made on the basis of the best available evidence. Evidence often is selectively presented or spun to advance (or undermine) a particular interest or cause.[54] Public opinion leveraged by powerful interest groups can operate upon ideologically aligned governments to produce policy momentum in the absence of good evidence, and policy stasis in its presence.[55] And governments and politicians seeking (re)election are conditioned to regulate based on 'political-electoral' considerations. These considerations sometimes can be more evidence-free than evidence-based.[56] For this reason, some commentators argue that evidence-based policy-making is an ideal more than a reality (the reality being that policy also is the product of intuitive appeal, tradition, politics and existing practice).[57] Yet it is an ideal worth striving for. Those responsible for diagnosing issues, and designing, implementing and evaluating regulation, should seek to do so on the basis of the best available evidence. It also is important that they understand the limitations of that evidence. Circumstantial evidence should be corroborated; scientific evidence should be verifiable and repeatable, and the potential biases and conflicts of those generating and interpreting the evidence should be identified and taken into account. Evidence also should reflect a diversity of viewpoints and opinions. This diversity often means, however, that decision-makers are presented with evidence from many different sources, in many different forms, and with different levels of assuredness. Assessing, weighing and balancing this diverse and sometimes contradictory evidence requires judgement. This observation—that the use of even expert scientific evidence requires judgement—reinforces one of the book's key themes— that regulation is both a science and an art.

Politics

The third gear is politics. 'Politics' is used here broadly and comprises many elements. 'Politics' consists of the national mood and public opinion, prevailing ideologies and the organisation and composition of government, the bureaucracy, interest groups and other political forces.[58] Politics also includes the energy exerted by regulatory actors advocating for their regulatory objectives or defending regulatory gains already secured. As Cohen, March and Olsen observed, the energy exerted by regulatory actors influences which issues are likely to be addressed, how and over what period of time.[59] Politics' inclusion as a gear emphasises its importance to the regulatory process, it being both a source of energy and a factor determining the extent to which that energy is converted into momentum. As Levi-Faur observed, '[k]nowledge, rationality, and reason are always mediated (not to say mobilized and abused) by political processes'.[60]

The more the politics of an issue are aligned, the quicker and smoother the passage of that issue through the stages of the regulatory policy cycle. An excellent example of this are the contrasting examples of gun control in the United States and Australia.[61] In the United States, policy movement has been slow and laborious despite regular mass-shootings, a reflection of a political landscape where public opinion on the issue is divided; constitutional protections and social institutions have created a culture supportive of individual rights generally, and the individual's right to bear arms in particular; and well-resourced and influential interest groups can leverage the US Presidential system's separation of executive and legislature, emphasis on states' rights and strong partisanship to prevent, delay and diminish action on the issue. In contrast, in Australia, strong and decisive gun control measures were introduced quickly in response to one mass-shooting. Unlike the United States, in Australia, strong public support for gun control, an absence of relevant constitutional protections and powerful interest groups, greater acceptance of government action prioritising the collective over the individual and a Westminster system of government and strong traditions of intergovernmental cooperation combined to facilitate bi-partisan action on the issue.[62]

Of the four gears, politics is the factor least capable of being influenced directly by policy and regulatory practitioners. It largely is an exogenous force that shapes the behaviour of even the most senior decision-makers. At the same time, however, it is something that those involved in the regulatory endeavour should be cognisant of and take into account as they move through the cycle's stages. Policy analysts should consider the political feasibility of the options they develop and recommend, and whether they are likely to receive the political support necessary for legislative adoption and budgetary support. Policy analysts, regulators and others involved in the process also should consider how affected parties and other interested groups might respond to the decisions they make and the actions they take, and prepare accordingly. Politically sensitive issues may require more time, effort and evidence to persuade people to participate in the endeavour, and to resist adversely affected groups' attempts to delay or derail the process.

Capability

The final gear is capability. The momentum with which an issue moves through the stages of the regulatory policy cycle—and the success of the entire regulatory endeavour—depends in large part on the integrity and capability of the persons undertaking it.[63] Persons engaged in the regulatory endeavour need a commitment to serving the public interest. Absent this commitment the process is apt to be captured or manipulated by private interests or political or bureaucratic self-interest. They also need the skills, competencies and knowledge to perform at a high level. These will vary according to the stage of the cycle, the nature of the issue and the particular role of the person in question. Looked at holistically, they include: leadership, negotiation and communication skills to steer and direct different interests towards a common goal; inter-personal and facilitation skills to conduct participatory processes fairly and respectfully; technical skills with which to understand the issue and the social, cultural, economic and political systems in which it is embedded; analytical skills to collect, assess, interpret and synthesise vast amounts of different and sometimes inconsistent evidence; problem-solving and program management skills to make and implement decisions effectively; and the judgement, discretion and political acumen to weigh and balance the various technical, social, economic and political considerations that go into making regulatory decisions.[64] The latter is particularly important. As Head observes: 'Policy decisions are not deduced primarily from facts and empirical models, but from politics, judgement and debate'.[65]

Concluding Insights and Implications

This chapter has explored a number of different theories that purport to explain the process by which public policy is made. These theories fall into two broad schools: the normative school, for whom policy-making is rational, analytical and orderly; and the positivist or empirical school, who observe that policy-making often is characterised by compromise, chance, expediency, power, influence and self-interest. The reality is that modern regulatory policy-making is likely to span all these theories; that policy-making is apt to be rational in places and messy and unpredictable in others; that some policy is the product of decisions made rationally and sequentially; other policy is the product of iterative trial and error; and other policy still is the product of the opportunism of skilled entrepreneurs taking advantage of changes in the political landscape to couple their preferred policy solution to a new or changed issue.

Notwithstanding this reality—and partly because of this reality—the book adopts the stagist regulatory policy cycle to examine the regulatory endeavour. The regulatory policy cycle provides a rational structure through which the regulatory endeavour can be described and explained, constructed and deconstructed, and its constituent stages examined and analysed. Real-world complexities cannot be ignored, however. For this reason, the book seeks to incorporate into its application of the cycle many of the real-world nuances, intricacies and complexities faced by regulatory policy-makers. This is achieved in part by incorporating into the cycle factors that influence the momentum with which an issue moves through it. It also is achieved by incorporating different perspectives and frameworks into the book's examination of each stage of the cycle.

Use of the regulatory policy cycle in this manner is emblematic of one of the book's core themes—that the regulatory endeavour is both a science and an art. The regulatory policy cycle is one of the systems that bring structure and order to the regulatory process. Tailoring the cycle to the issue at hand, identifying and incorporating the myriad of actors, interests and institutional dynamics into it, and adjusting the cycle when necessary to accommodate changed circumstances, information gaps, contested meanings and other uncertainties is the art. The science and art of employing the regulatory policy cycle is the focus of Part III of the book.

Notes

1. There are numerous theoretical frameworks that purport to explain the policy process or policy change. The theories discussed in this chapter were chosen because of the significant influence they have exerted over the field, and because they purport to explain the entire (or majority) of the policy process, as opposed to specific aspects of it. More specific theories are discussed elsewhere in the book, where relevant.

2. Herbert A Simon, *Administrative Behavior: A Study of Decision-Making Processes in Administrative Organization* (Macmillan Co, 1945). See also Herbert A Simon, 'A Behavioral Model of Rational Choice' (1955) 69 *Quarterly Journal of Economics* 99; Herbert A Simon, *Models of Man: Social and Rational: Mathematical Essays on Rational Human Behavior in a Social Setting* (Wiley, 1957).

3. The observation that people have 'bounded rationality' applies not only to policy-makers. It also applies to regulatees and other actors whose cooperation and support is required to regulate effectively.

4. Simon, *Administrative Behavior*, above n 2, xxiii, quoted in Wayne Parsons, *Public Policy: An Introduction to the Theory and Practice of Policy Analysis* (Edward Elgar, 1995) 275.

5. Simon, *Models of Man*, above n 2, 198.

6. Herbert A Simon, *The New Science of Management Decisions* (Harper, 1960).

7. Bounded rationality can be seen as the father of behavioural economics and the nudge techniques for changing behaviour it has spawned: Graham Mallard, *Bounded Rationality and Behavioural Economics* (Routledge, 2015). Nudge techniques are discussed in Chapter 8.

8. Charles E Lindblom, 'The Science of "Muddling Through"' (1959) 19 *Public Administration Review* 79.

9. Charles E Lindblom, 'Still Muddling, Not Yet Through' (1979) 39 *Public Administrative Review* 517. See also Charles E Lindblom and Edward J Woodhouse, *The Policy-Making Process* (Prentice Hall, 3rd ed, 1993) 27–32.

10. Nandini Rajagopalan and Abdul M A Rasheed, 'Incremental Models of Policy Formulation and Non-Incremental Changes: Critical Review and Synthesis' (1995) 6 *British Journal of Management* 289, 291.

11. John W Kingdon, *Agendas, Alternatives, and Public Policies* (Longman, 2nd ed, 2003). Kingdon developed this model to explain US federal policy-making. Zahariadis has since demonstrated its applicability to policy-making in other political systems, including Westminster parliamentary systems (United Kingdom) and European style presidential systems (France and Germany): Nikolaos Zahariadis, 'Ambiguity, Time and Multiple Streams' in P A Sabatier (ed), *Theories of the Policy Process* (Westview Press, 1999) 73.

12. Kingdon, *Agendas, Alternatives, and Public Policies*, above n 11, 165.

13. Ibid 179.

14. Harold D Lasswell, *The Decision Process: Seven Categories of Functional Analysis* (University of Maryland, 1956).

15. Garry D Brewer, 'The Policy Sciences Emerge: To Nurture and Structure a Discipline' (1974) 5 *Policy Sciences* 239.

16. Catherine Althaus, Peter Bridgman and Glyn Davis, *The Australian Policy Handbook* (Allen & Unwin, 5th ed, 2013) 34; Sarah Maddison and Richard Denniss, *An Introduction to Australian Public Policy: Theory and Practice* (Cambridge University Press, 2nd ed, 2013) 76.

17. Malcolm Sparrow, *The Regulatory Craft* (Brookings Institution Press, 2000) 137.

18. The evaluation stage in particular frequently is abbreviated, de-emphasised or by-passed, and stages are reversed when analysis is undertaken to substantiate a decision already made. Cosmo Howard, 'The Policy Cycle: A Model of

Post-Machiavellian Policy Making?' (2005) 64 *Australian Journal of Public Administration* 3.

19. Michael Howlett and M Ramesh, *Studying Public Policy: Policy Cycles and Policy Subsystems* (Oxford University Press, 1995) 12.
20. Althaus, Bridgman and Davis, *The Australian Policy Handbook*, above n 16, 2.
21. For an overview of the criticisms of stagist approaches, see: Robert Nakamura, 'The Textbook Policy Process and Implementation Research' (1987) 1 *Policy Studies Review* 142; Lindblom and Woodhouse, *The Policy-Making Process*, above n 9, 10–2; Hank C Jenkins-Smith and Paul A Sabatier, 'The Study of Public Policy Processes' in P A Sabatier and H C Jenkins-Smith (eds), *Policy Change and Learning: An Advocacy Coalition Approach* (Westview Press, 1993) 3–4. For a critique of these criticisms and a defence of stagist approaches, see Peter deLeon, 'The Stages Approach to the Policy Process: What Has It Done? Where Is It Going?' in P A Sabatier (ed), *Theories of the Policy Process* (Westview Press, 1999) 19.
22. For others who have reached the same conclusion, see: Wayne Parsons, *Public Policy: An Introduction to the Theory and Practice of Policy Analysis* (Edward Elgar, 1995) 80; deLeon, 'The Stages Approach to the Policy Process', above n 21; Peter Bridgman and Glyn Davis, 'What Use Is a Policy Cycle? Plenty, If the Aim Is Clear' (2003) 62 *Australian Journal of Public Administration* 98.
23. Bridgman and Davis, 'What Use Is a Policy Cycle?', above n 22.
24. The stages of the regulatory policy cycle are defined by reference to the regulatory activity undertaken. This can be distinguished from regulatory life-cycles that define the stages genealogically by reference to the agency's maturity and vibrancy. See discussion in Chapter 3, 44–5.
25. Tony Prosser, *The Regulatory Enterprise: Government, Regulation, and Legitimacy* (Oxford University Press, 2010) 233.
26. See discussion in Chapter 4 (Regulatory Space and Regulatory Regimes). See also: Jennifer Nash and Daniel E Walters, 'Public Engagement and Transparency in Regulation: A Field Guide to Regulatory Excellence' (Research Paper prepared for the Penn Program on Regulation's Best-in-Class Regulator Initiative, June 2015) 1–5; Renee A Irving and John Stansbury, 'Citizen Participation in Decision-Making: Is It Worth the Effort?' (2004) 64 *Public Administration Review* 55–65.
27. Cass R Sunstein, *Infotopia: How Many Minds Produce Knowledge* (Oxford University Press, 2006) 19. See also Cary Coglianese, 'Citizen Participation in Rulemaking: Past, Present, and Future' (2006) 55 *Duke Law Journal* 943; Julia Black, 'Talking about Regulation' [1998] (Spring) *Public Law* 77; Julia Black, 'Regulatory Conversations' (2002) 29 *Journal of Law and Society* 163.
28. See Chapter 4.
29. Julia Black, *Rules and Regulators* (Clarendon Press, 1997) 30–2; Black, 'Regulatory Conversations', above n 27.
30. Neil Gunningham and Peter Grabosky, *Smart Regulation: Designing Environmental Policy* (Clarendon Press, 1998) 386.
31. Regulatory legitimacy is discussed in detail in Chapter 6, 112–18.
32. Gunningham and Grabosky, *Smart Regulation*, above n 30.
33. Black, 'Talking about Regulation', above n 27, 104–5. See generally Christopher Hood and David Heald (eds), *Transparency: The Key to Better Governance* (Oxford University Press, 2006) 3.
34. For a general discussion of the disadvantages of participation, see Nash and Walters, 'Public Engagement and Transparency in Regulation', above n 26; Irving and Stansbury, 'Citizen Participation in Decision-Making', above n 26.

35. Irving and Stansbury, 'Citizen Participation in Decision-Making', above n 26; Jim Rossi, 'Participation Run Amok: The Costs of Mass Participation for Deliberative Agency Decisionmaking' (1997) 92 *Northwestern University Law Review* 173.
36. Some commentators refer to participatory biases leading to regulatory biases as a result of better informed and organized stakeholders having their voices heard disproportionally, see e.g., Robert Baldwin, *Rules and Government* (Clarendon Press, 1995) 139–40.
37. Rossi, 'Participation Run Amok', above n 35.
38. See e.g., Wendy E Wagner, 'Administrative Law, Filter Failure, and Information Capture' (2010) 59 *Duke Law Journal* 1321; Irving and Stansbury, 'Citizen Participation in Decision-Making', above n 26.
39. This categorization is borrowed from Nash and Walters, 'Public Engagement and Transparency in Regulation', above n 26. Nash and Walters, in turn, base their categories on Fung's 'democracy cube' in which he differentiates between the scope of participation, the intensity of communication and the extent of authority conferred on those participating: Archon Fung, 'Varieties of Participation in Complex Governance' (2006) 66 *Public Administration Review* 66.
40. Black, 'Talking about Regulation', above n 27, 100.
41. For a discussion of some of these processes, see Nash and Walters, 'Public Engagement and Transparency in Regulation', above n 26.
42. Sherry Arnstein, 'A Ladder of Citizen Participation' (1969) 35 *Journal of the American Institute of Planners* 216.
43. Julia Black, 'Proceduralizing Regulation: Part I' (2000) 20 *Oxford Journal of Legal Studies* 597; Julia Black, 'Proceduralizing Regulation: Part II' (2001) 21 *Oxford Journal of Legal Studies* 33; Ciara Brown and Colin Scott, 'Regulation, Public Law, and Better Regulation' (2011) *European Public Law* 467, 475–83.
44. There are numerous models for conducting these 'thicker' dialogues. They include: Hood, Rothstein and Baldwin's 'open process of institutionalized debate' about competing values: Christopher Hood, Henry Rothstein and Robert Baldwin, *The Government of Risk: Understanding Risk Regulation Regimes* (Oxford University Press, 2001) 184; Prosser's 'collaborative enterprise' in which the regulatee and other stakeholders who inhabit the broader regulatory space are part of the regulator's deliberative process: Prosser, *The Regulatory Enterprise*, above n 25, 5–6; and Black's 'thick proceduralization' based on deliberative models of democracy: Black, 'Proceduralizing Regulation: Part I', above n 43; Black, 'Proceduralizing Regulation: Part II', above n 43; Black, 'Regulatory Conversations', above n 27.
45. Patrick Bishop and Glyn Davis, 'Mapping Public Participation in Policy Choices' (2002) 61 *Australian Journal of Public Administration* 14.
46. Those familiar with Bishop and Davis's work will see that Table 5.1 is an adaption of a table they developed, tailored to the regulatory policy cycle and to which I have added dialogue (reflecting the thick participatory approaches discussed above) and removed 'consumer choice' (that relates to consumers' ability to influence service delivery mechanisms through their choice of service provider and which is not relevant to regulatory policy).
47. Black, 'Talking about Regulation', above n 27, 77–8.
48. See discussion of procedural legitimacy in Chapter 6, 114–15.
49. Thomas A Birkland, *An Introduction to the Policy Process: Theories, Concepts, and Models of Public Policy Making* (Routledge, 4th ed, 2016) 19. Framing is discussed in Chapter 7, 132–3.
50. Rob Watts, 'Truth and Politics: Thinking about Evidence Policy in the Age of Spin' (2014) 73 *Australian Journal of Public Administration* 34.

51. A pluralistic approach also eschews the positivist/constructionist knowledge debate. Pluralist definitions accept some knowledge is not objectively verifiable and is constructed by regulatory actors with an interest in the issue at hand. Even scientific knowledge can be shaped by the beliefs, values, ideologies and cognitive biases of these who interpret it: Ian Sanderson, 'Evaluation, Policy Learning, and Evidence-Based Policy Making' (2002) 80 *Public Administration* 1. Of course, the manner in which knowledge is constructed, and the assumptions and beliefs of those who construct it, may be relevant to the weight to be given to it.

52. Commission of the European Communities, 'Communication from the Commission on the Collection and Use of Expertise by the Commission: Principles and Guidelines' (COM(2002) 713 Final, 11 November 2002) 9. See also David Levi-Faur, 'Regulatory Excellence via Multiple Forms of Expertise' in C Coglianese (ed), *Achieving Regulatory Excellence* (Brookings Institution Press, 2017) 225.

53. For a discussion of how these biases can be mitigated, see Chapter 7, 144.

54. Watts, 'Truth and Politics', above n 50; Arie Freiberg and W G Carson, 'The Limits to Evidence-Based Policy: Evidence, Emotion and Criminal Justice' (2010) 69 *Australian Journal of Public Administration* 152.

55. Freiberg and Carson, 'The Limits to Evidence-Based Policy', above n 54.

56. Christopher Hood and Martin Lodge, 'Pavlovian Innovation, Pet Solutions and Economizing on Rationality? Politicians and Dangerous Dogs' in J Black, M Lodge and M Thatcher (eds), *Regulatory Innovation: A Comparative Analysis* (Edward Elgar, 2005) 138, 151.

57. See e.g., Watts, 'Truth and Politics', above n 50; Brian W Head, 'Three Lenses of Evidence-Based Policy' (2008) 67 *Australian Journal of Public Administration* 1, 9.

58. This is consistent with the definition employed by Kingdon is his multiple streams model. See discussion above at 82–3.

59. Michael D Cohen, James G March and Johan P Olsen, 'A Garbage Can Model of Organizational Choice' (1972) 17 *Administrative Science Quarterly* 1.

60. Levi-Faur, 'Regulatory Excellence via Multiple Forms of Expertise', above n 52.

61. Joshua Newman and Brian Head, 'The National Context of Wicked Problems: Comparing Policies on Gun Violence in the US, Canada and Australia' (2017) 19(1) *Journal of Comparative Policy Analysis: Research and Practice* 40.

62. Newman and Head's study also included Canada. Canada shares features of both the US and Australian political systems, and its approach to gun control treads a middle path as a result.

63. These match the findings of a study by the University of Pennsylvania's Penn Program on Regulation that identified three core attributes of regulatory excellence: integrity, empathetic engagement and stellar competence; see Cary Coglianese, 'Listening, Learning, Leading: A Framework for Regulatory Excellence' (Penn Program on Regulation, 2015).

64. For an attempt to develop a comprehensive statement of the capabilities required by modern policy and regulatory professionals, see Institute of Public Administration Australia, 'Policy Professional Capability Statement' (IPAA, 2014); Institute of Public Administration Australia, 'Regulatory Professional Capability Guide' (IPAA, 2015).

65. Head, 'Three Lenses of Evidence-Based Policy', above n 57, 9.

6 Bad, Better and Legitimate Regulation

Before exploring the stages of the regulatory policy cycle, it is important to understand what regulatory success looks like. 'Success' is an elusive concept. For the technocrat, success is measured in terms of effectiveness and efficiency: regulation succeeds when it delivers its policy objectives on time and on budget. But this technocratic answer is far too simple. Success is multi-dimensional. As McConnell reminds us, it has process, programmatic and political dimensions.[1] A policy may succeed on one dimension but fail on another. Success also is contestable. Like beauty, it is in the eye of the beholder. The question, 'what does success look like?' does not lend itself to easy answers. With this in mind, this chapter seeks to build a picture of regulatory success in three steps. First, we examine the causes of regulatory failure. Studying regulatory failure provides fertile ground from which to draw lessons about what went wrong and why, and about what might be done differently and better. Not surprisingly, many of these lessons have found their way into reforms designed to guide policy-makers and regulators on how better regulation can be designed and implemented. The core elements of these 'better regulation' reforms are explored in the second part of this chapter. These reforms largely focus on the legal and normative dimensions of the regulatory endeavour and, on their own, may be insufficient to effect behaviour change in situations where people are being asked to do things they would not otherwise choose to do. In these situations, something more generally is required. What constitutes that something more is explored in the third part of the chapter and is encapsulated in the concept of 'regulatory legitimacy'. This part constructs a framework for understanding how different actors in the regulatory space perceive the legitimacy (acceptability and credibility) of regulators and regulatory regimes. Regulatory legitimacy has a number of important implications for the regulatory endeavour which are discussed in the concluding part of the chapter.

Regulatory Failure

Regulatory failures are not accidents. They do not occur by chance. Each regulatory failure has a cause (and, in most cases, more than one cause). As Grabosky, in his seminal work on counterproductive regulation, observed: '[t]he ways in which efforts to produce regulatory compliance may become derailed are numerous and diverse, as are the generic pathologies which give rise to them'.[2] Authors who have studied regulatory failures have employed different ways to categorise these pathologies.[3] In this section we examine them by reference to the stages and, in some cases, sub-stages of the regulatory policy cycle. Employing the stages of the regulatory policy cycle enables the lessons of regulatory failure to be injected directly into our consideration of those stages in Part III of the book.

Poor Diagnosis

Regulation can fail because of a failure to properly diagnose the issue being regulated. Numerous factors can contribute to poor diagnosis. First, poor diagnosis may simply be the result of a lack of thought. Hancher and Moran refer to it often being done unthinkingly on the basis of customary assumptions and organisational routines.[4] Grabosky similarly refers to issue diagnosis failing to look beyond superficial, mechanistic doctrines of opportunity and deterrence.[5]

However, even diagnoses undertaken thoughtfully can fail. One reason is inadequate time. Frequently, regulation is designed under time pressures that prevent the issue being thoroughly analysed. The pressure to act quickly may be because of the speed with which the issue is moving and deteriorating (e.g. the need at the start of the global financial crisis to act quickly to restore confidence in the liquidity of financial institutions and to arrest a run on the banks), or because of a political need for government to be seen to be acting decisively in response to a perceived safety or security risk. An example of this is Hood's and Lodge's study of dangerous dog legislation implemented 'pavlovianly' in response to dog attacks on children which is then scaled back when found to be unnecessarily harsh in its enforcement or unnecessarily broad in its scope.[6]

Evidentiary problems are another factor leading to poor diagnosis. Evidence is the life-blood of good policy and regulatory analysis.[7] However, many policy and regulatory analysts find themselves with insufficient data about the issue and its broader environment from which to draw reliable inferences or, alternatively, too much data and without the skills and systems to convert the data into meaningful and useable information. In both situations, analysts are restricted in their ability to forensically examine the issue's various nuances and intricacies. This can lead to a tendency to oversimplify and overgeneralise, which Grabosky suggests is the most common pitfall in regulatory design.[8]

Another basic diagnostic shortcoming is failing to understand an issue's causal processes, the target audience's motivations and capabilities, and the numerous social, cultural and economic systems and sub-systems into which both are integrated, and which an intervention is likely to impact and potentially disrupt.[9] This failure, in turn, can result in unintended consequences that create other harmful behaviours. Arguably, there is no better example of this than Prohibition in the United States, where the failure to take into account entrenched socio-cultural practices led to the creation of a significant black market and the rise of organised crime on a scale not previously seen. Other examples include: risk regulation that leads people to switch to products risker than those being regulated (e.g. airport security measures that lead people to choose more dangerous road travel);[10] industry regulation that changes the benefit-cost ratio of activities and inhibits innovative entrepreneurial activity or, worse, leads businesses to cease existing productive activity;[11] and workers' rights and environmental regulation that displaces the harmful activity to another jurisdiction with lower standards, thus potentially causing greater harm when measured on a global scale.[12]

Poor diagnosis also may be the product of the preconceived ideas and biases of those undertaking it. Policy and regulatory analysts are not empty vessels waiting to be filled with data objectively obtained. Rather, analysts are individuals with existing values, beliefs and organisational and disciplinary perspectives that shape and colour how they view issues and events. Organisationally, government is highly structured and compartmentalised. Head and Alford, for example, refer to government departments and agencies as 'cultural fortresses' each with their own specialised functional and professional expertise.[13] Dery similarly observes that government agencies embody certain worldviews that can prevent awareness of alternative ways of conceiving of problems, events and processes.[14] The same lack of awareness can arise from disciplinary biases. A lack of workplace health and safety, for example, would be viewed by an economist through the prism of the market and likely be attributed to market failures caused by information asymmetries and unequal bargaining power. A labour lawyer, on the other hand, may view the same lack of workplace health and safety as an issue of fairness, equity and distributional justice and see its cause being the amoral market functioning exactly as intended.[15]

Policy and regulatory analysts also may have expectations or hypotheses about the issue being diagnosed that can make them susceptible to a range of cognitive biases, including: confirmation bias (interpreting evidence in ways that are partial to existing beliefs, expectations or hypotheses), disconfirmation bias (an inability to ignore prior beliefs when presented with counter-arguments or evidence) and prosecutorial bias (the selective treatment of evidence in ways that support the agenda of the institution in which the investigation or research is being conducted).[16] These ideological and professional predispositions and biases can prevent awareness of alternative ways of conceiving of issues, events and evidence, thus undermining the objectivity of the diagnosis.[17]

Poor Objective Setting

Poor diagnoses also can lead to poor objective setting, with the wrong audiences, behaviours or outcomes being targeted. However, objective setting can be found wanting even in the presence of excellent diagnosis. Political pressure, for example, can lead governments to commit to overly ambitious objectives that place pressure on all other actors involved in the regulatory endeavour. 'Zero-harm' targets are a classic example of this. Not only do they set unrealistic and unachievable targets (thereby guaranteeing non-delivery), they also can produce inefficient outcomes. Zero-harm targets can cause regulators to be unnecessarily aggressive in their enforcement efforts, and regulators and regulatees to invest in the issue disproportionally to the societal benefit.[18]

Poor objective setting also can be the product of governments' inability to reach consensus on the nature of the public interest to be served by a regulation. As Ayres and Braithwaite observed: 'When the state acts as an umpire between interest groups under a liberal-pluralist model, it is hard put to find a general justification that appeals to the plurality of interests, and it generally fails to do so'.[19] Moreover, even if government manages to find a set of words that enables all interest groups to read into them the delivery of their objectives and aspirations, they are likely to be expressed at a comparatively high level of abstraction and generalisation that masks rather than resolves policy differences.[20] Policy differences unresolved at the objective-setting stage are likely to raise their heads again during later stages.[21] An example of this was Australia's recent efforts to harmonise its various state (sub-national) workplace health and safety laws. The harmonisation project commenced with a broad and universally endorsed objective of making workplaces safer, reducing compliance costs for business and improving government efficiency. However, as the process moved from the generality of the harmonisation promise to policy particulars, stakeholders were confronted by the nature and extent of their differences and the threat harmonisation posed to previously hard-fought-for rights and benefits. The result was that support for aspects of the reform fractured, leading to harmonisation sapping changes being made to the laws.[22]

Poor Design

Obviously, a failure to properly diagnose the issue is likely to lead to a failure to design an appropriate regulatory intervention. For example, a failure to identify an issue's underlying causal factors could lead to the wrong selection of tools to address it, and a failure to understand the economic, social, cultural and political systems in which an issue is embedded can lead to countervailing effects that undermine achievement of the regulatory objectives.

The design stage also can be affected by a lack of imagination and creativity. We have observed that the ability of policy analysts to process all the information necessary to develop competing design solutions is bounded by the resources at their disposal, the time they have to do it and their own cognitive capabilities.[23] We also have seen that policy analysts can tend to work incrementally from existing policies, and can continue down well-worn institutional and ideational paths without adequate reflection.[24] Similarly, a solution from one jurisdiction can be transferred to, and adopted by, another jurisdiction without a proper appreciation of the social, cultural, economic and political differences between the two jurisdictions that could render it inappropriate.[25]

Poor design also may be the product of the organisational, disciplinary and personal biases of those undertaking it. We have seen that these biases can infect the diagnosis of an issue. They also can infect the design of its remedy by restricting designers to processes, institutions and instruments with which they are familiar and comfortable. Lawyers, for example, may have a tendency to look to laws (rules) as a solution, economists are likely to favour market-based mechanisms and communication professionals are likely to favour communication tools. These disciplinary predilections can blind policy analysts to the existence of other, potentially more effective design options.[26] To the extent that this is the case, this book's examination of regulatory options in Chapter 8 is an important step in addressing it.

Poor Design Selection

Generating a broad suite of realistic design alternatives does not necessarily mean the best alternative is always selected. We already have observed that our rationality is bounded and that our capacity to rank and choose the optimal design from among competing options is limited by our organisational and psychological environment. As Simon observed, this can lead decision-makers to 'satisfice' rather than select the optimal solution.[27] And we also have observed that design choice is vulnerable to the bureau building and shaping behaviour of regulators and other public officials, to capture by the industry being regulated, and to compromises struck between competing interest groups. And as Grabosky notes: '[c]ompromise, so often the lubricant of policy making in a democracy, gives rise to contradiction and neutralization'.[28]

Poor Implementation

Well-diagnosed and designed regulation can nevertheless fail if poorly implemented. The potential causes of poor implementation are many, and can be further sub-divided into poor regime deployment, poor enforcement and poor coordination. Poor regime deployment can take the form of inadequate resourcing of a new regulator or asking too much of it too soon.[29] For example, regulation can fail if a new regulator is not allowed adequate time to recruit and train its leaders and operational personnel, and to develop the cultural settings, governance structure and organisational processes needed for effective regulatory decision-making. Poor deployment can be the result of poor planning on the part of those charged with establishing the regulator or because of political pressure that prioritises speed of delivery and does not allow for proper planning to take place.

The regulatory failure literature is richest with respect to poor enforcement. Poor enforcement can take the form of either 'inappropriately lenient' enforcement or 'excessively strict' enforcement, to borrow Bardach's and Kagan's labels.[30] Inappropriately lenient enforcement results in behaviours continuing that should be modified, the issue not being addressed in a timely manner and the worsening of its impact or intractability.[31] Excessively strict enforcement, on the other hand, leads to behaviour being restricted that ought not to have been restricted, thus stifling otherwise productive and welfare-enhancing activities.[32] It also risks the regulation being perceived as draconian and punitive, unnecessary and burdensome or otherwise unreasonable and unfair by those whose compliance with it is sought. This can lead to confrontation and defiance which, in turn, reduces the incentive for voluntary compliance and possibly incentivises calculated non-compliance.[33]

The potential causes of poor enforcement are many. Some we have already discussed and need only be summarised here. They can include capture (either by private interests or well-organised public interest groups), regulator lethargy and the self-interested behaviours of the public servants and regulators charged with its implementation.[34] Other enforcement failures may be the result of poor regime application. These include failing to inform and educate regulatees on their obligations and how to comply with them, failing adequately to monitor for and detect instances of non-compliance and failing to act decisively to remedy and sanction non-compliances that are detected. And yet other failures may be the result of poor strategic judgment: for example, choosing to adopt a cooperative and facilitative approach to enforcement when a more coercive approach is warranted (and vice-versa).

Poor strategic judgements often are the result of failing to accurately triage the target audience's different attitudes, motivations and capabilities. The target audience rarely, if ever, is homogeneous. It is made up of persons and entities with different interests, values, capacities and capabilities. These differences mean that not all members of the target audience are likely to respond to regulation in the same manner. While some may respond rationally, others may respond irrationally and perversely. An example of this is the 'forbidden fruit effect' where regulatory prohibitions or restrictions entice the rebellious and curious to experiment with the prohibited activity, and the unscrupulous and criminal to exploit the opportunities this presents.[35] Alcohol regulation and censorship have both been found to create this effect.[36] Another example is the 'Peltzman effect', named after Chicago School of Economics Professor Sam Peltzman, who hypothesised the tendency of people to react to a safety regulation by being less careful, thus off-setting all or some of the regulation's intended benefit.[37] This effect has been observed with motorists (with respect to seat belts), patients (with respect to medical treatment), cyclists (with respect to helmets) and children (with respect to wearing safety gear).[38] Nor are all members of the target audience likely to respond consistently with the regulation's broader societal objectives. Some, for example, will be motivated to game the system and to explore for loop-holes and creative ways to comply with the regulation's let-ter but not its spirit (e.g. tax minimisation);[39] whereas others might comply ritualistically and unthinkingly with the letter of the law while 'missing its spirit, substance and foundation' (e.g. tick-box compliance).[40] Regulatory ritualism, as it has become known, has been observed in fields as diverse as finance and aged care homes.[41] Failure to appreciate these differences in motivations and capabilities—and to tailor regulation accordingly—can result in 'one-size-fits-none (or some)' regulation that not only fails to achieve its intended objectives, but exacerbates the situation.

Poor implementation also can result from poor coordination. The greater the number of moving parts in the regulatory regime (actors and instru-ments), the greater the risk of coordination problems. These coordina-tion problems can arise from non-state actors co-opted into the regulatory regime pursuing their own self-interest, but generally are most acute when regime responsibilities are poorly split among two or more government regulators creating blurred lines of responsibilities. Thompson refers to this as the problem of 'many hands',[42] and it can occur where different regula-tors undertake different aspects of the regulatory endeavour (e.g. separation of standard setting from enforcement), or where two or more regulators simultaneously regulate the same issue but according to different standards (as might occur in a federal system where national and sub-national govern-ments regulate the same issue). These blurred lines can create inconsistencies and confusion, overlap and duplication, gaps in coverage and the conditions for blame shifting, buck-passing and reduced accountability.[43]

Poor Monitoring, Evaluation and Adaptability

Not incorporating appropriate monitoring, evaluation and continuous improvement processes into the regulatory regime also can contribute to regulatory failure. As we have seen, not all regulatory initiatives generate the behavioural changes sought, and some can generate perverse responses and unexpected negative consequences. The failure to monitor and adjust for these unintended behaviours and consequences in a timely manner risks exacerbating and entrenching them.

More generally though, the regulatory environment is not static. It is dynamic and constantly changing. Regulators that do not adapt to, and evolve with, their changing environment risk regulatory drift, atrophy and obsolescence. 'Regulatory drift' refers to the failure of a regulator to adapt to changes in its environment that render existing interventions meaningless or counterproductive.[44] Changes in technology are some of the more com-mon causes of regulatory drift, and can be seen in many regulatory regimes' struggles to retain focus and relevance in the face of new web and app-based technologies that have revolutionised the markets for the goods and services they regulate, of which taxi services (disrupted by Uber) and accommo-dation (disrupted by Airbnb) are arguably the two most prominent. Left unchecked, regulatory drift can exacerbate into regulatory atrophy and decay, where the utility and legitimacy of the regulators' practices are called into question, and the institution itself becomes redundant and begins to erode before eventually being broken-up or replaced.[45] This end point is similar to that posited by Bernstein's 'life-cycle of regulation' discussed in Chapter 3.[46] According to Bernstein, regulators decline as they age, eventually reaching a point where they cease 'to keep pace with changes in technology, economic organization, and popular views about the proper scope of governmental activity'.[47] This state of 'old age' continues 'until some scandal or emergency calls attention dramatically to the failure of regulation and the need to redefine regulatory objectives and public policies'.[48]

So why may regulators fail to evaluate and adapt? It could be an omission in the design stage to incorporate appropriate monitoring and feedback mechanisms; it could be a failure of those responsible for receiving and interpreting the feedback to see or appreciate the significance of the warning signs and to respond to them in a timely manner (recalling that even experts can suffer from biases that lead them to interpret evidence consistent with existing expectations and hypotheses); or it could be the result of strategies employed by private interests vested in the status quo, or political or bureaucratic risk aversion that prioritises stability and predictability over flexibility and adaptability. Often, however, it simply is a product of workload demands and budgetary and time constraints: regulators often are not resourced to invest in self-examination at the expense of their primary regulatory functions.

Summing up Regulatory Failure

This discussion of regulatory failure has demonstrated that regulation fails in numerous ways and for numerous reasons. Most often, however, regulation fails because of poor planning, poor execution and bad politics.[49] The consequences of regulatory failure are far-reaching. Failures can cascade and exacerbate. A diagnosis failure leads to a design failure which, in turn, leads to an implementation failure and, collectively, all three can lead to a failure of public governance with the potential to undermine 'the credibility of government and governance under the rule of law'.[50]

As dark a picture of the regulatory endeavour that the regulatory failure literature at times paints (or, maybe more to the point, is used by those opposed to regulation to paint), there is a clear and strong silver lining to it. There is much governments and regulators can do to predict and prevent the causes of regulatory failure. The examples of regulatory failure discussed under each heading provide a checklist of potential causes of failure against which those responsible for the various stages of the regulatory policy cycle should be stress testing their efforts. After all, those causes are no longer unforeseeable. The regulatory failure literature also contains lessons for how those causes can be avoided in the future. These lessons are included in our discussion of the stages of the regulatory policy cycle in Part III. Some also comprise elements of better regulation reforms, to which the chapter now turns.

Better Regulation

Better regulation reforms were introduced in Chapter 2. They are an example of an idea that has taken flight globally. Today most modern regulatory systems are governed to some degree by policies and procedures designed to produce 'better' regulation.[51] But what does this mean? What constitutes 'better' regulation? A review of better regulation policies and procedures reveals three rationales underpinning the reforms. First, better regulation reforms are about producing regulation that functions more effectively and efficiently in the public interest than regulation that preceded it. Pursuant to this rationale, better regulation is not about setting less ambitious policy objectives, but is about finding the best way to achieve those ambitious objectives. Second, better regulation reforms are about reducing the compliance burden on private interests. This rationale continues to reflect the logic of the deregulation era of the 1980s, from which the better regulation reforms evolved. And third, better regulation reforms are about improving overall regulatory quality. This rationale views good quality regulation as an essential element of good governance and the rule of law. These three rationales combine to frame the better regulation reforms, namely that regulation should be: effective in achieving its regulatory objectives, parsimonious and burden business no more than is necessary to achieve those objectives, and developed and implemented in a manner that upholds public confidence in government and regulatory governance.

A review of better regulation policies and procedures also reveals three core elements common to most of them: (1) principles of good regulation, (2) analytical and procedural methods, and (3) system oversight. Each of these elements is discussed below.

Principles of Good Regulation

Across the various better regulation policies and procedures, numerous different labels are employed to describe the principles and attributes of 'good' regulation. Table 6.1 below summarises the most commonly found principles and attributes by reference to the three rationales for better regulation reforms identified earlier—effectiveness, parsimony and good governance.

This (long) list of principles reflects the complexity of the regulatory endeavour. The list combines principles that are primarily instrumental in nature (e.g. effectiveness and efficiency) with principles that accord with liberal democratic constitutional values (e.g. participation and consultation), reflecting the importance of both the 'what' and the 'how'. It also combines principles that are likely to operate in different directions: for example,

Table 6.1 Principles of Good Regulation

Effectiveness	Parsimony	Good Governance
Effective	Efficient/cost-effective	Participatory/consultative
Rational/evidence-based	Proportional	Accountable
Accessible/clear	Targeted	Transparent/open
Responsive/flexible	Necessary	Coherent
Certain/predictable		Consistent
Adaptive/anticipatory		Contestable/subject to
Adequately resourced		appeal
Coordinated		Fair/equitable
Timely		

flexibility with consistency, and certainty with responsiveness. How the principles are to be prioritised and applied is not automatically clear, however. They are not capable of a universal or formulaic application, and most do not lend themselves to objective analysis. Subjective considerations will always be present. Consensus on a definitive set of principles (and on their relative weightings) is likely to be difficult, if at all possible, given the number of interested actors with multiple and often competing values, interests and objectives. Trade-offs between the principles are likely to be the rule, not the exception. It is therefore important that the application of the principles is supported by good decision-making processes. This is where the better regulation reforms' second core element comes in.

Analytical and Procedural Methods

We saw in our earlier discussion that many regulatory failures are the result of poor planning, poor execution and bad politics. Better regulation reforms address these causes of failure by institutionalising into the regulatory process a range of analytical and procedural methods to resist political expediency, and to ensure regulation is based on a rational assessment of the best available evidence. The more frequently recommended methods are summarised in Table 6.2.

Of these methods, two have come to epitomise better regulation reforms: the use of alternative modes of regulation and regulatory impact assessments (RIAs). Indeed, such has been the focus of much of the academic and practitioner literature on these methods that one would be excused for thinking that they were the sum total of the reforms. However, as Table 6.2 clearly demonstrates, this is not the case. The better regulation reforms are much richer than just a more flexible set of regulatory initiatives and the use of cost-benefit analyses. The strength of the reforms lies not in any one method, but in their use in combination and, in particular, the combining of analytical methods to improve how regulation is designed, implemented

Table 6.2 Analytical and Procedural Methods for Producing Better Regulation

Stage	Analytical/Procedural Method
Overall	Whole-of-government regulatory policy
	High-level official responsible for policy
	Designated oversight body
	Evidence-based policy-making
Define	Participatory/consultative processes
	Rational analytical tools
	Use of expert advice
Design	Use of alternative modes of regulation
	Education/information
	Incentive- or market-based tools
	Performance-based standards
	Self- or co-regulation
Decide	Regulatory impact assessments
	Cost-benefit analyses
	Multi-criteria analyses
Implement	Effective deployment
	Accessible regulatory standards
	Well-resourced/organised regulator
	Risk-based enforcement
	Responsive regulation
	Regulatory co-ordination
Evaluate	Post-implementation reviews
	Periodic evaluations

and maintained with participatory processes that not only inform those processes, but also build support and respect for the regulatory endeavour and for regulatory governance more broadly.[52]

System Oversight

Concerns about the manner with which better regulation reforms are implemented has led many governments to establish dedicated oversight units.[53] The mandate of these units varies from jurisdiction to jurisdiction. Some are limited to championing that jurisdiction's better regulation reforms; others to developing, monitoring and enforcing guidelines that give effect to the reforms; and others still have mandates that extend to improving the quality of the regulatory system more broadly. The latter generally involves facilitating better coordination and cooperation among and between regulators to minimise duplication, overlap and inconsistencies, and monitoring the total stock of regulation to ensure the cumulative effect of multiple regulatory regimes does not overwhelm those subject to them.[54]

The mechanisms employed by these units to secure compliance with the better regulation reforms also can differ. They range from the central promulgation of common methodologies and procedural standards to be adopted by all departments and agencies, through to requiring departments and agencies proposing new regulations to have their proposal's compliance with those methods and standards vetted and signed-off by the central unit. Another approach is to publically benchmark government compliance with the standards to create a competitive dynamic and reputational imperative to comply.[55] This also can be achieved by having the central unit's assessment of the quality of RIAs made publically available. Finally, an increasingly popular method is for governments to set numeric targets. These tend to be expressed as reductions either in the compliance burden or in the total stock of regulations.[56]

Summing up Better Regulation

Better regulation reforms comprise a suite of initiatives designed to improve regulatory decision-making. They range from participatory processes and *ex-ante* assessments of regulatory options, through to risk-based enforcement and *ex-post* evaluations. Each of the initiatives on their own is not new or unique to better regulation reforms. Their strength lies, however, in their cumulative effect. Better regulatory decision-making is more likely than not to emerge from transparent participatory processes that employ evidence-based analytical methods and rational processes implemented in a targeted, proportional and accountable manner. As Meuwese and Popelier observe, 'the normative force of combining several tools in one transparent regime should not be underestimated'.[57] Notwithstanding their prominence, however, their use does not appear to have significantly quietened the complaints of business that regulation remains too costly and burdensome, or of public interest groups that regulation remains ineffective in addressing many of the challenges faced by society today. This may, in part, be the result of deficiencies in their operationalisation.[58] However, it is also a reflection that rationality and normative force alone is not sufficient to ensure the credibility and acceptability of regulatory institutions and the regulations they produce and enforce. Generally, something more is required. What this 'something more' might entail is the focus of the next section.

Regulatory Legitimacy

Regulation is about modifying behaviours. It is about motivating and, in some cases, requiring people to do something different to what they are currently doing and what they understand to be their best interests. A growing body of research establishes that legitimacy is essential to a regulator's ability to obtain behaviour change in these circumstances.[59] Majone goes so far as to suggest that legitimacy has replaced coercive power as the essential resource of policy-makers.[60] This makes understanding how legitimacy is constructed critically important to the regulatory endeavour.[61]

Central to dictionary definitions of 'legitimacy' are notions of acceptability and credibility; of actions that are proper and justifiable by reference to accepted rules, principles or standards.[62] Suchman (in one of the more frequently cited definitions) defines legitimacy as 'a generalised perception or assumption that the actions of an entity are desirable, proper, or appropriate within some socially constructed system of norms, values, beliefs, and definitions'.[63] But socially constructed by whom? According to whose values and beliefs should a regulator be perceived as acceptable or credible for it to be legitimate? And by what norms, principles or standards do these people assess whether a regulator's actions are proper or justified? It is to these questions that we now turn.

Legitimacy Communities

'Legitimacy communities' is a term that has evolved to describe groups of persons in whose eyes it is important for an organisation to be perceived to be legitimate. In the case of a regulator, these persons are the actors occupying the regulatory space with it. Four legitimacy communities are of primary importance to regulators. First and foremost, there are the regulatees—the persons whose behaviour is sought to be modified. Regulation can require these persons to comply with policies and laws with which they do not agree and which run counter to their perception of their interests. Research establishes that these people are more likely to comply with regulations they perceive to be legitimate, credible and acceptable.[64] Second, are those for whose benefit governments regulate. It is important that these people too perceive the regulatory regime and the regulators within it to be legitimate, credible and acceptable, and that they have trust and confidence in them. This trust and confidence provides regulators with stability and support, and contributes to public confidence in government and public governance more broadly. Third, are the actors whose active participation and resources are required for the regulation to achieve its objectives. As we have seen, this group includes other regulators, public sector agencies that perform regulatory or support functions, and private sector and non-governmental organisations who make valuable contributions to policy development and regulatory design and implementation.[65] Fourth, there are persons whose support (more so than their active participation) is important for the regulator to secure and maintain the resources and authority needed to discharge its regulatory mission, especially when a crisis or other event places those resources and authority under threat. These persons include political superiors, department heads, oversight bodies, the media and even the courts.[66] The participation and support of these later communities is more likely if they perceive the regulator to be credible and the most appropriate entity to undertake the functions entrusted to it.[67]

Each of these legitimacy communities is important to a regulator's ability effectively to discharge its regulatory responsibilities, and to a regime's ability to deliver its objectives. However, given each legitimacy community is likely to have different perspectives and interests in the regulatory endeavour, how each community perceives regulatory legitimacy also is likely to be different. It is to how these different perceptions are constructed and framed that the chapter now turns.

Legitimacy Domains and Dimensions

Legitimacy is actor and context specific. As Black observes, legitimacy 'lies as much in the values, interests, expectations and cognitive frames of those who are perceiving or accepting the regime as they do in the regime itself'.[68] As a result, attempting to frame a definition of legitimacy capable of applying across all legitimacy communities would be an exercise in futility. Rather, the focus should be on understanding the different domains and dimensions of legitimacy, and their relative importance to different legitimacy communities. There are four broad types or domains of legitimacy—legal, normative, pragmatic and cognitive—each with multiple dimensions.[69] Each of these legitimacy domains and their dimensions is discussed below.

Legal Legitimacy

For state regulators, the clarity and scope of their legislative mandate, and the legal validity of the laws they enforce and their institutional arrangements, are central to their acceptability and credibility.[70] They are an authoritative declaration by the people's elected representatives that the regulator is in the public interest,[71] and the conferral of state-sanctioned coercive power legitimates its use of force.[72] However, a legislative mandate and legal validity, on their own, may not suffice to clothe a regulator with legitimacy in the eyes of some of its legitimacy communities. This might be the case where one or more communities perceive the regulator, the regulatory regime or the laws they administer to be unfair, unjust or inappropriate because, for example, they were established autocratically and without engagement with affected parties, were established in breach of previously given commitments or impose regulatory standards that are impractical or onerous to implement.

Legal legitimacy also is unlikely to be sufficient on its own where the regulator has autonomy and discretion to determine how it discharges its mandate. Let us assume that a regulator validly created, and with a clear legislative mandate, is considered legitimate on establishment by its key legitimacy communities. That legitimacy might be lost, however, depending on how the regulator discharges its mandate.[73] For example, a regulator that exercises its powers in a heavy-handed draconian manner in response to complaints from the public may be seen as credible and appropriate by those for whose benefit it regulates, but may be seen as lacking in fairness (and therefore acceptability) by those it directly regulates. Alternatively, a regulator that partners with the industry it regulates in the development of regulatory standards may be seen as credible by that industry, but may be perceived by those for whose benefit it regulates as too close to, and possibly captured by, that industry. A regulator also can lose legitimacy in the eyes of the government that conferred its legislative mandate upon it if it fails to discharge its regulatory responsibilities in accordance with that government's expectations or, in the case of a change of government, in accordance with the expectations of its new political masters. As such, it might be better to think of the legislative mandate creating a presumption of legitimacy.[74] Whether that presumption is affirmed or rebutted is determined by reference to the other legitimacy domains.

Normative Legitimacy

Normative legitimacy, as its name suggests, reflects a legitimacy community's assessment of the regulator and its activities against a set of normative criteria important to that legitimacy community. As with many aspects of the regulatory endeavour, different commentators have developed different ways and nomenclature for categorising these criteria.[75] Notwithstanding these differences, the normative criteria against which legitimacy communities assess a regulator's legitimacy can be distilled into six dimensions: consequential, procedural, structural, expertise, role and personal.[76]

Consequential legitimacy: Nothing breeds legitimacy like success, and nothing destroys it like failure. As a result, most (if not all) legitimacy communities are likely to assess a regulator's legitimacy by reference to what they accomplish—the outcomes they deliver, the efficiency with which they are delivered and any unintended consequences produced along the way. Measuring the outcomes of regulatory initiatives is inherently difficult, however, either because there are no objective metrics for doing so, or the metrics that exist lag the regulatory initiative or are unable to isolate the impact of the initiative from other variables. As a result, legitimacy communities also tend to assess a regulator's legitimacy by reference to the outputs produced to deliver the outcomes (e.g. information and guidance; enforcement actions).

Procedural legitimacy: Procedural legitimacy focuses on whether the regulatory outcomes and outputs are produced by proper means and procedures. There are four main components of procedural legitimacy. The first component is the use of rational analytical processes in which the problem is clearly defined, relevant facts gathered and options developed and compared according to their value and consequences. Use of the regulatory policy cycle is a good example of such a process. Other examples include the use of RIAs and checklists that convey structure, system and competence.[77] The second component is procedural fairness, which Tyler argues is the main determinant of legitimacy—even more so than whether regulation leads to outcomes that accord with that community's self-interest or personal sense of substantive justice.[78] Tyler's work establishes that people assess procedural fairness by four criteria: opportunities for participation, neutrality of the decision-maker, quality of interpersonal treatment (respect, politeness; treatment with dignity) and trust in the motives of the regulator (that the regulator's focus is on their needs, concerns and well-being).[79] The third component is whether decision-making processes are transparent, timely and decisive, and the fourth is whether persons aggrieved by a decision are provided with reasons for the decision and an opportunity to challenge or appeal it (which also relates to Tyler's criteria of interpersonal treatment).

Structural legitimacy: Structural legitimacy focuses on whether the overall organisational form conveys the message that the regulator 'is acting on collectively valued purposes in a proper and adequate manner'.[80] This extends to the regulator being established in a manner that ensures its independence and impartiality; that it is resourced to perform its role effectively and efficiently; and that there are mechanisms to hold it accountable for both the decisions it makes and the manner with which it makes them.

Expertise legitimacy: Expertise legitimacy focuses on whether the organisation has the expertise, problem-solving capacity and judgement to enable it to make decisions fairly and independently.[81] Baldwin, Cave and Lodge observe that the weight given to expertise legitimacy increases with the difficulty and complexity of the decisions to be made, and that expertise legitimacy is particularly important where the regulator 'has to consider a number of competing options or values and come to a balanced judgment on incomplete and shifting information'.[82]

Role legitimacy: For most legitimacy communities, it is important that the roles performed by the regulator are not only authorised by the legislature, but also are appropriate in the circumstances. We already have observed that regulatory regimes that fail to evolve with the external environment risk regulatory drift, atrophy and obsolescence. Dangers also exist if regulators evolve too quickly and assume roles with no clear connection to their primary regulatory role or, worse, a role that might be perceived by some to conflict with that primary regulatory role. This is sometimes referred to as 'conversion' where existing institutions are redeployed to serve new goals, functions or purposes.[83] Conflicting roles can impact assessments of a regulator's legitimacy. Such conflicts can arise when the one entity acts as both industry promoter and industry regulator.[84] And in regulatory regimes where regulatory roles are divided among different regulators, conflicts can arise when the various regulators do not function in a cooperative and coordinated manner.[85]

Personal legitimacy: Whereas expertise legitimacy is based on an assessment of the regulator's overall capability and capacity, personal legitimacy is based on an evaluation of the regulator's leaders and whether they are perceived to be visionary, charismatic and inspirational.[86] Personal legitimacy is the least tangible of the normative criteria, yet its importance cannot be denied. Numerous studies on leadership highlight the important role personal leadership can play in building trust internally and externally, engendering a moral and ethical culture, and securing staff and stakeholder (legitimacy community) commitment to the organisation's mission and vision.[87] It also has been found to be an important factor for regulators seeking to repair damaged legitimacy.[88]

Cognitive Legitimacy

Cognitive legitimacy exists when legitimacy communities accept the regulator as necessary or inevitable such that its existence is no longer debated. Cognitive legitimacy has strong links with sociological institutionalism discussed in Chapter 3, namely that legitimacy attaches to institutions that reflect accepted cognitive frames of what is credible and appropriate. There are two forms of cognitive legitimacy—one based on comprehensibility; and one based on taken-for-grantedness.[89] Legitimacy based on comprehensibility is when the regulator's role makes sense—that the nature of the issue is one that should be addressed, and the regulator and the regulation it administers is the most logical and obvious way of addressing it. Legitimacy based on taken-for-grantedness, on the other hand, describes a situation where the regulator is accepted as necessary or inevitable based on prevailing economic, social and cultural models; where its presence is 'so deeply rooted it is barely questioned'.[90] Workplace health and safety and environment protection regulation are good examples. Whereas there was once a time when the need for such regulation (and regulators) was fiercely debated, today workplace health and safety and environment protection are shared community goals, and no self-respecting business would now argue there should be no such laws (although the debate around what constitutes 'good' regulation in these areas continues). Suchman argues that cognitive legitimacy is the most powerful source of legitimacy;[91] Black similarly suggests that while cognitive legitimacy is perhaps the subtlest form of legitimacy, it also is the most resilient.[92]

Pragmatic Legitimacy

Pragmatic legitimacy is based on each legitimacy community's self-interest. We already have observed that regulation perceived to be unfair, unjust or inappropriate can lead to defiance and non-compliance. However, even reasonable regulatory requirements can fail to motivate people to comply if the manner of their administration and enforcement do not connect with those persons' concerns and values.[93] Suchman identifies three dimensions of pragmatic legitimacy: dispositional legitimacy that rests on the community's perception that the regulator shares their values and has their best interests at heart; influence legitimacy that rests on the community's perception that the regulator is responsive to their interests and capable of being influenced by them; and exchange legitimacy that rests on the community's belief that the regulator will produce policies and outcomes aligned to their interests.[94] Black observes that pragmatic legitimacy often is excluded from legal accounts of regulation, principally because it is seen as illegitimate.[95] However, to ignore it is to ignore the reality of human behaviour and the role played by self-interest in determining how different communities assess a regulator's legitimacy.

Summing up Regulatory Legitimacy

Table 6.3 summarises the domains and dimensions of regulatory legitimacy.[96] The framework provides a useful tool with which to construct and deconstruct how different legitimacy communities perceive the legitimacy of regulators and the regulatory regimes they administer.

That different legitimacy communities combine and prioritise the various legitimacy domains and dimensions differently is illustrated by recent research into the Victorian (Australia) Environment Protection Authority. That research revealed that regulatees (businesses required to change their behaviour) viewed regulatory legitimacy primarily as an aspect of the rule of law (legal legitimacy) and good governance practices (normative legitimacy, with a focus on role clarity, procedural fairness and efficiency); those

Table 6.3 Constituent Elements of Regulatory Legitimacy

Domain/Type	Dimension	Attributes
Legal legitimacy	Legislative mandate	Regulator and its actions are authorised by the legislature through democratic processes
	Legal validity	Rules, institutional arrangements and decisions are legally valid
Normative legitimacy	Consequential	Regulator is effective and efficient in producing desired outcomes and outputs
	Procedural	Regulator's procedures are rational, open and fair; its decisions transparent and subject to appeal
	Structural	Institutional arrangements ensure independent, impartial, effective and accountable decision-making
	Expertise	Regulator possesses technical and regulatory expertise to enable it to come to fair, independent and balanced decisions
	Role	Roles performed by the regulator are appropriate, relevant and consistent
	Personal	Regulator's leaders are perceived to be visionary, charismatic and inspirational

(Continued)

Table 6.3 (Continued)

Domain/Type	Dimension	Attributes
Cognitive legitimacy	Comprehensibility	Regulator's role makes sense; it is logical and obvious
	Taken-for-grantedness	Regulator's role and presence is taken as a given; necessary or inevitable
Pragmatic legitimacy	Dispositional	Regulator shares the legitimacy community's values and has their best interests at heart
	Influence	Regulator is responsive to legitimacy community's interests and capable of being influenced by them
	Exchange	Regulator will produce policies and outcomes aligned to legitimacy community's interests

for whose benefit the regulation is made (community groups) viewed legitimacy in substantive policy terms (cognitive and pragmatic legitimacy) and whether they had been heard and their concerns taken on board (normative legitimacy, with a focus on procedural fairness); and other regulators and government actors viewed legitimacy primarily through legal and normative lenses that mirror the principles of better regulation to which they themselves are subject.[97]

Concluding Insights and Implications

This chapter commenced by examining the causes of regulatory failure. We observed that those causes are not accidents; that if regulation fails, it fails because persons responsible for the regulatory endeavour—the public servants that diagnose the issue and prescribe a response, the decision-makers that approve it and the regulators that implement it—failed to predict and prevent the causes of that failure. Of course, not all causes are easy to predict or prevent. As we saw, some may be situated in the subconscious of those whose behaviour the regulation is seeking to change, or deeply embedded in the social, cultural and economic systems in which the issue is situated. And in some situations, governments and regulators may choose not to act to eliminate or mitigate a potential cause of failure, either because the likelihood of the cause materialising is considered too low, the cost too great or doing so might interfere with important social values such as individual autonomy and liberty. But deciding not to act is different to saying that it could not be prevented.

Next, the chapter examined better regulation reforms. This revealed a suite of initiatives designed to ensure regulation is effective and efficient, and developed and implemented in accordance with good governance principles. Our discussion of regulatory legitimacy then highlighted that the debate about what constitutes 'good' regulation has moved beyond regime effectiveness and efficiency. It now also is a matter of values, interests, expectations and beliefs.

Regulatory legitimacy recognises that being able to modify the behaviour of others—which is at the heart of the regulatory endeavour—requires more than the use of state-sanctioned coercive powers; that it requires those whose behaviour is to be modified (and others whose resources and support are required) to accept the regulator and the regulatory regime as acceptable and credible; proper and appropriate; justified and desirable. This means that legitimacy is not something that simply can be bestowed by the state. Regulatory legitimacy needs to be actively built and maintained and, if necessary, repaired.[98]

The best substantive strategy for building and maintaining regulatory legitimacy is regulatory success. This entails avoiding the causes of regulatory failure which, as we have observed, are predictable and preventable. Looking for potential points or causes of failure therefore should be part of the regulatory design process, as should taking appropriate steps for avoiding them.[99] Suggestions for avoiding these causes of failure can be found in the regulatory failure literature itself. They also can be found in the better regulation reforms. Central to these reforms is use of rational decision-making tools to ensure regulation is necessary, targeted and proportionate. Other substantive strategies include: adopting inclusive participatory and consultative processes; improving training and resources to increase expertise and competency; and introducing effective oversight and accountability mechanisms.[100] Which of these (and other) strategies to employ, in what order and with what emphasis, will depend on the legitimacy domains and dimensions of most importance to its key legitimacy communities. This makes understanding the interests, values, motivations and perceptions of those communities an important component of the issue diagnosis and design stages of the regulatory process.[101]

That different legitimacy communities are likely to perceive legitimacy differently poses a challenge for regulators; a challenge accentuated by legitimacy's dynamic nature. Simultaneously satisfying all legitimacy communities' different legitimacy claims often is impossible, and satisfying only one legitimacy community's claims risks alienating the holders of conflicting claims. As Black observes: 'What may be necessary to maintain the regulators' legitimacy for one audience may be contrary to that which is necessary to maintain it for another'.[102] The challenge for regulators is to design participatory and deliberative processes to resolve these conflicts and, where that is not possible, to acknowledge the tensions inherent in conflicting legitimacy claims and to deal with them transparently.[103] As with many other aspects of the regulatory endeavour, balances may need to be struck and trade-offs made.

In conclusion, this chapter's examination of regulatory failure, better regulation reforms and the concept of regulatory legitimacy reinforces the complexity and difficulty of the regulatory endeavour. Designing and implementing regulation that is good and legitimate is a significant challenge. The potential sources of failure are many, as are the prescriptions to overcome them. There is no 'single' best approach. Legitimate regulation requires a combination of tools, principles and approaches tailored to the problem and actors involved. And the selection and tailoring of those tools, principles and approaches involves the exercise of judgement and discretion. How this may be done successfully is the focus of the rest of this book.

Notes

1. Allan McConnell, *Understanding Policy Success: Rethinking Public Policy* (Palgrave Macmillan, 2010).
2. P N Grabosky, 'Counterproductive Regulation' (1995) 23 *International Journal of the Sociology of Law* 347, 347.
3. See, e.g., ibid, Grabosky, who classifies them into: bad science (which he describes as poor problem diagnosis and poor solution design); bad planning (underestimating the time required, complexity involved and spill over effects); bad implementation (resource inadequacy; lack of coordination; and oversight failure); and bad politics (which he describes as the contradictions and neutralization introduced by the compromise often needed to obtain the cooperation and consent to proceed with the policy); Organisation for Economic Co-operation and Development, *Reducing the Risk of Policy Failure: Challenges for Regulatory Compliance* (OECD, 2000) organizes the reasons for regulatory failure or non-compliance into three categories: the degree to which the target group knows of and comprehends the rules, the degree to which the target group is willing to comply and the degree to which the target group is able to comply with the rules; Julia Black, 'Learning from Regulatory Disasters' (LSE Law, Society and Economy Working Paper No 24/2014, London School of Economics and Political Science Law Department, 2014) identifies six causes that contribute to regulatory disasters: individual and group incentives; organisational dynamics of regulators, regulated operators and the complexity of the regulatory system; weaknesses, ambiguities and contractions in regulatory strategies; misunderstandings of the problem and potential solutions; communication problems and conflicting messages and trust and accountability structures.
4. Leigh Hancher and Michael Moran, 'Organizing Regulatory Space', in L Hancher and M Moran (eds), *Capitalism, Culture and Economic Regulation* (Oxford University Press, 1989) 293.
5. Grabosky, 'Counterproductive Regulation', above n 2, 363.
6. Christopher Hood and Martin Lodge, 'Pavlovian Innovation, Pet Solutions and Economizing on Rationality? Politicians and Dangerous Dogs' in J Black, M Lodge and M Thatcher (eds), *Regulatory Innovation: A Comparative Analysis* (Edward Elgar, 2005) 138.
7. Evidence-based policy-making is discussed in Chapter 5, 91–3.

8. Grabosky, 'Counterproductive Regulation', above n 2, 356–8.
9. Ibid 357.
10. Garrick Blalock, Vrinda Kadiyali and Daniel H Simon, 'The Impact of Post-9/11 Airport Security Measures on the Demand for Air Travel' (2007) 50 *Journal of Law and Economics* 731, 751–2.
11. Grabosky, 'Counterproductive Regulation', above n 2, 351–2.
12. Ibid 353.
13. Brian W Head and John Alford, 'Wicked Problems: Implications for Policy and Management' (2015) 47 *Administration & Society* 711, 719.
14. David Dery, *Problem Definition in Policy Analysis* (University Press of Kansas, 1984) 92–3.
15. Eric Windholz and Graeme Hodge, 'Conceptualising Social and Economic Regulation: Implication for Modern Regulators and Regulatory Activity' (2012) 38 *Monash University Law Review* 212, 229–32.
16. Jeremy A Blumenthal, 'Expert Paternalism' (2012) 64 *Florida Law Review* 721; Oren Perez, 'Can Experts Be Trusted and What Can Be Done about It? Insights from the Biases and Heuristics Literature' in A Alemanno and Anne-Lise Sibony (eds), *Nudge and the Law: A European Perspective* (Hart Publishing, 2015) 115.
17. Dery, *Problem Definition in Policy Analysis*, above n 14, 92–3.
18. Grabosky, 'Counterproductive Regulation', above n 2, 355–6.
19. Ian Ayres and John Braithwaite, *Responsive Regulation: Transcending the Deregulatory Debate* (Oxford University Press, 1992) 87.
20. Christopher Pollitt and Peter Hupe, 'Talking about Government: The Role of Magic Concepts' (2011) 13 *Public Management Review* 641.
21. Eric Windholz and Graeme Hodge, 'The Magic of Harmonisation: A Case Study of Occupational Health and Safety in Australia' (2012) 34 *The Asia Pacific Journal of Public Administration* 137; Eugene Bardach, *The Implementation Game: What Happens after a Bill Becomes Law* (MIT Press, 1977).
22. Windholz and Hodge, 'The Magic of Harmonisation', above n 21.
23. See discussion of bounded rationality in Chapter 5.
24. See discussion of incrementalism in Chapter 5, and of institutional and ideational theories in Chapter 3.
25. David P Dolowitz and David Marsh, 'Learning from Abroad: The Role of Policy Transfer in Contemporary Policy-Making' (2000) 13 *Governance* 5, 17–20; Organisation for Economic Cooperation and Development, *Reducing the Risk of Policy Failure*, above n 3, 21–2.
26. See, e.g., Robert Baldwin, 'Better Regulation: Tensions Aboard the Enterprise' in S Weatherill (ed), *Better Regulation* (Hart Publishing, 2007) 40–4; Ciara Brown and Colin Scott, 'Regulation, Public Law, and Better Regulation' (2011) 17 *European Public Law* 467, 471–2, and the reports cited therein.
27. See discussion of bounded rationality in Chapter 5.
28. Grabosky, 'Counterproductive Regulation', above n 2, 360.
29. Ibid, 359; Julia Black, 'Learning from Regulatory Disasters', above n 3, 7.
30. Eugene Bardach and Robert A Kagan, *Social Regulation: Strategies for Reform* (Institute for Contemporary Studies, 1982) 15.
31. Grabosky, 'Counterproductive Regulation', above n 2, 350.
32. Ibid 352.
33. Organisation for Economic Cooperation and Development, *Reducing the Risk of Policy Failure*, above n 3, 19.
34. See the discussion of private interest theories in Chapter 3, 43–51.
35. Grabosky, 'Counterproductive Regulation', above n 2, 349; Dwight Filley, 'Forbidden Fruit: When Prohibition Increases the Harm It Is Supposed to Reduce' (1999) 3 *The Independent Review* 441.

36. Sam Sieber, *Fatal Remedies: The Ironies of Social Intervention* (Plenum Publishing, 1981); Bruce Yandle, 'Bootleggers and Baptists: The Education of a Regulatory Economist' (1983) 7 *Regulation* 12; Cassandra Davis and Elizabeth Howlett, 'From Apples to Alcopops: The Forbidden Fruit Effect on Supersized Alcoholic Beverages' (2012) 40 *Advances in Consumer Research* 1105.

37. Sam Peltzman, 'The Effects of Automobile Safety Regulation' (1975) 83 *Journal of Political Economy* 677.

38. See, e.g., Wiel Janssen, 'Seat-Belt Wearing and Driving Behaviour: An Instrumented-Vehicle Study' (1994) 26 *Accident and Analysis Prevention* 249; Sam Peltzman, 'Offsetting Behaviour, Medical Breakthroughs, and Breakdowns' (2011) 5 *Journal of Human Capital* 302; Barbara A Morrongiello, Beverly Walpole and Jennifer Lasenby, 'Understanding Children's Injury-Risk Behaviour: Wearing Safety Gear Can Lead To Increased Risk Taking' (2007) 39 *Accident Analysis & Prevention* 618; Ross Owen Phillips, Aslak Fyhri and Fridulv Sagberg, 'Risk Compensation and Bicycle Helmets' (2011) 31 *Risk Analysis* 1187.

39. Grabosky, 'Counterproductive Regulation', above n 2, 349; Doreen McBarnet, 'It's Not What You Do but the Way That You Do It: Tax Evasion, Tax Avoidance and the Boundaries of Deviance', in D M Downes (ed), *Unravelling Criminal Justice* (MacMillan, 1992) 247; Doreen McBarnet, 'When Compliance Is Not the Solution but the Problem: From Changes in Law to Changes in Attitude' in V Braithwaite (ed), *Taxing Democracy: Understanding Tax Avoidance and Evasion* (Ashgate, 2003) 229; Valerie Braithwaite, *Defiance in Taxation and Governance: Resisting and Dismissing Authority in a Democracy* (Edward Elgar, 2009).

40. Christine Parker and John Braithwaite, 'Regulation' in P Cane and M Tushnet (eds), *The Oxford Handbook of Legal Studies* (Oxford University Press, 2003) 119, 135.

41. John Braithwaite, Toni Makkai and Valerie Braithwaite, *Regulating Aged Care: Ritualism and the New Pyramid* (Edward Elgar, 2007); John Braithwaite, *Regulatory Capitalism: How It Works, Ideas for Making It Work Better* (Edward Elgar, 2008) ch 6; Michael Power, *The Audit Society: Rituals of Verification* (Oxford University Press, 1997); Cheryl L Wade, 'Sarbanes-Oxley Five Years Later: Will Criticism of SOX Undermine Its Benefits?' (2008) 39 *Loyola University Chicago Law Journal* 595, 597.

42. Dennis F Thompson, 'The Moral Responsibility of Public Officials: The Problemm of Many Hands' (1980) 74 *American Political Science Review* 905.

43. Grabosky, 'Counterproductive Regulation', above n 2, 359–60; Black, 'Learning from Regulatory Disasters', above n 3, 10–1.

44. Jacob S Hacker, 'Policy Drift: The Hidden Politics of US Welfare State Retrenchment' in W Streeck and K Thelen (eds), *Beyond Continuity: Institutional Change in Advanced Political Economies* (Oxford University Press, 2005) 40; Wolfgang Streeck and Kathleen Thelen, 'Introduction: Institutional Change in Advanced Political Economies' in W Streeck and K Thelen (eds), *Beyond Continuity: Institutional Change in Advanced Political Economies* (Oxford University Press, 2005) 1, 24–36.

45. Hacker, 'Policy Drift', above n 44; Streeck and Thelen, 'Introduction', above n 44, 24–5.

46. See Chapter 3, 44–5.

47. Marver H Bernstein, *Regulating Business by Independent Commission* (New York, 1955) 94.

48. Ibid 95.

49. Grabosky, 'Counterproductive Regulation', above n 2.

50. Organisation for Economic Cooperation and Development, *Reducing the Risk of Policy Failure*, above n 3, 10.

51. See, e.g., *United Kingdom*: Better Regulation Taskforce, *Principles of Good Regulation* (2003); Better Regulation Taskforce, *Regulation—Less Is More: Reducing Burdens, Improving Outcomes: A BRTF Report to the Prime Minister* (2005); *United States*: *Regulatory Planning and Review*, Executive Order 12866, 58 Fed Reg 51735 (30 September 1993); *Improving Regulation and Regulatory Review*, Executive Order 13563, 3 CFR 3821 (18 January 2011); *Retrospective Review of Regulation*, Executive Order 13610, 3 CFR 28469 (10 May 2012); *Australia*: Council of Australian Governments, *Best Practice Regulation: A Guide for Ministerial Councils and National Standard Setting Bodies* (2007); Department of Prime Minister and Cabinet, *The Australian Government Guide to Regulation* (2014); Department of Prime Minister and Cabinet, *Regulator Performance Framework* (2014); *European Union*: European Commission, *Better Regulation Guidelines* (EC, 2015); European Commission, *Better Regulation 'Toolbox'* (EC, 2015); *Canada*: Government of Canada, *Cabinet Directive of Regulatory Management* (2012); OECD: *Reducing the Risk of Policy Failure*, above n 3; *Recommendations of the Council on Regulatory Policy and Governance* (OECD Publishing, 2012); *Best Practice Principles for Regulatory Policy: The Governance of Regulator* (OECD Publishing, 2014).

52. Anne Meuwese and Patricia Popelier, 'Legal Implications of Better Regulation: A Special Issue' (2011) 17 *European Public Law* 455.

53. *United Kingdom*: Better Regulation Executive within the Cabinet Office; *United States*: Office of Information and Regulatory Affairs within the White House's Office of Management and Budget: *Australia*: Office of Best Practice Regulation within the Department of Prime Minister and Cabinet; *European Commission*: Regulatory Scrutiny Board within the Secretariat-General to the Commission; *Canada*: Regulatory Affairs Sector within the Treasury Board Secretariat.

54. These central units are in addition to the exhortations found in better regulation policies and procedures for individual government departments and regulatory agencies to assume responsibility for regularly reviewing and proactively managing its stock of regulation and the cumulative burden it imposes. See, e.g., Organisation for Economic Co-Operation and Development, *Recommendations of the Council on Regulatory Policy and Governance*, above n 51, 12; United States, *Improving Regulation and Regulatory Review*, Executive Order 13563, 3 CFR 3821 (2011); *Retrospective Review of Regulation*, Executive Order 13610, 3 CFR 28469 (2012); Government of Canada, *Cabinet Directive on Regulatory Management* (October 2012).

55. See, e.g., Organisation for Economic Co-Operation and Development, *OECD Regulatory Policy Outlook 2015* (OECD Publishing, 2015) 127.

56. An example of the former is the commitment of European governments to reduce the administrative burden on business by 25%, measured using the Standard Cost Model that quantifies the cost of the time needed to comply with a regulation's administrative obligations; Commission of the European Communities, *Commission Working Document: Measuring Administrative Costs and Reducing Administrative Burdens in the European Union* (14 November 2006). An example of the latter is the United Kingdom Government's 'one in, two out' rule for business regulation—that is, for every new regulation that imposes a cost on business, existing regulation with double the cost to business will need to be repealed or modified; United Kingdom Government, *2010 to 2015 Government Policy: Business Regulation* (2015).

57. Meuwese and Popelier, 'Legal Implications of Better Regulation', above n 52, 456.
58. See, e.g., Baldwin, 'Better Regulation', above n 26, 22, who discusses how tensions inherent in better regulation reforms can lead to compromises in how they are operationalised; Patricia Popelier, 'Governance and Better Regulation: Dealing with the Legitimacy Paradox' (2011) 17 *European Public Law* 555, who argues that better regulation reforms as operationalised lack the qualities of representativeness, transparency, accountability and enforceability that gives legitimacy to decision-making.
59. See, e.g., Tom R Tyler, *Why People Obey the Law: Procedural Justice, Legitimacy and Compliance* (Princeton University Press, 2nd ed, 2006); Valerie Braithwaite, Kristina Murphy and Monika Reinhart, 'Taxation Threat, Motivational Postures, and Responsive Regulation' (2007) 29 *Law and Policy* 137; Julia Black, 'Constructing and Contesting Legitimacy and Accountability in Polycentric Regulatory Regimes' (2008) 2 *Regulation & Governance* 137; Kristina Murphy, Tom R Tyler and Amy Curtis, 'Nurturing Regulatory Compliance: Is Procedural Justice Effective When People Question the Legitimacy of the Law?' (2009) 3 *Regulation & Governance* 1; Julia Black, 'Legitimacy and the Competition for Regulatory Share' (LSE Law, Society and Economy Working Paper 14/2009, London School of Economics and Political Science, Law Department, 2009) 25.
60. Giandomenico Majone, 'Regulation and Its Modes' in G Majone (ed), *Regulating Europe* (Routledge, 2006) 11; Giandomenico Majone, 'From the Positive State to the Regulatory State: Causes and Consequences of Changes in Modes of Governance' (1997) 17 *Journal of Public Policy* 139, 161.
61. See Eric Windholz, 'The Evolution of a Modern (and More Legitimate) Regulator: A Case Study of the Victorian Environment Protection Authority' (2016) 3 *Australian Journal of Environmental Law* 17 on which this section draws.
62. See, e.g., *Oxford Online Dictionary*<www.oxforddictionaries.com> accessed 23 April 2015; *Macquarie Dictionary* (Macquarie Library, 4th ed, 2005) 817; *The Oxford Thesaurus* (Oxford University Press, 2nd ed, 1997) 257.
63. Mark C Suchman, 'Managing Legitimacy: Strategic and Institutional Approaches' (1995) 20 *Academy of Management Review* 571, 574.
64. See references, above n 59.
65. See discussion of regulatory regimes in Chapter 4.
66. This community accords with Moore's 'authorising environment, the support of which, according to Moore, is necessary for public managers to create value'. Mark H Moore, *Creating Public Value: Strategic Management in Government* (Harvard University Press, 1995) 118.
67. Majone, 'From the Positive State to the Regulatory State', above n 60, 161.
68. Black, 'Constructing and Contesting Legitimacy and Accountability', above n 59, 145.
69. This framework builds upon the work of Mark Suchman, who identified three primary forms of organisational legitimacy that he labelled moral, pragmatic and cognitive; Suchman, 'Managing Legitimacy', above n 63. Although developed from an organisational management perspective, Suchman's analysis is, as Black observes, consistent with the regulatory compliance literature; Black, 'Constructing and Contesting Legitimacy and Accountability', above n 59, 144.
70. This is to be distinguished from the case of non-state regulators such as exist in transnational regimes. Such regulators necessarily lack legal legitimacy and must look to the other legitimacy domains for their legitimacy; Black, 'Legitimacy and the Competition for Regulatory Share', above n 59, 9.
71. Moore, *Creating Public Value*, above n 66, 17.

72. John Benington and Mark H Moore, 'Public Value in Complex and Changing Times' in J Benington and M H Moore (eds), *Public Value: Theory and Practice* (Palgrave Macmillan, 2011) 1, 6; Bronwen Morgan and Karen Yeung, *An Introduction to Law and Regulation* (Cambridge University Press, 2007) 4.

73. Tony Prosser, *The Regulatory Enterprise: Government, Regulation, and Legitimacy* (Oxford University Press, 2010) 8.

74. Moore, *Creating Public Value*, above n 66, 30.

75. See, e.g., Suchman who identifies four dimensions: consequential, procedural, structural and personal; Suchman, 'Managing Legitimacy', above n 63, 579–82; Majone who identifies two dimensions: substantive and procedural; Giandomenico Majone, 'Regulatory Legitimacy' in G Majone (ed), *Regulating Europe* (Routledge, 1996) 286; a distinction also employed by Moore, *Creating Public Value*, above n 66, 163–7; Baldwin who identifies five normative criteria: legislative mandate, accountability, due process, expertise and efficiency; Robert Baldwin, *Rules and Government* (Clarendon Press, 1995) 41–9; and Black who summarises normative assessments of regulatory legitimacy into four main claims: constitutional, justice, functional or performance-based and democratic; Black, 'Constructing and Contesting Legitimacy and Accountability', above n 59, 145–6.

76. See Suchman, 'Managing Legitimacy', above n 63, 579–82.

77. Madalina Busuioc and Martin Lodge, 'The Reputational Basis of Public Accountability' (2016) 29(2) Governance 247.

78. Tyler, *Why People Obey the Law*, above n 59, 269–76. See also Kristina Murphy, 'Turning Defiance into Compliance with Procedural Justice: Understanding Reactions to Regulatory Encounters through Motivational Posturing' (2016) 10 *Regulation & Governance* 93.

79. Tyler, *Why People Obey the Law*, above n 59, 276.

80. Suchman, 'Managing Legitimacy', above n 63, 581 quoting J W Meyer and B Rowan, 'Institutionalized Organisations: Formal Structure as Myth and Ceremony' in W W Powell ad P J DiMaggio (eds), *The New Institutionalism in Organisational Analysis* (University of Chicago Press, 1991) 41, 50.

81. Majone, 'Regulatory Legitimacy', above n 75, 286.

82. Robert Baldwin, Martin Cave and Martin Lodge, *Understanding Regulation: Theory, Strategy, and Practice* (Oxford University Press, 2nd ed, 2012) 29.

83. Streeck and Thelen, 'Introduction', above n 44, 26–9, 31.

84. An example of this was the Deepwater Horizon oil spill in the Gulf of Mexico. In that case, the regulator was responsible for both licensing drilling operators and collecting royalties from them, and regulating their safety and environmental performance. Reports into the disaster found that royalty generation dominated safety and environmental concerns; Black, 'Learning from Regulatory Disasters', above n 3, 5.

85. Recent research reveals that within regulatory regimes, the assessments of each regulator's legitimacy is, to a degree, impacted by the nature of that division, and the manner with which the regulators cooperate in the discharge of their regulatory responsibilities; Windholz, 'The Evolution of a Modern (and More Legitimate) Regulator', above n 61.

86. Suchman, 'Managing Legitimacy', above n 63, 581–2.

87. Angelo Mastrangelo, Erik R Eddy and Steven J Lorenzet, 'The Importance of Personal and Professional Leadership' (2004) 25 *Leadership & Organization Development Journal* 435; Erik R Eddy, Steven J Lorenzet and Angelo Mastrangelo, 'Personal and Professional Leadership in a Government Agency' (2008) 29 *Leadership & Organization Development Journal* 412.

88. Windholz, 'The Evolution of a Modern (and More Legitimate) Regulator', above n 61.

89. Suchman, 'Managing Legitimacy', above n 63, 582–3.
90. Black, 'Constructing and Contesting Legitimacy and Accountability', above n 59, 145.
91. Suchman, 'Managing Legitimacy', above n 63, 583.
92. Black, 'Constructing and Contesting Legitimacy and Accountability', above n 59, 145.
93. Parker and Braithwaite, 'Regulation', above n 40, 128.
94. Suchman, 'Managing Legitimacy', above n 63, 578–9.
95. Black, 'Constructing and Contesting Legitimacy and Accountability', above n 59, 146.
96. This table is a modified version of the table originally published in Windholz, 'The Evolution of a Modern (and More Legitimate) Regulator', above n 61.
97. Ibid.
98. Suchman, 'Managing Legitimacy', above n 63, 585–99.
99. Black, 'Learning from Regulatory Disasters', above n 3, 17.
100. Baldwin, Cave and Lodge, *Understanding Regulation*, above n 82, 33–4.
101. See Chapter 7 (Diagnosis) and 8 (Design).
102. Julia Black, 'Talking about Regulation' [1998] (Summer) *Public Law* 77, 95.
103. Prosser, *The Regulatory Enterprise*, above n 73, 4.

Part III

Regulatory Design and Practice

7 Define

Agenda-Setting, Issue Diagnosis and Objective Setting

This chapter examines the define stage of the regulatory policy cycle. The define stage refers to the processes by which the issue is defined, its causes and key attributes diagnosed and the desired future state—the regulatory objectives—is set. These processes require an investment of resources, time and effort by the government department or agency charged with the task. This, in turn, presumes a decision to make this investment. How this decision is made involves consideration of how issues enter or become part of the regulatory policy cycle—what is described in the public policy literature as 'agenda-setting'. Agenda-setting is a critical component of the regulatory policy process. How an issue first appears on the government's agenda plays a significant role in how it is subsequently defined and diagnosed. This chapter therefore starts by examining how the policy agenda is set before moving on to issue diagnosis and objective setting.

Agenda-Setting

When discussing agenda-setting, it is necessary to differentiate between two types of agendas. Kingdon, whose multiple streams model of policy-making was discussed in Chapter 5, refers to these as the 'governmental agenda' (being issues with respect to which governments pay attention) and the 'decision agenda' (being the issues selected by government for active consideration).[1] Issues on the decision agenda are those that go through the regulatory policy cycle. But to understand how issues reach the decision agenda and enter the policy cycle, it is first necessary to understand how the governmental agenda is set from which the decision agenda is drawn.

Governmental Agenda

Kingdon's explanation of how issues become matters about which governments pay attention focuses on three critical elements of agenda-setting: an event or change in circumstances that triggers a (re)assessment of an issue, entrepreneurs who leverage that trigger to their advantage and the use of framing to persuade people the issue is something about which they should care and governments should act. Each of these elements is considered below, following which the special position of the media in agenda-setting is discussed.

Triggering Mechanisms

For an issue to emerge on the governmental agenda there first needs to be a 'trigger' that leads persons to reassess an existing issue or to discover a new issue.[2] According to Kingdon, this trigger could be an occurrence that changes the nature or image of an issue or its solution, or a development in the political sphere that changes the way the issue is perceived.[3] This has parallels with Baumgartner's and Jones' model of 'punctuated equilibrium'. Baumgartner and Jones argue there is a point of 'policy equilibrium' around which government and interest groups coalesce, and policy change tends to be gradual and incremental. This policy equilibrium is only punctuated when a significant external shock affects either the 'policy image' (the shared view of the policy community of the issue and its solution) or the 'policy venue' (the institutions through which decision-making takes place).[4]

Triggers that change an issue's 'policy image' can take a variety of forms. The trigger could be a change in an established indicator or benchmark used to measure the existence or magnitude of an issue. An increase in workplace injuries will focus attention on workplace health and safety, an increase in pedestrian fatalities on road safety and an increase in unemployment or business insolvencies on the state of the economy.

Alternatively, the trigger could be a crisis such as that which befell the global financial system in the late 2000s,[5] a scandal such as the 2012 rigging of the Libor (London Interbank Offered Rate),[6] a natural catastrophe such as Hurricane Katrina that claimed more than 1000 lives[7] or an industrial disaster such as the 2010 Deepwater Horizon oil spill that killed eleven people and wreaked environmental damage across the Gulf of Mexico.[8] Crises, scandals, catastrophes and disasters focus the public's attention on a new, changed or previously unseen issue, causing them to reassess the risks associated with that existing issue or to question the robustness and adequacy of existing regulatory regimes.

The triggering event need not be large or catastrophic to gain the public's and government's attention, however. Small and local events also can act as triggers. An example of this was the murder of a young boy by his father in Melbourne, Australia, that transformed the previously thought of private issue of domestic violence into an issue of public and national significance.[9] Nor need the event be sudden and immediate. Issues can emerge on the agenda gradually as changes in indicators and events become a pattern, and knowledge moves from contested to consensus. Ecological change such as global warming arguably is the most prominent recent example of this.

Scientific and technological developments also can act as triggers. The invention of the motor car, radio, television, the internet and genetic engineering are but a few examples of scientific and technical developments that created new products and new and complex economic, social and moral issues attracting the public's and government's attention. And more recently we have seen the emergence of robotics, nanotechnology and technology enhanced sharing platforms create new products and disrupt existing markets. The speed with which these technologies have been commercialised and the changes they are making to our existing economic, social and cultural systems—which for some are opportunities and for others risks—have thrust them on to the governmental agenda.

Social progress too can trigger issues appearing on the governmental agenda. The 1960s and 1970s, for example, saw social movements place a range of issues including environmentalism, women's and indigenous rights, and racial equality, on the governmental agenda of many liberal Western democracies. And today history is repeating itself with same-sex marriage and the rights of gays and transgender people appearing on governmental agendas. Movements for social change succeed by altering an issue's visibility, scope and intensity—in particular by increasing the number of people concerned about the issue and the strength of emotion with which that concern is expressed.

The trigger for an issue appearing on the governmental agenda also can be feedback on the adequacy of existing institutional or regulatory arrangements. Externally, this feedback could come from actors subject to or impacted by the regulatory regime, or from court cases, non-governmental reports and media stories that question the manner with which the regime is operating and the outcomes it is achieving. Alternatively, the feedback might be generated internally and relate to concerns visible only to those within government or the regulatory agency. Efficiency concerns often fall into this category. Finally, the trigger might be part of the regular maintenance of government institutions and activities. Examples of this are sunset clauses in existing regulation that trigger a review of that regulation absent any concerns being expressed about it.

Finally, an issue can appear on the governmental agenda—not because of a change in the issue itself—but because of a change in what Kingdon refers to as the political stream (and Baumgartner and Jones as the policy venue). The political stream refers to the prevailing political processes, forces and climate. It includes the national mood (public opinion), prevailing ideologies, organised political forces, the composition of government and the bureaucracy and the processes through which interest groups are given voice and consensus is built. Changes in the national mood (e.g. growth of environmental consciousness); changes in or within government (e.g. from a conservative to a progressive government); or the emergence of new interest groups (e.g. well-funded and organised environmental lobby groups) can combine to elevate an existing issue (e.g. the environment) on to the governmental agenda.

Entrepreneurs and Promoters

Not all changes in indicators, and not all events, result in an issue gaining traction on the governmental agenda. Something more generally is required. For Kingdon, this 'something more' was the policy entrepreneur: individuals and groups who leverage an occurrence, event or development to promote an issue or policy solution on to the governmental agenda. These entrepreneurs or issue promoters (as they are sometimes also called) can take many forms. They can include governments and elected politicians;[10] bureaucrats, regulators and policy officials;[11] sectorial, ideological and cause based interest groups;[12] concerned individuals;[13] academics, researchers, consultants, think tanks and other non-governmental organisations;[14] international and transnational bodies;[15] and social commentators and journalists.[16] Some of these entrepreneurs and promoters act selflessly in the public interest, perceiving the issue made prominent by the trigger to be unfair or threatening to society or a section of society; others may act in their private self-interest, perceiving the issue to be a threat to their personal or commercial interests; and others still may act for mixed motives, promoting their preferred policy solution (and their interests) on to the governmental agenda.[17]

Of course, not all policy entrepreneurs and promoters operate for the same cause. Frequently, agenda-setting is contested between those who seek to expand the agenda by creating or increasing community concern about an issue and those who seek to maintain the status quo.[18] Cobb and Coughlin refer to these two types of actors as 'expanders' and 'containers' respectively.[19] The ability of these competing groups to influence the governmental agenda largely is dependent on their comparative ability to mobilise support for their cause from within the policy community and from the public more broadly.[20] And their ability to mobilise this support, in turn, will vary (at least in part) according to the logic and cogency of their arguments, and the weight and strength of the evidence in support of them (which is, in part, dependent upon the resources at their disposal and their level of expertise). However, facts alone, no matter how objective and scientific, often are not enough to gain traction and momentum. Also important is how those facts are presented and framed.

Framing

Framing is the process by which competing agenda-setting actors seek to give meaning to facts and to make sense of a situation. Framing starts from the proposition that

> Public problems are not like games or puzzles, with neatly defined rules and ready solutions. They are mental constructs, abstractions from reality shaped by our values, perceptions and interests. Problems are "not objective entities in their own right, 'out there' to be detected as such, but are rather the product of imposing certain frames of reference" on reality.[21]

There are a number of tools available to persons seeking to impose their frame on an issue. First is adopting a label that captures the essence of the issue sought to be communicated. This is usually done through the use of a metaphor, catch-phrase or symbol. Labelling cuts through what often is a cluttered informational environment by providing persons whose rationality is 'bounded' with a quick, shorthand device to simplify the complex and ambiguous, and to interpret and make sense of the otherwise contradictory and unmanageable.[22] Labelling also communicates an intended emotional state. Language has an emotional quality or valence. That quality can be positive, generating a strong attractiveness and, with it, a greater potential to mobilise support; or it can have a negative quality and low attractiveness that can be used to generate opposition to changes sought by others.[23] And labelling selects and characterises. The name or label applied to a situation highlights what the person applying the label wants the recipient to see and diverts attention away from what they do not want the recipient to see. In so doing, the process of selection also creates categories—of what is in and what is out; of what is normal and what is abnormal; of what is preferred and what is not preferred.[24] The utility of labelling to simplify, categorise and convey different understandings of an issue is illustrated by the contrasting labels applied to a number of contemporary issues: 'pro-life' or 'pro-choice' to characterise the abortion debate; 'affirmative action' or 'preferential treatment' to characterise hiring practices; and 'illegal arrival' or 'refugee' to characterise persons crossing national borders to escape war.

A second tool is selectivity. As we already have observed, agenda-setting often is contested and adversarial. There is no obligation on persons engaged in the debate to make full disclosure. As a result, framing involves the selective use of information, with competing actors highlighting (and sometimes exaggerating) information that supports their preferred frame or perspective, and ignoring or discrediting information that does not. Framing also involves competing actors selecting and highlighting those dimensions of an issue that are most salient and relevant to the target audience.[25] Rochefort and Cobb identify seven such dimensions: causality (and issues of culpability and blame allocation); severity (extent, timing and impact of consequences); incidence (whether growing, stable or declining); novelty (is it unprecedented or trailblazing); proximity (whether personally relevant to the target audience or of general societal concern); crisis (level of urgency); and problem population size, frequency and nature (are they considered deserving or undeserving; familiar or strange; mainstream or outcasts).[26] Other potential dimensions include important values such as freedom, liberty, equality and fairness, as well as existing policy paradigms (economic; social; legal) and political ideologies (right vs left; capitalist vs socialist vs communist).

The final tool is story-telling. Story-telling (or what is sometimes referred to as the narrative) moves beyond the use of labels and metaphors, to explain what is happening, why and how, and what might be done going forward to rectify the situation.[27] Van Hulst and Yanow refer to it as providing the 'plot line'.[28] And like the plot line in a movie, a good story has victims and villains; people to praise and people to blame; and prospects for redemption. It ties the elements together in a manner that is both logical and causal, and motivational and persuasive. It produces 'both a model *of* the world . . . and a model *for* subsequent action in that world'.[29]

The Role of the Media

No discussion of framing would be complete without a discussion of the role of the media. Debate has long raged about the impact of the media on public policy processes, and agenda-setting in particular. Studies reveal that the media is more than a neutral medium for information dissemination, and that it can impact which issues get on the agenda and the speed with which they move up it, sometimes significantly.[30] It is therefore important that its role is understood and taken into account.

The main mechanism through which the media impacts agenda-setting is by influencing public opinion. The media makes events, incidents and issues visible. In doing so, the media performs a valuable democratic role by giving persons outside the political mainstream an opportunity to be heard.[31] The media also can take events previously thought of as private and make them issues of public concern. A good illustration of this is Nelson's 1984 study of the manner with which the media publicised the growing professional literature on child abuse, placing it on the public and governmental agenda.[32] The media also operates directly upon political actors. Studies reveal that policy-makers, and politicians in particular, can overstate the extent to which public opinion is influenced by the media. As a result, politicians and other policy-makers may be more likely than the general public to be influenced by what appears in the media.[33]

The media also acts as a gatekeeper. They select what is 'newsworthy' and in so doing steer and direct public attention towards some events, issues and ideas, and away from others.[34] There is no definitive set of criteria according to which the media considers something to be 'newsworthy', although, consistent with our discussion of framing, human interest, victims and villains, conflict, deviance and impact are likely to be considered by the media to have 'news value', as are stories that question established authority.[35]

The media also plays an important interpretive role. They can be a powerful framer and amplifier of events, issues and incidents. Cohen's *Folk Devils and Moral Panic* provides an excellent example of this. Cohen studied how the media amplified and sensationalised incidents of fighting between youth gangs, turning what objectively were minor events into a perceived crisis threatening social order and requiring urgent government action.[36] Cohen's example also demonstrates the darker side of the media's involvement. The media's business model requires it to present issues in a manner that attracts an audience. As Parsons observes, the media, by being 'in the business of "manufacturing" news are also involved in the production of problems'.[37] This, Edelman argues, leads the media to treat the public as an audience for which it produces a spectacle by constructing and reconstructing social problems into a succession of threats and reassurances.[38]

The media also provides an arena in which rival entrepreneurs, promoters, interest groups and other regulatory actors compete to have their framing of an issue adopted by others. And the media set the rules of this competition. As we already have observed, frames with human interest, conflict, deviance and impact, and which question established authority, are more likely to succeed in gaining media attention. Finally, the media itself can act as an issue or solution promoter partnering with politicians, professionals, academics and other experts to form coalitions to advocate for specific policy reforms. An example of this is the prominent role played by the media in a number of countries advocating for the introduction of mandatory reporting of child abuse and sex offender registers.[39]

Whether an issue attracts the attention of the media not only influences whether it appears on the governmental agenda, but also the speed with which it moves up that agenda and crosses over on to the decision agenda. And it is to the decision agenda that we now turn.

Decision Agenda

The previous discussion explained how an issue might appear on the governmental agenda. However, not every issue that gains a government's attention is acted upon by that government. Governments have limited resources. The number of issues that compete for a government's attention usually exceeds that government's capacity to deal with them with the result that, at any given point of time, only a few issues are chosen for active consideration and elevated on to the decision agenda.

Several commentators have sought to distil the dimensions or criteria against which issues are filtered before emerging on the decision agenda.[40] First and foremost of these are the issue's political dimensions. Mass appeal is the best vehicle to obtain the attention of political decision-makers.[41] The larger the number of people paying attention to the issue, and the larger the number of people demanding action with respect to it, the more likely it will be prioritised for action. Governments also tend to put issues through a 'political risk calculation', and are more likely to act on issues perceived to be electorally popular and to avoid issues that are likely to be unpopular with its support base, or which run counter to the positions of powerful vested interests.[42] In this regard, agenda-setting, like other aspects of the regulatory endeavour, is susceptible to power influences, with stronger, better organised voices being heard over smaller, less well-organised voices. Second are the issue's substantive dimensions—its size, scale and complexity. The greater the number of people affected by the issue and the larger the scale and intensity of that affect, the more likely governments are to act upon it. Operating in the opposite direction, however, can be the issue's complexity and uncertainty. Governments can be reluctant to take on issues if uncertain about its causes, its interconnectedness with other issues and their ability to tackle it successfully. In this regard, issues linked to a plausible solution are more likely to make their way on to the decision agenda than an issue without a solution.[43] Third are the issue's operational and budgetary dimensions—the resources, time and cost required to define, diagnose, design and implement a response to the issue. Governments have limited resources. Governments therefore need to be confident, first that the issue's politics, size and scale is such (compared to other issues) to warrant the investment of its limited resources and, second, of its ability to generate a return on that investment within a reasonable timeframe (which time-frame increasingly is defined by the electoral cycle).

The manner in which these criteria are applied, by whom and through which institutions will vary from political system to political system.[44] What is clear, however, is that while non-governmental actors have significant influence over the shape of the governmental agenda, government actors (executive, legislature, department heads, policy analysts) have greater influence over the shape of the decision agenda. This means that issues that resonate with government actors' own ideas, preferences, ideologies and worldviews are more likely to appear on the decision agenda than issues that do not.[45] An example of this is climate change, which more readily appears on the decision agenda of progressive left-leaning governments than it does on those of conservative right-leaning governments.

What also is clear from this discussion is that the manner with which an issue appears on the decision agenda may not be the only or most appropri-ate representation of the issue, its solution or the objectives that ought to be set. The governmental agenda and, ultimately, the decision agenda, is shaped by people and groups that actively compete to impose their under-standing and perspective of the issue or its solution upon the public and government decision-makers. This creates an incentive for these actors to present or frame the issue or solution in the most persuasive way. We have seen this can be achieved through the use of labels, symbols and stories, evidence presented logically and coherently, as well as by evidence presented selectively to overstate and exaggerate their position or to misrepresent and discredit the position of opponents. Indeed, Zahariadis goes so far as to sug-gest that systematic distortion, misrepresentation and the selective presenta-tion of information—and not rational argument—is the principal method by which issues gain the attention of policy-makers.[46] Therefore, while the issue appearing on the government's decision agenda, and upon which the government has decided to consider taking action, provides a convenient and sensible starting point for its subsequent analysis (it can be thought of as a hypothesis to be confirmed, refuted or replaced), those responsible for undertaking that analysis should do so cognisant of how it has been devel-oped and with a healthy level of skepticism of the tactics and motives of those who have promoted it to this point.

Issue Definition and Diagnosis

In order for governments to know what action to take with respect to an issue, the issue first needs to be independently defined, its causes diag-nosed and its effects understood. The importance of this step cannot be over-emphasised. It provides the foundations for all subsequent steps in the regulatory policy cycle. As Ackoff observes: '[w]e fail more often because we solve the wrong problem than because we get the wrong solution to the right problem'.[47] Issue definition and diagnosis is both a science and an art: a mix of systematic process and subjective judgement; method and intuition.[48] In this section, the systematic process is represented as a series of sequential steps. As with the regulatory policy cycle itself, breaking down the definitional and diagnostic process into its constituent parts enables it to be explained and examined without being overwhelmed by its complexity. However, and again consistent with the regulatory policy cycle, reality is unlikely to be this ordered; some steps may overlap; some may be conducted concurrently; and some may be abridged or overlooked. The process also is likely to be iterative, with the findings of subsequent steps being fed back into earlier steps which are then repeated. The definitional and diagnostic steps employed in this book are: assigning the issue for analysis, clarifying the initial issue hypothesis, mapping the regulatory space, conducting a causal analysis, future thinking and issue confirmation. These steps are not unique to this book. They are common to many public policy texts.[49] What this book does do, however, is tailor those steps to cater for the unique nature of regulatory policy issues and the regulatory policy cycle within which the issue definition and diagnosis stage sits.

Before examining each step, it is important to emphasise the value of engaging actors occupying the regulatory space in the process of diagnosing and defining the issue. Up to this point meaningful participation in the regulatory policy process has been absent. Agenda-setting is competitive and adversarial. The promoters of competing frames speak at and past each other, not to each other. Issue definition and diagnosis provides the first opportunity for regulatory actors to engage in what this book previously has described as 'thick' participation or dialogue,[50] and what Schön and Rein refer to as 'frame reflection', where relevant actors reflect upon how they and others perceive and frame the issue, and through this reflection or mutual learning, a common understanding of the issue emerges (or different frames move closer together).[51]

Assigning the Issue for Analysis

The first step in the process is assigning the issue to an analyst or team of analysts to define and diagnose. This first step frequently is overlooked in explanations of the regulatory policy process. This is somewhat surprising given its importance. The body to which an issue is assigned for diagnosis says a lot about how the government perceives the issue. Government has a choice to assign the issue to a government department or agency with existing responsibilities for the issue, to an independent institution such as a law reform or industry commission, or to a bespoke body created specifically for the purpose. Assigning the issue to an independent or bespoke body generally reflects the seriousness with which the government views the issue, the government's assessment that existing institutions are unlikely to be (or to be perceived to be) sufficiently independent to conduct a robust analysis or the government's willingness to consider solutions that are not beholden to existing bureaucratic structures and divisions of power.

The nature and composition of the body to which the issue is assigned also says a lot about how the government decision-maker perceives the issue and its solution. Government is highly structured and compartmentalised. Head and Alford refer to government departments and agencies as 'cultural fortresses' each with their own specialised functional and professional expertise.[52] The selection of government agency (or the composition of a bespoke body) therefore reflects a choice of the functional, professional or cultural lens through which the issue diagnosis is to be conducted. For example, assigning an issue to an economic centric body such as Treasury implies a preference for a market-orientated solution, assigning the issue to a service portfolio such as health or education implies a preference for a more interventionist approach and assigning it to a law reform commission suggests a preference for a rule-based solution.

Whichever body is assigned the issue, however, it would behove that organisation to bring different skills and organisational and disciplinary perspectives to bear upon its diagnosis. Doing so maximises the prospects that all or most dimensions of the issue will be identified, and their analysis will benefit from a more robust (and less siloed) approach.

Clarifying the Issue Hypothesis

Next, the persons to whom the issue is assigned for analysis need to clarify the issue hypothesis. As noted above, the issue appearing on the government's decision agenda, and upon which the government is considering taking action, provides the starting point for the analysis and can be thought of as a hypothesis to be confirmed, refuted or replaced. However, the decision by government to give active consideration to regulating an issue often is made amidst competing conceptions of the issue, its causes and solution. It is therefore important to understand what the government decision-maker believes to be the nature of the issue justifying regulatory intervention by the state. Is it a problem to be solved, an opportunity to be grasped or a risk to be eliminated or mitigated? And if it is a problem, does government perceive it to be economic or social in nature, or a combination of both? It also is helpful to obtain from the government decision-maker what they understand to be the parameters and scope of the issue and any drivers, barriers or other factors important to its resolution. These could include, for example, key stakeholders whose support the government considers essential to any solution's political feasibility and any overarching government policies that must be taken into account (for example, budgetary policies; human rights commitments).

Some commentators counsel caution at this step, arguing that analysts should not probe too deeply for the government decision-maker's understanding of the issue.[53] These commentators argue that this knowledge can lead analysts (consciously or subconsciously) to provide the answer sought (or which they think is sought) by that decision-maker, thereby undermining the objectivity of the analysis. However, no analysis is purely objective. There is a political dimension to every issue. Ignoring this knowledge creates a professional risk for analysts that their conclusions and recommendations may be perceived to be politically naïve. Analysts should err on the side of maximising their understanding of the decision-maker's understanding of the issue. The risks that this understanding can bias the subsequent analysis can be guarded against better than the risks of not knowing. How this bias can be guarded against is discussed under 'Issue Confirmation' below.

Mapping the Regulatory Space

As discussed in Chapter 4, regulatory issues do not exist in a vacuum. They exist within a regulatory space with boundaries, contours, atmosphere and occupants. Mapping this space is the next step in defining and diagnosing the issue. The initial boundaries for this mapping exercise are provided by the issue hypothesis. However, those conducting the analysis should be cognisant of the limitations inherent in the manner with which the hypothesis was developed, and be prepared to expand or contract the boundaries of the space if appropriate.

A useful starting point for this mapping exercise are existing government interventions. This should cover interventions by all levels of government and all policy instruments. It also should include relevant actors occupying the regulatory space, and their interests, values and positions, interrelationships and interdependencies, commonalities and differences. Figures 4.1 to 4.3 (in Chapter 4) are illustrative of this mapping.

A number of techniques and methods exist to identify actors and their interests, values and positions. They include identifying actors involved in the process by which the issue emerged on the governmental or decision agenda, examining related historical decision-making, conducting media searches and other environmental scans on the issue and employing 'snowball' or 'reputation' methods, in which an initial set of actors are asked to identify other potentially interested actors.[54]

Depending on the issue, this mapping exercise is apt to identify large numbers of regulatory actors. Aggregating and categorising these actors is a useful way to manage this volume, and a useful system of categorisation are the legitimacy communities discussed in Chapter 6, namely: the persons likely to be regulated under any regulatory solution (potential regulatees); the likely beneficiaries of that regulation; actors whose active participation and resources are likely to be required for the regulation to achieve its objectives; and persons whose support is important to secure and maintain the resources and authority needed to implement the regulatory solution.[55]

It also can be helpful to map each actor's (or group of actors') level of interest in an issue against their power to facilitate or frustrate government attempts to regulate it. Doing so produces four categories of actors: 'players' who have both a significant interest in the issue and significant power to influence it; 'subjects' who have an interest in the issue but little power; 'context-setters' who have power but little interest; and the 'crowd' who have both little interest and little power.[56] These categories of actors are shown in Figure 7.1, together with a brief description of how governments might choose to approach each group.

As can be seen, categorising actors in this manner can help identify those whose buy-in is required to maximise the prospects of regulatory success, and whose opinions therefore should be given greater weight. Some 'players' and 'context-setters', for example, may have sufficient influence (political or practical) that regulatory success cannot be achieved without their support or active participation. These players are sometimes described in the literature as having 'veto' power. It is with these actors that compromises frequently have to be made, first in order for the regulatory policy to be adopted and, then, for it to be implemented effectively. Early identification of these actors can assist with the development of an appropriate participation (and negotiation) strategy.

Finally, it is important to identify the systems, customs and conventions that define and shape the regulatory space. These include: existing regulatory regimes and other forms of social and contractual control; the institutions through which decision-making occurs; the issue's history and how that history has shaped its current trajectory and the distribution of power among regulatory actors (recall historical institutionalism); and the different (and interdependent) socio-cultural, economic, political, legal and constitutional systems and sub-systems in which the target behaviour resides. The latter in

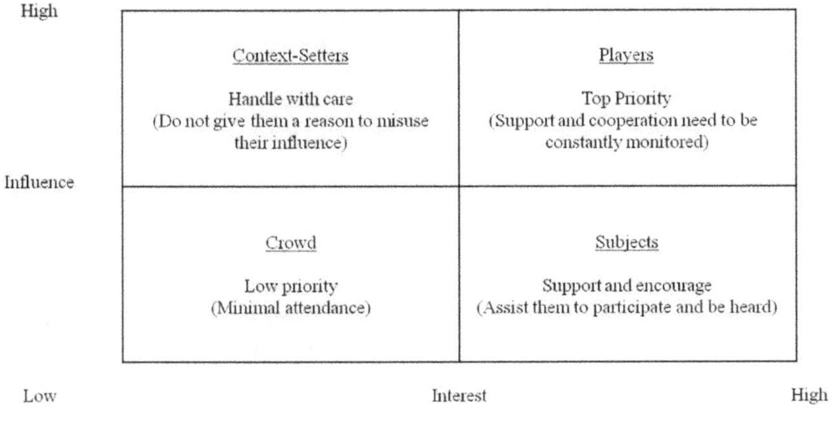

High		
	Context-Setters	Players
	Handle with care	Top Priority
	(Do not give them a reason to misuse their influence)	(Support and cooperation need to be constantly monitored)
Influence		
	Crowd	Subjects
	Low priority	Support and encourage
	(Minimal attendance)	(Assist them to participate and be heard)
Low	Interest	High

Figure 7.1 Regulatory Actor Influence-Interest Matrix[57]

particular is not always easy to identify, but as we have seen, is very important to ensure unintended consequences are identified and avoided.

Causal Analysis

Having confirmed the nature and boundaries of the issue, and mapped its regulatory space, the next step is to conduct a causal analysis. A causal analysis works from the assumption that the occurrence, event or incident that acted as the trigger for the issue being placed on the governmental agenda (and now the decision agenda) is a symptom or effect for which there are one or more causes. The importance of this causal analysis cannot be overstated. As we have observed, failing to look beyond the superficial and simplistic to understand the underlying causes of an issue is a frequent cause of regulatory failure.[58]

Numerous methodologies exist for identifying these causes (or causal inferences).[59] These range from the empirical and statistical to the discursive and judgmental. The choice of methodology will depend on the size, scale and importance of the issue; the time, budget and expertise available to do it; and, critically, the available data and its form. For example, a significant statistical database that can be interrogated may lend itself to a path analysis—a specialised form of regression analysis that yields estimates of the pattern and magnitude of a relationship between a dependent variable (the effect) and one or more independent variables (the potential causes).[60] However, absent a rich statistical database, discursive and judgmental techniques would need to be employed. An example of a discursive and judgemental technique is the 'five whys' approach, pursuant to which the policy analyst asks 'why' an occurrence, event or incident happened, and for every cause identified in answer to that question asks 'why' again, repeating the exercise five times.[61]

Backward and Forward Mapping

Common to these causal analytical techniques is the need for policy analysts to shift their focus 'backwards' to identify causal factors and influences, and through this process to break the issue down into smaller more manageable components.[62] This is called 'backward mapping' in the policy literature. Often missed, however, is the need to also 'map forward'. Forward mapping asks what other effects are produced by each identified cause—which can be answered by asking what would be the effects if this cause did not exist? This has the advantage of identifying how regulating each cause might affect other issues and other systems.[63] This type of 'systems thinking' makes visible the consequential effects of solutions that alter identified causes and, in doing so, potentially avoids unintended consequences of the type we have seen can cause regulatory failure.

A simple example to illustrate how backward and forward mapping work. Let us assume the issue is people smoking. To start the backward mapping, we ask—why do some people choose to smoke? Answers to this question include: peer pressure, smoking looks 'cool' and to relieve boredom and stress.[64] Let us take one of these answers—smoking looks 'cool'—and again ask, 'why'? The answer to this question may be because it is shown in movies, advertised at sporting events, their role models smoke and because people smoke when socialising in bars and nightclubs. Now, let us take the last of these answers—people smoking in bars and nightclubs—and again ask 'why'? Answers to this 'why' might be because workplace health and safety laws give owners of these venues the discretion to allow smoking, and international tourists expect it and would be lost without it. This backward mapping exercise is represented in Figure 7.2.

Now let us take smoking in bars and nightclubs and map it forward. What would be the effects if this cause did not exist—if people were not able to smoke in bars and nightclubs? Potentially, smokers and their friends might choose not to go to bars and nightclubs. This would impact the profitability of those venues, possibly causing them to lay off staff and spend less with other businesses that provide them with goods and services. This, in turn, could lead to increased unemployment and reduce the overall level of economic activity. It also might incentivise entrepreneurs to develop other venues at which people could smoke and socialise (such as private clubs) or new products which smokers could consume while at a bar or nightclub (such as e-cigarettes). The creation of these new venues and products may further disrupt existing economic and socio-cultural systems, creating both new opportunities and new risks. This forward mapping exercise is represented in Figure 7.3.

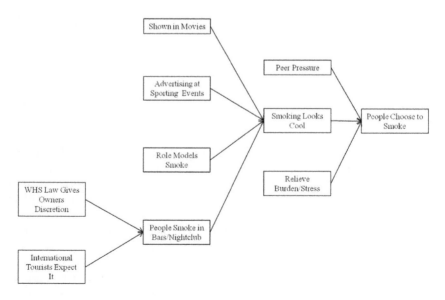

Figure 7.2 Illustrative Backward Mapping of Causes for Why People Smoke

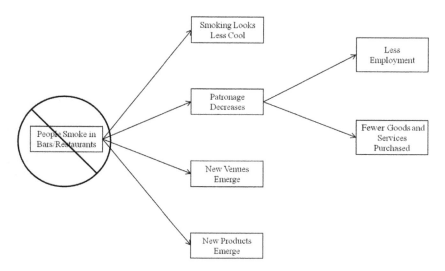

Figure 7.3 Illustrative Forward Mapping of Effects of Banning Smoking in Bars

Classifying Causes

Depending on the issue, the number of causes identified by the mapping can be very large. Classifying the causes can provide much needed structure, as well as a basis for prioritising them for attention. One way to classify causes is according to their proximity and force. Wagner, for example, identifies five types and levels of causes: primary causes that set off the effect and are closest to it physically and temporally; secondary causes whose effect is to create a primary (or another secondary) cause; contributory causes that exacerbate the effect of other causes; common causes that are systemic in nature and effect multiple issues; and episodic or special causes that are not present systemically but occur intermittently and unpredictably. In our simple 'people smoking' example, the answers to the first 'why' question are primary causes, and the answers to the second and third set of 'why' questions are secondary causes. An example of a common cause might be workplace health and safety laws that grant bar and nightclub owners (and all other employers) discretion to allow smoking, and a major sporting event that attracts international tourists unaccustomed to smoking restrictions is an example of an episodic cause. As simple as this example might initially have appeared, it clearly demonstrates the interconnectedness of causes and effects, and the complexity of causal analyses.

Future Thinking

Causal analyses tend to be 'point in time' exercises. However, the issue being diagnosed rarely is static. It is constantly evolving, sometimes maintaining its historical trajectory, sometimes changing in nature and intensity as a result of changes in the regulatory space, and sometimes simply in response to gaining the interest and attention of government.[65] In the regulatory context, it is not uncommon for actors responsible for an issue to act pre-emptively to address its causes to reduce the likelihood of government regulation. Self-regulation is one such response.[66]

Regulatory policy analysts need to consider how future changes in the regulatory space, actors' motivational postures and the institutions in and through which they operate may alter the nature of the issue. Again, there are a number of techniques for doing this, of which scenario-building arguably is the most common and prevalent.[67] Scenario-building involves constructing a number of possible futures and assessing whether the issue worsens, ameliorates or even disappears under each scenario. This 'future thinking' has a number of advantages. First, it may either reinforce or qualify the need for action, depending on whether the future changes are likely to intensify or lessen the issue. Second, it may identify factors or potential causal mechanisms not considered under the 'business-as-usual' scenario. And third, it enables analysts to identify the extent to which any regulatory intervention may need to accommodate future changes, thereby broadening the search for alternative solutions.

Issue Confirmation

The final step is to synthesise the mapping exercise, causal analysis and future thinking into a holistic model of the issue: of its various causal mechanisms and their direction, force and effect; of the actors, institutions and systems impacting, and impacted by, those causal factors; and of the potential future scenarios in which the issue may play out. This synthesis process should include a 'consistency check' for gaps, tensions and contradictions.[68] For example, the results of the causal analysis may identify system effects impacting actors not identified in the regulatory space mapping exercise; and the future scenarios may require the boundaries of the mapping exercise to be broadened. Processes also should be employed to guard against potential conflicts and cognitive biases in the analytical process. These include 'introspective, meta-cognitive techniques' to encourage policy analysts to identify and address biases in their research; 'cognitive forcing techniques' that include checklists and guidelines to help analysts resist biases; and 'deliberative decision-making mechanisms' that challenge analysts (and, indeed, all participants in the process) to consider and take into account other points of view.[69] As a result of these consistency checks and anti-bias processes, additional information or analysis may be required, making the synthesis process iterative in nature.

Once these consistency checks are completed, the finalised holistic model should provide a clearly stated definition and diagnosis of the issue upon which the next stages of the regulatory policy cycle may proceed. That the issue may be stated with clarity is not the same, however, as saying its definition and diagnosis are objectively verifiable or universally agreed. It is therefore important, when putting together the issue model, to identify the evidence in support of each of its elements, and the confidence level that attaches to that evidence, remembering that some causes and effects will be based on circumstantial evidence and the inferences drawn from it, and others on evidence scientifically obtained and verifiable.[70] Differences of opinion and perspectives of key actors also should be noted, as should key assumptions and hypotheses, especially when choices are being made between alternative plausible interpretations of the facts or on the basis of incomplete or opinion or anecdotal evidence.

Objective Setting

Having defined and diagnosed the issue, the final component in this stage is to describe the desired future state. This is done in the form of regulatory objectives. Clear and concise objectives provide all regulatory actors with a 'north star' with which to navigate the remainder of the regulatory policy cycle. Without clear objectives, it is impossible to devise a rational and meaningful strategy. Clarity of objectives also is important to harnessing, steering and directing the support of regulatory actors whose coordinated participation is critical to successful regulatory design and implementation. A clear objective also aids regulatory decision-making. It provides a reference point according to which competing values are balanced or traded-off, and from a legal perspective, it is something to which courts may have recourse when interpreting regulatory requirements that may not be clear on their face or reasonable in their application. Finally, the regulatory objectives are important measures against which the regulation's operation and the regulator's performance can be evaluated.

Regulatory objectives generally are expressed at two levels: primary or high level objectives specify what the regulatory initiative as a whole should achieve; and operational or secondary objectives specify the changes that need to occur for the high level objectives to be achieved. Operational objectives should reflect the logic of the initiatives employed to address the issue's causal drivers. This, however, only can be done after those regulatory initiatives have been designed and agreed upon (which is done in the next stages of the regulatory policy cycle). To define operational objectives earlier (e.g., by setting a high prosecution target), risks predetermining or at least prejudicing the selection of those interventions (e.g., by implicitly requiring an injection of (additional) prosecutorial resources). For this reason, our focus at this stage is on the regulatory policy's primary or high level policy objectives.[71]

Primary regulatory objectives should be both broad and S.M.A.R.T. Broad in the sense that they should allow for the consideration of a range of alternative regulatory options and not favour or prejudice a particular solution. And S.M.A.R.T. in the sense that they should be: specific (precise and concrete enough not to be open to varying interpretations by different actors); measurable (such that their attainment can be verified); achievable (ambitious but realistic); relevant (should link directly to the issue and its causes); and time-bound (should be deliverable by a fixed date or time).[72] S.M.A.R.T. criteria differentiate an objective from a vision. 'A tobacco-free world' is a vision; a ten percent reduction in the number of people smoking over the next two years is a high level policy objective. It is specific, measurable, achievable, relevant and time-bound, and broad in that it does not specify or suggest how that reduction is to be achieved.

Concluding Insights and Implications

This chapter commenced by examining how issues become matters which governments choose to give serious consideration to regulating and therefore enter the regulatory policy cycle. Our examination revealed that this 'agenda-setting' rarely is a rational exercise of prioritising issues for action based on an agreed set of objective criteria. Rather, agenda-setting is a contested process involving evidence and emotion; ideas and institutions; and competing interests employing their power and influence to construct and frame issues to advance their worldview and understanding to the exclusion of others. How an issue is first framed provides the initial hypothesis for the issue's definition and diagnosis, and a first mover advantage for those whose frame is adopted. Once a particular definition is adopted and internalised, changing it involves not only presenting another plausible definition of the issue, but also discrediting the existing definition and changing sometimes entrenched paradigms.[73]

Next we examined the process by which the issue's causes and effects are diagnosed, and its initial definition confirmed, revised or replaced. A number of methodologies and techniques were identified to guide and structure this analysis. These methodologies combine systematic approaches with judgement and creativity, reinforcing one of the book's key themes—that regulation is both a science and an art. How the issue is defined and its causes diagnosed has important implications for the remaining stages of the regulatory policy cycle. It provides the reference point from which regulatory objectives are set, and regulatory solutions are designed, implemented and evaluated.

The definition and diagnosis of the issue emanating from this stage may not be agreed upon by all relevant actors. Some actors may disagree on the existence or nature of an issue, others may disagree about its causes and effects and others still may disagree on whether the issue is appropriate for government intervention (for example, on moral or ideological grounds). Some commentators refer to issues about which agreement on their existence, nature and causes cannot be reached as 'wicked problems'.[74] Wicked problems are thought to be intractable problems for which there is no solution.[75] This book does not subscribe to the view that there are issues without solutions, just as it does not subscribe to the view that there are regulatory failures for which there are no causes. Issues may be difficult to define and diagnose and solutions may be difficult to identify and design. But this does not mean a solution does not exist. Rather, it means that we do not presently have the knowledge or technology to fully diagnose the issue's causes and effects with sufficient precision and confidence to design an effective solution. However, this only makes improving our knowledge and understanding of the issue the first step in its resolution. In some situations, regulatory analysts may need to progress in the absence of consensus, on the basis of limited, incomplete or contested evidence, accepting that the issue's definition and diagnosis may change with changes in our knowledge and understanding, and that addressing the issue may require trial and error, incremental progress and a long-term focus—a product of our bounded rationality and the very definition of Lindblom's incrementalism and mutual successive adjustment.

There always will be a degree of uncertainty in every issue diagnosis. The issues with which governments have to grapple 'are the result of various interacting forces, not all of which may be known, the nature and relevance of which changes over time, and the interaction between which will be only imperfectly understood'.[76] Whether this uncertainty is such as to warrant a decision not to proceed to the design stage of the regulatory policy cycle falls to be decided by the same criteria applied to determine whether an issue should be diagnosed in the first place—that is, its political, substantive and administrative dimensions—albeit freshly defined. Is the issue of sufficient size, scale and importance to warrant further investment in its resolution? Does the diagnosis provide sufficient confidence that its causes (and their effects) are both understood and capable of being addressed? Do the regulatory objectives warrant the investment required to realise them? If the answer to all three questions is 'yes', then the issue proceeds to the design stage. If the answer to one or more questions is 'no', then the appropriate action may be to return the issue to the governmental agenda for ongoing monitoring. And if the answer to the questions is 'we do not know'—as might be the case with a wicked problem—then a choice may need to be made. At this early stage of the regulatory policy cycle, application of a form of the precautionary principle may be warranted: namely, that the absence of certainty and consensus is not a reason not to proceed in circumstances where the evidence raises reasonable grounds for concern and where the consequences of not acting may be large or irreversible.[77]

Notes

1. This is similar to Cobb's and Elder's distinction between the 'systemic agenda' (all societal problems meriting public attention and within governmental jurisdiction) and the 'institutional agenda' (issues selected by government for potential policy action); Roger W Cobb and Charles D Elder, *Participation in American Politics: The Dynamics of Agenda-Building* (John Hopkins Press, 2nd ed, 1983) 8–86.

2. For a general discussion of triggering mechanisms, see Larry N Gerston, *Public Policy Making: Process and Principles* (M E Sharpe, 3rd ed, 2010) ch 2.
3. John W Kingdon, *Agendas, Alternatives, and Public Policy* (Longman, 2nd ed, 2003) 203–4.
4. Frank R Baumgartner and Bryan D Jones, *Agendas and Instability in American Politics* (University of Chicago Press, 2nd ed, 2009).
5. See, e.g., Julia Black, 'Paradoxes and Failures: "New Governance" Techniques and the Financial Crisis' (2012) 75 *Modern Law Review* 1037.
6. See, e.g., David Hou and David Skieie, 'LIBOR: Origins, Economics, Crisis, Scandal, and Reform' (Staff Report No 667, Federal Reserve Bank of New York, March 2014).
7. See, e.g., Select Bipartisan Committee, United States Congress, *A Failure of Initiative: Final Report of the Select Bipartisan Committee to Investigate the Preparation for and Response to Hurricane Katrina* (2006).
8 See, e.g., Julia Black, 'Learning from Regulatory Disasters' (LSE Law, Society and Economy Working Paper 24/2014, London School of Economics and Political Science, Law Department, 2014).
9. See, e.g., Kathy Landvogt, 'Looking Back, Going Forward' (2016) 11 *Good Policy* 9; Victoria, Royal Commission into Family Violence, *Report* (2016).
10. Kingdon observed that during elections, politicians and political parties promote issues they believe resonate with the electorate; Kingdon, *Agendas, Alternatives, and Public Policy*, above n 3, 61–5.
11. Recent research reveals policy officials demonstrate a high degree of instrumentality in steering the policy process, that they nurture policy ideas over long timeframes and actively seek to place policy ideas on the government's agenda; Kathleen Mackie, 'Success and Failure in Environment Policy: The Role of Policy Officials' (2016) 75 *Australian Journal of Public Administration* 291.
12. See discussion of Interest Group Theory in Chapter 3.
13. The role played by a particular person in moving issues on to and up the governmental agenda was considered to be important or very important in fifteen of Kingdon's twenty-three case studies. Of these, the most prominent was Ralph Nader, the consumer advocate who elevated vehicle safety on to the US governmental agenda; Kingdon, *Agendas, Alternatives, and Public Policy*, above n 3, 180.
14. Spector and Kitsuse observed that social problems are constructed by individuals or groups who consider existing social conditions to be unjust, immoral or harmful, and are promoted by professionals and academics involved in analysing and dealing with them; Malcolm Spector and John I Kitsuse, *Constructing Social Problems* (Cummings Publishing, 1977). Hass similarly notes the important agenda-setting role played by networks of professionals with recognised expertise in the policy area; Peter M Hass, 'Introduction: Epistemic Communities and International Policy Coordination' (1992) 46 *International Organization* 1, a topic touched on in the discussion of Ideational Theories in Chapter 3.
15. Majone observes that a notable share of the work of international organisations such as the OECD and the WHO is explicitly aimed at influencing the agendas of member states; Giandomenico Majone, 'Agenda-Setting' in M Moran, M Rein and R E Goodin (eds), *The Oxford Handbook of Public Policy* (Oxford University Press, 2008) 247.
16. The role of the media is discussed in detail below.
17. See the discussion public and private interest theories of regulation in Chapter 3.
18. This is a specific manifestation of Interest Group Theory discussed in Chapter 3.

19. Roger W Cobb and Joseph F Coughlin, 'Are Elderly Drivers a Road Hazard? Problem Definition and Political Impact' (1998) 12 *Journal of Aging Studies* 411, 417–18.
20. 'Policy community' is used here broadly to refer to all actors with an interest in the policy issue. It also is used by some commentators to refer to close, stable, cooperative relationships between interest groups, politicians and bureaucrats focused on a specific issue; for a discussion of the different usages see Michael M Atkinson and William D Coleman, 'Policy Networks, Policy Communities and the Problems of Governance' (1992) 5 *Governance* 154.
21. Catherine Althaus, Peter Bridgman and Glyn Davis, *The Australian Policy Handbook* (Allen & Unwin, 5th ed, 2013) 58 citing David Dery, *Problem Definition in Policy Analysis* (University Press of Kansas, 1984) 4.
22. Merlijn van Hulst and Dvora Yanow, 'From Policy "Frames" to "Framing": Theorizing a More Dynamic, Political Approach' (2016) 46 *American Review of Public Administration* 92, 97. See also Deborah A Stone, *Policy Paradox: The Art of Political Decision Making* (Norton, 3rd ed, 2011) 157.
23. Robert Henry Cox and Daniel Béland, 'Valence, Policy Ideas, and the Rise of Sustainability' (2013) 26 *Governance* 307–28.
24. Hulst and Yanow, 'From Policy "Frames" to "Framing"', above n 22. See also Martin Rein and Donald A Schön, 'Problem Setting in Policy Research' in C H Weiss (ed), *Using Social Research in Public Policy Making* (Lexington Books, 1977) 235, 238–9.
25. Robert Entman, 'Framing: Toward Clarification of a Fractured Paradigm' (1993) 43(4) *Journal of Communication* 51, 52.
26. David A Rochefort and Roger W Cobb, 'Problem Definition: An Emerging Perspective', in D A Rochefort and R W Cobb (eds), *The Politics of Problem Definition: Shaping the Policy Agenda* (University Press of Kansas, 1994) 15.
27. Deborah A Stone, 'Causal Stories and the Formation of Policy Agendas' (1989) 104 *Political Science Quarterly* 281; Elizabeth A Shanahan, Mark K McBeth and Paul L Hathaway, 'Narrative Policy Framework: The Influence of Media Policy Narratives on Public Opinion' (2011) 39 *Politics & Policy* 373.
28. Hulst and Yanow, 'From Policy "Frames" to "Framing"', above n 22, 101. See also Stone, 'Causal Stories and the Formation of Policy Agendas', above n 27.
29. Hulst and Yanow, 'From Policy "Frames" to "Framing"', above n 22, 98 (emphasis in original).
30. The impact of the media on the agenda-setting process is issue and context specific. For a review of the literature see Maxwell McCombs, *Setting the Agenda: The Mass Media and Public Opinion* (Polity Press, 2004); Stefaan Walgrave and Peter van Aelst, 'The Contingency of the Mass Media's Political Agenda-Setting Power: Towards a Preliminary Theory' (2006) 56(1) *Journal of Communication* 88; Katrin Voltmer and Sigrid Koch-Baumgarten, 'Mass Media and Public Policy: Is There a Link?' in S K Baumgarten and K Voltmer (eds), *Public Policy and Mass Media: The Interplay of Mass Communications and Political Decision-Making* (Routledge, 2010) 1; Peter van Aelst and Stefaan Walgrave, 'Minimal or Massive? The Political Agenda-Setting Power of the Mass Media According to Different Methods' (2011) 16 *International Journal of Press/Politics* 295; Stuart Soroka et al, 'Mass Media and Policymaking' in E Araral et al (eds), *Routledge Handbook on Public Policy* (Routledge, 2013) 201.
31. Iris Korthagen, 'Who Gets on the News? The Relation between Media Biases and Different Actors in News Reporting on Complex Policy Processes' (2015) 17 *Public Management Review* 617.

32. Barbara J Nelson, *Making an Issue of Child Abuse* (University of Chicago Press, 1984).
33. Aeron Davis, 'Investigating Journalist Influence on Political Issue Agendas at Westminster' (2007) 24 *Political Communication* 181; Aelst and Walgrave, 'Minimal or Massive?', above n 30.
34. Wayne Parsons, *Public Policy: An Introduction to the Theory and Practice of Policy Analysis* (Edward Elgar, 1995) 107. A number of commentators observe that this gatekeeping role is being diluted by the growth of the Internet that provides additional, unfiltered avenues of mass communication. See, e.g., Neuman W Russell et al, 'The Dynamics of Public Attention: Agenda-Setting Theory Meets Big Data' (2014) 64(2) *Journal of Communication* 193.
35. Joachim F Staab, 'The Role of News Factors in News Selection: A Theoretical Reconsideration' (1990) 5 *European Journal of Communication* 423; Korthagen, 'Who Gets on the News?', above n 31. These selection criteria are part of what is referred to as 'media logic'—the process of news-making that also includes the media's aims and production norms; David L Altheide and Robert P Snow, *Media Logic* (Sage, 1979).
36. Stanley Cohen, *Folk Devils and Moral Panics: The Creation of the Mods and Rockers* (MacGibbon and Kee, 1972).
37. Parsons, *Public Policy*, above n 34, 107.
38. Murray Edelman, *Constructing the Political Spectacle* (Chicago University Press, 1988) 1.
39. See, e.g., Bob Lonne and Nigel Parton, 'Portrayals of Child Abuse Scandals in the Media in Australia and England: Impacts on Practice, Policy, and Systems' (2014) 38 *Child Abuse & Neglect* 822.
40. See, e.g., Cobb and Elder, *Participation in American Politics*, above n 1; Brian W Hogwood and Lewis A Gunn, *Policy Analysis for the Real World* (Oxford University Press, 1984) 91–9; Althaus, Bridgman and Davis, *The Australian Policy Handbook*, above n 21, 51–2.
41. Cobb and Elder, *Participation in American Politics*, above n 1, 161–2.
42. Althaus, Bridgman and Davis, *The Australian Policy Handbook*, above n 21, 52.
43. Kingdon, *Agendas, Alternatives, and Public Policies*, above n 3, 202; Althaus, Bridgman and Davis, *The Australian Policy Handbook*, above n 21, 51.
44. Francesco Zucchini, 'Government Alternation and Legislative Agenda Setting' (2011) 50 *European Journal of Political Research* 749 who examines the impact on agenda-setting of different systems of parliamentary democracy.
45. Martin Lodge, Kai Wegrich and Gail McElroy, 'Dodgy Kebabs Everywhere: Variety of Worldviews and Regulatory Change' (2010) 88 *Public Administration* 247.
46. Nikolaos Zahariadis, *Ambiguity and Choice in Public Policy: Political Decision Making in Modern Democracies* (Georgetown University Press, 2003) 18.
47. Russell Ackoff, *Redesigning the Future: A Systems Approach to Societal Problems* (Wiley, 1974) 8.
48. Eugene Bardach and Eric M Patashnik, *A Practical Guide for Policy Analysis: The Eightfold Path to More Effective Problem Solving* (CQ Press, 5th ed, 2016) xvi.
49. See, e.g., Wil A H Thissen, 'Diagnosing Policy Problem Situations' in W A H Thissen and W E Walker (eds), *Public Policy Analysis: New Developments* (Springer, 2013) 65; Bardach and Patashnik, *A Practical Guide for Policy Analysis*, above n 48.
50. See Chapter 5, 89–90.
51. Donald A Schön and Martin Rein, *Frame Reflection* (Basic Books, 1994) ch 7.

52. Brian W Head and John Alford, 'Wicked Problems: Implications for Public Policy and Management' (2015) 47 *Administration & Society* 711, 719.
53. See, e.g., Travis P Wagner, 'Using Root Cause Analysis in Public Policy Pedagogy' (2014) 20 *Journal of Public Affairs Education* 429, 434; Bardach and Patashnik, *A Practical Guide for Policy Analysis*, above n 48, 11–2.
54. See, e.g., John M Bryson, 'What to Do When Stakeholders Matter: Stakeholder Identification and Analysis Techniques' (2004) 6 *Public Management Review* 21; Leon M Hermans and Wil A Thissen, 'Actor Analysis Methods and Their Use for Public Policy Analysts' (2009) 196 *European Journal of Operational Research* 808; Thissen, 'Diagnosing Policy Problem Situations', above n 49, 85–6.
55. See Chapter 6, 112–13.
56. Colin Eden and Fran Ackerman, *Making Strategy: The Journey of Strategic Management* (Sage Publications, 1999) 121–5; 344–6.
57. Adapted from ibid Stakeholder Consultation Tools, 121–5; 344–6; European Commission, *Better Regulation 'Toolbox'* (EC, 2016) 313 (Tool 50: Stakeholder Consultation Tools).
58. See the discussion of poor diagnosis as a cause of regulatory failure in Chapter 6, 101–2.
59. In many cases, it is not possible to establish causation objectively, only to infer causation from estimates or informed judgements about the relationships among variables; William N Dunn, *Public Policy Analysis: An Introduction* (Pearson, 4th ed, 2008) 167–9.
60. See, e.g., ibid 168–9.
61. For a more detailed explanation of the approach, see Wagner, 'Using Root Cause Analysis in Public Policy Pedagogy', above n 53. There is no magic to the number five, other than to keep what could be an infinite process within reasonable bounds. It is possible that the causal analysis could be exhausted in less than five questions.
62. Rein and Schön, 'Problem Setting in Policy Research', above n 24, 244–6; Schön and Rein, *Frame Reflection*, above n 51, 204; Richard F Elmore, 'Backward Mapping: Implementation Research and Policy Decisions' (1980) 94 *Political Science Quarterly* 601.
63. Richard F Elmore, 'Forward and Backward Mapping: Reversible Logic in the Analysis of Public Policy' in K Hanf and T Toonen (eds), *Policy Implementation in Federal and Unitary Systems* (Springer Netherlands, 1985) 33.
64. This is not intended to be an exhaustive list of causes. For a more comprehensive examination of the causes, see Hans Jurgen Eysenck and J L Eaves, *The Causes and Effects of Smoking* (Sage Publications, 1980).
65. This later response is known as the Hawthorne or observer effect, in which individuals modify or improve an aspect of their behaviour in response to their awareness of being observed. The term was coined in 1958 by Henry A Landsberger who, when analyzing the results of experiments at the Hawthorne Works to assess worker productivity under different light conditions, observed that worker productivity seemed to improve, not as a result of different lighting, but as a result of the motivational effect on the workers of the interest being shown in them; Henry A Landsberger, *Hawthorne Revisited: Management and the Worker, Its Critics, and Developments in Human Relations in Industry* (Cornell University, 1958).
66. Self-regulation is discussed in Chapter 8, 161–2.
67. For an overview of scenario-building, see Wil A H Thissen, 'Diagnosing Policy Problem Situations', above n 49, 65, 81–3; Warren E Walker, Vincent A W J Marchau and Jan H Kwakkel, 'Uncertainty in the Framework of Policy Analysis' in W A H Thissen and W E Walker (eds), *Public Policy Analysis: New*

Developments (Springer, 2013) ch 9. See also Kees van der Heijden, *Scenarios: The Art of Strategic Conversation* (Wiley, 1996) ch 6.

68. For techniques that can be employed to conduct a consistency check, see Dunn, *Public Policy Analysis*, above n 59, 95.

69. For an overview of these techniques, see Jeremy A Blumenthal, 'Expert Paternalism' (2012) 64 *Florida Law Review* 721.

70. For a discussion of types of evidence, see Chapter 5, 91–3.

71. Operational objectives are discussed in Chapter 9 (Decide Stage) at 215.

72. European Commission, 'How to Set Objectives', *Better Regulation Toolbox* (EC, 2015) 80 (Tool 13: How to Set Objectives).

73. Christoph Knill and Jale Tosun, *Public Policy: A New Introduction* (Palgrave Macmillan, 2012) 99.

74. Rittel and Webber are acknowledged as having coined the term; H W J Rittel and M Webber, 'Dilemmas in a General Theory of Planning' (1973) 4 *Policy Sciences* 155. There is no consensus on what exactly constitutes a 'wicked problem', although the following related characteristics appear to be common to most definitions: that the issue is technically or morally complex; its causes and effects uncertain; and there is a high level of disagreement amongst relevant actors about the nature of the issue that makes consensus or compromise unlikely (Joshua Newman and Brian Head, 'The National Context of Wicked Problems: Comparing Policies on Gun Violence in the US, Canada and Australia' (2017) 19(1) *Journal of Comparative Policy Analysis: Research and Practice* 40).

75. Rittel and Webber, 'Dilemmas in a General Theory of Planning', above n 74; Robert Durrant and Jerome Legge Jr, '"Wicked Problems", Public Policy, and Administrative Theory: Lessons from the GM Food Regulatory Area' (2006) 38 *Administration & Society* 309, 310; Althaus, Bridgman and Davis, *The Australian Policy Handbook*, above n 21, 54.

76. Julia Black, 'Critical Reflections on Regulation' (2002) 27 *Australian Journal of Legal Philosophy* 1, 4.

77. For a discussion of the precautionary principle, see Mike Feintuck, 'Precautionary Maybe, but What's the Principle? The Precautionary Principle, the Regulation of Risk, and the Public Domain' (2005) 32 *Journal of Law and Society* 371.

8   Design

Regime Variables; Option Generation

This chapter examines the design stage of the regulatory policy cycle. The design stage refers to the processes by which plausible alternative regulatory regimes for delivering the regulatory objective are formulated. This stage is critical to the success of the regulatory endeavour. We previously have observed that the design stage can be compromised by the organisational, disciplinary and personal biases of those undertaking it, with the result that analysts can tend to work incrementally from existing polices, continue down well-worn institutional paths and restrict themselves to instruments and tools with which they are familiar and comfortable.[1] Avoiding these causes of failure requires analysts to broaden their horizons to understand the richness of the design options available to them. This is the purpose of this chapter. First, the chapter explores the key regulatory design variables: who should regulate; whom should be regulated; how; to what standards; and through what institutional arrangements. This examination reveals that within each variable there exists a rich array of different instruments and arrangements from which regulatory designers can choose to construct alternative regulatory regimes. The construction of these regulatory regimes is the focus of the second part of the chapter. This part examines how and from where regime design ideas can be generated, and the principles that should guide this process. The output of this stage should be a broad and manageable set of plausible, feasible and flexible regime options. The processes and principles by which these options are then assessed and compared, and the regulatory regime to be implemented is chosen, is the focus of Chapter 9.

Regime Design Variables

In Chapter 4 the concept of the regulatory regime was introduced. That chapter explained that regulatory regimes refer to networks of actors involved in regulating an issue, the aggregate activities undertaken by those actors to modify the behaviour of the target audience and the norms, principles, rules and decision-making processes through which those actors and activities are coordinated. Chapter 4 also explained that regulatory regimes can be thought of as having four dimensions: size and scope (being the issues and objectives assigned to it); structure (being the regulatory instruments and actors within it, and the institutional arrangements through which they are coordinated and held to account); and style (the manner with which the regulator discharges its role and responsibilities). Regime size and scope (issues and objectives) were addressed in Chapter 7; regime style will be addressed in Chapter 10. In this and the next chapter we focus on regime structure.

The starting point for examining regime structure is our definition of regulation. In Chapter 1 we defined regulation to be 'a structured process undertaken by or under the auspices of government designed to modify the behaviour of persons or entities according to defined standards'. This definition identifies five key regulatory design variables. They are (in the order in which they will be considered in this chapter): (1) defined standards; (2) who should regulate (being government or those auspiced by government); (3) whom to regulate (the 'persons or entities'); (4) the mechanisms of behaviour modification; and (5) the institutional (structural) arrangements that give effect to the regulatory process. Within each of these variables reside a variety of options. Understanding the richness of these options is critical to being able to engage in the innovative and creative design thinking needed to address the increasingly complex issues confronting modern societies.

Defined Standards

Standards are an expression of the regulatory objective. They set out what needs to be done or achieved. Different commentators employ different systems to categorise standards.[2] Generally speaking, these systems tend to differentiate between a standard's legal operation (whether it is mandatory or consensual) and its character and application (whether it is prescriptive or outcome-orientated; and whether it applies to inputs, outputs, processes or principles). Each of these dimensions is considered below.

Legal Operation

Standards can be mandatory or consensual. Mandatory standards operate with the force of law. They include standards developed by government and enshrined in legislation, and standards developed by non-government bodies and incorporated into legislation by reference.[3] Legislation can be primary (passed by the legislature) or delegated (made by bodies to whom the legislature has conferred rule making authority). Legislation (primary and delegated) is sometimes called 'hard law', and is differentiated from 'soft law' instruments that are designed to assist compliance and to which sanctions for non-compliance do not attach directly.[4] Regulatees have no choice but to comply with mandatory standards.

Consensual standards, on the other hand, operate by virtue of the regulatee agreeing to comply with them. They generally operate as a contract between those promulgating them (often an industry or professional body) and the person or entity agreeing to comply with them (being a member of that body). Consensual standards can also operate through their persuasive, or what Black refers to as their 'halo', effect.[5] The 'halo' comes from being promulgated by industry or professional leaders, or from being endorsed or recognised in a manner that confers benefits or privileges on those that comply with them. Examples include professional accreditation schemes for accountants that operate as criteria for employment and enable the holder to charge higher fees in the market place,[6] and fair trade and responsible forestry management certification schemes that enable standard compliant entities to differentiate themselves positively in the market place.[7]

At one level, the difference between mandatory and consensual standards is a matter of form over substance: for mandatory standards to apply, a person must choose to engage in the activity to which those standards attach; and to the extent a monopoly governs a particular activity (as occurs with many professions), the standards promulgated by that monopoly are mandatory for persons choosing that activity. The key difference between mandatory and consensual standards resides in the consequences that attach to non-compliance. Breaches of mandatory standards generally are sanctioned through courts and tribunals, and attract criminal, civil or administrative penalties.[8] Consensual standards, on the other hand, are generally sanctioned by the industry or professional body in accordance with the contract between that body and the person or entity, and generally involve the loss of benefits that attach to being compliant with that body's standards.

Character and Application

The legal operation of a standard is not determinative of its character or application. Both mandatory and consensual standards can be either prescriptive or outcome-orientated. They also can apply to inputs, outputs, processes and principles. It is to these attributes of standards that we now turn.

PRESCRIPTIVE STANDARDS

Prescriptive standards, as their name suggests, prescribe how something is to be done, usually with a high level of specificity. Prescriptive standards come in many different forms. Some operate directly upon the person or entity by, for example, mandating that they engage in certain conduct (e.g. education and training); prohibiting them from engaging in certain conduct (e.g. driving beyond the speed limit); or only permitting conduct with the permission of the state. That permission could come in the form of a licence, authorisation, registration, permit, accreditation or certification.[9] Only being permitted to drive a car when licensed is an example. Other standards operate indirectly upon the person or entity by targeting products, processes, markets or transactions they engage in. The application of prescriptive standards to the inputs and outputs of manufacture and commerce is one of the more prominent examples of this. Prescriptive standards have been applied to plant and equipment (e.g. mandatory technology, materials and engineering requirements); work processes (e.g. maximum hours of work; minimum hours of rest; staffing ratios; lifting and load limits); and product specifications (e.g. mandatory weight, size and other product dimensions).

The main advantage of prescriptive standards is certainty. Prescriptive standards do not require regulatees to expend resources searching for solutions; the standards tell them exactly what they need to do to comply. This also makes it easier for regulators to administer and enforce compliance with them. Realising these advantages, however, is dependent on the standards being accessible (easy-to-locate), clear (easy to understand), precise (capable of being applied without interpretation and discretion), comprehensible (reflective of a widely accepted cause and effect relationship) and consistent (with other regulatory standards with which the regulatee must comply).[10] These criteria should be familiar to the reader by now, reflective as they are of better regulation principles and normative dimensions of legitimate regulation discussed in Chapter 6.

The main disadvantage of prescriptive standards is their inflexibility, rigidity and frequent complexity. By prescribing what is to be done, and not the outcome to be achieved, prescriptive standards provide little incentive for regulatees to engage with the regulation's underlying objective and rationale. As a result, they do not encourage regulatees to innovate to develop more effective and less costly regulatory solutions and technologies.[11] Prescriptive standards also can date quickly, especially in times of rapid social and technological change.[12] This disadvantage can be compounded by cumbersome and slow processes to change standards, which often is the case if the standards are legislated or developed through broad participatory and consensus based processes.[13]

Prescriptive standards also can be difficult to draft well. The nature of language is such that even the most carefully drafted standard can include ambiguities and gaps that only become visible when the unusual and unexpected arises in their application, or when dissected by lawyers and other advisers employed by those motivated to resist or game the system.[14] Regulatory draftspersons can respond to this risk in one of two ways. Either they can choose to inject even greater detail and specificity into the standard, or they can choose to draft the standard in more general and less specific language. However, both options have their disadvantages. Greater specificity can lead to greater complexity, and risks making compliance more costly for those motivated to comply, and more easily gamed by those who are not so motivated. Less specificity, on the other hand, risks prescriptive standards losing their main advantage—certainty—and becoming subjective and contingent. This, in turn, creates the risk that the standard as applied may become over-inclusive and prohibit valuable, welfare enhancing activities; or under-inclusive and permit conduct intended to be prohibited.[15]

Prescriptive standards are best suited to issues that are comparatively simple, and about which there is consensus about their causes and means of addressing them and little scope for innovation.[16] In times of rapid technological, commercial or societal change, however, these conditions rarely exist (or exist for long). This led regulatory practitioners and scholars to search for more flexible alternatives.

OUTCOME-ORIENTATED STANDARDS

Outcome-orientated standards, as their name suggests, articulate the outcome to be achieved, not how it is to be achieved. Outcome-orientated standards recognise that many regulatory issues do not have 'one-size-fits-all' solutions—that solutions need to be tailored to a variety of different regulatees operating in a variety of different circumstances, and that this is best done by each regulatee (with its knowledge advantage) rather than by government or the regulator. Outcome-orientated standards provide regulatees with the flexibility to develop their own customised methods to achieve the substantive outcome; to align regulatory compliance with good business practices; to evolve and adapt those methods to changing circumstances and technology; and to innovate and go beyond compliance if conditions permit.

Outcome-orientated standards that focus on an output are commonly referred to as *performance-based standards*. A common form of performance-based standard specifies how a product must perform before it can be sold or used. Australia's heavy vehicle standards are an excellent example. Whereas in the past, heavy vehicle standards prescribed what a vehicle should look like (i.e., its mass, length and other dimensions), today they specify how a vehicle must perform on the road (i.e., they should be stable and able to turn, stop and travel safely).[17] Performance-based standards also can be applied to industrial output. Emission standards are an example of this. They set quantitative limits on the permissible amount of specific air pollutants that may be emitted by sources such as vehicles, factories and power plants.[18]

A more recent application of outcome-orientated standards has been to systems and processes employed by business. These are called *process- (or systems or management) based standards*.[19] The focus here is on management having in place processes and systems to ensure regulatory compliance (usually through detecting, assessing and addressing sources of harm and risk in their operations). They are used mainly in industries where outputs are the product of complex, technical processes, and where the potential sources of harm and risk are many and not readily observable. Examples include Hazard Analysis and Critical Control Points ('HACCP') systems required in the food industry,[20] and safety case management systems increasingly being required of major hazard facilities.[21]

A third type of outcome-orientated standard is the *principle-based standard* which, as its name suggests, expresses the outcome to be achieved as a principle. Examples of principle-based standards can be found in environmental regulation, where the outcome frequently is expressed in terms such as 'ecologically sustainable development', 'intergenerational equity' and 'biological diversity',[22] and in financial regulation, where the outcome generally is expressed as a requirement to act 'fairly', 'with integrity' and 'in the best interests of the client'.[23]

The three types of outcome-orientated standards—performance-, process-, and principle-based—can be thought of as sitting on a continuum, differentiated by their distance to the regulatory objective and level of abstraction. Principle-based standards are closest to the objective, and frequently are an expression of the objective itself. Performance- and process-based standards, on the other hand, are more removed from the objective, and rely for their efficacy on there being a causal connection between the output or process and the regulatory objective. Principle-based standards also tend to be expressed at higher levels of abstraction, making them the most flexible (and most uncertain) of outcome-orientated standards.

Advocates of outcome-orientated standards claim they have four main advantages over prescriptive standards: first, that they are more durable and able to adapt more easily to changing circumstances; second, that they are more concise and therefore more accessible; third, that they are less burdensome (a result of the flexibility afforded regulatees); and fourth, that they are more effective.[24] This effectiveness is said to stem from focusing regulatees on the outcome to be achieved and the regulatory objective to be attained. This, it is argued, fosters greater substantive compliance, avoids ritual compliance and makes gaming more difficult. Two critical assumptions underpin the effectiveness claim, however.

The first assumption is that regulatees are motivated and capable of complying with outcome-orientated standards. Outcome-orientated standards require businesses to be committed to both the regulatory objective and to the processes and systems they implement to advance it.[25] This is not always the case, however, especially in circumstances where the regulatory objective does not align with business and management imperatives.[26] In these situations, effective enforcement of the standard takes on increased importance. Outcome-orientated standards also require regulatees to interpret what the standard requires and to translate it into concrete action. This might be a reasonable expectation in the case of large regulatees with the resources to keep up to date with the state of knowledge about potential problems and their solutions, and to retain experts to advise on complex issues. In the case of small to medium-sized regulatees, this is a more optimistic assumption. Outcome-orientated standards can impose significant information costs upon them.[27] This can lead to calls from small to medium-sized (and sometimes even large) regulatees for regulators to provide them with greater certainty (clarity and prescription), and to regulators responding to these calls by producing detailed 'how to comply' and, in some cases, 'deemed to comply' or 'safe harbor' guidance.[28] However, a number of risks attach to the generation of this authoritative guidance. First, this guidance can operate as 'a de facto system of prescriptive regulation', with the result that outcome-orientated standards lose their main advantage—their flexibility.[29] Its proliferation also increases the complexity of the regulatory regime, and risks inconsistency and inaccessibility 'as each new piece of guidance expresses another "good idea" but the overall sum of guidance is never assessed'.[30]

The second assumption is that regulators are effective in detecting non-compliance when it occurs. Regulators' main role under outcome-orientated standards is to monitor and audit the regulatee's systems, processes and outputs to determine whether the actions they have taken meet the standard.[31] Moreover, regulators have the added challenge of ensuring consistency of interpretation and application across different regulatees operating in different circumstances—consistency being a common criteria of better and legitimate regulation. This requires the regulator to have a higher level of knowledge and understanding of the regulatees and activities being regulated than under prescriptive standards. It also requires regulators to be proactive and diligent in their supervision. However, a number of recent high profile failures reveal that this has not always been the case, with outcome-orientated standards being implemented with a 'light touch' that placed too much reliance on regulatees behaving responsibly and in furtherance of the regulatory objective.[32] Outcome-orientated standards should not automatically be equated with light-touch enforcement, however. They also can be applied with a 'heavy hand'. The manner and intensity of regulatory supervision should be a reflection of, among other things, the regulator's assessment of, and trust in, a regulatee's motivation and capability to comply with the standards.[33]

Summing up Defined Standards

The current empirical research does not support broad claims that outcome-orientated standards are consistently more effective and less burdensome than prescriptive standards.[34] This should not be a surprise, however. Our discussion of regulatory standards has highlighted that prescriptive and outcome-orientated standards each have strengths and weaknesses that make them better suited for some issues, and not for others. The certainty provided by prescriptive standards makes them suitable for regulating issues that are relatively simple and environments that are relatively stable. The regulation of complex issues and dynamic environments, on the other hand, can benefit from the greater flexibility provided by outcome-orientated standards. Outcome-orientated standards, however, are more prone to different and inconsistent interpretations and the uncertainty that creates. This discussion highlights one of the main tensions inherent in designing regulatory regimes, namely that between certainty and flexibility. And as with many aspects of the regulatory endeavour, the solution often lies in striking a balance between these competing principles, and in having a combination of both prescriptive and outcome-orientated standards. Very few regulatory regimes today rely wholly on either prescriptive or outcome-orientated standards. Most regimes are a combination of the two, with prescriptive standards being used to 'fill out' outcome-orientated standards, and desired outcomes being used to focus the application of prescriptive standards.[35] Care must be taken, however, to avoid creating a dysfunctional and unnecessarily complex regulatory scheme with overlapping standards of different legal and practical effect. Each type of standard has its own logic, and they must be combined in a manner that is complimentary and mutually reinforcing.[36]

Who Should Regulate?

It may seem out of place in a book titled 'Governing through Regulation' to ask the question—who should regulate? 'Government, of course', would be many people's instinctive response. But as with much in the field of regulation, simple questions often do not have simple answers. As we observed in Chapter 4, numerous actors occupying the regulatory space with government regulate or are capable of regulating. We also observed that it can be useful to think in terms of regulatory regimes—of networks of actors involved in regulating an issue. Regulation, according to this book's definition, is undertaken 'by or under the auspices of government'. A number of different regulatory models are captured by this phrase. It is useful to think of these models as sitting on a continuum with wholly government regulation at one end, self-regulation at the other end, and a variety of co- and poly-centric regulatory models in between. Each of these regulatory models is considered below.

Government Regulation

Government regulation is where government acts directly upon regulatees to modify their behaviours. Government regulation has a number of advantages. First, it operates with the force of law. As such, its prescriptions and proscriptions cannot easily be ignored. Second, it sets minimum standards for community safety and security, and provides certainty for markets and those that engage in them. Third, it serves a strong expressive role. It is an authoritative declaration that regulation is in the public interest, and communicates with the authority of the state behaviours that are considered unacceptable, or only acceptable if certain safeguards are met. In doing so, it provides the community with reassurance that the government is discharging its primary role of protecting and providing for the community.

Government regulation also is frequently criticised. Major criticisms include that it is: expensive to administer and costly to enforce; that it imposes high and unnecessary administrative and compliance burdens on those required to comply with it; that it tends to be complex, inflexible and unnecessarily broad; that it stifles innovation and entrepreneurialism; and that it is prone to capture. It is undoubtedly true that there are examples of government regulation that have exhibited some (and maybe all) of these attributes. However, these criticisms relate to how government regulation is designed and implemented; and do not (even collectively) operate as an argument against government regulation *per se*. As such, these criticisms operate as a list of things for government to avoid when regulating—things that the suggestions in this book have learned from. The closest we come to arguments against government regulation *per se* can be found in neo-liberalism and free-market ideologies that lionise the market and demonise government, and which gave birth to the deregulatory era of the 1980s.[37] But even adherents to these views do not call for there to be no government regulation; only that free markets be preferred to government regulation, and that if government must regulate, that it do so in the most flexible and least interventionist manner possible.[38]

Self-Regulation

At the other end of the spectrum to government regulation is self-regulation. Self-regulation is where the regulatees themselves (without any direct government involvement or assistance) are responsible for developing and implementing the regulatory regime. This is a narrow definition of self-regulation. Other commentators include within the ambit of self-regulation, regimes where government delegates public policy functions to private actors or where government performs an active and overt substantive or supporting role.[39] As will be seen, this book treats such regimes as co-regulatory. They are discussed below.

There are two types of self-regulation. First, is what some call 'voluntary' or 'pure' self-regulation, but for reasons that will soon become apparent, we prefer to call 'tacit' self-regulation.[40] Tacit self-regulation exists where individual businesses (and, in some cases, industries) voluntarily adopt and implement specific policies that amount to some form of self-restraint on their conduct.[41] They might do this to win consumer confidence, secure a competitive advantage, to deflect community concerns or to pursue goals of social responsibility. Examples include voluntary codes of conduct administered by individual businesses and industry associations.[42] But even here government performs a role. First, the existence of the regime reflects government's benign acceptance and tacit agreement (thus its name). Government could intervene to regulate, but chooses not to. This state of affairs generally continues until an external 'shock' triggers community calls for government to play a more direct role.[43] Second, government performs an indirect regulatory role. Self-regulatory regimes must comply with general law requirements, including prohibitions against engaging in anti-competitive conduct and consumer protection legislation.

The second type of self-regulation is coerced self-regulation, which, as its name suggests, is developed in response to threats of government regulation. That threat could be implied or expressed; general or specific. It could constitute a vague statement that the government may consider regulation if the regulatees (often an industry or profession) do not put in place adequate self-regulatory measures; or a commitment to regulate by a specific date if specified actions are not taken or a quantitative target is not met. The existence of this threat is important. The stronger and more explicit the threat, the more likely self-regulation will operate in the public interest and not in the regulatees' self-interest.[44] Press regulation is an excellent example of coerced self-regulation. The United Kingdom's Press Complaints Commission described its establishment in 1991 as having occurred with a 'Damoclean Sword—in the shape of . . . statutory controls—dangling menacingly over free press'.[45]

The risk that self-regulation may operate in the private interests of those who develop and implement it is the main argument advanced against its use. Indeed, nearly all other criticisms of self-regulation are an extension of this core criticism. These other criticisms include that self-regulation may be misused to erect barriers to entry and to facilitate other anti-competitive conduct; may not be adequately resourced, funded and enforced with the result that non-compliance goes undetected, and those that are detected receive only modest sanctions; and finally, that it lacks the level of transparency and accountability that normally attaches to the exercise of public power.[46]

On the other side of the ledger, self-regulation (implemented well) is said to offer a number of advantages over government regulation. These include: better targeted and more flexible and practical regulation by virtue of the superior knowledge and expertise of the regulatees (who are also the regulators); regulation that is more adaptive to changing industry circumstances and technology because it is not beholden to the more formal processes of government; lower cost regulation to both regulatees (as a result of its better targeting, flexibility and adaptability) and to government (as the regulatees bear the administration and enforcement costs that otherwise would fall to it); more effective enforcement by peers incentivised to ensure a level playing field; and higher and more sustainable levels of compliance, a product of regulatory standards that are aligned to industry practices and norms and which, by virtue of the manner of their development, are 'owned' by, and perceived to be reasonable, appropriate and legitimate to, those who have to comply with them.[47] Not surprisingly, some of these advantages mirror the benefits of outcome-orientated standards that delegate to the regulatee how best to achieve specified outcomes.[48]

Self-regulation operates best where the regulatees form a relatively cohesive and stable industry or profession that shares common values, standards and interests, and where those interests align with the broader public interest. It is not well-suited to industries and professions characterised by members that are transitory or less readily identifiable and accessible. Nor is it well-suited to issues with high risk over which the community expects governments to exercise some direct control and oversight. In these cases, some level of government involvement is considered appropriate. This bring us to the next regulatory model.

Co-Regulation

Between the extremes of government regulation and self-regulation lie a variety of co-regulatory models. Co-regulation exists where government and regulatees cooperate in the development and implementation of the regulatory regime. Co-regulation may relate to all regulatory tasks, or to some only; and may be the product of genuine cooperative arrangements, or the result of government coercion.[49] This broad definition encompasses a wide variety of co-regulatory models. Four common co-regulatory models are described below, in ascending order according to the level of government involvement.

Facilitated co-regulation is where government assists with the development or administration of regulatory standards that operate through voluntary (non-statutory) codes and other mechanisms. An example of this type of co-regulation is the chemical industry's Responsible Care Program, a voluntary collaborative program between the chemical industry and governments (at both international and domestic levels) to implement safe chemical management programs and to drive continuous improvement and excellence in environmental, health, safety and security performance.[50] Another example is Australia's ePayments Code that regulates electronic consumer payment transactions, credit card transactions and internet and mobile banking. The Code was developed cooperatively by credit providers and government, is administered by the government's financial regulator, the Australian Industry and Securities Commission, but operates on a voluntary (non-statutory) basis.[51]

Next is *devolved co-regulation*. This is where the applicable standards are made by regulatees pursuant to a statutory framework that specifies the standard making institution and makes compliance with its standards a pre-requisite for market entry. Regulation of professionals such as medical practitioners, lawyers and architects generally adopt this model.[52] Closely associated to devolved co-regulation is *delegated co-regulation*. This is where government delegates standard-setting and enforcement to a private body, but retains an audit and appellate role to ensure the regime operates effectively and in the public interest. Stock-market regulation is an example of delegated co-regulation. Most stock-market regulation is undertaken by privately run stock-markets or exchanges that govern their members contractually, but do so under the supervision of a government regulator with powers (that vary from jurisdiction to jurisdiction) to approve (and disapprove) exchange rules, to undertake inquiries into their operations, and to hear appeals from their decisions.[53]

And finally, there is *enforced co-regulation*.[54] This is where government sets outcome-orientated standards, the regulatee develops and puts in place systems to comply with those standards, and the regulator oversees and audits those systems to ensure they are appropriate and functioning effectively. Examples of enforced co-regulation are the safety case management systems increasingly being required of major hazard facilities and the food industry's hazard analysis and critical control points (HACCP) system.[55]

Co-regulation promises the best of both government regulation and self-regulation, while minimising the disadvantages of each. By empowering regulatees and co-opting their expertise and infrastructure, co-regulation promises regulation that is better targeted, more flexible, less burdensome and more effective than government regulation, with the protection that government involvement provides against the system being captured, compromised or manipulated by regulatee self-interest. Co-regulation is ideally suited to situations where solely government regulation is considered unnecessary, too burdensome or too heavy-handed; self-regulation is considered inadequate compared to the risks (or the community's perception of the risks); and where the regulatees themselves possess the expertise, knowledge and infrastructure needed to regulate effectively and efficiently.

To be effective, co-regulation requires the commitment of all co-regulators. It requires regulatees to take responsibility for their own performance, and government to actively monitor and oversee the manner in which they discharge those responsibilities. Government should regularly review coregulatory arrangements to ensure those to whom it has delegated regulatory responsibilities remain representative of those being regulated, and that the co-regulatory regime continues to reflect industry realities and community expectations.

Co-regulatory regimes have grown in number and prominence, partly in response to the better regulation reform movement's drive for the use of more flexible and less prescriptive modes of regulation, and partly in response to an increase in issues that are too complex and complicated for governments to regulate on their own. This complexity also is leading governments to think beyond traditional regulatory paradigms—which brings us to the next regulatory model.

Poly-Centric Regulation

Poly-centric modes of regulation look beyond government and those being regulated to include other actors occupying the regulatory space. Some of these actors may already be regulating the issue (remembering government rarely regulates on to a blank slate); others may have the resources and potential to do so. Co-opting or enlisting these actors into the regulatory endeavour in a coordinated and synergistic manner is one of the key advantages of thinking in terms of regulatory governance and regulatory regimes.

The simplest poly-centric model is tripartism. Tripartism is where the government regulator, those being regulated and persons representing those for whose benefit the regulatory regime exists cooperate in the development, administration or enforcement of the regulatory regime. Examples include workplace health and safety regulatory regimes that include both employer and worker representatives, and environmental regulatory regimes that include both industry and environmental public interest groups.[56] From simple tripartite models can be built poly-centric regimes of various complexity with multiple actors enlisted or co-opted to perform a variety of regulatory roles.[57] Gunningham and Grabosky refer to third parties co-opted into regulatory roles as surrogate or quasi-regulators.[58] The tobacco control regulatory regime discussed in Chapter 4 is an excellent example of such a poly-centric regulatory regime.

The advantages of poly-centric regulatory regimes are many. First, they can be more effective and efficient than more narrowly conceived regimes. More effective because they enable greater resources, knowledge and skills to be applied to achieving the regulatory objective; and more efficient because those resources are not paid for by the state, freeing up state resources to be applied to those aspects of the regulatory endeavour that only government can (or should) perform.[59] Including multiple actors also guards against the regulatory endeavour being captured by or unduly influenced by any one interest group. Their inclusion also enables them to act as fire-alarms should they detect regulatory drift, inefficiency, incompetence or self-serving behaviours on the part of the government regulator.[60] Including third parties as surrogate or quasi-regulators also can enhance regime legitimacy, especially if those third parties are perceived to be more credible and acceptable than government. In tobacco control regulatory regimes for example, doctors may be perceived as more acceptable and credible anti-smoking messengers than governments addicted to the taxes smokers pay.

Of course, these advantages come at a cost and with risk. Most obvious is the risk that these actors will use their involvement in the regime to advance their private interests and not the public interest. There also are administrative costs and risks. The more actors co-opted into the regulatory regime, the greater the complexity and the greater the costs of building and maintaining systems to coordinate their contributions in a manner that is consistent and synergistic. And with multiple actors comes risks of duplication, overlap and inconsistency if those systems do not function well. Poly-centric regimes work best when those co-opted into the regime have convergent interests in achieving the regulatory objective. Absent convergent interests, third parties can become irritants and counterproductive.

Summing up Who Should Regulate?

In this section, we examined four regulator models: government regulation; co-regulation (by government and regulatees); poly-centric regulation (by government, regulatees and third parties); and self-regulation (by regulatees alone). With respect to self-regulation, we observed that contrary to its name, it does not occur without any government involvement. Government is always there, albeit sometimes hidden in the shadows. 'Pure' self-regulation in the sense of there being no government involvement, however subtle, arguably does not exist. Similarly, there is unlikely to be 'pure' government regulation in which no other actor plays a role, however minor. The reality may be that the extremities of 'pure' government regulation and 'pure' self-regulation exist only in the world of theory. This means that in most cases the challenge confronting regulatory designers is to define an appropriate mix of government, regulatee and third party involvement in the regulatory regime.

Whom to Regulate?

Regulation operates by modifying the behaviour of 'persons and entities'. We refer to these 'persons and entities' as 'regulatees'. Identifying potential regulatees and understanding their relationships, attitudes, motivations and capabilities is an essential component of the regulatory endeavour. Different systems have been developed to classify and describe regulatees. The simplest systems classify regulatees according to their legal form; more sophisticated systems classify them according to their strategic influence, or their attitudes, motivations and capability to comply.

Legal Form

All behaviour and all activity ultimately is the function of human agency.[61] Thus, persons are the base unit regulatee. Persons can act individually or in groups. These groups broadly take two forms. First, there are groups that have no separate legal existence independent of their members. These groups exist only by virtue of the agreement of their members, and are recognised by the law only to the extent that agreement constitutes a legally enforceable contract. Examples of groups with no separate legal existence include unincorporated partnerships, firms and associations. A group without a separate legal existence generally cannot be regulated directly; regulation of its activities occurs through regulation of each of its individual members.

The second type of group is a separate legal entity with an existence independent of its members. Legal entities can be created directly by government (e.g. government departments, agencies and statutory corporations), or by private and non-governmental organisations pursuant to registration or incorporation processes prescribed by the state. Corporations and incorporated associations and partnerships are common examples of the latter. Separate legal entity status is important for regulation. It provides a distinct entity upon which obligations and duties can be imposed and enforced. This, in turn, enables separate regulation of the legal entity and of its individual members. An example of this can be found in corporations' regulation where the corporation, and its directors, officers and members, each are separately regulated.

Classifying regulatees according to their legal form is of limited practical use. Classifying regulatees according to their strategic influence, and motivations and capability, is more instructive.

Strategic Influence: Primary, Intermediary and Collective Targets

A useful way of conceptualising regulatees is to differentiate between primary and intermediary targets. The primary target is the person or entity closest to the regulatory objective, and whose behaviour ultimately must be changed in order to achieve that objective. Intermediary targets are persons or entities that stand between the regulator and the primary target and which are capable of exercising strategic influence over the primary target.[62] The identity of intermediary targets usually comes from the issue's causal analysis, and usually are persons or entities capable of influencing a factor causing the primary target's behaviour. Thus, potential intermediaries will vary from issue to issue, and according to how the regulatory objective is defined.

A simple example to illustrate. If the regulatory objective is to reduce the number of people smoking, the primary regulatory target is the smoker, and government can act directly upon smokers to modify their behaviour by, for example, prohibiting them from smoking or providing them with information on the health effects of smoking. However, as our discussion of regulatory space in Chapter 4 revealed, there are other actors with the capacity to influence a person's decision to smoke. These actors include health promotion foundations, medical professionals, community leaders and role models, family and friends, tobacco manufacturers and retailers, insurance companies and the operators of restaurants, bars and other venues at which people congregate. These other actors have the capacity to exercise strategic influence over the smoker and those considering smoking (the primary target), and can be thought of as intermediaries whose support and resources governments can enlist to modify the primary target's behaviour.

These intermediaries are not neutral conduits, however. Each has their own interests and perspectives. Some such as doctors and other medical professionals may be aligned to the regulatory objective, willing to assist and only require information to steer them in the appropriate direction; others such as community leaders and role models may be sympathetic but need to be persuaded or incentivised to cooperate; and others still such as tobacco manufacturers and retailers may be hostile to the entire endeavour and may need to be coerced and compelled. In each of these cases, the behaviour of the intermediary needs to be modified, making them 'intermediary targets' of the regulatory endeavour.

For some issues, it can be difficult to differentiate between primary and intermediary targets. This increasingly is the case with complex commercial arrangements involving multiple actors and multiple interactions. This has seen some regulatory regimes alter their focus away from individual responsibility and individual targets (primary or intermediary) and towards collective responsibility and collective targets. 'Chain of responsibility' regulation is an excellent example of this. Chain of responsibility regulation applies where the relevant activity consists of a chain or series of interdependent and interlocking steps, with each step undertaken by a different person or entity. In these situations, chain of responsibility regulation seeks to modify the behaviour of each person or entity responsible for a step in the process, usually by imposing obligations on them not to contravene the applicable legal standard themselves, and not to encourage, coerce or countenance another actor in the chain to do so. Chain of responsibility regulation most commonly is applied to industries with a high degree of contracting and sub-contracting, such as road transportation and clothing manufacture.[63]

Another approach to collective targeting is to impose concurrent and overlapping regulatory duties on multiple regulatees. Workplace health and safety laws are a good example of this. They impose concurrent and overlapping duties on all persons and entities whose acts or omissions are capable of affecting the health, safety and welfare of persons at work. These persons include those for whose business or undertaking the work is done; the directors and officers with effective control over those businesses or undertakings; and other persons who carry out specific activities relevant to the conduct of work at a workplace. This latter group includes designers, manufacturers and suppliers of plant, equipment and substances used at the workplace. Corporation law adopts a similar approach and imposes a series of mutually reinforcing duties upon the corporation (as a separate legal entity) and its directors and officers, making the corporation liable for the actions of its directors and officers and, in certain circumstances, directors and officers liable for the actions of the corporation.

Target Segmentation: Attitudes, Motivations and Capability

Marketers have long known that targeted and tailored strategies are often more effective and efficient in changing behaviour than 'one-size-fits-all' campaigns. Dividing the target population into smaller groups that can be targeted effectively is known as 'segmentation'. Effective segmentation involves identifying those attributes shared by a sub-group of the target population that makes them likely to respond similarly to regulatory interventions. The variables used to segment a population will vary with the issue, its context and, of course, the nature of the target population. Typical segmentation variables include geographic variables (e.g. urban; regional); demographic variables (e.g. age; gender; education; nationality, religion; race); commercial variables (e.g. occupation; income; industry); and psychographic variables (e.g. social class; lifestyle; values; personality traits).[64] In the context of a definition of regulation based on behaviour change, particularly instructive are behavioural variables. Behavioural segmentation divides the target population on the basis of their attitudes and motivations both to the issue being regulated and to government's role in regulating that issue. A regulatee's attitudes and motivations can be an indicator of the ease or difficulty with which its behaviour can be modified. And as we have seen, not identifying and allowing for different regulatee motivations and capabilities in the design of a regulatory regime can lead to regulatory failure.[65]

Plotting regulatee willingness and capability to comply on a two-by-two matrix provides a useful framework through which to explore these variables (see Figure 8.1). As can be seen, doing so produces four broad types of regulatees: *leaders* who are compliant and prepared to perform to higher standards than required by the regulatory regime; the *reluctant* who also are compliant but are intent on doing no more than the regime's mandated minimum; the *incompetent* who are willing to comply but do not have the capability to do

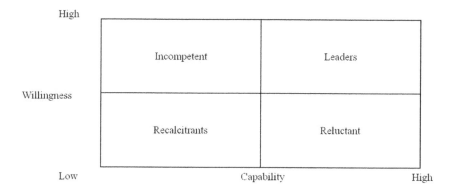

Figure 8.1 Regulatee Types

so; and finally, the *recalcitrant* who do not want to comply and have no interest in investing in the skills, resources and capability to do so.[66]

The simplicity of the matrix belies the complexity of its substance. Regulatees do not fit neatly into one of the four boxes. As Ayres and Braithwaite described colourfully:

> Regulatory actors also have multiple selves: they can be nice guys or tough guys, self-interested or public-spirited, professional or unprofessional, diligent or lazy, intelligent or confused.[67]

Moreover, to say that a particular regulatee is or is not willing to comply tells us nothing about why. Why regulatees may or may not be willing to comply lends itself to different explanations. It is an area on which much research has been conducted.[68] Feldman, in an effort to summarise this research, identifies five motivational approaches or models that he labels: (1) the incentive-driven model—where the decision to comply or not comply is based on a rational cost-benefit calculation; (2) the reason-driven model—where the decision to comply is dependent on the regulatee being convinced of the wisdom of compliance over non-compliance; (3) the socially-orientated model—where the decision to comply is dependent on the regulatee's social identity and need to belong (and thus to act consistently with prevailing norms); (4) the moral-orientated model—where the decision to comply is motivated by what is moral and fair; and (5) the citizenship-orientated model—where the regulatee complies with the law simply because that is what good citizens do (regardless of the law's content).[69] Understanding these deeper behavioural drivers of regulatee behaviour can significantly improve the targeting of regulatory interventions.

Summing up Whom to Regulate?

This section commenced by highlighting the importance of there being a distinct legal entity on to which regulatory responsibilities can be attached. It also identified opportunities for innovative regulatory design created by being able to regulate a legal entity separately from its directors, officers and members. Such opportunities also flow from thinking in terms of primary, intermediary and collective targets. Such is the complex nature of modern society that regulatory regimes targeting one actor in isolation are unlikely to be effective. Regulatory regimes that seek to allocate duties and responsibilities across all actors with the ability to influence the issue at hand increasingly are the norm. Effective targeting of these various actors can be enhanced by better understanding their different attitudes, motivations and capabilities. Different regulatee attitudes, motivations and capabilities suggest different combinations of change mechanisms may be required to modify their behaviour. For example, incentives to reward and encourage the leaders; persuasion and incentives to convert the reluctant; assistance to help the incompetent; and coercion to compel the recalcitrant. It is to these change mechanisms that we now turn.

Mechanisms of Behaviour Modification

Regulation is about modifying behaviour. Over time, different systems for classifying the mechanisms through which regulation modifies behaviour have been developed.[70] Five key behaviour modification mechanisms can be distilled from this previous work. They are coercion, incentives (and disincentives), persuasion, assistance and nudges. The nature, key characteristics and main advantages and disadvantages of each of these behaviour change mechanism are explored below. Examples of regulatory tools representative of each mechanism also are given. Few regulatory tools are one dimensional, however. Most tools can be thought of as a hydra, simultaneously leveraging more than one behaviour change mechanism to effect the desired regulatory change.

Coercion

Coercion is the behaviour change mechanism most commonly associated with regulation. Coercive mechanisms generally have three elements. The first is defined standards, which we have already explored.[71] The second element is mechanisms to detect non-compliance with those standards. These mechanisms are discussed in Chapter 10 (Implementation). Our focus here is on the third element—the sanctions that attach to those non-compliances. Sanctions (or more precisely, the fear of sanctions) are central to a coercive mechanism's deterrence effect.[72] Sanctions for breaches of consensual standards come in the form of contractual remedies such as damages, injunctions and orders that persons perform their contractual obligations. However, the sanctions most commonly associated with coercive mechanisms are state based and formal. These generally fall into one of three categories: criminal, civil and administrative.[73]

Criminal sanctions traditionally have been designed to punish—imprisonment and fines being the classic examples. Over time, however, legal systems have evolved a range of complimentary sanctions designed to prevent further breaches and to remedy existing breaches. Examples of these non-punitive sanctions include community service orders, probationary and supervisory orders, and training, compensation and restoration orders. The power to issue criminal sanctions invariably is vested in courts, and made after a trial initiated by the regulator or another prosecuting authority at the regulator's instigation. The imposition of criminal sanctions traditionally requires the prosecution to prove both the *actus reus* (the wrongful act) and *mens rea* (a guilty mind—that the act was undertaken knowing it was wrong), and to do so beyond reasonable doubt. In the regulatory arena, however, criminal offences that are strict liability are not uncommon.[74] Strict liability offences do not require the prosecution to establish *mens rea*. However, to protect the blameless, they frequently are accompanied by defences exculpating or reducing the liability of persons who exercised due diligence or took all reasonably practicable measures.[75]

Civil sanctions also are imposed by courts (or tribunals) at the instigation of the regulatory agency. They can include pecuniary (monetary) penalty orders, compensation orders, declarations of non-compliance and disqualification from holding certain offices. Civil sanctions generally exist for commercial and corporate offences to which the state has chosen not to attach the stigma (and consequences) of a criminal conviction.[76] While some criminal and civil sanctions look very similar (e.g. fines and pecuniary penalty orders), there are important differences in their application. First, civil sanctions operate to a lower standard of proof, usually the balance of probabilities. Second, because there is no criminal conviction, it is more common for the regulator and offender to negotiate and agree upon the final form of civil sanctions. This makes their pursuit less resource intensive than criminal sanctions, freeing up limited regulatory resources for other purposes.[77]

Unlike criminal and civil sanctions, administrative sanctions are imposed by a regulator without recourse to a court or tribunal. This gives them the advantage of being immediate and cheap to administer, features rarely associated with court-based processes. Examples include official warnings and cautions, fines and other monetary penalties, infringement, improvement and prohibition notices, enforceable undertakings, adverse publicity orders and licence conditions, suspensions or revocations. Administrative sanctions generally do not require *mens rea* and often operate to a lower standard of proof.

Regulatory regimes also can provide for sanctions to be initiated and, in some cases, imposed by non-state actors. Australian workplace health and safety legislation, for example, empowers workplace parties to order unsafe work to cease and, in some jurisdictions, empowers those parties to initiate criminal proceedings for breach of the legislation.[78] Empowering private actors to initiate criminal proceedings tends to be the exception rather than the rule, however. More common is empowering private actors to bring civil actions for damages resulting from a breach of the standards. Corporations law is a good example of this, with company members (shareholders/stockholders) being able to bring civil actions against directors whose breaches of statutory duties have caused them loss.[79] Use of private actions in this manner has the advantage of sparing public resources. However, such actions have the disadvantage of being sporadic and uncoordinated, with the result they may not focus upon and target the most pressing issues and concerns viewed from a broader, societal perspective. Court processes—state and privately initiated—also tend to be slow to develop coherent and robust principles that can be used by others to inform and guide their compliance efforts.

Coercive mechanisms have a number of advantages. Compared to other behaviour change mechanisms, coercive mechanisms are more straightforward to formulate and serve a strong expressive role. They communicate with the authority of the state that certain behaviour is considered unacceptable, or acceptable only if certain safeguards are met. Coercive mechanisms also can be designed to operate with immediate effect, thereby enabling governments to position themselves as strong and decisive protectors of the public.[80]

Coercive mechanisms also have disadvantages. They frequently are criticised for being blunt and over-inclusive, and for imposing unnecessarily high compliance costs on those subject to them. Many of these criticisms, however, are more correctly directed to prescriptive standards and old fashioned command and control style enforcement that historically have been the backbone of coercive mechanisms. The use of outcome-orientated standards and more flexible and modern regulatory styles can ameliorate many of these criticisms.[81] Coercive mechanisms also can be expensive to administer and enforce. They require systems to detect and correct instances of non-compliance. Generally these come in the form of inspectorates, audits and other methods of policing the conduct of regulatees, and judicial and administrative mechanisms to correct and sanction non-compliance. These systems can become adversarial and legalistic, resulting in increasingly formal, expensive and lengthy processes. This, in turn, can undermine constructive regulator-regulatee relationships and the beneficial cooperation they can produce or, worse, breed defiance and resistance that can lead to non-compliance.[82]

The advantages and disadvantages of coercive mechanisms combine to suggest they are best applied to issues of higher risk, impact or significance with respect to which the community expects strong and decisive state action. For issues that do not meet these criteria, more flexible and facilitative mechanisms may be appropriate. It is to these mechanisms that we now turn.

Incentives (and Disincentives)

Incentives (and disincentives) assume individuals make rational benefit-cost decisions on whether to comply with regulatory standards. They then operate to influence those decisions by increasing the benefits or decreasing the costs of compliant behaviours (through incentives), or reducing the benefits or increasing the costs of non-compliant behaviours (through disincentives).[83]

Incentives and disincentives can be direct and indirect. Examples of direct incentives and disincentives include tax credits, differential tax rates, rebates, bounties, grants, subsidies and levies that confer a direct financial benefit or detriment on the regulatee.[84] Examples of indirect incentives include awards and certification systems that can be used by regulatees positively to differentiate themselves in the market place, thereby better positioning themselves to generate increased sales and revenue.[85] Government contracts also can operate as an indirect incentive by making compliance with certain standards a prerequisite of doing business with the government.[86]

Just as incentives and disincentives can operate on both sides of the benefit-cost equation, so too can they operate on both the supply and demand sides of markets by targeting producers and consumers respectively. Incentives and disincentives used to address pollution and the causes of climate change illustrate this well.[87] Examples of incentives and disincentives targeting producers include: tax deductions, grants and subsidies to incentivise investments in renewable energy or pollution reducing technologies; tax rebates for reducing the emission of pollutants; levies for landfills; and putting a price on carbon emissions and other pollutants through taxes or the creation of tradeable permits and markets through which to trade them (i.e., emission trading schemes). Examples of incentives and disincentives targeting consumers include rebates on purchases of more resource efficient appliances (e.g. water efficient washing machines; energy efficient light bulbs); discount energy charges at off-peak times or for renewable energy; and differential tax rates (e.g. on leaded and unleaded petrol). Many of these incentives and disincentives are grounded in economic theories of regulation and designed to address market failures: sometimes by creating a market where it did not exist, but more often by altering the costs and benefits of certain actions to account for their externalities.[88]

Establishing incentives tends to be more complex and challenging than establishing a coercive regime. Incentives need to be carefully targeted at the right actors and at the right level to incentivise desired behaviours while avoiding undesirable behaviours and rorts of the type that can doom regulation to failure.[89] This can require detailed modelling which can place onerous information demands on regulatees, and can make government and the regulator vulnerable to manipulation or capture by regulatees in a superior informational position.[90] It also can require complex judgements to be made. This detail and complexity often finds its way into detailed, complex and sometimes prescriptive rules and standards (with all their disadvantages—see above discussion) and which generally require sophisticated audit and compliance mechanisms to ensure non-compliance is detected, and manipulation and rorting of the system is guarded against. The need for these mechanisms can result in incentive mechanisms coming to resemble coercive mechanisms.[91] As Braithwaite observes with respect to the use of financial incentives over coercive mechanisms:

> One form of detailed policing of corporate conduct would be substituted for another. . . . Economism [the use of incentives] therefore does not eliminate the need for government inspectors; it merely replaces inspections by technical experts with inspections by experts in financial deception.[92]

Once established, however, many incentive mechanisms such as tax credits, differential tax rates and rebates are largely self-executing, the tailoring of the incentive to individual circumstances having been done at the design stage. They do not require constant negotiations with regulatees, or the exercise of significant regulatory discretions. This can make them cheaper to administer, and less prone to regulatory capture (at least at the administration stage). They also allow for greater flexibility and innovation on the part of regulatees— incentivising them to go beyond compliance with standards that might only be met under a more coercive and prescriptive regime. This assumes, of course, an economically rational regulatee. Compared to coercive mechanisms, incentives are less likely to operate upon the irrational, irresponsible and ill-informed who arguably are in the most need of having their behaviour regulated. Nor are they likely to operate with the same immediate effect as coercive mechanisms. Understanding the nature of an incentive and how best to modify operations to take advantage of it can take time.[93] Finally, incentives can lack the expressive clarity of coercive mechanisms, especially when directed at the producers of socially harmful activities such as pollution. Whereas coercive mechanisms unambiguously communicate the unacceptability of the activities they prohibit or restrict, incentives can appear counter-intuitive by financially supporting the very activity that is sought to be eliminated or reduced.[94]

Incentives operate to modify behaviour through the provision of tangible benefits and costs that appeal to regulatees' hip pockets. The next mechanism operates through less tangible means that appeal to their hearts and heads.

Persuasion

Regulation can seek to persuade persons and entities to act in accordance with defined standards by appealing to their motivations, interests, values, beliefs and preferences. Persuasive mechanisms seek to influence behaviour without recourse to coercive or incentive driven interventions. Rather, persuasion works by cajoling, exhorting or convincing the regulatee to act in a manner consistent with the regulatory objective.[95] In this regard, persuasion has parallels with our discussion of framing in Chapter 7. Persuasion involves framing the regulatory objective in a manner designed to illicit the desired behavioural response. Depending on the regulatee and its motivation to comply, this might involve an appeal to the regulatee's self-interest (e.g. by providing new information that alters the way the regulatee perceives, weighs and balances the benefits and costs of alternative courses of action). In other cases, it might involve an appeal to the regulatee's altruism or sense of community (e.g. by appealing to intangible values such as justice, equality, fairness or morality; or to important societal concerns such as safety and security). And in others still, it may be an appeal to the regulatee's instincts to comply with (or exceed) societal norms. Studies have shown that providing people with data that compares their performance with the norm encourages those people to change their behaviour to improve their performance.[96]

Persuasion can take many forms. It can take the form of direct communications with regulatees though letters, emails or texts; advertising through traditional and social media; and coordinated marketing campaigns that simultaneously leverage multiple communication formats and channels. In some cases, it might involve the use of facts, figures and statistics; in others the use of images, symbols, labels and stories. In some cases, the communication might come direct from government or the regulator; in other cases, they may use influential intermediaries, such as community leaders, role models and family and friends.

Persuasion, targeted properly and executed well, can be effective to change behaviour or, at least, to motivate people to consider changing their behaviour. But on its own, it is unlikely to lead to wide-spread and sustained change. Persuasion works best when coupled with other behaviour change mechanisms, whether that be reinforcing the deterrent effect of coercive mechanisms or the benefits of an incentive.

Coercion, incentives and persuasion all assume the regulatee needs to be imposed upon, incentivised or convinced in some way to behave in accordance with regulatory standards. In some instances, however, the regulatee wants to comply but does not have the knowledge, skills or resources to do so. This often is the case with small to medium-sized businesses. In this situation, what they require is assistance.

Assistance

Assisting regulatees to understand and comply with regulatory standards is an integral part of modern regulatory regimes. Like other behaviour change mechanisms, assistance can come in many forms. Its most common forms are information and advice, training and education and resources and infrastructure.

INFORMATION AND ADVICE

Governments are the primary source of information and advice in most regulatory regimes. Before regulators take enforcement action against regulatees, it is incumbent on the regulator (or another government agency) to inform the regulatee of the regulatory standards to which it is subject.[97] The rule of law requires no less.[98] However, this increasingly is seen as a minimum requirement. Regulators also are being called upon to ensure regulatees understand their regulatory duties and obligations,[99] and to provide regulatees with advice and guidance about how best to comply with them.[100] Examples of this type of information include formal interpretative guidelines, rulings and codes of practice, as well as less formal how to guides and other more generic information. This information is sometimes referred to as 'soft law'. While sanctions do not directly attach to non-compliance with this type of information, it still has legal effect by being part of the 'state of knowledge' against which the reasonableness of regulatee actions are assessed for tortious and statutory duty of care liability.[101]

Regulatees are not the only recipients of government information and advice. Governments also can provide information and advice to persons with whom regulatees might deal, to assist those persons to make better informed decisions about whether (and how) to deal with the regulatee. This information can range from making publically available regulatory disclosures made to government,[102] to the publication of comparative performance data and league tables of both better and poorer performing regulatees,[103] through to the 'naming and shaming' of regulatees that fail to comply with regulatory standards or who have been successfully prosecuted.[104] Used in this way, information provision acts as a complement to the primary (usually coercive) mechanisms that impose standards on the regulatees.

Of course, governments are not the only source of information. Non-government organisations and the private sector also are an important source of information and advice that can be co-opted into the regulatory endeavour. For example, industry and worker representative bodies can be funded to provide 'how to comply' advice to their members, and non-government organisations can be funded to provide information and advice to members of the public. Consumer advice bureaus and community legal and financial advice centres are examples of this. There also are a range of non-government and private organisations that publish league tables on the performance of regulatees, including against regulatory standards. University rankings, credit ratings and financial analyst and consumer reports are examples of these.

Regulatees also can be enlisted (or maybe more correctly, conscripted) to provide information. For example, regulatees can be compelled to provide information to consumers and others with whom they transact to address information asymmetries that might exist between them. Often referred to as disclosure regulation, this form of regulation is today ubiquitous with modern regulatory regimes that have consumer, worker, investor or environment protection as their objectives. Examples include consumer product ingredient, nutritional and country of origin labelling; corporate prospectus and continuous disclosure requirements; and community 'right to know' and 'truth in lending' laws.[105] Disclosure regulation is an example of a hydra regulatory tool. It operates coercively by forcing regulatees to make disclosure; incentivises them to improve their performance by providing a basis upon which market participants can assess and compare their performance; and assists those other market participants to make better informed decisions.[106]

TRAINING AND EDUCATION

At one level, training and education can be thought of as a specific channel through which information and advice is provided. However, training and education is much more than the mere transmission of information and advice. It is about building in regulatees the skills, competencies and capabilities they need to comply with their regulatory duties and obligations. Training and education can be provided by the regulator. More commonly, however, training and education is provided by non-government organisations and private sector bodies. Educational institutions are active providers of training, as are industry associations and unions to their members. The market for this training and education is strengthened (and in some cases, created) by regulatory requirements that mandate training and education or the attainment of certain skills and competencies for specified professions, trades and undertakings (e.g. doctors, lawyers, electricians and gas fitters).

RESOURCES AND INFRASTRUCTURE

Governments and regulators also can assist regulatees to comply with regulatory standards by providing them with the resources and infrastructure needed to do so. Resources can include equipment (or grants or subsidies to purchase equipment), as well as subsidised access to expert advice on how to comply. In the workplace health and safety field, for example, some regulators run programs where they subsidise the costs of external consultants to conduct risk assessments and make recommendations, and also provide subsidies and grants for the purchase of safety equipment recommended by those consultants. As can be seen, there is an overlap between this type of assistance and some incentives.

In some cases, government and regulator assistance extends beyond resources for a specific regulatee, to infrastructure for an entire industry or market. The law is one of the most important pieces of infrastructure provided by the state. Property rights, tort and contract law, and judicial and alternative dispute resolution mechanisms are but a few of the legal structures that enable people to interact, invest and trade with one another with certainty and confidence.[107] Government infrastructure also is important in circumstances where, absent government intervention, a market would not form or, if it did, it would not operate effectively or efficiently.[108] Examples include emissions trading schemes that create markets for externalities,[109] the use of auctions and tender systems for the efficient allocation of scarce resources such as land, fishing entitlements and logging rights,[110] and government loan guarantee, workers' compensation and medical insurance schemes that address cost and other barriers that prevent some people from accessing those markets at an affordable price.[111]

Finally, governments can assist regulatees to comply with regulatory standards by designing solutions into the infrastructure. Often referred to as structural regulation, design solutions do not so much assist regulatees as compel them 'to act in accordance with the desired regulatory pattern'.[112] A good example of this is road design. The use of speed humps and roundabouts compels drivers to slow down, and the use of concrete bollards, highway dividers and other physical barriers ensures drivers travel only where they are permitted by road rules.[113] Other examples of structural regulation (or regulation by design, as it is sometimes also called) include requiring the installation of speed limiters, alcohol interlock devices and automatic braking systems on cars to improve road safety; pay-as-you-earn and withholding taxes to reduce tax evasion; and the use of filtering and screening technologies to control access to content on the internet.[114]

Assistance mechanisms have an important advantage compared to other behaviour change mechanisms: they are practical and direct. Whereas coercive mechanisms tell regulatees what to do, and incentives and persuasion encourage them to do it, assistance mechanisms help them do it. Of course, to be effective, assistance mechanisms need to be well targeted and effectively implemented. Information and advice, and training and education, need to be carefully prepared to ensure they are relevant and intelligible to those to whom they are directed. This, in turn, requires those communicating the information to understand their (different) audience's attitudes, motivations and needs, and existing levels of understanding and knowledge. Information also needs to be provided to people cognisant that their rationality is bounded, and their ability to process and absorb it is limited.[115] Providing people with too much information, or information that is too complex, can overwhelm, intimidate and cause people to disregard the information or, worse, to disengage from the regulatory process.[116] Resources too should be targeted to those who need them the most and who can afford them the least. Infrastructure also needs to be carefully designed to achieve its objective without creating unintended adverse consequences, such as moral hazard problems in the case of insurance schemes.[117]

Assistance mechanisms assume regulatees are motivated to comply, whether by coercion, incentives or persuasion. Assistance mechanisms also assume regulatees will comply if properly informed, skilled and resourced. This is a rational assessment based on regulatees acting rationally. But as we have seen, not all decisions are rational. Our rationality is bounded and we act under various cognitive biases. This is where nudge techniques come in.

Nudge

Nudge techniques are the product of the coming together of two schools of thought. The first school is the 'context' model of behaviour change that emphasises the importance of context in determining the choices people make. The second school of thought is behavioural economics that combines lessons from psychology with those of economics and posits that people make 'poor' decisions because of a range of cognitive biases. Cognitive biases are tendencies to think in ways that lead to systematic deviations from standards of rational decision-making. Important cognitive biases identified by behavioural economists include present or current moment bias (the tendency for people to have a stronger preference for more immediate payoffs relative to later payoffs), status quo bias (the tendency of people to like things to stay the same), inertia bias (the tendency of people when given a choice to act or to do nothing, to choose to do nothing) and omission bias (the tendency to judge harmful actions as worse and more morally reprehensible than equally harmful omissions).[118] Contextualists and behavioural economists combine to argue that cognitive biases are both predictable and capable of being leveraged by changing the context in which decisions are made—that is, they can be acted upon to 'nudge' people to make the 'right' decision.[119]

What actually constitutes a 'nudge' is a question of some controversy. Like many regulatory fashions that have preceded it, many people have sought to rebadge and reinvigorate traditional regulatory techniques by attaching the 'nudge' label to them, leading Kosters and Van der Heijden to observe 'there is no clear definition of what makes for a nudge, and how nudging differs from other governance interventions'.[120] The most frequently cited definition of a 'nudge' comes from Sunstein and Thaler, whose book, *Nudge: Improving Decisions about Health, Wealth, and Happiness*, made nudges the regulatory technique *du jour*. Their definition provides that a nudge

> is any aspect of the choice architecture that alters people's behaviour in a predictable way without forbidding any options or significantly changing their economic incentives. To count as a mere nudge, the intervention must be cheap and easy to avoid. Nudges are not mandates.[121]

This definition tells us what nudges are, and what they are not. Looking first at what they are not. Nudges do not coerce, adjust financial incentives or attempt to rationally persuade. This is not to say that understanding and leveraging known cognitive biases and the context within which choices are made cannot make other behaviour change mechanisms more effective. Clearly they can.[122] However, nudges are more than traditional modes of regulation, behaviorally informed. Nudges differ from traditional behaviour change mechanisms in three important ways: first, they focus on altering the 'choice architecture'—the context and environment in which decisions are made; second, they leverage predictable patterns of irrationality (cognitive biases); and third, they respect the autonomy of the individual by leaving them free to choose a different—'not right'—path.[123] Examples of successful architecture changing nudges include: increasing the number of people choosing to consume healthy food by (amongst other things) placing healthy food at eye level and in easy reach (e.g. at the cash register desk);[124] significantly increasing the proportion of people agreeing to donate their organs by redesigning organ donation forms from opt-in to opt-out;[125] and eliciting more honest disclosures on official forms by positioning the declaration and signature box at the start of a form rather than at the end.[126]

Nudge techniques have found favour with many governments in recent years.[127] They promise governments effective outcomes with comparatively little cost and bureaucracy, and without overt restrictions on individual liberty. Nudge techniques are not without their critics, however.[128] Many nudge techniques rely for their effectiveness on their covert nature. Why? Because drawing people's attention to the fact that the context in which they are making decisions is being altered to influence them to make a choice other than that which they might otherwise have made can lead to rebellious and counterproductive behaviour. Their covert nature, however, raises issues of transparency, accountability and ultimately, legitimacy.

Nudge techniques rely on experts designing interventions to nudge people to make the 'right' choices, as judged by those experts. While most regulatory interventions rely to some degree on expert determinations of what is the preferred course of action and desired regulatory outcome, nudge techniques differ because of their covert nature. Nudge techniques generally do not benefit from the discussion and debate that informs other regulatory techniques. Whereas other behaviour change mechanisms should, and in most cases are, developed with the benefit of public participation, this is not the case with many nudge techniques. This results in greater trust and faith being placed in the expertise and public interest mindedness of those designing the nudge than is the case with other regulatory interventions. Sunstein and Thaler justify this greater trust in two ways. First, they have recourse to what they refer to as their new movement, 'libertarian paternalism'. Paternalism refers to the legitimacy of governments influencing people's behaviour in order to make their lives longer, healthier and better. Libertarian refers to the requirement that this be done in a manner that is liberty-preserving, namely, that there be a cheap and easy 'opt-out' that enables the target to choose a different (non-right) course of action.[129] Second, Sunstein and Thaler argue that nudge techniques should be confined to circumstances where they can clearly do good and no harm: circumstances where the 'nudgers' have higher levels of expertise, the 'nudgees' have few opportunities for feedback and learning, the differences in preferences among those being nudged are small or easily detected and the nudge does not impinge upon the exercise of constitutional rights.[130]

However, there is a fine line between nudge and shove; influence and manipulation. This is especially the case if the course of action towards which the person is being nudged is not cheap and easy to avoid as required by Thaler and Sunstein. This could be the case if the alternative is not obvious (because it may be hidden in the manner in which government chooses to present the choices), or the costs of exercising the choice are not small (e.g. requires the person to invest a disproportionate amount of time to implement, or requires the use of technology which the person is not familiar or comfortable using). And there is much to be concerned about in Thaler and Sunstein's 'libertarian paternalism'. 'Nudgers' are just as susceptible to cognitive biases as those they are trying to nudge, and just as prone to capture and manipulation by private interests as other government and policy officials. They also are at risk of succumbing to 'the temptation to impose their own vision of the good' upon those they consider less sophisticated, rational and able, and to extending their well-meaning interventions far beyond the limited circumstances envisaged by Thaler and Sunstein.[131]

Thaler and Sunstein were not blind to these risks, and suggested two primary safeguards against ill-motivated and ill-considered nudges. First, was the ability of the nudgee to 'opt-out'. They considered this an important corrective.[132] However this is a weak safeguard, especially given Thaler's and Sunstein's own admission that people often are poor decision-makers (because of inertia bias, for example). Second, Thaler and Sunstein counsel that nudges should be governed by the 'publicity principle'—that government should refrain from selecting a policy that it would not be able or willing to defend publicly to its own citizens.[133] However, a mere ability or willingness to defend is insufficient. As Koster and Van der Heijden note, '[w]ithout disclosure this [defence] cannot be contested'.[134] Rather, actual defence (explanation and deliberation) is required. Some have argued that this requires nudges' covert nature to be compromised, and for them to be subject to transparent regulatory impact assessment processes.[135] However, if nudges cannot retain their effectiveness if exposed to this level of public scrutiny, then the requisite transparency should occur in another forum. Many nudges are presently subjected to random control trials to test the comparative effectiveness of different types of nudges. The use of these trails has been borrowed from the pharmaceutical industry, and could be extended to the use of ethics committees of the type that oversee pharmaceutical trails, and university and hospital research involving human participants.[136] Whatever the mechanism though, what is important is that nudge techniques should be accompanied by strong accountability and transparency mechanisms.

Summing up Mechanisms of Behaviour Modification

Our examination of behaviour change mechanisms reveals that the regulatory 'tool box' is indeed rich. Traditional conceptions of regulation as coercively enforced rules belong to a bygone era. Modern regulation also incentivises, persuades, assists and nudges. Today's regulatory designers have an extensive menu of change mechanisms and instruments from which to choose and build. This variety is testimony to the innovation that exists within government. However, the richness of the tool box and size of the menu also can be daunting. The choice can overwhelm and intimidate, leading some to stay with the known and familiar (which often are rule based mechanisms coercively enforced). Creating an environment that supports a consideration of all possible mechanisms (and combinations of mechanisms) is critical to the regulatory design process. How this might be done is discussed in the second part of this chapter.

Institutional (Structural) Arrangements

Regulatory regimes can be structured in different ways. In poly-centric regimes in particular, the options are numerous. Guidance on structuring regulatory regimes (and the government regulators within it) is found in both the theoretical and empirical literature. The theoretical literature points to a number of institutional design options that facilitate regulation in the public interest and guard against capture or manipulation by private interests. Similarly, the literature on regulatory failure contains many suggestions for how regimes can be structured to avoid the cause of those failures. In this section, we consider these lessons under the following structural dimensions: the organisational form of the government regulator; the vertical structures that govern the relationship between the regulator and those that oversee it; and the horizontal structures that govern its interactions with other regulators and actors part of the regulatory regime.

Organisational Form

Regulators take a variety of forms.[137] Some are established as distinct functions within departments; others are created as legal entities separate from departments. Some are created by legislation; others by executive order; and others still may be companies incorporated under general corporations law provisions. Some operate under the direct control of a minister; others under the hierarchical control of a department; and others still enjoy formal independence from both. Some focus on a single issue or industry; others on multiple issues or industries.[138] Such is their variety that a detailed discussion of each would be confusing, cumbersome and of limited utility. A more instructive way to approach a discussion about organisational form is to focus on the following three key questions: (1) should the government establish a new regulator or add to the responsibilities of an existing regulator; (2) should the regime be implemented by a single regulator or through a network of regulators; and (3) should the regulator be established as an independent agency or housed within an existing government department. Each of these questions is considered below.

NEW OR EXISTING REGULATOR

Creating a new regulator generally is more expensive than adding responsibilities to an existing regulator. New regulators require internal administrative structures and systems to be established. These include the internal governance, information, finance, human resources and other systems required for day-to-day functioning. They also require specialist regulatory and technical expertise to be developed. These systems and expertise may already exist in an established regulator. Leveraging them would be more cost-effective than establishing them afresh in a new regulator. However, adding responsibilities to an existing regulator involves other costs and risks. It invariably involves re-engineering the existing regulator to some extent. This is not always easy. As Knill and Tosun observe, one constant across an otherwise diverse research literature is that institutional change rarely takes place in a smooth and unproblematic way.[139] Existing institutional arrangements, structures and routines often do not lend themselves to easy modification. As our discussion of institutional theories in Chapter 3 revealed, existing institutions constrain options for future change and adaption. Adding new roles and responsibilities to an existing regulator also creates risks of role confusion if the new regulatory role does not align well with the regulator's existing responsibilities. As we have seen, role confusion can undermine regulatory legitimacy.[140] The greater the change required to existing institutional arrangements, the greater the implementation challenge and risk, and the greater the case for a new regulator. However, creating too many new regulators can lead to an unnecessarily crowded regulatory space with multiple regulators performing similar functions. In Victoria, Australia, for example, there are at least six regulators with public safety responsibilities.[141] This creates the potential for overlapping jurisdictions or, worse, gaps in jurisdiction.

SINGLE REGULATOR OR REGULATORY NETWORK

The second question is whether the policy should be implemented by a single regulator performing all relevant regulatory tasks, or by a network of regulators each performing one (or a few) main regulatory tasks?[142] For example, in a networked regulatory regime, one regulator may inform and educate regulatees on their duties, responsibilities and obligations; another may administer grants and other programs to assist them to comply with those obligations; and yet another regulator may be responsible for enforcing compliance with those obligations. Each structural approach has its advantages and disadvantages. Housing all regulatory functions in the one regulator enables synergies in administration and information management to be realised, reduces inefficient duplication and overlap of functions and minimises the risks of issues falling between networked agencies. Single issue or industry regulators also facilitate greater technical specialisation in that issue or industry. This can improve effectiveness. However, housing all regulatory functions and tasks in the one regulator can result in role confusion if those functions and tasks are not well-aligned.

Regimes with multiple, networked government regulators, on the other hand, allow each regulator to specialise in a particular regulatory task. Linking these specialist regulators enables greater specialisation and expertise to be applied to the regulatory endeavour. Multiple regulators also can act as a check and balance on each other, thereby minimising risks of failure or capture of any one regulator. The division of responsibilities between regulators also means that should one regulator fail, the consequences of that failure can be contained and possibly compensated for by the continued activities of other regulators. However, using regulatory networks has its own costs and risks. First there are the costs associated with multiple regulators duplicating head office and other functions. Second, there are the costs of coordinating the functions and activities of the multiple regulators. And third, there are risks of that coordination failing: of inconsistency and incoherence, duplication and overlap, and the potential for blame-shifting and buck-passing should gaps in coverage emerge.

Which structure to adopt will depend in large part on the regulatory policy to be implemented. Policies that are narrow in scope and functions lend themselves more readily to implementation by a single regulator than do polices that are broad in scope and require different and potentially conflicting functions to be performed. Having said that, one lesson that can be drawn from the regulatory literature is that role clarity is more important than size. Size rarely is identified as a cause of regulatory failure; role confusion is.[143] Many large regulators operate successfully. Central to their success is a clear statement of purpose—a touchstone that links and connects the variety of regulatory tasks they undertake.[144] For example, in many jurisdictions, large workplace health and safety and environmental regulators operate successfully across multiple industries and hazards. Their regulatory mission—protecting workers and the environment (respectively)—provides a clear statement of purpose around which staff undertaking their various tasks can mobilise and align.[145] However, when that clarity is lost, such as when the safety regulator also assumes an industry support and promotion role (as was the case with the regulator responsible for safety on the Deepwater Horizon oil rig),[146] the consequences can be disastrous, and can far exceed the costs of establishing and maintaining separate regulators.

INDEPENDENT OR DEPARTMENTAL REGULATOR

The third question is whether the regulator should sit within an established government department or ministry, or whether it should be established as a specialist agency separate and independent from the central bureaucracy?[147] One would be excused for thinking this question largely moot. Such has been the growth of independent regulatory agencies that today, they are generally accepted as the most appropriate vehicle for regulatory administration and enforcement.[148] However, given the up-front costs and complexities associated with establishing independent regulatory agencies, and the accountability risks associated with them (discussed below), an examination of their benefits and advantages is warranted.

Advocates of independent regulatory agencies claim they have four main advantages over centralised bureaucracies.[149] First, independent regulatory agencies are said to produce better (more effective and efficient) outcomes. The source of this advantage is two-fold. First, is the greater managerial autonomy enjoyed by independent regulatory agencies. Advocates argue this makes them more agile than (slow and cumbersome) government departments. Second, is the specialist regulatory, technical and subject-matter expertise independent regulatory agencies can develop, and the scope for innovation and experimentation this affords. The extent to which independent regulatory agencies produce better outcomes than government departments is, however, open to debate. Empirical research is still in its infancy and based mainly on case studies. While this remains the case, for many independent regulatory agencies, delivery of its promise will continue to be assumed rather than proved.[150] It also may mean that the explanation for the growth of independent regulatory agencies might lie in its other advantages.

The second advantage is the promise of more consistent implementation over time. The investment of money, time and effort required to create a separate and independent regulatory agency (and the investment that would be required to dismantle it once created) is said to communicate a 'credible commitment' that the agency, and the regulatory policy choice it reflects, will withstand (or at least is better positioned than a centralised department to withstand) the influence of alternating governments beholden to the electoral cycle.[151] This institutional signal is particularly important to rational actors as it enables them to plan and invest with a greater level of policy certainty.[152]

Third, the use of an independent regulatory agency can enhance regulatory legitimacy. Independent regulatory agencies have strong cognitive legitimacy and taken-for-grantedness. They increasingly are seen as the logical, obvious and necessary choice for a regulator, such that a regulatory regime absent an independent regulatory agency to coordinate, administer and enforce it may lack 'the symbolic rewards of reform'.[153]

The fourth main advantage attributed to independent regulatory agencies is that they are better insulated from political interference.[154] The extent to which this is the case, however, is dependent on the agency enjoying an appropriate degree of autonomy. Autonomy means more than the absence of direct or formal political or departmental control.[155] Autonomy is the ability to make decisions on their merits consistent with the public interest enshrined in the agency's mandate free from external interference. Of course, with autonomy comes risk. Most notable of these are the risks of regulatory capture (by the businesses it is designed to regulate),[156] regulatory drift (that the agency will pursue outcomes different from those set for it by government), regulatory atrophy (that the agency will fail to keep pace with changes in the regulatory environment) and regulatory failure (that the agency otherwise will fail to perform its responsibilities to the standards expected of it). Independent regulatory agencies are also said to create a democratic deficit—that placing authority in the hands of bodies that are independent of politicians by definition, undermines the authority and power of those politicians—the people's elected representatives.[157] The existence of these risks highlights the importance of regulators being subject to effective oversight and accountability mechanisms. Striking an appropriate balance between autonomy and accountability is one of regulatory design's most important challenges. This challenge is discussed in the next section.

Vertical Structures

Vertical structures determine the relationship between the regulator and those that oversee it. Regulatory agencies that are independent (in the sense of not being subject to direct control by a Minister or hierarchical control by a government department) generally are thought to enjoy greater autonomy than centralised government departments. But 'independence' and 'autonomy' are slippery concepts. What constitutes formal (or what the literature sometimes calls de jure) independence, and the extent to which it is a measure of autonomy (or actual or de facto independence), is a question that has been much studied recently.[158] Measures of formal independence generally focus on the agency head and board (how they are appointed; the length of their terms; the manner with which they can be removed); the agency's level of financial autonomy (is it funded by fees and charges levied on those it regulates, or is it dependent on budget appropriations susceptible to political adjustment); the breadth of the agency's discretion (to set its own policies and procedures; to determine and impose sanctions);[159] and the extent the legislature or executive is empowered to direct the agency in the exercise of that discretion (either generally or with respect to specific decisions). Some studies find formal independence to be very important, some of moderate importance and some of little or no importance.[160] Other studies have found that formal independence can be counterproductive and generate incentives to comprise the agency's actual independence by, for example, appointing politically compliant individuals into leadership positions.[161]

What is clear from this research, though, is that while structuring a regulator to afford it a high degree of 'formal' independence may be a necessary condition of autonomy, rarely is it sufficient. Other factors also are important. These include the rule of law (the extent to which politicians (and society) respect the formal independence of an agency); whether the agency is a member of a regulatory network (being a member of a network can afford an agency a degree of independence from political interference—there being safety in numbers—but also can limit its autonomy by requiring some decisions to be made collectively); the issue's political salience (the more politically sensitive the issue, the more willing politicians may be to attempt to exercise control over the agency's management of it); the ease or difficulty with which the legislature or executive can amend the regulator's mandate, structure or operations (to control or influence management of an issue); the regulator's level of experience relative to other actors (greater experience gives the regulator authority and legitimacy in the eyes of other actors); and the power and influence of other actors occupying the regulatory space (how their involvement in the regime is structured and whether they have the power to effectively veto regulatory action).[162]

Autonomy needs to be balanced with accountability. 'Accountability' itself is a broad and elusive concept. At a minimum, accountability requires regulators to give an 'account' of themselves—to explain what they have achieved and how they have achieved it. Broader concepts extend to the allocation of blame, mechanisms for redress and the keeping of power in check.[163] Accountability can be achieved through different institutional oversight mechanisms.[164] First, there is accountability to the legislature. Regulators can be required to report to the legislature periodically, and to appear before committees of the legislature to answer questions. Second, there is legal accountability—requiring regulators to provide persons affected by their decisions with reasons, and providing those persons with the right to challenge the legality or merits of that decision in a court of law or other tribunal. Third, there is accountability to the executive. At its simplest level this involves the regulator giving an account to its responsible Minister. This can be achieved through both formal and informal briefings, as well as periodic reporting. Regulators also can be structured in a manner that subjects them to broader forms of executive review. For example, the regulator could be made subject to the oversight of agencies established within the executive to ensure the integrity of government decision-making more broadly. These 'integrity agencies' include ombudsman, government audit functions, anti-corruption bodies and human rights and privacy commissions.[165] They also can include special purpose commissions and inquiries established to inquire into issues of significant public concern.

This brings us to the fourth accountability mechanism—the public itself. Regulators are subject to the oversight of interest groups, the media and the public more broadly. The advent of social media in particular has provided a powerful vehicle through which members of the public can hold regulators accountable. These groups operate as 'fire-alarms' alerting both politicians and integrity regulators to concerns about the manner with which a regulator is discharging its responsibilities.[166] Regulators can be structured to facilitate these 'fire-alarms' by, for example, being required to report publically on their performance, and being subject to freedom of information laws that confer on members of the public a right to access information in the possession of government.

Our discussion of vertical structures commenced by stating that they are about the relationship between the regulator and those that oversee it. However, the discussion revealed that the key dimension of that relationship—the balance between autonomy and accountability—also is impacted by the regulator's relationship with other actors in the regulatory space. This brings us to the manner with which its relationships with these other actors are structured.

Horizontal Structures

Horizontal structures reflect and shape the regulator's relationship with its co-regulators and the non-government actors it co-opts into the regulatory regime. Realising the benefits and mitigating the risks of their involvement requires effective coordination.[167] This includes a clear statement of each actor's role and responsibilities, open lines of communication, forums for raising and resolving issues and an integrated implementation structure.[168] It also involves structuring the regime in a manner that guards against actors advancing their private interests at the expense of the public interest. There are a number of horizontal structural options that can be employed in this regard. They include: establishing the regulator with a board that is representative of all relevant interest groups (to create a check against the regulator being captured by any one interest group); the use of regulatory networks (to guard against the capture or self-interest of any one regulator); the use of multi-industry regulatory agencies (to reduce the influence any one industry can have on the regulator); and ensuring the regulator has independent access to relevant industry knowledge and technical expertise (to guard against unhealthy reliance on, and capture by, industry).

Summing up Institutional (Structural) Arrangements

The presence of so many structural factors, dimensions and options highlights the complexity of regime design. Looking at organisational form and vertical and horizontal structures separately assists us to navigate this complexity. Reality is more complicated, however. Structural choices within each dimension are interdependent. Accountability, for example, can be addressed through both vertical and horizontal structures. And the degree to which vertical structures afford a regulator a degree of autonomy can determine the extent to which the regulator is free to determine its horizontal relationship with other actors in the regulatory regime. Structural choices also involve trade-offs. Strengthening autonomy may weaken accountability; concentrating multiple functions in one regulator may strengthen efficiency but create role confusion; and dividing functions amongst different regulators may provide each with greater role clarity but also may create overlap, duplication and the conditions for 'turf wars'. How these trade-offs are to be made, and which values and goals are to be prioritised, cannot be decided in the abstract. They are content and context specific. What is important, however, is that these trade-offs are recognised and made transparently.[169]

Finally, it is important to remember that a regulator's institutional arrangements are not limited to its formal structural elements. They also include its organisational dynamics. These include the diversity and mix of the regulator's staff's professional and disciplinary backgrounds, employee mobility (and the extent to which the revolving door is allowed to operate), the manner with which the regulator is organised internally (e.g. by task or function; issue or industry) and its governance and other internal systems. Recognising the impact of these organisational elements is important. While the regulator itself may not be in a position to determine (or even influence) its formal structure (at least initially),[170] it usually is in a position to determine the manner with which it organises itself internally. Some of the internal aspects of regulator design are explored under 'Regime Deployment' in Chapter 10.

Generating Regulatory Options

Understanding the richness of choice within each regime variable is the first step in designing a regulatory regime. Using this knowledge to generate a set of regime options is the next step. The choices within each variable means that there are literally hundreds of possible combinations of variables—and therefore of regulatory regimes. Clearly not all combinations can be considered. So where should we start? What should be the goal? And to where should we look for ideas? These are (some of) the questions considered in this section.

Principles and Criteria

The goal of this stage of the regulatory policy cycle is to develop a set of alternative regulatory options that can be assessed and compared. But what principles and criteria should guide the development of these options? A review of better regulation guidance reveals key five criteria: that the set of options should be broad, manageable, plausible, feasible and flexible. Let us look at each of these criteria in a little more detail.

Broad: Regulatory designers should start very broad. Initially, the widest range of realistic regulatory options should be considered. These should range from the classical and traditional to the new and innovative; from the interventionist and coercive to the flexible and facilitative. A useful way to do this is to explore the boundaries of the regime variables examined in this chapter. The options could explore alternative regulator models (including government, co-regulation, self-regulation and poly-centric regulation); the use of different standards (prescriptive, outcome-orientated and a mix of the two); and alternative behaviour change mechanisms. For example, there could be options that rely primarily on coercive mechanisms, options that employ a complimentary mix of coercive and non-coercive mechanisms (that is, incentives, persuasion, assistance and nudges), and others that rely primarily on non-coercive mechanisms. And with respect to the targets of those mechanisms, there could be options that seek to operate directly upon the primary target, and others that seek to modify the primary target's behaviour through the strategic use of intermediaries. Designers also should remember to include a 'do nothing' option, or what Bardach and Patashnik more accurately describe as the 'let present trends continue' option.[171] It provides a benchmark against which all other options can be compared.

Manageable: Having started out broad, the next step is to reduce the number of options to a manageable number. But what is a manageable number? There is no fixed numerical answer to this question. The number will vary according to the nature, importance, size and complexity of the issue, the degree of ambition inherent in the regulatory objectives and the time and resources available to both generate the options, and to undertake their subsequent analysis. The more important and novel the issue, and the greater the change required, the larger the number of options that should proceed to the decide (selection) stage. At the same time, however, that number should not be so large as to impose an unreasonable and unnecessary burden on those charged with assessing and comparing them. Remember, our rationality—and therefore our ability to assess and compare alternative options—is bounded.[172]

Plausible: Each option has (or should have) a 'program' or 'intervention logic' that explains how the option's interventions and initiatives address the issue's causal drivers. To understand an option's intervention logic, it can be useful to map the option against the issue's causal map. Doing so gives a sense of whether the option addresses (or is likely to address) the issue's key causal factors. Weick refers to this as 'sensemaking', which he observes is driven by plausibility rather than accuracy.[173] Plausibility involves assessing whether the option is capable of addressing the causes of the issue in a manner that will achieve the regulatory objective. This assessment combines judgments about the clarity, consistency, coherence and completeness of the intervention logic. Only options with a clear, consistent, coherent and largely complete intervention logic should proceed to the next stage.

Feasible: The options should be feasible—legally, technically and politically. Legally they need to be within the government's jurisdiction to enact and implement. This is a particularly important issue in federal systems where legislative and executive powers are divided between different levels of government, and in jurisdictions that have Bills or Charters of Rights that protect fundamental rights from government interference. Technically, the option should be capable of being implemented within existing institutional, technological and resource constraints. This does not mean that some 'out-of-the-box' options should not proceed and that options involving changes to existing institutional arrangements, or requiring an injection of additional resources, should not be considered. What it does mean, however, is that the options should not be fanciful or so politically naïve that the credibility of the option generation process is undermined in the eyes of those who will be asked to choose from amongst them. This brings us to feasibility's third dimension—political feasibility. The options should reflect an understanding of the political environment in which they will be considered and subsequently implemented. Options that clearly would fail to garner the necessary political support to be enacted or implemented should be discarded. And options known to be favoured by the government of the day should be included. What should be avoided however, is constructing a set of options made up only of the government's preferred option and a clearly unsuitable strawman.[174] A cross-section of plausible and feasible options is important for both the effectiveness and legitimacy of the process.

Flexible: The options should be flexible and adaptable. While some aspects of the regulatory regime may need to be hard-coded in legislation—usually the primary regulatory targets, the standards of behaviour required of the target and the organisational form of the government regulator (or regulators)—other aspects should remain flexible and adaptable to the possible futures in which the regime may need to operate. This is especially important in times of uncertainty, or rapid technological, economic and social change. Options also need to be flexible and adaptable to the different attitudes, motivations and capabilities of those being regulated.[175] We have observed that regulatees can respond differently to regulatory strategies. This has two important consequences for regulatory design. First, designing on the basis of one (even dominant) motivational and capability model is likely to be only partially successful and could potentially lead to negative, unintended consequences amongst regulatees with different motivational postures. Second, regulation that speaks individually to each regulatee is likely to be cumbersome, complex and difficult to enforce (assuming it is possible to draft in the first place).[176] For many issues, the regulator rather than regulatory designer is better placed to speak with many voices.[177] For this reason, options should err on the side of providing regulators with a flexible suite of regulatory tools and the discretion to choose when and how to use them to target different regulatee's attitudes, motivations and capabilities.

Process and People

So how do we develop this broad yet manageable set of plausible, feasible and flexible regulatory options? The answer is a combination of systematic method and creativity (another reflection that modern regulatory practice is both a science and an art). As Sparrow observes with respect to problem-solving generally, without some reasonable degree of methodological rigour, analysts tend to slip back into old habits, built on old assumptions.[178] At the same time, however, it is not something that can be totally systematised. Imagination and creativity also are essential ingredients, and these require a degree of flexibility. How systems and creativity can be combined to generate regulatory options is the focus of this section.

Idea Generation

There are three broad avenues available to analysts to generate regime ideas: building upon existing initiatives; learning and borrowing from other countries or industry sectors; and conducting an open-minded search for new ideas. Ideally, all three should be explored. Let us look briefly at each.

Existing initiatives are a common starting point for idea generation (assuming, of course, that the issue already is being regulated). As we have observed, policy designers often work incrementally from existing initiatives in a series of successive adjustments.[179] However, the fact that what has been done to date has failed to produce the desired results means that there needs to be an honest appraisal of those initiatives—of what has worked and what has not worked, and why.[180] It also means that examining existing initiatives can only be a starting point. It should never be an end point. There also needs to be a search for new ideas.

Other countries and industry sectors can be a rich source of new ideas. As we have seen, studying regulatory failures in other countries and sectors enables valuable lessons to be drawn to inform current design options.[181] Also valuable is scanning other countries and sectors for successful new regulatory processes, instruments and institutions. There is a vast body of research on how policies, processes, instruments and institutions are transferred from one country or sector to another.[182] Common to this research is a strong note of caution—not all policy transfer is successful. Dolowitz and Marsh identify three common causes of policy transfer failure: insufficient information about how the regulatory policy operates in its home country or sector (which they call 'uninformed transfer'); not transferring critical elements of what made the regulatory policy successful in its home country or sector ('incomplete transfer'); and insufficient attention being paid to the different economic, social, political and ideological contexts of the transferring and borrowing countries or sectors ('inappropriate transfer').[183] The lesson from this is that policies, processes, instruments and institutions should only be borrowed from other countries or sectors after careful and thoughtful analysis.

The third option generation process calls for an open-minded search for new ideas. The issue diagnosis, and the causal analysis in particular, is a good place to start this search. Different methodologies can be employed to give varying degrees of structure to the search. These range from relatively unstructured activities in which persons from different fields and disciplines are brought together to brainstorm ideas in a largely spontaneous debate about the issue and its potential solutions, through to more structured activities in which techniques such as scenarios and other foresight and forward looking tools are used to focus discussions.[184] It also can be useful to review existing forward looking material produced by government departments and agencies, industry and professional associations, research groups and think-tanks.

Participatory Processes

Every effort should be made to ensure the option generation process is undertaken through participatory processes—to ensure the honest appraisal of existing initiatives; to critically evaluate the suitability and applicability of ideas from other countries and sectors; and to inform the open-minded search for new ideas. Moreover, these processes should be inclusive and dialogical.[185]

The participation process should cast a wide net. Bringing a diverse set of skills, experiences and organisational and disciplinary perspectives to the design process is one of the best ways to inject fresh and creative thinking into the process, and to challenge entrenched ways of seeing the world. Participants should include those persons who are likely to be affected by any new regulatory initiative (either as a beneficiary or prospective duty holder), and persons whose support and resources may be required to effectively implement the options. It also should include regulators of regimes that may be impacted by the options, as well as other regulators who have relevant resources that may be co-opted into any new regime. Relevant experts also should be included, both academic and field.

To obtain maximum value, these persons should be engaged through processes that encourage a dialogue amongst participants and a genuine exchange of ideas about how the issue might best be regulated. Bringing different actors' diverse knowledge, expertise, perspectives and ideas to bear through processes of genuine dialogue should enable a wider variety of alternative design options to be generated and considered, and a higher quality and more robust set of final options to be developed. It also contributes to the legitimacy of the process and the credibility of the options it produces.

Concluding Insights and Implications

This chapter has explored the processes by which regime design options are generated. We have seen that regulatory design can suffer from a failure to think laterally and creatively and to explore a wide range of options. This chapter has sought to address this by: first, deconstructing the regulatory endeavour into its component parts (design variables) to understand the choices that exist within each; and second, exploring how these variables might be combined into a broad and manageable set of alternative regime options.

Our examination of regime design variables revealed that within each variable there are a variety of different instruments, processes and institutional arrangements from which to choose. We also observed that each of these instruments, processes and institutional arrangements has strengths and weaknesses, and advantages and disadvantages, which makes them better suited to some issues and circumstances, and less well-suited to others. Our discussion of each regime variable concluded by observing that combinations are likely to be more effective that single variants. The same logic applies equally across variables. It is important to think in terms of complementary and synergistic combinations of regime variables that leverage each other's strengths and mitigate their weaknesses, while avoiding combinations that are incompatible or counterproductive. Leveraging strengths should make the regime more effective; compensating for weaknesses more resilient; and avoiding counterproductive combinations more efficient.[186]

We then observed that combining regime variables in this manner to form alternative regulatory options can be a daunting, challenging and complex exercise. This chapter has provided those charged with this responsibility with guidance on where to start; where to go to for ideas; and what questions they should be asking. This discussion highlighted the importance of looking beyond the familiar and safe, and to explore for new and innovative ideas. It also emphasised the utility of employing inclusive participatory processes to both assist with the generation of new ideas and to assess their plausibility. This discussion also revealed that meeting the challenges of regime design involves combining systematic methods with creativity; science with art. Leveraging the ingenuity of the past—and fostering the creativity of today—is key to meeting the regulatory challenges of the future.

This chapter's approach to option generation has followed a largely technically rational and systematic path consistent with those found in better regulation guides. The next step in the regulatory policy process—settling on the regime design to be implemented—also can benefit from the application of technically rational decision-making processes. However, as we are about to see, compared to option generation, it also has a much more overt political dimension.

Notes

1. See the discussion of poor design in Chapter 6, 103–4.
2. See e.g., Julia Black, '"Which Arrow?" Rule Type and Regulatory Policy' [1995] (Spring) *Public Law* 94; Robert Baldwin, Martin Cave and Martin Lodge, *Understanding Regulation: Theory, Strategy, and Practice* (Oxford University Press, 2012) 296–8; Colin Scott, 'Standard-Setting in Regulatory Regimes' in R Baldwin, M Cave and M Lodge (eds), *The Oxford Handbook of Regulation* (Oxford University Press, 2010) 104.
3. Examples of non-government standard-setting bodies whose standards are commonly incorporated into legislation include the International Organization for Standardization (ISO) and the International Accounting Standards Board (IASB). For a discussion of non-government standard-setting bodies, see, Tim Büthe and Walter Mattli, *The New Global Rulers: The Privatization of Regulation in the World Economy* (Princeton University Press, 2011); Craig N Murphy and Joanne Yates, *The International Organization for Standardization (ISO): Global Governance through Voluntary Consensus* (Routledge, 2009); Kristina Tamm Hallström, *Organizing International Standardization: ISO and the IASC in Quest of Authority* (Edward Elgar, 2004).
4. Soft law instruments are discussed at 175–6 (re assistance). See also: Robin Creke and John McMillan, 'Soft Law v Hard Law' in L Pearson, C Harlow and M Taggart (eds), *Administrative Law in a Changing State: Essays in Honour of Mark Aronson* (Hart Publishing, 2008) 377.
5. Julia Black, 'Decentering Regulation: Understanding the Role of Regulation and Self-Regulation in a "Post-Regulatory" World' (2001) 54 *Current Legal Problems* 103, 116–17.
6. Numerous countries have schemes to differentiate qualified accountants that have attained a high level of professional competence from other persons who provide accounting services. Commonly referred to as CPAs (Certified Public Accountants in the USA; Certified Practising Accountants in Australia and the UK; and Chartered Professional Accountants in Canada).
7. Fairtrade International is a non-government organisation that certifies use of its 'fair trade' logo on products that conform to its economic, social and environmental standards. The Forestry Stewardship Council too is an international non-government organisation, and it certifies use of its logo by organisations that conform to its nine standards for responsible forest management. For a general discussion of certification schemes, see: Tim Bartley, 'Certification as a Mode of Social Regulation' in D Levi-Faur (ed), *Handbook on the Politics of Regulation* (Edward Elgar, 2011) 441.
8. Sanctions are discussed at 170–2.

9. See Anthony I Ogus, *Regulation: Legal Form and Economic Theory* (Hart Publishing, 2004) ch 10; Arie Freiberg, *The Tools of Regulation* (Federation Press, 2010) ch 7.

10. Colin S Diver, 'The Optimal Precision of Administrative Rules' (1983) 93 *Yale Law Journal* 65; Cass R Sunstein, 'Problems with Rules' (1995) 83 *California Law Review* 953.

11. John Braithwaite, 'Rules and Principles: A Theory of Legal Certainty' (2002) 27 *Journal of Legal Philosophy* 47, 60–5. Baldwin, Cave and Lodge observe that this places the onus to innovate upon the regulator, and may be appropriate in circumstances where the regulator has expertise and knowledge unavailable to regulatees: Baldwin, Cave and Lodge, *Understanding Regulation*, above n 2, 297.

12. Braithwaite, 'Rules and Principles', above n 11, 57; Sunstein, 'Problems with Rules', above n 10, 993–4.

13. Robert Baldwin, *Rules and Government* (Clarendon Press, 1995) 167–74.

14. This has been identified as a cause of regulatory failure. See discussion at Chapter 6, 105–6.

15. Sunstein, 'Problems with Rules', above n 10, 992, 995.

16. Braithwaite argues that precise rules more consistently regulate simple issues, and principles more consistently regulate complex issues: Braithwaite, 'Rules and Principles', above n 11.

17. There are, for example, longitudinal performance standards that relate to the vehicle's startability, gradeabilty, acceleration capability and ability to track on a straight path; and directional performance standards that relate to the vehicle's frontal and tail swing, swept path, and rollover threshold. For a full list and description of the heavy vehicle standards, see: National Transport Commission, *Performance-Based Standards Scheme: The Standards and Vehicle Assessment Rules* (National Transport Commission, 2008).

18. See, e.g., US's *Clean Air Act* 42 USC § 7411 (2013). It authorizes the US EPA to set numerical emission standards for stationary sources such as power plants and factories. An example of such a standard is *Standards of Performance for Petroleum Refineries* 40 CFR § 60 subpart J (2008).

19. See, e.g., Cary Coglianese and David Lazar, 'Management-Based Regulation: Prescribing Private Management to Achieve Public Goals' (2003) 37 *Law & Society* 691; Neil Gunningham and Darren Sinclair, 'Organisational Trust and the Limits of Management-Based Regulation' (2009) 43 *Law & Society Review* 865.

20. For information on HACCP, see: Karen L Hulebak and Wayne Schlosser, 'Hazard Analysis and Critical Control Point (HACCP) History and Conceptual Overview' (2002) 22 *Risk Analysis* 547; Sara E Mortimore and Carol A Wallace, *HACCP: A Food Industry Briefing* (Wiley Blackwell, 2nd ed, 2015).

21. For information on safety case management systems, see Andrew Hopkins, 'Explaining "Safety Case"' (Working Paper 87, Regulatory Institutions Network, April 2012); Neil Gunningham, 'Designing OSH Standards: Process, Safety Case and Best Practice' (2007) 5(2) *Policy and Practice in Health and Safety* 3.

22. See, e.g., the principles enshrined in the *Environment Protection Act 1970* (Vic).

23. Julia Black, 'The Rise, Fall and Fate of Principles Based Regulation' (LSE Law, Society and Economy Working Paper 17/2010, London School of Economics and Political Science, Law Department, 2010) 5–8, summarises principles commonly found in financial regulation.

24. See, e.g., Braithwaite, 'Rules and Principles', above n 11; Robert Baldwin, 'Why Rules Don't Work' (1990) 53 *Modern Law Review* 321; Black, 'The Rise, Fall and Fate of Principles Based Regulation', above n 23.

25. Gunningham and Sinclair, 'Organisational Trust', above n 19. Regulatee motivation and capability is discussed in more detail under 'Whom to Regulate?' below.

26. Julia Black, 'Learning from Regulatory Disasters' (LSE Law, Society and Economy Working Paper 24/2014, London School of Economics and Political Science, Law Department, 2014) 12; Julia Black, 'Paradoxes and Failures: "New Governance" Techniques and the Financial Crisis' (2012) 75 *Modern Law Review* 1037, 1046.

27. Rex Deighton-Smith, 'What Do We Mean by "Rethinking Regulation"' (2008) 67 *Australian Journal of Public Administration* 41, 51.

28. 'Deemed to comply' and 'safe harbour' guidance operate as 'shields' against enforcement action. 'Deemed to comply' guidance is produced by the regulator and, while not mandatory, deems regulatees acting in accordance with it to have complied with corresponding legislative and regulatory requirements. 'Safe harbor' guidance, on the other hand, generally is produced by industry and 'confirmed' by the regulator as a compliant application of the standards. See ibid; Black, 'The Rise, Fall and Fate of Principles Based Regulation', above n 23, 9–10.

29. Julia Black, Martyn Hopper and Christa Band, 'Making Success of Principles-Based Regulation' (2007) 1 *Law and Financial Markets Review* 191, 196–200; Deighton-Smith, 'What Do We Mean by "Rethinking Regulation"', above n 27. See also Cary Coglianese, Jennifer Nash and Todd Olmstead, 'Performance-Based Regulation: Prospects and Limitations in Health, Safety, and Environment Protection' (2003) 55 *Administrative Law Review* 705, 712.

30. Black, Hopper and Band, 'Making Success of Principles-Based Regulation', above n 29, 197.

31. What is being described here is enforced co-regulation—see discussion at 163.

32. These include the global financial crisis, the Deepwater Horizon oil rig disaster, the 'leaky buildings' of New Zealand and the Pike River mining disaster in New Zealand. See Black, 'Learning from Regulatory Disasters', above n 26, 12; Black, 'Paradoxes and Failures', above n 26, 1046; Peter J May, 'Performance-Based Regulation and Regulatory Regimes: The Saga of Leaky Buildings' (2003) 25 *Law and Policy* 381; Neil Gunningham, 'Lessons from Pike River: Regulation, Safety and Neoliberalism' (2015) 26 *New Zealand Universities Law Review* 736.

33. This point is discussed further under 'Regulatory Strategies' in Chapter 10.

34. See, e.g., Sharon Gilad, 'Process-Orientated Regulation: Conceptualization and Assessment' in D Levi-Faur (ed), *Handbook on the Politics of Regulation* (Edward Elgar, 2011) 423, 432; Black, 'Paradoxes and Failures', above n 26, 1044.

35. Braithwaite, 'Rules and Principles', above n 11; Black, 'The Rise, Fall and Fate of Principles Based Regulation', above n 23, 5.

36. Black, Hopper and Band, 'Making Success of Principle-Based Regulation', above n 29, 200; Julia Black, 'Forms and Paradoxes of Principles-Based Regulation' (2008) 3 *Capital Markets Law Journal* 425, 453.

37. See Chapter 2, 22–4.

38. Gunningham, 'Lessons from Pike River', above n 32.

39. See, e.g., Margot Priest, 'The Privatization of Regulation: Five Models of Self-Regulation' (1997–1998) 29 *Ottawa Law Review* 233, who encompasses within her conception of self-regulation regimes where government actively sets the standards and imposes sanctions for their breach; Black, 'Decentering Regulation', above n 5, who includes as self-regulation, regimes where

government approves the standards or sets the framework within which they are formulated and enforced; Ian Bartle and Peter Vass, 'Self-Regulation and the Regulatory State: A Survey of Policy and Practice' (Research Report No 17, Centre for the Study of Regulated Industries, University of Bath, 2005), who include within their conception of self-regulation, regimes where government devolves or delegates statutory powers or duties to the self-regulatory body or otherwise facilitates the endeavour.

40. My use of 'tacit' differs from that of Bartle and Vass who use it to describe self-regulation in response to government threats: Bartle and Vass, 'Self-Regulation and the Regulatory State', above n 39. We see nothing tacit in a threat, and prefer to describe regulation in response to a threat as 'coerced' self-regulation, which is the second type of self-regulation discussed below.

41. Numerous definitions of tacit self-regulation exist. This is based on the definition in National Consumer Council, *Models of Self-Regulation: An Overview of Models in Business and the Professions* (NCC, 2000) 7.

42. For examples, see Bartle and Vass, 'Self-Regulation and the Regulatory State', above n 39, 69–71.

43. Ibid 3.

44. Black, 'Decentering Regulation', above n 5, 118.

45. Introduction to the Press Complaints Commission's 10 Year Book cited in Ian Bartle and Peter Vass, 'Self-Regulation within the Regulatory State: Towards a New Regulatory Paradigm' (2007) 85 *Public Administration* 885, 895.

46. For further discussion of these disadvantages, see: Bartle and Vass, 'Self-Regulation within the Regulatory State', above n 45; Anthony I Ogus, 'Rethinking Regulation' (1995) 15 *Oxford Journal of Legal Studies* 97; Neil Gunningham and Joseph Rees, 'Industry Self-Regulation: An Institutional Perspective' (1997) 19 *Law & Policy* 365; Priest, 'The Privatization of Regulation', above n 39, 268–71.

47. For further discussion of these advantages, see references, above n 46.

48. See discussion at 157–9.

49. A review of the literature reveals that 'co-regulation' is another term with variable meanings. Levi-Faur, for example, restricts it to regulatory arrangements 'grounded in cooperative techniques' and would exclude more coercive arrangements: David Levi-Faur, 'Regulation and Regulatory Governance' in D Levi-Faur (ed), *Handbook on the Politics of Regulation* (Edward Elgar, 2011) 3, 10.

50. See, e.g., Andrew A King and Michael J Lenox, 'Industry Self-Regulation without Sanctions: The Chemical Industry's Responsible Care Program' (2000) 43 *Academy of Management Journal* 698.

51. See Australian Securities & Investment Commission, 'ePayments Code' (ASIC, 29 March 2016) <http://asic.gov.au/for-consumers/codes-of-practice/epayments-code/>.

52. This is sometimes referred to as 'statutory self-regulation'. See Bartle and Vass, 'Self-Regulation and the Regulatory State', above n 39, 63.

53. Priest, 'The Privatization of Regulation', above n 39, 259–61.

54. This type of regulation is sometimes referred to as 'meta-regulation'. 'Meta-regulation' is another term to which different meanings are applied. For example, some commentators use it more broadly to refer to any oversight of regulatory decision-making which could include, in addition to government oversight of private regulation, one government body oversighting the regulatory decision-making of another government body (see, e.g., Christine Parker, 'Meta-Regulation: Legal Accountability for Corporate Social Responsibility' in D McBarnet, A Voicilescu and T Campbell (eds), *The New Corporate*

Accountability: Corporate Social Responsibility and the Law (Cambridge University Press, 2007) 207). See generally, Baldwin, Cave and Lodge, *Understanding Regulation*, above n 2, 146–57; Freiberg, *The Tools of Regulation*, above n 9, 33–7.

55. See discussion: above n 20; above n 21.
56. Ian Ayres and John Braithwaite, *Responsive Regulation: Transcending the Deregulatory Debate* (Oxford University Press, 1992) ch 3.
57. For a discussion of the different roles third parties can play, see the discussion of regulatory regimes (Chapter 4, 74–6) and behaviour change mechanisms (at 170–81).
58. Neil Gunningham and Peter Grabosky, *Smart Regulation: Designing Environmental Policy* (Clarendon Press, 1988) 15, 93, 408–13. See also: Peter Grabosky, 'Using Non-Governmental Resources to Foster Regulatory Compliance' (1995) 8 *Governance* 527; Colin Scott, 'Analysing Regulatory Space: Fragmented Resources and Institutional Design' [2001] (Summer) *Public Law* 329; Peter Grabosky, 'Beyond *Responsive Regulation*: The Expanding Role of Non-State Actors in the Regulatory Process' (2013) 7 *Regulation & Governance* 114.
59. Gunningham and Grabosky, *Smart Regulation*, above n 58, 408–9.
60. Mathew McCubbins, Roger Noll and Barry Weingast, 'Administrative Procedures as Instruments of Political Control' (1987) 3 *Journal of Law, Economics, and Organization* 243.
61. Freiberg, *The Tools of Regulation*, above n 9, 59.
62. See Black, 'Paradoxes and Failures', above n 26, 1048–52 who refers to intermediary targets as 'gatekeepers'.
63. For a general discussion, see, Michael Rawling, 'A Generic Model of Regulating Supply Chain Outsourcing', in C Arup et al (eds), *Labour Law and Labour Market Regulation* (Federation Press, 2006) 520.
64. For a discussion of these variables, see Nancy R Lee and Philip Kotler, *Social Marketing: Changing Behaviors for Good* (Sage Publications, 2016) 130–3.
65. See Chapter 6, 105–6.
66. These labels are borrowed from Neil Gunningham, *Mine Safety: Law, Regulation and Policy* (The Federation Press, 2007) 50–9.
67. Ayres and Braithwaite, *Responsive Regulation*, above n 56, 31.
68. See, e.g., Robert Kagan and John T Scholz, 'The Criminology of the Corporation and Regulatory Enforcement Strategies' in K Hawkins and J M Thomas (eds), *Enforcing Regulation* (Kluwer-Nijhoff, 1984) 67; Ayres and Braithwaite, *Responsive Regulation*, above n 56, 23–30; Valerie Braithwaite et al, 'Regulatory Styles, Motivational Postures and Nursing Home Compliance' (1994) 16 *Law & Policy* 363; Valerie Braithwaite, 'Games of Engagement: Postures within the Regulatory Community' (1995) 17 *Law & Policy* 225; Valerie Braithwaite, Kristina Murphy and Monika Reinhart, 'Taxation Threat, Motivational Posture, and Responsive Regulation' (2007) 29 *Law & Policy* 137.
69. Yuval Feldman, 'Five Models of Regulatory Compliance Motivation: Empirical Findings and Normative Implications' in D Levi-Faur (ed), *Handbook on the Politics of Regulation* (Edward Elgar, 2011) 335.
70. See, e.g., Anne Schneider and Helen Ingram, 'Behavioral Assumptions of Policy Tools' (1990) 52 *Journal of Politics* 510, who classified policy tools into five behavioural modification mechanisms: authority tools, incentive tools, capacity tools, symbolic and hortatory tools and learning tools; Terence Daintith, 'The Techniques of Government' in J Jowell and D Oliver (eds), *The Changing Constitution* (Clarendon Press, 3rd ed, 1994) 209 who classified government interventions into three categories—*imperium* (commands through law), *dominium* (incentives through wealth) and suasion (persuasion through

information); Evert Vedung, 'Policy Instruments: Typologies and Theories' in M L Benemmans-Videc, R C Rist and E Vedung (eds), *Carrots, Stick and Sermons: Policy Instruments and Their Evaluation* (Transaction Publishers, 1998) 21 who employs the familiar 'carrots, sticks and sermons' classification; Bronwen Morgan and Karen Yeung, *An Introduction to Law and Regulation: Text and Materials* (Cambridge University Press, 2007) ch 3, who classify regulatory tools according to the behaviour change modalities of command, competition, communication, consensus and code (architecture).

71. See discussion at 154–9.
72. Deterrence is discussed in Chapter 10 at 230–2.
73. See generally Freiberg, *The Tools of Regulation*, above n 9, 215–57.
74. The relationship between criminal law and regulation is one that has troubled a number of commentators. Ogus, for example, draws a distinction between criminal conduct that is 'wrongful in itself' (*mala in se*) and conduct that cannot be so categorised and is subject to specific proscription (*mala prohibita*), and refers to the use of criminal sanctions to enforce regulatory standards as 'quasi-criminal': Ogus, *Regulation*, above n 9, 79–81.
75. Ibid 81–9.
76. Kenneth Mann, 'Punitive Civil Sanctions: The Middleground between Criminal and Civil Law' (1991–1992) 101 *Yale Law Journal* 1795.
77. Peta Spender, 'Negotiating the Third Way: Developing Effective Process in Civil Penalty Litigation' (2008) 26 *Companies and Securities Law Journal* 249; Michelle Welsh, 'The Regulatory Dilemma: The Choice between Overlapping Criminal Sanctions and Civil Penalties for Contraventions of the Directors' Duty Provisions' (2009) 27 *Companies and Securities Law Journal* 370.
78. For a discussion of these provisions, see Richard Johnstone, Elizabeth Bluff and Alan Clayton, *Work Health and Safety Law and Policy* (Lawbook Co, 3rd ed, 2012) 507–46, 736–42.
79. See, e.g., Andrew Keay and Joan Loughrey, 'An Assessment of the Present State of Statutory Derivative Proceedings' in J Loughrey (ed), *Directors' Duties and Shareholder Litigation in the Wake of the Financial Crisis* (Edward Elgar, 2013) 187.
80. Baldwin, Cave and Lodge, *Understanding Regulation*, above n 2, 107. While this is the case, drafting the standard to be applied and the rules according to which it is to be enforced can take considerable time, especially if the processes to do so are legislative or highly participatory.
81. Regulatory styles are discussed in Chapter 10.
82. Gunningham and Grabosky, *Smart Regulation*, above n 58, 45; J Braithwaite and T Makkai, 'Trust and Compliance' (1994) 4 *Policy and Society* 1.
83. Incentives and disincentives often are referred to as 'economic instruments', and if the instrument affects the cost or price of a good or service, as 'market-based instruments'.
84. See Ogus, *Regulation*, above n 9, ch 11; Freiberg, *The Tools of Regulation*, above n 9, ch 5.
85. See discussion of certification systems at 155.
86. Ian Harden, *The Contracting State* (Open University Press, 1992). See also Baldwin, Cave and Lodge, *Understanding Regulation*, above n 2, 116–17; Freiberg, *The Tools of Regulation*, above n 9, 132–6.
87. For an overview of some of these incentives and disincentives, see Nathaniel O Keohane, Richard L Revesz and Robert N Stavins, 'The Choice of Regulatory Instruments in Environmental Policy' (1998) 22 *Harvard Environmental Law Review* 313; Gunningham and Grabosky, *Smart Regulation*, above n 58, 69–83. See generally, Jody Freeman and Charles D Kolstad (eds), *Moving to Markets in Environmental Regulation: Lessons from Twenty Years of Experience* (Oxford University Press, 2007).

88. See discussion of economic theories of regulation in Chapter 3.
89. See also Chapter 6, 105–6 for a discussion of such rorts and failures.
90. See Chapter 3, 44 for a discussion of these risks.
91. Baldwin, Cave and Lodge, *Understanding Regulation*, above n 2, 112.
92. John Braithwaite, 'The Limits of Economism in Controlling Harmful Corporate Conduct' (1982) 16 *Law and Society Review* 481, 595.
93. Ibid; See also Baldwin, Cave and Lodge, *Understanding Regulation*, above n 2, 113.
94. Baldwin, Cave and Lodge, *Understanding Regulation*, above n 2, 114.
95. Karen Yeung, 'Government by Publicity Management: Sunlight or Spin' [2005] (Summer) *Public Law* 360, 369–71.
96. See, e.g., Cabinet Office Behavioural Insights Team, *Applying Behavioural Insights to Reduce Fraud, Error and Debt* (Cabinet Office, 2012), which found people were encouraged to pay their taxes when compared with a peer norm, and the more proximate the norm to the person (e.g. town vs nation), the greater the impact; P Wesley Schultz et al, 'The Constructive, Destructive and Reconstructive Power of Social Norms' (2007) 18 *Psychological Science* 429 found providing consumers with feedback on their energy consumption in the form of a happy face for those consuming less than the average, and with a sad face for those consuming more than the average, led to an overall reduction in energy consumption.
97. This expectation is enshrined in most jurisdictions' better regulation principles, and regulator codes and guides issued under them. See Chapter 6, 108–11.
98. It is generally accepted that the rule of law requires rules to be clear and publically accessible. See, e.g., Joseph Raz, *The Authority of Law* (Oxford University Press, 2nd ed, 2009) 214.
99. Information and advice about the source, nature, importance and consequences of the regulatory issue can be used to change attitudes about the issue being regulated; and information about the benefits of compliance or the consequences of non-compliance can convince regulatees of the merits of complying with the regulatory standards. There clearly is an overlap between the provision of this type of information and advice, and persuasion discussed above.
100. See, e.g., The United Kingdom's Department for Business Enterprise & Regulatory Reform, 'Regulator's Compliance Code: Statutory Code of Practice for Regulators' (17 December 2007) [5.2]—[5.4]. 'How to comply' information and advice is particularly important for small to medium-sized businesses whose capacity to keep informed of regulatory developments may be limited.
101. See generally Creke and McMillan, 'Soft Law v Hard Law', above n 4.
102. An example of this is the publication by corporate regulators of documents filed with them by companies.
103. The Australian Taxation Office, for example, publishes an annual list of Australia's largest companies, their income, taxable income and the tax payable on that income (available at<www.ato.gov.au>). The Australian Taxation Offices states that publication of the list is part of its efforts to ensure corporate taxpayers pay the correct amount of tax.
104. Yeung, 'Government by Publicity Management', above n 95, 372–6. See Matthew S Johnson, 'Regulation by Shaming: Deterrence Effects of Publicizing Violations of Workplace Safety and Health Laws' (Sanford School of Public Policy, Duke University, 29 September 2016), who found that 'naming and shaming' workplaces that breached workplace health and safety laws improved health and safety compliance in workplaces within the same industry and geographic region.
105. For a discussion of these and other forms of disclosure regulation, see Freiberg, *The Tools of Regulation*, above n 9, 167–9; Ogus, *Regulation*, above n 9, 126–44. 'Right to know' laws oblige employers, manufacturers and government

authorities to provide workers and communities with information about chemicals to which they may be exposed. See, e.g., Neil Gunningham and Amanda Cornwall, 'Legislating the Right to Know' (1994) *Environment and Planning Law Journal* 274; James T Hamilton, 'Pollution as News: Media and Stockmarket Reactions to the Capital Toxic Release Inventory Data' (1995) *Journal of Environmental Economics and Management* 98. 'Truth in lending' laws require lenders to disclose to prospective borrowers information about the costs and terms of borrowing in a standardised manner that facilitates comparison, see, e.g., Alvin C Harrell, *The Law of Truth in Lending* (ABA Book Publishing, 2014).

106. Yeung, 'Government by Publicity Management', above n 95, 367–9.
107. Ogus, *Regulation*, above n 9, ch 12.
108. See discussion of market failure in Chapter 3, 36–8.
109. For a discussion of emission trading schemes, see Baldwin, Cave and Lodge, *Understanding Regulation*, above n 2, ch 10.
110. See Freiberg, *The Tools of Regulation*, above n 9, 114–17.
111. State-based workers' compensation schemes are a good example of this. By mandating insurance cover be taken out, they ensure all workers are adequately insured; by underwriting and managing the scheme, they ensure all employers can obtain insurance at a reasonable price (something not assured in a competitive market); and by transparently linking insurance premiums to the employer's safety performance (usually measured in the number and value of claims), the schemes also act as an inventive for employers to improve their future safety performance.
112. Roger Brownsword, 'Code, Control and Choice: Why East Is East and West Is West' (2005) 25 *Legal Studies* 1, 11.
113. Martin Friedland, Michael Trebilcock and Kent Roach, 'Regulating Traffic Safety' in M L Friedland (ed), *Securing Compliance: Seven Case Studies* (University of Toronto Press, 1990) 165, 254–62.
114. For a discussion of these and other forms of design or structural regulation, see Freiberg, *The Tools of Regulation*, above n 9, ch 8.
115. Bounded rationality is discussed in Chapter 5.
116. Cass R Sunstein, 'Informational Regulation and Informational Standing: *Akins* and beyond' (1999) 147 *University of Pennsylvania Law Review* 613, 627; Janet A Weiss, 'Public Information' in Lester M Salamon and Odus V Elliot (eds), *The Tools of Government: A Guide to the New Governance* (Oxford University Press, 2002) 217, 229; David Weil et al, 'The Effectiveness of Regulatory Disclosure Policies' (2006) 25 *Journal of Policy Analysis and Management* 155, 161.
117. See discussion in Chapter 3, 37.
118. For an overview of cognitive biases, see: Daniel Kahneman, Paul Slovic and Amos Tversky, *Judgment under Uncertainty: Heuristics and Biases* (Cambridge University Press, 1982); Jonathan Baron, *Thinking and Deciding* (Cambridge University Press, 4th ed, 2007); Dan Ariely, *Predictably Irrational: The Hidden Forces That Shape Our Decisions* (Harper Collins, 2008).
119. Paul Dolan et al, 'Mindscape: Influencing Behaviour through Public Policy: The Practical Guide' (Institute for Government, 2010) 1–2.
120. Mark Kosters and Jeroen Van der Heijden, 'From Mechanism to Virtue: Evaluating Nudge-Theory' (2015) 21 *Evaluation* 276, 286.
121. Richard H Thaler and Cass R Sunstein, *Nudge: Improving Decisions about Health, Wealth, and Happiness* (Penguin Books, 2009) 6.
122. See discussion, above n 96, with respect to the use of comparative data in support of coercive tax avoidance mechanisms, and to persuade people to reduce energy consumption.

123. Alberto Alemanno and Alessandro Spina, 'Nudging Legally: On the Checks and Balances of Behavioural Regulation' (2014) 12 *International Journal of Constitutional Law* 429, 438. The ability of the regulatee to 'opt-out' differentiates nudges from structural design regulation (discussed above) that remove or limit choices.

124. See, e.g., Andrew Hanks, David Just and Brian Wansink, 'Smarter Lunchrooms Can Address New School Lunchroom Guidelines and Child Obesity' (2013) 162 *The Journal of Paediatrics* 867; Floor M Kroese, David R Marchiori and Denise T D de Ridder, 'Nudging Healthy Food Choices: A Field Assessment at the Train Station' (2016) 38 *Journal of Public Health* 133.

125. See, e.g., Eric J Johnson and Daniel Goldstein, 'Do Defaults Save Lives?' (2003) 302 *Science* 1338.

126. See, e.g., Lisa L Shu et al, 'Signing at the Beginning Makes Ethics Salient and Decreases Dishonest Self-Reports in Comparison with Signing at the End' (2012) 109 *Proceedings of the National Academy of Sciences* 15197.

127. Behavioural insights (or economics) teams have been established in the White House Office of Information and Regulatory Affairs (to which Sunstein was appointed administrator), the United Kingdom's Cabinet Office (to which Thaler acts in an advisory capacity), the Australian Government's Department of Prime Minister and Cabinet, and the European Commission has established a Behavioural Studies for European Policies Program. See Kosters and Van der Heijden, 'From Mechanism to Virtue', above n 120, 277.

128. See, e.g., Daniel M Hausman and Brynn Welch, 'Debate: To Nudge or Not to Nudge' (2010) 18 *The Journal of Political Philosophy* 123; Patrick Brown, 'A Nudge in the Right Direction? Towards a Sociological Engagement with Libertarian Paternalism' (2012) 11 *Social Policy and Society* 305; Tom Goodwin, 'Why We Should Reject "Nudge"' (2012) 32 *Politics* 85; Evan Selinger and Kyle Whyte, 'Is There a Right Way to Nudge? The Practice and Ethics of Choice Architecture' (2011) 5 *Sociology Compass* 923; Mark D White, *The Manipulation of Choice: Ethics and Libertarian Paternalism* (Palgrave Macmillan, 2013); Riccardo Rebanato, *Taking Liberties: A Critical Examination of Libertarian Paternalism* (Palgrave Macmillan, 2012).

129. Thaler and Sunstein, *Nudge*, above n 121, 5.

130. Ibid 249–51.

131. Baldwin, Cave and Lodge, *Understanding Regulation*, above n 2, 124–5.

132. Thaler and Sunstein, *Nudge*, above n 121, 244.

133. Ibid 246–9. The 'publicity principle' was espoused by legal philosopher John Rawls as a formal precondition to the use of power: John Rawls, *A Theory of Justice* (Clarendon Press, 1971).

134. Kosters and Van der Heijden, 'From Mechanism to Virtue', above n 120, 281.

135. Alberto Alemanno and Anne-Lise Sibony, 'Epilogue: The Legitimacy and Practicality of EU Behavioural Policy-Making' in A Alemanno and A Sibony (eds), *Nudges and the Law* (Hart Publishing, 2015) 325, 335. Regulatory impact assessments are discussed in Chapter 9.

136. For a discussion of different frameworks and checks and balances for ensuring the responsible use of nudge techniques, see generally: Alemanno and Spina, 'Nudging Legally', above n 123; Pelle G Hansen and Andreas M Jespersen, 'Nudge and the Manipulation of Choice: A Framework for the Responsible Use of the Nudge Approach to Behaviour Change in Public Policy' (2013) 3 *European Journal of Risk Regulation* 3.

137. They also can take a variety of names including agency, board, commission, office and authority. For examples of different names applied to different types of regulatory agencies, see Organisation for Economic Co-Operation and Development, *Distributed Public Governance: Agencies, Authorities and*

Other Government Bodies (OECD, 2002); Koen Verhoest et al, *Government Agencies: Practices and Lessons from 30 Countries* (Palgrave Macmillan, 2012).

138. For a discussion of the growth of agencies over the past thirty years across thirty countries and the different forms they can take and functions they can perform, see Verhoest et al, *Government Agencies*, above n 137.

139. Christoph Knill and Jale Tosun, *Public Policy: A New Introduction* (Palgrave Macmillan, 2012) 167.

140. See the discussion of role legitimacy in Chapter 6, 115.

141. These are Victoria Police, WorkSafe Victoria, Transport Safety Victoria, Energy Safe Victoria, Transport Accident Commission and Environment Protection Authority.

142. Regulatory tasks are discussed in Chapter 10, 227–30.

143. See Chapter 6, 125 n 84.

144. Mark H Moore, *Creating Public Value: Strategic Management in Government* (Harvard University Press, 1995) 89. See also Christopher Carrigan and Lindsey Poole, 'Structuring Regulators: The Effects of Organizational Design on Regulatory Behaviour and Performance' (Research Paper prepared for the Penn Program on Regulation's Best-in-Class Regulator Initiative, June 2015) 20–2.

145. Moore, *Creating Public Value*, above n 144, 89–94.

146. See Chapter 6, 125 n 84.

147. The differences between and among Parliamentary and Presidential systems (and the inconsistency with which terms are sometimes used) requires some generalisations to be made here. Strictly speaking, in Parliamentary systems, there is a distinction between a ministry and a department. A ministry is under the direct control of a minister who is an elected member of Parliament, and a department is guided and controlled by a secretary who is a public servant answerable to a Minister. In Presidential systems, there generally are Departments (not Ministries) headed by Secretaries who generally are nominated by the President and confirmed by the legislature. In this section, the term 'department' is used to refer to both a ministry and a department, 'Minister' to refer to both a Minister and a Secretary.

148. Jacint Jordana, David Levi-Faur and Xavier Fernandez i Marín, 'The Global Diffusion of Regulatory Agencies: Channels of Transfer and Stages of Diffusion' (2011) 44 *Comparative Political Studies* 1343; Fabrio Gilardi, 'The Institutional Foundations of Regulatory Capitalism: The Diffusion of Independent Regulatory Agencies in Western Europe' (2005) 598 *Annals of the American Academy of Political and Social Sciences* 84; Verhoest et al, *Government Agencies*, above n 137; Christopher Pollitt et al, 'Agency Fever: Analysis of an International Policy Fashion' (2001) 3 *Journal of Contemporary Policy Analysis* 271.

149. For a discussion of these benefits and advantages, see: Mark Thatcher and Alec Sweet Stone, 'Theory and Practice of Delegation to Non-Majoritarian Institutions' (2002) 25 *West European Politics* 1; Fabrizio Gilardi, *Delegation in the Regulatory State: Independent Regulatory Agencies in Western Europe* (Edward Elgar, 2008); Verhoest et al, *Government Agencies*, above n 137; Organisation for Economic Co-Operation and Development, *Distributed Public Governance*, above n 137.

150. Mattia Guidi, 'The Impact of Independence on Regulatory Outcomes: The Case of EU Competition Policy' (2015) 53 *Journal of Common Market Studies* 1195, 1199; Verhoest et al, *Government Agencies*, above n 137, 4.

151. The 'credible commitment' basis of 'agentification' was argued most strenuously by Majone, and has since gained wide acceptance. See, eg, Giandomenico

Majone, 'The Rise of the Regulatory State in Europe' (1994) 17 *West European Politics* 77; Giandomenico Majone, *Regulating Europe* (Routledge, 1996) 40–4; Giandomenico Majone, 'Temporal Consistency and Policy Credibility: Why Democracies Need Non-Majoritarian Institutions' (European University Institute Working Paper No 1996/57, 1996); Giandomenico Majone, 'Independent Agencies and the Delegation Problem: Theoretical and Normative Dimensions' in B Steuenberg and F van Vught (eds), *Political Institutions and Public Policy* (Kluwer, 1997) 139; Giandomenico Majone, 'The Regulatory State and Its Legitimacy Problems' (1999) 22 *West European Politics* 1; Mark Thatcher, 'Delegation to Independent Regulatory Agencies: Pressures, Functions and Contextual Mediation' (2002) 25 *West European Politics* 125; Fabrizio Gilardi, 'Policy Credibility and Delegation to Independent Regulatory Agencies: A Comparative Empirical Analysis' (2002) 9 *Journal of European Public Policy* 873.

152. This is an example of rational choice institutionalism. See Chapter 3, 52–3.
153. Gilardi, 'The Institutional Foundations of Regulatory Capitalism', above n 148, 90. This is an example of sociological institutionalism. See Chapter 3, 53–4.
154. This insulation operates both ways: agencies allow politicians to shift the responsibility and blame for difficult and unpopular decisions to the agency, thereby creating a buffer between them and the controversial decision: Thatcher, 'Delegation to Independent Regulatory Agencies', above n 151; M P Fiorina, 'Legislative Choice of Regulatory Forms: Legal Process or Administrative Process' (1982) 29 *Public Choice* 33, 46.
155. Tony Prosser, *The Regulatory Enterprise: Government, Regulation, and Legitimacy* (Oxford University Press, 2010) 224–5.
156. This too works both ways—autonomy insulates independent regulatory agencies from the consequences of their political overseers being captured.
157. Majone, 'The Regulatory State and Its Legitimacy Problems', above n 151; Thatcher and Sweet, 'Theory and Practice of Delegation to Non-Majoritarian Institutions', above n 149.
158. See, e.g., Gilardi, 'Policy Credibility and Delegation to Independent Regulatory Agencies', above n 151; Chris Hanretty and Christel Koop, 'Measuring the Formal Independence of Regulatory Agencies' (2012) 19 *Journal of European Public Policy* 198; Chris Hanretty and Christel Koop, 'Shall the Law Set Them Free? The Formal and Actual Independence of Regulatory Agencies' (2013) 7 *Regulation & Governance* 195; Guidi, 'The Impact of Independence on Regulatory Outcomes', above n 150.
159. McCubbins, Noll and Weingast refer to legislatures including 'deck-stacking' devices in a regulator's enabling legislation that are designed to curtail or bias decision-making towards particular outcomes. Examples of deck-stacking devices include prescriptive consultation procedures and governance structures that preference the holders of particular views: McCubbins, Noll and Weingast, 'Administrative Procedures as Instruments of Political Control', above n 60. See also: Jonathan R Macey, 'Organizational Design and Political Control of Administrative Agencies' (1992) 8 *Journal of Law, Economics, and Organization* 93.
160. Hanretty and Koop, 'Shall the Law Set Them Free?', above n 158, 197–8 and the studies cited therein.
161. Laurenz Ennser-Jedenastik, 'The Politicization of Regulatory Agencies: Between Partisan Influence and Formal Independence' (2016) 26 *Journal of Public Administration Research and Theory* 507.
162. Martino Maggetti, 'De Facto Independence after Delegation: A Fuzzy-Set Analysis' (2007) 1 *Regulation & Governance* 271; Hanretty and Koop, 'Shall

the Law Set Them Free?' above n 158; Carrigan and Poole, 'Structuring Regulators', above n 144.

163. See generally: Richard Mulgan, *Holding Power to Account: Accountability in Modern Democracies* (Palgrave Macmillan, 2003); Mark Bovens, Robert E Goodin and Thomas Schillemans, *The Oxford Handbook of Public Accountability* (Oxford University Press, 2014).

164. This section adopts the categories employed by Gabrielle Appleby, Alexander Reilly and Laura Grenfell, *Australian Public Law* (Oxford University Press, 2nd ed, 2014) ch 7. They also provide a useful description of the application of these institutional oversight mechanisms in the Australian context.

165. 'Integrity agencies' is the term employed by Levi-Faur, 'Regulation and Regulatory Governance', above n 49, 13. McCubbins, Noll and Weingast refer to them as 'police-patrols' in McCubbins, Noll and Weingast, 'Administrative Procedures as Instruments of Political Control', above n 60.

166. McCubbins, Noll and Weingast, 'Administrative Procedures as Instruments of Political Control', above n 60.

167. These benefits and risks have been discussed in several places already. See, e.g., Regulatory Regimes (Chapter 4, 74–5); and Participation (Chapter 5, 86–90).

168. Knill and Tosun, *Public Policy*, above n 139, 165.

169. Carrigan and Poole, 'Structuring Regulators', above n 144, 11.

170. While a new regulator is likely to have little or no say over its original structure, it is likely to be consulted on, and therefore have some influence over, subsequent structural decisions.

171. Eugene Bardach and Eric M Patashnik, *A Practical Guide to Policy Analysis: The Eightfold Path to More Effective Problem Solving* (Sage, 5th ed, 2016) 21.

172. See Chapter 5, 79–81 for a discussion of bounded rationality.

173. Karl E Weick, *Sensemaking in Organizations* (Sage Publications, 1995) 55–61.

174. Dewetz, as far back as 1969, warned of the dangers of 'implicitly presenting the relevant choice as between an ideal norm and an existing "imperfect" institutional arrangement' in Harold Dewetz, 'Information and Efficiency: Another Viewpoint' (1969) 12 *Journal of Law and Economics* 1, 1.

175. P N Grabosky, 'Counterproductive Regulation' (1995) 23 *International Journal of the Sociology of Law* 347, 364.

176. Feldman, 'Five Models of Regulatory Compliance Motivation', above n 69.

177. How regulators might choose to speak with many voices is discussed under 'Regulatory Style' in Chapter 10.

178. Malcolm K Sparrow, *The Regulatory Craft: Controlling Risks, Solving Problems, and Managing Compliance* (Brookings Institution Press, 2000) 135.

179. See the discussion of incrementalism in Chapter 5, 81–2.

180. Sparrow, *The Regulatory Craft*, above n 178, 151.

181. See the discussion of regulatory failure in Chapter 6, 100–8.

182. Numerous different labels are used to describe these processes. They include 'policy transfer', 'lesson drawing', 'policy learning' 'and 'policy diffusion', to name but a few. See generally: Giandomenico Majone, 'Cross-National Sources of Regulatory Policymaking in Europe and the United States' (1991) 11 *Journal of Public Policy* 79; Richard Rose, 'What Is Lesson-Drawing?' (1991) 11 *Journal of Public Policy* 3; Peter J May, 'Policy Learning and Failure' (1992) 12 *Journal of Public Policy* 331; David P Dolowitz and David Marsh, 'Learning from Abroad: The Role of Policy Transfer in Contemporary Policy-Making' (2000) 13 *Governance* 5, 17–20; Fabrizio Gilardi, 'Who Learns from What in Policy Diffusion Processes?' (2010) 54 *American Journal of Political Science* 650.

183. Dolowitz and Marsh, 'Learning from Abroad', above n 182, 17–20.

184. For an overview of brainstorming (and like) techniques, see Michael Michalko, *Cracking Creativity: The Secrets of Creative Genius* (Ten Speed Press, 2001) ch 9; William N Dunn, *Public Policy Analysis: An Introduction* (Pearson, 4th ed, 2008) 107–15. For an overview of foresight and forward looking tools, see European Commission, 'Towards Standards in Forward Looking Activities for the EC' (Policy Brief No 14, European Forum on Forward Looking Activities) <http://ec.europa.eu/research/innovation-union/pdf/expert-groups/effla-reports/effla_pb_14_-_towards_a_foresight_standard.pdf>.
185. See discussion of participatory process in Chapter 5, 86–90.
186. Neil Gunningham, 'Compliance, Enforcement and Regulatory Excellence' (Paper prepared for the Penn Program on Regulation's Best-in-Class Regulator Initiative, June 2015) 11.

9 Decide

Regime Assessment and Selection

This chapter examines the decide stage of the regulatory policy cycle. The decide stage refers to the processes by which the regulatory regime to be implemented is selected. Two schools of thought dominate debate about how regulatory options are (or maybe more to the point, should be) selected: the technical rationalist school, for whom regime selection should be a systematic, analytical and evidence-based process of choosing the best option employing technical calculation methods such as cost-benefit and multi-criteria analyses; and the political rationalist school, for whom regime selection is a political process of consensus and coalition building employing political calculation methods of consultation, deliberation and negotiation. This chapter begins by examining the technical rationalist model of regime selection, after which the politically rational approach is discussed. The chapter concludes that while regime selection has both a technical and political component, politics is the master, and technical analysis the servant. The implications of this for the next stage of the regulatory policy cycle—regime implementation—are then discussed.

Technically Rational Regime Selection

Technically rational decision-making refers to the use of systematic, analytical and evidence-based processes for selecting among different courses of action. In a technically rational world, the positive and negative effects of alternative courses of action are compared, and the course of action with the highest net benefit is chosen. Technically rational decision-making is the approach advocated by better regulation reforms, and the regulatory impact assessment (RIA) is the instrument most commonly associated with those reforms.[1]

Regulatory Impact Assessments

RIAs require proponents of new regulation to systematically and critically assess the positive and negative effects of a range of regulatory options and to recommend the option with the greatest net societal benefit. Most jurisdictions with modern economies have detailed policies and procedures to guide regulatory policy analysts through the assessment process.[2] It is not the purpose of this chapter to replicate this guidance or to attempt to develop a consolidated ideal. Rather, this section's focus is on both explaining and critiquing the approach: identifying its main components, strengths and weaknesses, and issues which persons not familiar with them should be aware.

The core element of a RIA is the use of technical analytical methods to assess each option's net societal benefit. A review of different jurisdictional RIA guides reveals the use of different analytical methods. These include cost-benefit analysis, multi-criteria analysis, cost-effectiveness analysis and least-cost analysis.[3] Of these, the two most prominent are cost-benefit analysis and multi-criteria analysis.

Cost-benefit analysis is the analytical technique most commonly associated with RIAs. A cost-benefit analysis monetises the costs and benefits of each regulatory option and recommends the option with the greatest net monetary value. Cost-benefit analyses' main advantage is their use of a common unit of measurement (monetary value) to measure costs and benefits and compare alternative options. However, they have several limitations. First among these is the dubious assumption that intangibles such as health, safety, security and human rights can be measured in monetary terms. While economists have developed several methods to value these intangibles— including placing a statistical value on a human life—these measures are far from perfect, and can vary significantly depending on the methodology employed.[4] Second is its disregard of distributional effects. Cost-benefit analysis places economic efficiency (measured in terms of wealth maximisation) above all other values.[5] However, recommending the option with the greatest net benefit says nothing about whether that benefit is fairly, equitably or justly distributed. And third, measuring and monetising costs and benefits is an estimation process, not an exact science. The objectivity of the top line measure masks the subjectivity of many of its parameters and underlying assumptions. These include the hypotheses upon which intangibles such as health, safety and security are monetised (which often are based on preference based studies of people's willingness to pay money to acquire those intangibles and predicted behavioural responses to proposed regulatory instruments); business estimates of the costs to them of complying with regulatory requirements (which estimates, it has been observed, can be exaggerated); and the period over which benefits are calculated and the rate at which future benefits are discounted (the longer the period and the lower the rate, the greater the net benefit).[6] Cost-benefit analyses also are criticised for not being truly participatory. Consultation as part of a cost-benefit analysis tends to focus on collecting information from affected parties about the costs and benefits of regime components, rather than generating a genuine dialogue about the nature of the issue, regulatory objectives and the merits of alternative options for achieving those objectives.[7]

The limitations inherent in the use of cost-benefit analyses has led to them being used less frequently, and to multi-criteria analyses being used more frequently.[8] Multi-criteria analysis is an analytical technique that assesses regulatory options against a number of different criteria. The standard procedure for conducting a multi-criteria analysis consists of three steps: (1) identifying the criteria against which the regulatory option should be assessed and weighting them according to their relative importance; (2) scoring each option against those criteria; and (3) summing those scores, and selecting the option with the highest score. Multi-criteria analyses enjoy a number of advantages over cost-benefit analyses. First, they do not rely on monetisation for their efficacy. They enable regulatory effects to be measured and assessed both qualitatively and quantitatively. This is especially valuable with respect to intangibles such as health, safety and security. Second, they allow for a wide range of criteria to be employed beyond just efficiency. The weighting and scoring processes in particular enable consideration of the distributional effects of the options to be considered, and for the options effects on a broad range of social and democratic values to be taken into account, including social cohesion, fairness, equity, justice and human rights. Third, the weighing process allows for a more nuanced analysis by recognising that some impacts may be more important than others: for example, that the impact on small businesses may be more important than the impact on large businesses; and that the impact on individual health and welfare may be more important than the impact on trade and investment. And fourth, multi-criteria analyses facilitate more meaningful participation. The process of selecting, weighing and scoring the criteria lends itself to thicker forms of dialogue and to an exchange of ideas and perspectives than does the one-way transmission of cost-benefit data.

Like all regulatory processes, RIAs have their strengths and weaknesses.[9] A RIA's strength lies in combining analytical methods with participatory processes.[10] The use of analytical methods provides structure and injects discipline into the decision-making process, ensuring the positives (benefits) and negatives (costs) of each option are considered. They also encourage evidence-based policy-making and reduce the role of intuition and ideology.[11] By standardising the decision-making process, RIAs facilitate consistent decision-making. They also can improve transparency by making their assessments of the advantages and disadvantages of different regulatory options public, and accountability by making governments respond to those public assessments.[12] And the use of participatory processes both informs the technical analysis and provides affected parties with a degree of procedural fairness which enhances the legitimacy of the process and the regime it recommends, thereby building support for its effective implementation.

As for RIAs' weaknesses, many of the more commonly heard criticisms relate more to cost-benefit analyses than they do to RIAs *per se.* This is unfortunate given the increasing prominence of alternative analytical methods such as multi-criteria analyses. However, even RIAs employing multi-criteria analytical techniques can fail to live up to their promise. First, RIAs often fail properly to consider a broad range of realistic regulatory options. We already have examined one reason for this—that the organisational, disciplinary and personal biases of those responsible for generating options can see them tread well-worn institutional paths, and restrict themselves to instruments with which they are familiar and comfortable.[13] Another reason is that RIAs generally are triggered at the legislative or rule-making stage. By this stage, the government usually has publically committed itself to a particular approach and considered and rejected any alternatives. This can lead to criticisms that RIAs are expensive public relations processes to justify decisions already made.[14] Second, while RIAs utilising multi-criteria analysis employ both quantitative and qualitative measures, the quantitative (that usually relate to costs) can tend to dominate the qualitative (that usually relate to benefits), with the result that, in practice, costs are overestimated, benefits underestimated and unquantified values 'often forgotten, or even denigrated, once all the numbers have been crunched'.[15]

Third, those conducting RIAs can tend to assume perfect (or near perfect) implementation. This can have the opposite effect to that observed above, namely, that benefits can be overstated and costs understated. As Baldwin, Cave and Lodge observe, '[a]ny analysis of the need to regulate will be skewed if it is assumed that regulatory techniques will operate perfectly'.[16] RIAs conducted by the same persons who developed the options being assessed are particularly susceptible to this. Those designing regime options can be over-confident, over-enthusiastic and over-estimate the effectiveness and robustness of the design options they are proposing, and may be unable to see weaknesses and potential causes of failure. They also can be blind to and biased against ideas generated elsewhere and that are unfamiliar to them. It is therefore important that safeguards are included in the decision-making process to guard against these biases undermining the process. We have already touched on some of these safeguards in our discussion of anti-bias processes in the context of issue diagnosis.[17] Other safeguards can be found in the system oversight mechanisms that form part of many better regulation reforms, such as requirements that RIAs be vetted and signed off by a central unit.[18] RIAs also should be conducted by persons independent from the option designers, and from those who may be asked to implement the final regime option (lest those persons succumb to the temptation to choose the option that advances their organisational or personal interests). Grabosky goes even further and argues for an 'institutional sceptic, whose role it is to pose the hard questions'.[19]

Fourth, RIAs are costly and time consuming to do well. They require both skilled analysts and high quality data. The analytical methods employed, and the rigour with which they are employed, should match the complexity, size and scale of the issue, and the size, scale and permanency of any solution. The more difficult it is to adjust a solution, or to alter course once set, the more robust should be the assessment and selection process.[20] Unfortunately, however, political imperatives of speed over process can sometimes result in RIAs being conducted without the time and resources needed to carefully assess each option.

This brings us to the fifth weakness—that RIAs can be sacrificed for political expediency. Many guidelines allow for RIAs to be dispensed with or abridged in exceptional circumstances. Originally designed to cater for situations of genuine urgency when there is no time to develop and carefully assess multiple options, the exceptional circumstance exemption also can be used to shield governments from RIAs that could be politically embarrassing. Australian Governments, for example, have employed the exceptional circumstances exemption to shield policies implementing election promises from scrutiny. The most notable of these was the refusal of the Labor Government in 2009 to submit its A\$43 billion proposal to build a national broadband network to a RIA.[21]

And even when conducted, RIAs are subject to 'political adjustment'. We have observed that an RIA is an estimation process heavily dependent on its methodology, assumptions and parameters. These usually are set in conjunction with the government agency commissioning it. It should therefore not be surprising that they tend to produce results supportive of the commissioning government's policy direction. An example on point are the duelling RIAs produced to support and critique the harmonisation of Australia's workplace health and safety laws. The RIA produced by the Australian Government (the proponent of the laws) estimated a net annual benefit *nationally* of A\$753 million with a one-off transition cost of A\$875 million; whereas the RIA commissioned by the Victorian Government (a critic of the laws) estimated a cost to business in that *one state* of A\$3.4 billion over five years.[22] This example reinforces the political context in which RIAs are conducted. However, the use of technically rational processes can mask these political considerations. For this reason alone, RIAs should be approached with an appropriate level of skepticism. It also is a reason why the RIA process should be subject to some form of central oversight mechanism to guard against (or at least make transparent) some of the more glaring instances of 'political adjustment'.

While RIAs frequently fall short of the ideal, they nevertheless can be useful inputs into decision-making processes. However, they should be used cognisant of their limitations. Several of these limitations relate to the ability of political considerations to compromise the technical rationality that some herald as the RIA's defining feature. This brings us to the second school of thought.

Politically Rational Regime Selection

The political rationalist school of thought sees regime selection taking place through political calculation methods such as consultation, deliberation and negotiation. The objective of these methods is not to identify the 'best' solution, but to build a sufficiently broad coalition in support of an option that enables government to move forward in the direction of that solution.

Viewed in this way, politically rational regime selection shares much in common with Lindblom's 'muddling through', where the need for political consensus and agreement is paramount, and progress is achieved through a process of mutual adjustment and negotiation.[23]

Politically rational decision-making processes place great importance on understanding the logic of the political environment in which decisions are made. This includes not only the institutions of government and the bureaucracy, but also the processes through which interest groups are given voice and consensus is built, and the social, economic, political and ideological forces that operate upon them.[24] Hood, Rothstein and Baldwin, for example, suggest that risk regulation regimes are shaped by three main contextual forces (that reflect three of the key regulatory theories discussed in Chapter 3), namely: 'market-failure' pressures for governments in liberal-capitalist societies to adopt proportionate responses to correct serious failures in markets; 'opinion-responsive' pressures for liberal-democratic governments to respond to general public opinion; and 'interest-driven' pressures for governments to respond to organised interest groups.[25] They also describe the latter force as the issue's politics, as it reflects the distribution of power among groups interested in the issue. These three forces have strong parallels with Haines' three risk dimensions that she argues determines the shape of government action, namely: actuarial risk that is calculated using technically rational analytical methods, socio-cultural risk that reflects societal perceptions of risk and political risk to a government's prospects of re-election.[26] Haines associates political risk with failing to regulate consistent with socio-cultural risk. However, it also could arise from regulating contrary to the interests of groups with resources capable of being mobilised at an election. It also will be recalled that Haines observed that of the three risks (or pressures for change), it was the technically rational actuarial risk that was most often compromised to better manage socio-cultural and political risks.

These forces are not exhaustive. Others factors also may influence regime shape. Hood, Rothstein and Baldwin (again consistent with the key regulatory theories discussed in Chapter 3) give as examples 'ideas' and the advocates of those ideas, and the significant role played by institutional forces and processes which they describe as forming a 'barrier or membrane' between contextual factors and regime design.[27] Political and ideological considerations internal to the body (or bodies) involved in choosing the design of the regime also can be important. We have observed that different government organisations (and different functional and disciplinary units within an organisation) have their own way of seeing the world.[28] Those charged with conducting the RIA may see the issue and its solution very differently from those engaged with the day-to-day management of the issue, and with the central unit that may be required to vet and sign-off on the RIA. In these situations, the final regime shape is likely to be influenced by the relative ability (politically and administratively) of these organisations (or units within organisations) to control or influence the design selection process.[29]

What is needed is a tool that can assist government decision-makers to align these forces and to fashion a regulatory policy and regime with sufficient political support for its adoption and implementation. It is to such a tool that we now turn.

Explanation-Based Assessments

Explanation-based decision-making argues that in practice, options are assessed against the cogency of the explanation in support of it, and that the option chosen is the one with the most compelling explanation.[30] But compelling to whom? The theory as normally espoused says the explanation must be convincing to the ultimate decision-maker. But in the context in which we are examining the application of the theory, what is required is a platform from which government can elicit the political support of those whose active engagement in policy development and implementation is needed, or at least to quieten or soften the voices of the harshest critics.[31] These persons comprise the legitimacy communities explored in Chapter 6: the regulatees; the persons for whose benefit the regulatees are being regulated; those whose active participation and resources are required to regulate effectively; and those whose support is important for the regulator to secure and maintain the resources and authority needed to discharge its regulatory mission.[32] And especially important amongst these communities are actors with 'veto' power—the 'players' and 'context-setters' whose level of influence (political or practical) is such that progress cannot be achieved without their support.[33] A compelling explanation provides the platform from which to build political support among these communities and actors.

So what makes an explanation compelling? Three factors are particularly influential. First is the evidence in support of the explanation. This would include the technical calculations made as part of the RIA. Explanation-based assessments thus incorporate rather than replace RIAs. Second is the strength of the intervention logic—the clarity, consistency and coherence with which the option's proposed interventions address the issue's causal drivers. And third is how the option is framed. We discussed framing in Chapter 7 in the context of agenda-setting.[34] The same principles apply here. The strength of an explanation is determined (in part) by the labels used to describe it. Pollitt and Hupe, for example, refer to 'magic concepts of government' that have the ability to dilute and obscure differences and conflicting interests and assist governments to form coalitions across traditional ideological divides.[35] 'Harmonisation' is an example of such a concept. After all, who does not want more harmony?[36] Describing the option using dimensions that resonate with the target audience also is important. Often the most salient dimensions are found in the non-quantifiable benefits and values frequently devalued in the RIA process, such as safety and security, social cohesion and the protection of fundamental rights. And finally there is the story. Evidence is more persuasive and compelling when presented in story form.[37] But the story is more than facts and figures logically presented. It is the plot line that gives them meaning. The strength of a story lies in its ability to take the logical and causal and make it motivational and persuasive: to explain what is happening, why it needs to be addressed and, critically in the present context, what might be done going forward to improve the situation. And the more coherent and compelling the story attached to an option, the more likely that option will be selected.

If, as has been suggested here, the goal of politically rational decision-making is not to select the best solution, but to build sufficient political support to move forward in the direction of that solution, then what is important is for the explanation to speak to many audiences (legitimacy communities). In this regard, it is important to remember that each explanation—and, in particular, the intervention logic and story attached to it—will manifest a different set of causal mechanisms and relationships, and will emphasise different causal consequences. Those impacted by the options will ascribe different meanings to each option and explanation according to their goals, interests and values. The goal is to construct an explanation into which each audience (community; interest group) can read the delivery of their objectives and aspirations, and which each can interpret positively as favouring the positions they advocate. Of course, no one explanation (and therefore option) is likely to resonate equally with all audiences. Balances will need to be struck and compromises made to fashion an option with an explanation that resonates with enough people that a sufficiently broad coalition in support of that option can be built. As such, the use of explanation-based assessments is iterative and dynamic, as is the case with all negotiations. Options and explanations evolve and adapt in a symbiotic relationship. Government decision-makers consult and negotiate with relevant communities to explore different explanations and options upon which consensus and agreement may be built. Explanations are continually refined and adapted to appeal to a sufficiently broad audience, and options are continually adjusted to match those explanations. At the end of the day, decision-makers choose the option that best fits the explanation that enables a sufficiently broad coalition in support of that option to be forged. Viewed this way, political rationality is not so much a process of selecting an option from amongst those generated previously, but a process of fashioning a regime by adjusting, refining and in some cases, combining elements of those options to garner sufficient political support to enable government to progress with it.

Concluding Insights and Implications

This chapter has explored the processes by which the regulatory regime to be implemented is selected. Two approaches have been examined: the technically rational approach that relies predominately on systematic, analytical and evidence-based processes and technical calculation methods; and the politically rational approach that relies predominately on political processes of consensus and coalition building and political calculation methods of consultation, deliberation and negotiation. The chapter also introduced the concept of explanation-based assessments. Assessing options by reference to the cogency of their explanation brings technical and political rationality together. Explanation-based assessments recognise that the option must be capable of achieving the regulatory objective, and that analytical techniques such as RIAs and intervention logics are important inputs. However, explanation-based assessments also recognise that obtaining the political consensus and agreement necessary to move forward involves building coalitions made up of groups with different values, interests and perspectives, and that constructing an explanation that simultaneously speaks to those different values, interests and perspectives is crucial. As Edelman observed many years ago, the language used to communicate a policy can be just as important as its substance.[38]

It is clear from this discussion that both technically rational and politically rational approaches have their role, and both need each other. Technique without politics is naïve; and politics without technique is a mess.[39] And while Birkland is correct that policy initiatives are designed 'both through technical analysis and through the political process, to achieve a particular goal',[40] what also is clear is that of the two approaches, politics is the master and technical analysis the servant.[41] This observation has three important implications for regime implementation.

First, the output from this stage comprises both the technical specification of the chosen regime design and the political agreements and understandings made to forge consensus for its adoption. The technical specification should clearly articulate the key elements of the regulatory regime to be implemented: who will be the regulators; whom will be regulated; to what standards; and through which behaviour change mechanisms, instruments and institutional arrangements. The specification also should clearly articulate the regime's intervention logic (how the elements of the initiative address the issue's causal drivers), and the operational objectives linked to the intervention logic. Unlike the primary or high-level objectives set in conjunction with the issue's diagnosis, operational objectives generally are defined in terms of the intervention's deliverables and outputs, and the behaviour changes required to be seen for the primary regulatory objective to be realised.[42]

The agreements and understandings made to forge the political consensus needed to move forward with the selected regime are no less important. Disappointing these agreements and understandings, and the expectations they create, can be a source of implementation failure just as much as failing to deliver the regime's technical components. Disappointing them can lead actors to withdraw their support and resources or otherwise act in a manner that undermines achievement of the regulatory objectives. Both the technical specifications and the political agreements and understandings need to be communicated to those responsible for implementing the regime.

Second, the regulatory regime that emerges from this stage is likely to be sub-optimal. We have observed that our rationality is bounded: that our ability to gather and process the information necessary to rank and choose the best or optimal solution from among competing policy options is restricted by our organisational environment (e.g. time, resource and information constraints) and the cognitive biases under which we operate. This, Simon tells us, can lead regulatory designers to 'satisfice'—to adopt the course of action that is 'good enough' from the limited options available.[43] And the efficacy of this 'satisficing' regime may be impacted by the compromises made to obtain the political consensus and agreement to move forward. As Grabosky reminds us, '[c]ompromises, so often the lubricant of policy making in a democracy, gives rise to contradiction and neutralization'.[44]

And third, the regime is likely to be fragile. As difficult as it may be to obtain consensus, it can be equally difficult to maintain it. The compromises struck to achieve progress may prove to be illusory; the contradictions and neutralisation they create debilitating. The labels and stories employed to frame the selected option more often mask than resolve policy differences. Eventually one must move from the abstraction of labels and stories to the details of processes and programs—which is where the oft-quoted proverb warns us the devil resides. At this point the compromises that enabled different groups to come together in support of an option may became a potential source of conflict when those groups are confronted with the nature and extent of their differences. This leaves the regime vulnerable to the pressure which these groups can bring to re-litigate those aspects of the regime with which they disagree.

All of this means the option selected is unlikely to be the final regime model, and that politicians, policy-makers and regulators need to be prepared to make adjustments as new and better information comes to hand and the inability of the regime simultaneously to meet all expectations becomes evident. Indeed, it can be prudent to include a post-implementation review (say, one year down the track) as part of the implementation plan— which brings us to the next stage of the regulatory policy cycle.

Notes

1. It sometimes also is referred to as a regulatory impact analysis (also RIA), or just an impact analysis (IA). RIAs became vogue during the deregulation era of the 1980s having been championed by the Reagan administration in the United States, and at the time were perceived to have an anti-regulatory bias. Their use has not slowed the growth of regulation however, leading Revesz and Livermore to conclude that any anti-regulatory bias is 'historical rather than conceptual': Richard L Revesz and Michael A Livermore, *Retaking Rationality: How Cost-Benefit Analysis Can Better Protect the Environment and Our Health* (Oxford University Press, 2008) 10.
2. See, e.g., *EU*: European Commission, 'Better Regulation "Toolbox"' (EC, 2016); *United Kingdom*: UK Department of Business, Energy and Industrial Strategy, 'Regulatory Impact Assessments: Guidance for Government Departments and

Business Regulation' (June 2016); *United States*: Executive Order 12866, *Regulatory Planning and Review*, 58 Fed Reg 51735 (30 September 1993) and Executive Order 13563, 3 C.F.R. 3821, *Improving Regulation and Regulatory Review* (18 January 2011); *Australia*: Department of the Prime Minister and Cabinet, 'The Australian Government Guide to Regulation' (March 2014) and Council of Australian Governments, 'Best Practice Regulation: A Guide for Ministerial Councils and National Standard Setting Bodies' (October 2007). For an overview of RIA policies and guidance in a range of OECD countries, see Rex Deighton-Smith, Angelo Erbacci and Celine Kauffmann, 'Promoting Inclusive Growth through Better Regulation: The Role of Regulatory Impact Assessment' (OECD Regulatory Policy Working Papers No 3, OECD Publishing, 2016). See also the collection of essays in Claire A Dunlop and Claudio M Radaelli (eds), *Handbook of Regulatory Impact Assessment* (Edward Elgar, 2016).

3. For an overview of these (and other) analytical methods, see European Commission, 'Better Regulation "Toolbox"', 380–3 (Tool 55: Using Analytical Methods to Compare Options or Assess Performance).

4. See generally Frank Ackerman and Lisa Heinzerling, *Priceless: On Knowing the Price of Everything and the Value of Nothing* (New Press, 2004). For a discussion of the merits and criticisms of methods for valuing a statistical life, see: W Kip Viscusi, 'The Devaluation of Life' (2009) 3 *Regulation & Governance* 103; Marion Fourcade, 'The Political Valuation of Life' (2009) 3 *Regulation & Governance* 291.

5. Economists generally work with two concepts of economic efficiency—Pareto efficiency and Kaldor-Hicks efficiency: C G Veljanovski, *Economic Principles of Law* (Cambridge University Press, 2007) 32–3. A policy is Pareto efficient if 'all parties benefit, or none is harmed, by a reallocation of resources, goods, or assets, or a change in the law', and it is Kaldor-Hicks efficient 'if those that gain can in principle compensate those that have been "harmed" and still be better off'. Kaldor-Hicks efficiency provides the theoretical underpinning for cost-benefit analysis. It focuses on utilitarian wealth maximisation and is not concerned with individual justice and fairness.

6. See Eric Windholz, 'Revisiting the COAG Case for OHS Harmonisation' (2013) 5 *Journal of Health and Safety, Research and Practice* 9–16.

7. Ciara Brown and Colin Scott, 'Regulation, Public Law, and Better Regulation' (2011) *European Public Law* 467, 475–83. Participation is discussed in more detail in Chapter 5, 86–90.

8. European Commission, 'Better Regulation "Toolbox"' (EC, 2016) 381. See also Deighton-Smith, Erbacci and Kauffmann, 'Promoting Inclusive Growth through Better Regulation', above n 2.

9. For a detailed examination of these strengths and weaknesses, see generally: Robert Baldwin, Martin Cave and Martin Lodge, *Understanding Regulation: Theory, Strategy, and Practice* (Oxford University Press, 2nd ed, 2012) ch 15; Robert W Hahn, *In Defense of the Economic Analysis of Regulation* (AEI-Brookings Joint Center for Regulatory Studies, 2005); Frank Ackerman and Lisa Heinzerling, 'Pricing the Priceless: Cost-Benefit Analysis of Environmental Protection' (2002) 150 *University of Pennsylvania Law Review* 1553.

10. Brown and Scott, 'Regulation, Public Law, and Better Regulation', above n 7.

11. Revesz and Livermore, *Retaking Rationality*, above n 1.

12. Cass R Sunstein, *Risk and Reasons: Safety, Law, and the Environment* (Cambridge University Press, 2002) 35.

13. For a discussion of 'poor design', see Chapter 6, 103–4.

14. Brown and Scott, 'Regulation, Public Law, and Better Regulation', above n 7, 481–2; Windholz, 'Revisiting the COAG Case', above n 6, 11; Ackerman and

Heinzerling, 'Pricing the Priceless', above n 9, 1577; Christopher Carrigan and Stuart Shapiro, 'What's Wrong with the Back of the Envelope? A Call for Simple (and Timely) Benefit-Cost Analysis' 10 *Regulation & Governance* [first published 26 April 2016; DOI: 10.1111/rego.12120; print edition forthcoming].

15. Ackerman and Heinzerling, 'Pricing the Priceless', above n 9, 1579. See also Hahn, *In Defense of the Economic Analysis of Regulation*, above n 9, 11–13.
16. Baldwin, Cave and Lodge, *Understanding Regulation*, above n 9, 23.
17. See 'Issue Confirmation' in Chapter 7, 144–5.
18. See 'System Oversight' in Chapter 6, 110–11.
19. P N Grabosky, 'Counterproductive Regulation' (1995) 23 *International Journal of the Sociology of Law* 347, 362.
20. European Commission, 'Better Regulation "Toolbox"' (EC, 2016) 54–5 (Tool 9: How to Undertake a Proportionate IA).
21. Kevin Morgan, 'Australia's NBN: Come Hell or High Water' (2012) 19 *Agenda: A Journal of Policy Analysis and Reform* 69.
22. Windholz, 'Revisiting the COAG Case', above n 6, 10–1.
23. See Chapter 5, 81–2.
24. This is similar to Kingdon's political stream discussed in Chapter 5, 82–3.
25. Christopher Hood, Henry Rothstein and Robert Baldwin, *The Government of Risk: Understanding Risk Regulation Regimes* (Oxford University Press, 2001) ch 4.
26. See discussion in Chapter 3, 39–41.
27. Hood, Rothstein and Baldwin, *The Government of Risk*, above n 25, 68–9.
28. See Chapter 6, 102.
29. Robert Baldwin, *Rules and Government* (Clarendon Press, 1995) 167–74.
30. See, e.g., Nancy Pennington and Reid T Hastie, 'A Theory of Explanation-Based Decision Making' in G A Klein et al (eds), *Decision Making in Action: Models and Methods* (Ablex, 1993) 188; David H Jonassen, *Learning to Solve Problems: A Handbook for Designing Problem-Solving Learning Environments* (Routledge, 2011) 64–71.
31. Murray Edelman, *The Symbolic Uses of Politics* (University of Illinois Press, 1964) 114; Murray Edelman, *Politics as Symbolic Action: Mass Arousal & Quiescence* (Institute for Research on Poverty, 1971) 70.
32. See discussion in Chapter 6, 112–13.
33. See discussion in Chapter 7, 140.
34. See Chapter 7, 132–3.
35. Christopher Pollitt and John Hupe, 'Talking about Government: The Role of Magic Concepts' (2011) 13 *Public Management Review* 641.
36. Eric Windholz and Graeme Hodge, 'The Magic of Harmonisation: A Case Study of Occupational Health and Safety in Australia' (2012) 34 *Asia Pacific Journal of Public Administration* 137; Pollitt and Hupe, 'Talking about Government', above n 35, also give 'accountability' and 'governance' as examples.
37. Nancy Pennington and Reid Hastie, 'Evidence Evaluation in Complex Decision Making' (1986) 51 *Journal of Personality and Social Psychology* 242; Nancy Pennington and Reid Hastie, 'Explaining the Evidence: Test of the Story Model for Juror Decision Making' (1992) 62 *Journal of Personality and Social Psychology* 189; David A Rettinger and Reid Hastie, 'Content Effects of Decision Making' (2001) 85 *Organizational Behaviour and Human Decision Processes* 336.
38. Murray Edelman, *Political Language: Words That Succeed and Policies That Fail* (Academic Press, 1977).
39. Adapting the maxim attributed to Law Professor Karl Llewellyn that 'technique without morals is a menace; but morals without technique is a mess' cited by

Cass R Sunstein, *Conspiracy Theories and Other Dangerous Ideas* (Simon and Schuster, 2014) 153.

40. Thomas A Birkland, *An Introduction to the Policy Process: Theories, Concepts, and Models of Public Policy Making* (Routledge, 4th ed, 2016) 299.

41. Beryl A Radin, *Beyond Machiavelli: Policy Analysis Reaches Midlife* (Georgetown University Press, 2nd ed, 2013) 125.

42. These objectives also should be S.M.A.R.T. (specific; measurable; achievable; relevant; and time-bound. See Chapter 7, 145–6.

43. See the discussion of bounded rationality in Chapter 5, 79–81.

44. Grabosky, 'Counterproductive Regulation', above n 19, 360.

10 Implement
Regime Deployment, Application and Execution

Implementation, simply put, is the carrying out of the regulatory policy. However, implementation is far from simple. Effective implementation involves carrying out a variety of different and complex functions in a strategic and coordinated manner. These functions fall into two broad groups. The first is regime deployment, which involves putting in place the legislative, administrative, governance and organisational arrangements required to get the regime to a point where it is ready to be operationalised. The second is regime application, which involves operationalising the regime to modify behaviours to achieve the regulatory objectives. Regime application, in turn, involves undertaking the core tasks expected of a regulator, setting the overall regulatory strategy to govern how those tasks are to be undertaken and the 'street level' execution of that strategy. As with other aspects of the regulatory endeavour, there is no one-size-fits-all model for implementing regulation. Differences in the regime's technical specifications and associated political agreements and understandings (the outputs of the decide stage) will lead to different implementation approaches and strategies. Differences in implementation also can arise from differences in the economic, social, cultural and political environments in which the regime will operate. These differences can impact the resources available to the regulator, the level of cooperation that can be expected from actors within the regulatory space and the motivation and preparedness of regulatees to change their behaviour to meet the regulatory standards set for them. Because of these differences, this chapter focuses on key issues relevant to the implementation of all regulatory regimes (irrespective of size, scope and structure), some of the more prominent strategic approaches for applying regulation and principles that should guide their application. First, though, it is necessary to make a preliminary comment about the manner with which regulators should approach the implementation stage.

Open and Inclusive Participatory Processes

This book examines implementation through a predominately state-centric top-down lens. This is consistent with the book's conception of regulation being undertaken by or under the auspices of government, and of regulatory regimes being coordinated by a government regulator. It also is consistent with the empirical literature that finds implementation tends to be hierarchical, with directions flowing downward through a chain of delegation.[1] This is not to say that implementation is always or exclusively hierarchical. In co- and poly-centric regulatory regimes, with multiple regulators and other persons providing resources and support to the regulatory endeavour, effective regulatory implementation necessarily requires partnering with these persons. This is particularly valuable in situations where disagreement about the nature of the issue, ambiguity with respect to the regulatory objectives and differences about the means for achieving those objectives remain.[2] These disagreements, ambiguities and differences can derail or at least slow implementation. An inclusive implementation process can assist to find common ground, identify potential risks and pitfalls and chart better implementation paths.[3] However, including actors with different values, interests and perspectives in the implementation process risks the implementation stage becoming a contested, negotiated and political process. Those dissatisfied with the regulatory policy, its objectives or means are apt to use their participation in the implementation stage as an opportunity to renegotiate and modify the regulatory policy and its objectives. A number of studies have found that significant deviations from policy objectives can occur during the implementation stage.[4] The expectations, participation and input of these actors therefore needs to be carefully managed through the implementation process to guard against this risk.

Regime Deployment

Regime deployment is about making the regulatory policy and the chosen regulatory regime 'operationable'. There are three main components to regime deployment: formally transposing the policy into the tangible form, putting in place appropriate governance arrangements and developing the regulator's organisational capability, capacity and culture.

Formal Transposition

Formally transposing the regulatory policy into tangible form involves three main activities. The first activity is drafting and enacting legislation to provide the legal framework for the regulatory activities. The mechanics of this activity will vary with each jurisdiction's legal, legislative and constitutional rules, norms and practices. The activity includes legislating the regulatory standards and, depending on the policy and regime, creating a new regulatory agency and conferring on it all the vestiges of a separate (possibly legal) identity, or expanding the functions of an existing agency. It also includes conferring on the agency the legislative powers, privileges and discretions necessary to perform the functions assigned to it. These commonly include legal powers to enter, search and seize; to inspect documents and question witnesses; to licence certain activities; to issue prohibition or improvement notices; and to sanction non-compliance though fines, injunctions, enforceable undertakings and corrective advertising, for example. They also should include powers necessary to undertake less coercive behaviour change mechanisms, including to provide grants, information and other forms of assistance.

The second activity is putting in place the core systems and infrastructure required for the regulator to function (assuming a new regulator is being established). This includes the physical infrastructure and resources needed for the regulator to function (e.g. premises, furniture, computers, consumables, etc.), and establishing finance, human resources, information management and other administrative systems. This activity is relatively straightforward and does not differ significantly from what is required when establishing any new organisation.

A more complicated and context specific activity is determining the regulator's internal structure. This is the third activity. In the field of organisational and management studies, the traditional view was that 'structure follows strategy'—that is, the strategy chosen by the organisation determines its organisational structure.[5] More modern theories, however, recognise that the relationship between structure and strategy is more complex and iterative, and that in some situations structure follows strategy and in others, strategy follows structure.[6] In this regard, it is important to keep in mind that 'structure' is not limited to the creation of administrative and functional units, but extends to the lines of authority, communication and information flows through and between those units. The flow of information is central to strategy development, as are the functional, disciplinary and organisational perspectives brought to the task, and the distribution of decision-making authority. Each of these structural choices constrains and shapes future strategic choices. And at the point of initial organisational creation—when many strategic choices remain to be made—their impact is likely to be even more profound.

So what are the structural choices available to a new regulator? A review of how regulators structure themselves identifies a number of common dimensions. These include structuring by regulatory task (e.g. some regulators may have an information and education branch; a support and assistance branch; a licensing and authorisation branch; and an enforcement and prosecution branch); functionally (e.g. some regulators will have a data analytic branch; a marketing and communications branch; a scientific branch; a program development and problem-solving branch; an enforcement branch; and a legal branch); geographically (e.g. by region); by issue (e.g. an environmental regulator may organise itself around the areas of the environment for which it is responsible such as land, water and air; and a workplace health and safety regulator by hazards such as musculoskeletal diseases, bullying and other psychological stressors, chemical and dangerous goods, etc.); and by regulatee (e.g. some regulators may organise themselves around industry sectors such as telecommunications, utilities, manufacturing and retail, or by the size of the regulatee—small, medium and large—size being a proxy for capability).

These dimensions are not mutually exclusive, however. Many regulators operate under a matrix-structure in which staff are organised across multiple dimensions. Head office, for example, may be organised by task or function, and the field inspectorate by region, issue or regulatee. Matrix structures enable synergies to be realised, gaps to be avoided and holistic and comprehensive programs and interventions to be designed and implemented. However, matrix structures with overlapping roles and responsibilities can create role confusion, inefficient task duplication and a lack of accountability. Matrix structures therefore require a degree of organisational and cultural maturity that new regulators are unlikely to possess when initially being established. At this stage, simplicity can be a more valuable commodity than sophistication.

Good Governance Arrangements

The second component of regime deployment is putting in place good governance arrangements. Good governance arrangements assist to ensure regulation is implemented effectively, efficiently and in the public interest, and that risks, errors and potential causes of failure are identified and minimised. Good governance also is central to building and maintaining regulatory legitimacy. Common to all legitimacy communities is an expectation that regulation will be applied and administered in accordance with the law, consistently, fairly and equitably, and in a manner that is transparent and accountable.[7] Numerous good governance guides exist: many of general application; some specific for regulators.[8] It is not the purpose of this section to replicate this guidance. Rather, in this section we focus on governance's five key elements, as distilled from this guidance: accountable decision-making, performance measurement, information management, risk management and probity.

Accountable Decision-Making

Legislation establishing a regulator often will confer powers upon the regulatory body itself (to be exercised by its Board acting collectively) or upon a designated individual (e.g. Minister; Department Secretary; Administrator). However, the number, type and frequency of regulatory decisions usually is such that one body or person is incapable of making them all, or at least not in a manner that is effective and efficient. Effective implementation therefore requires that decision-making powers be delegated to others within the regulator. These delegations create lines of authority within the organisation. The nature of these lines—to whom authority is given, how much, the conditions that attach to their exercise and the manner with which they are controlled and oversighted—impact not only how those powers are exercised, but also the regulator's broader organisational culture.[9] Effective systems for making, maintaining and administering these delegations therefore is a crucial part of regime deployment. These systems should extend to training delegates on the proper exercise of their powers to ensure decision-making is exercised in accordance with the regulator's authorising legislation, regulatory policy and procedural and administrative law requirements. The exercise by delegates of their decision-making powers also should be subject to quality assurance processes to confirm their proper exercise, and to review upon the request of persons aggrieved or otherwise adversely affected by the decision. And for this to occur, there needs to be a minimum standard of documentation (and document retention) in relation to administrative processes and decisions. While often considered bureaucratic red-tape, proper documentation is essential to support good decision-making today, to improve the consistency of decision-making over time and to ensure accountability and transparency.

Performance Measurement

Central to good governance arrangements is an effective system to generate information about the regime's performance. Performance measurement facilitates effective internal management, can be used to demonstrate to legitimacy communities that regulatory objectives are being achieved effectively and efficiently and is an essential input into any evaluation of the regime. What should be measured by this system is normally defined by reference to the regime's intervention logic, and generally includes the intervention's outputs, the impact of these outputs on the causal drivers to which they are directed (i.e. the operational objectives) and progress towards the regime's primary regulatory objectives. We have discussed that regulatory objectives should be S.M.A.R.T.[10] The indicators employed to measure progress against those objectives should be R.A.C.E.R.: relevant (in the sense of being closely linked to the regulatory objectives); accepted (by both the regulator's staff whose individual performance may be assessed by reference to those indicators, and the actors and communities on whose support and resources the regime relies); credible (in the sense of being easy to understand and interpret); easy to monitor (data can be collected in a timely manner and, ideally, at low cost to both regulator and regulatees); and robust (against manipulation).[11] Indicators that meet these criteria generally are quantitative measures of effectiveness and efficiency. This has seen performance measurement systems criticised for much the same reason as cost-benefit analyses, namely that they privilege these economic values over less readily quantifiable democratic and social values such as accountability and transparency, and equity and fairness.[12] There is merit to these criticisms, and just as RIAs have broadened their focus and increasingly are applying multi-criteria analyses,[13] so too should performance measurement systems seek to develop measures and frameworks that incorporate democratic and social values into their analyses. Doing so can only serve to enhance their legitimacy.

Information Management Systems

The central input into a performance measurement system is information. As we have observed on a number of occasions, information is the lifeblood of the regulatory endeavour. Information is central to issue diagnosis and regulatory objective setting, and to regime design, assessment and selection. Timely, accurate, reliable and comprehensive information also is essential to a regulator's ability to identify, analyse and prioritise issues to be addressed, to design and implement initiatives to address those issues and to monitor the progress of those initiatives. Information management systems therefore need to be carefully designed to ensure relevant data is captured and securely stored, and that it can be retrieved and interrogated in a meaningful and timely manner to assist decision-making.

Risk Management Systems

Risk management is another essential element of good governance arrangements. All regulatory regimes require robust risk management processes to identify and mitigate risks to the effective, efficient and legitimate achievement of its regulatory objectives. These risks fall into two broad types: internal risks that impact the regulator's ability to administer the regulatory regime; and external risks that affect regulatees' and other actors' willingness to comply with regulatory requirements or otherwise cooperate with the regulatory endeavour.[14] Effective risk management processes enable a regulator to adjust its strategies, activities and actions to reflect new or increased risks (and equally, redundant or reduced risks). These processes should span the entire scope of the regime's functions, and ideally should be developed cooperatively with those with whom the regulator partners in the discharge of its regulatory responsibilities. These risk management processes should include clear triggers for escalating issues internally to the regulator's most senior management and, if necessary, to its political overseers. A regulatory regime without a robust risk management system is a folly.

Probity

The final good governance element is probity. Probity refers to practices and systems designed to ensure the honesty and integrity of the regulatory regime. Examples of good probity practices include policies and procedures with respect to: preventing and reporting fraud, corruption and misconduct, including protections for whistleblowers; privacy and the proper use of official information; conflicts of interest, including rules for accepting gifts, benefits and hospitality; and rotating staff through functions where the risk of over-familiarisation with, or capture by, regulatees is considered high. There also should be induction and periodic training of staff on those policies and procedures, and audits and reviews of operations to ensure compliance (and to detect and investigate instances of non-compliance) with them. In high risk areas, dedicated integrity units to detect, investigate and prevent misconduct also may be appropriate.

Organisational Capability, Capacity and Culture

In Chapter 5 we identified capability as one of the gears that drives issues through the regulatory policy cycle. We observed that regulators need the capability to develop and implement regulatory strategies (and individual interventions) to address the multiple, overlapping and increasingly complex issues confronting modern society. We also observed that to do this effectively involves a mix of skills, knowledge and competencies. These include negotiation and communication skills, inter-personal and facilitation skills, technical and analytical skills, and problem-solving and program management skills; as well as good judgement and political acumen.[15]

Bringing these attributes to bear upon the regulatory endeavour is the domain of organisational studies, the details of which are outside the scope of this book. Having said that, two elements are worthy of mention. The first element is capacity. The regulator or regulators (remembering that different stages and regulatory tasks may be undertaken by different organisations) must be adequately and appropriately resourced. This includes human resources (persons with the appropriate mix of skills and competences discussed above) and financial and technical resources. The latter includes appropriate information technology and data gathering mechanisms, analytical decision-making tools and technologies, and monitoring, evaluation and performance measurement tools.

The second element is culture. The public interest underpinning the regulatory endeavour needs to be inculcated into and throughout the relevant regulatory organisations. This usually is expressed in each organisation's mission and vision. Each organisation also needs to create a culture conducive to delivering that mission and vision. Generally, this should be a culture that is positive, constructive, solution and outcome-orientated, and that encourages, empowers and supports its staff to operate in an open, respectful, decisive, confident and accountable manner.[16] Creating this culture is multi-dimensional. A critical element is the regulator's internal organisational dynamics. These dynamics include the manner with which the regulator is structured internally, its governance arrangements, lines of authority, communication and information flows and other internal systems. It also extends to the diversity and mix of its staff's professional and disciplinary backgrounds; its routines and organisational controls; how work is organised and roles are defined; and the manner with which these factors are translated at an individual level in the form of performance targets, supervisory arrangements and work group design.[17] There is a management adage that 'culture eats strategy for breakfast'.[18] What this discussion makes clear is that organisational structure is important to both.

Summing up Regime Deployment

This section has examined the main activities involved in deploying a regulatory regime. Many of these activities are not unique to the regulatory endeavour. Indeed, many are not unique to the public sector, and reflect steps that should be employed to deploy any major initiative—public or private. As a result, some may have appeared obvious and not worthy of specific mention. However, the number of times they are missed or implemented poorly instructs otherwise (as our examination of the causes of regulator failure revealed). Administratively, regime deployment is a comparatively straightforward task. It does, however, require systematic and rigorous planning. This, in turn, requires sufficient time for the administrative design features to be agreed upon, documented and put in place. The temptation to take shortcuts must be resisted. As we observed in our discussion of regulatory failure, many problems with regime implementation can be traced to poor deployment, whether that be caused by poor planning or the political prioritisation of speed over proper process.[19] Conceptually, regime deployment is more challenging. Determining the appropriate internal structure, recruiting staff with the right mix of skills and competencies and putting in place appropriate governance arrangements, lines of authority and other systems to support a positive, constructive, confident and outcome-orientated culture are complex, complicated and critical decisions that shape the manner with which the regime is applied—which brings us to the next implementation function.

Regime Application

Having put the regulatory regime in place, the next step is to apply that regime to modify behaviours to achieve the regulatory objectives. Regime application comprises three interrelated elements: the regulatory tasks that need to be undertaken; the regulatory strategy that governs (steers and directs) the manner with which those tasks are undertaken; and the 'street level' execution of that strategy. Each of these elements is discussed below.

Regulatory Tasks

As we have observed on numerous occasions, each regulatory regime is different. As a result, each regime is likely to be applied differently. Notwithstanding this, there are four core regulatory tasks common to most (if not all) regulatory regimes.[20] These are informing and educating regulatees and other parties about the regulatory regime and its requirements; administering the regime and supporting regulatees to comply with it; enforcing compliance and sanctioning non-compliance; and monitoring regime performance and adjusting accordingly. Each of these tasks is briefly elaborated upon below.

Inform and Educate

The first core task is informing and educating regulatees and other actors about the regulatory regime and their obligations, rights and duties under it. This should extend to explaining the rationale for the regime and the regime's objectives, and the importance of those objectives being achieved and the consequences if they are not. As we have seen, building a shared understanding of the regime's societal and normative value can aid compliance, at least among some regulatees.[21] It also should extend to explaining the regulator's role, responsibilities and powers, and its regulatory strategy for securing and enforcing compliance. Forewarning regulatees in this manner enhances regulatory legitimacy.[22]

Administer and Support

The second core task is administering the regime and supporting regulatees to comply with its requirements. The exact nature of these tasks will depend on the behaviour change mechanisms and regulatory tools employed by the regime. It could include, for example, setting standards and prescribing rules for certain activities; licensing, registering or otherwise authorising regulatees to engage in certain activities; administering grants and other incentive schemes; and providing regulatees with advice and guidance on how to comply. It also could include partnering with regulatees and other actors to develop innovative ways to eliminate or mitigate persistent risks and hazards, or to overcome institutional and other barriers to compliance. Depending on the regime, some of these tasks may be hard-coded in legislation, in which case the regulator's discretion is limited to how to undertake the tasks, not whether to undertake them; whereas in other regimes, the regulator may be empowered but not obliged to undertake some of these tasks, in which case the regulator has a discretion as to which tasks to undertake, when and in what circumstances and combinations. How the regulator exercises this discretion will be influenced by its choice of regulatory strategy (discussed below).

Enforce and Sanction

The next core task is enforcing compliance with the regulatory standards. Enforcement generally has four key elements. The first element is detecting non-compliance. The detection techniques available to the regulator will depend on the nature of the regulatory regime and the powers and privileges conferred upon it by its authorising legislation. They can include: inspections, surveillance and system reviews; surveys and other forms of self-assessment; third party audits and assessments; reports received from other government agencies and regulatory authorities; intelligence gleaned from publically available information and data; and reports from members of the public, industry and non-government organisations, other regulatees and whistleblowers from within offending regulatees. The second element is stopping the non-compliant activity and preventing further harm. This may be achieved by inspectors issuing prohibition notices, or by court issued injunctions. The third element is remedying any damage the non-compliant activity may have caused. Many regimes empower regulators to order (or to apply to a court for an order) that the offending regulatee fix any problems it has created. Such powers are frequently found in environmental regulation, for example, and can include clean up notices, restoration orders and orders that a person destroy, neutralise or treat the pollutant or other environmental hazard it has created.[23] And the fourth and final element is sanctioning the offending regulatee. Depending on the nature of the regime, sanctions can range from imprisonment and fines, to licence conditions or revocation, through to naming and shaming devices such as adverse publicity orders. In addition to punishing the offender, sanctioning helps level the playing field financially for those regulatees who have made the financial investments to be compliant, and acts as general deterrent for those who might be considering evading their regulatory responsibilities.

Monitor and Adjust

The fourth core task comprises two steps: monitoring and adjusting. Monitoring is the continuous and systematic process of gathering data to assess whether regime implementation is 'on track'—whether the interventions are being implemented in accordance with the implementation plan, and whether the changes they are effecting are likely to be sufficient to realise the regulatory policy's operational and primary objectives.[24] Adjusting is altering regime implementation in response to those assessments. We already have discussed the importance of effective performance measurement and information management.[25] Monitoring is only as effective as the relevance, reliability and robustness of its indicators, and the quality of the data with which those indicators are measured. The adjustment component, however, is as much a mindset as it is an informational, assessment and modification system. 'Continuous improvement' is another name for this function, and it demands a willingness on the part of the regulator to reflect critically on what it is doing, and how it might be done better. After all, there is no point to monitoring if there is not a willingness to act in response to its findings. Adjustments might relate to the instruments and processes employed by the regulator in the performance of its core regulatory tasks (discussed above), or to the regulator's broader strategic approach (discussed below). More substantive changes to the regime architecture (e.g. to include new enforcement mechanisms or to impose duties and obligations on actors presently not regulated) are normally beyond the mandate and power of the regulator, however. Paradigm shifting changes of this magnitude generally are returned to policy-makers to examine, and made after a more holistic evaluation of the regime.[26] Evaluation is discussed in Chapter 11.

Summing up Regulatory Tasks

This discussion of regulatory tasks reveals that regulators do much more than administer regulatory standards and enforce compliance with them. They also inform, educate and support people to comply with those standards. Each of these tasks is not an independent operation, however. The tasks are interrelated and form one overall regulatory process. Moreover, some tasks overlap. Inspections, for example, can be used both to inform, educate and support regulatees to comply with the regulatory standards, and to detect, remedy and sanction instances of non-compliance. And how one set of tasks is undertaken can impact the effectiveness of other tasks, both positively and negatively. For example, the provision of education, information and support can create constructive relationships that motivate regulatees to cooperate with the regulator's administration and enforcement activities. And fair and constructive enforcement processes can engender cooperation and knowledge sharing that facilitates regime administration, whereas enforcement that is perceived to be punitive and inconsistent, on the other hand, can alienate regulatees, impede knowledge sharing and make regime administration more difficult.[27]

Regulatory Strategy

Listing regulatory tasks tells us little about how they should be executed. Should they be performed with a 'heavy' or 'light' hand; proactively or reactively; rigidly or flexibly? The answer to these questions resides in the regulatory strategy adopted by the regulator. A regulator's choice of strategy is a powerful statement to regulatees and other actors about how they can expect the regulator to interact with them. Early regulatory literature focused on styles of enforcement, and drew a distinction between 'deterrence' approaches that command compliance and 'facilitative' approaches that encourage and assist compliance.[28] This changed in the early 1990s when Ayres and Brathwaite put forward their model of 'responsive regulation' that advocated a place for both deterrence and facilitative approaches in the one regulatory regime. Responsive regulation can be thought of as the father of modern regulatory approaches, and has since been followed by other approaches that similarly advocate for more flexible and sophisticated approaches to regulatory implementation. These include Gunningham's and Grabosky's smart regulation, Sparrow's problem-based approach, risk-based regulation and Baldwin's and Black's really responsive regulation. Each of these strategies is discussed below, starting with deterrence and facilitative approaches.

Deterrence Approaches

Deterrence approaches, as their name suggests, focus on government efforts to deter non-compliance. Classic deterrence models posit that persons and entities primarily are motivated to comply by the fear of legal sanctions that attach to non-compliance.[29] More modern deterrence theories, consistent with expanding notions of regulation and of regulatory space, have identified that associated social and economic sanctions also can play an important role. These include the social stigma and reputational damage that can attach to breaches of the law, the commercial losses that can flow from such damage and the direct economic costs of defending regulatory charges. In some situations, fear of these social and economic sanctions can be more important than formal legal sanctions in motivating a regulatee to comply.[30]

The effectiveness of sanctions in achieving a deterrent effect is dependent on: (1) the perceived severity of the sanction (i.e. does it outweigh the perceived benefits of non-compliance and alter the 'cost-benefit analysis' in favour of compliance); (2) the perceived certainty of the sanction (i.e. the probability of detection and punishment—the greater the perceived risk of apprehension, the greater the effect on behaviour exerted by the sanction); (3) the motivation of non-compliance (e.g. cost-saving; laziness; defiance/rebellion); and (4) the perceived swiftness (celerity) of the sanction (i.e. the proximity of the sanction to the non-compliance—if it is too distant, it may be discounted). The emphasis on perception here is important. As Freiberg observes, modern deterrence is not an objective quality but depends on regulatees understanding the standards with which they must comply and the regulatory practices through which they will be enforced.[31] This means that for maximum impact, coercive mechanisms generally are coupled with persuasion, education and information that reinforces the importance of complying with the regulatory standards, the breadth and effectiveness of the mechanisms in place to detect non-compliance and the severity and celerity of the sanctions that attach to non-compliance. Indeed, today's reality is that pure command and control regimes are unlikely to exist. Even modern police forces employ a range of non-coercive methods to encourage and facilitate compliance with the law.

Implemented well, deterrence approaches can effectively control activity the state has determined does not meet community standards. Its reliance on legal standards and the force of law provides a clear and authoritative statement of what is and is not acceptable, and provides the community with the assurance that comes from knowing decisive, prompt and forceful action is being taken for its protection and benefit. But deterrence approaches are not without their disadvantages. Many of the disadvantages attributed to deterrence approaches echo the disadvantages and weaknesses of prescriptive standards and coercive change mechanisms: that they are inflexible and inefficient; costly to comply with and costly to administer; and that they deter not only non-compliant behaviour, but also welfare enhancing innovation and risk-taking.[32] This is not surprising. Command and control regimes that enforce prescriptive standards through the rigid and formalistic use of coercive behaviour change mechanisms traditionally have been the most common manifestation of a deterrence approach. We have observed, however, that many of these disadvantages can be ameliorated by the use of outcome-orientated (and less prescriptive) regulatory standards enforced with less intensity and greater discretion. Indeed, representations of command and control regimes today tend to be 'more of a caricature than an accurate description of the operation of any particular regulatory system'.[33]

More generally though, deterrence approaches are, by their very nature, adversarial in character. As a result, they make it more difficult to develop constructive relationships between regulator and regulatees. They can create a climate of mistrust that can undermine compliance, and can lead to an increasing reliance on courts (rather than candid discussions between regulator and regulatee) to resolve differences about how issues should be addressed.[34] Moreover, deterrence approaches that subject the willing and able regulatee (leaders, to use the parlance of regulatee types from Chapter 8) to high levels of prescription, intrusive and strong enforcement can generate resentment, undermine the legitimacy of the regulatory regime in their eyes and, somewhat perversely, reduce their motivation to comply.[35]

Deterrence approaches also are criticised on efficiency grounds. Deterrence approaches work best with rational actors and those that are generally law abiding. They generally are less effective in changing the behaviour of those who are motivated to game the system, or are irrational. In this regard, we have seen that the more legalistic and rigid the regulatory regime, the greater the opportunity for those intent on gaming the system to discover loopholes or creative ways to comply.[36] And the concept of 'rationality' has been shown to be especially problematic in corporate settings. Numerous factors impact decision-making within a corporation. These include their internal reward systems (and the extent to which they reward risk taking), the structures through which messages are communicated up and down the organisation and the level of understanding of the regulatory environment at different levels of the organisation. These factors can lead corporations to respond to regulation differently than assumed by rational decision-making models.[37] And finally, deterrence approaches are criticised on equity grounds. Deterrence approaches impact small regulatees disproportionately. Significant financial penalties can undermine their viability more so than for larger firms. Penalties also are felt more 'personally' in smaller firms than in larger organisations with multiple and diffuse points of responsibility and accountability.[38]

Facilitative Approaches

Fear of sanctions is not the only factor motivating compliance. There is a rich body of research that emphasises that compliance is a plural, dynamic and interactive process involving (in addition to classic deterrence theory), social, economic and normative dimensions. Social responsibility, reputation management, ethics, an internalised sense of duty and general law abidedness all play an important role.[39] These economic, social and normative dimensions provide the foundation for facilitative regulatory approaches.

A facilitative implementation style, as its name suggests, focuses on encouraging and assisting regulatees to comply with their regulatory obligations. The different regulatee attitudes, motivations and capabilities discussed in Chapter 8 are especially relevant here. Segmenting the regulatee population according to their motivation and capability to comply enables the regulator to select and tailor facilitative (non-coercive) behaviour change mechanisms to each regulatee: for example, incentives and disincentives to regulatees for whom the decision to comply (or not) is based on a rational cost-benefit calculation, persuasion to those whose decision to comply is based on their being convinced of the fairness and appropriateness of the regulatory regime and assistance to those willing to comply but without the capability to do so.

Facilitative approaches allow the regulatee greater flexibility to determine how to comply with the regulatory standards, and to go beyond compliance if circumstances permit. This flexibility generally means compliance is less burdensome for the regulatee. Facilitative approaches also generally are less costly on the regulator to administer than prescriptive deterrent approaches, although we did see in Chapter 8 that incentives can be very complex to administer and enforce. Facilitative approaches also can develop constructive relationships between regulator and regulatee. Constructive relationships improve information flows between the two and can encourage regulatees to think constructively about different modes of compliance, and of performing at a higher level than called for by the regulatory standards.[40]

Facilitative approaches work best with regulatees motivated to comply and prepared to change their behaviour to do so. They are less likely to change the behaviour of recalcitrant and uncooperative regulatees not disposed to voluntary compliance.[41] For this reason, facilitative approaches should not totally eschew coercive mechanisms. Facilitative approaches should include a threat of sanctions, albeit one that exists in the background to be invoked only in the more extreme cases.[42]

Responsive Regulation

The idea that deterrence and facilitative approaches can and should co-exist in the one regulatory regime is one of the fundamental underpinnings of Ayres' and Braithwaite's *Responsive Regulation*.[43] As the authors explain: 'To reject punitive regulation is naïve; to be totally committed to it is to lead a charge of the Light Brigade. The trick of successful regulation is to establish a synergy between punishment and persuasion'.[44] Responsive regulation seeks to achieve this synergy by matching the regulator's response to the regulatee's willingness and capability to comply reflected in its compliance behaviour. To guide this matching of responses to motivations, Ayres and Braithwaite developed two 'enforcement pyramids'—one to be applied by governments to entire industries (the enforcement strategies pyramid); and one to be applied by regulators to individual regulatees (the enforcement instruments pyramid). Examples of these pyramids are shown in Figures 10.1 and 10.2, respectively.[45]

According to Ayres and Braithwaite, regulation should start at the bottom of each pyramid and from the presumption that regulatees are virtuous and will respond to facilitative strategies such as persuasion and assistance. After this starting point, regulation becomes a dialogic exercise. Regulatees who cooperate and behave as desired remain at the bottom of the pyramid. However, regulatees who do not cooperate and who fail to behave as desired are met with an escalation of enforcement activity. Escalation continues up the enforcement pyramid until compliance is achieved, at which point a consistent demonstration from that regulatee that it is now inclined

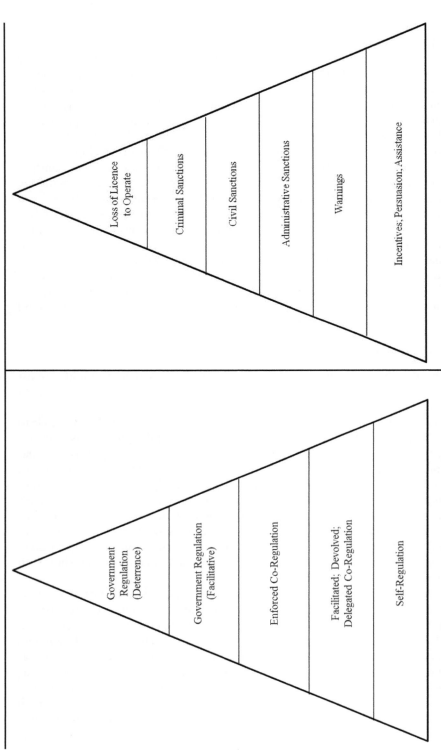

Figure 10.1 Example of an Enforcement (Strategies) Pyramid

Government
Regulation
(Deterrence)

Government Regulation
(Facilitative)

Enforced Co-Regulation

Facilitated; Devolved;
Delegated Co-Regulation

Self-Regulation

Figure 10.2 Example of an Enforcement (Instruments) Pyramid

Loss of Licence
to Operate

Criminal Sanctions

Civil Sanctions

Administrative Sanctions

Warnings

Incentives; Persuasion; Assistance

to comply and behave as desired may be responded to by a de-escalation of regulatory activity down the pyramid and a less punitive approach. Ayres and Braithwaite refer to this as 'tit-for-tat' enforcement.[46] This enables the regulator to focus its enforcement efforts on those regulatees who are less responsive or willing to comply. Doing so reduces the compliance burden on the compliant by sparing them the rod, and ensures more efficient use of the regulator's limited resources, although the costs involved in operationalising the pyramid—of monitoring individual regulatee attitudes and behaviour, and training and equipping staff to analyse, interpret and respond in a nuanced and considered manner—should not be underestimated.[47]

Transparent use of the pyramid is essential to its successful use—it is only when regulatees know that the regulator ultimately will respond to continued non-compliance through punitive means that there is an incentive to comply at the earlier stages. Transparent use of the pyramid also has other benefits. It provides clear guidance on which breaches are likely to be met with which responses, and what circumstances might trigger escalation up the pyramid. This provides a degree of procedural fairness, and improves consistency of outcomes. This, in turn, engenders trust and confidence in the fairness and equity of the regime, which we have observed is an important element of better and legitimate regulation.

Responsive regulation (and in particular, the enforcement instruments pyramid) has had a profound influence on regulatory practice around the world.[48] It is not without its critics and limitations, however.[49] Three limitations in particular have resulted in responsive regulation's practical application sometimes varying in important ways from that theorised by Ayres and Braithwaite. The first limitation is that not all issues are suitable for this approach. Some risks are (or are perceived to be) so severe in terms of their frequency, magnitude and permanency of harm that it would be inappropriate to assume virtuosity on the part of all regulatees and to start with the least interventionist approach. Terrorism (and airport security) is one such example. Adopting the least interventionist approach in such cases threatens regulatory legitimacy. As our discussion of risk in Chapter 3 revealed, there will be circumstances where community expectations of safety and security and a government's political need to be responsive to those expectations will shape how an issue is perceived, and the adequacy of the response.[50]

Second, responsive regulation assumes an ongoing relationship and dialogue between regulator and regulatee. However, this is not always the case. This can be because the regulatory environment is dominated by small, diffuse or logistically difficult (mobile or remote) regulatees with whom the regulator is not sufficiently resourced to engage on an ongoing basis.[51] It also might be the case because culturally, the regulatees are adversarial, litigious and generally suspicious of, and hostile to, the creation of such a relationship.[52] The less frequent and intense the regulator-regulatee interaction, and the less knowledge the regulator has about the regulatee's willingness and ability to comply, the less practicable responsive regulation becomes.[53]

And third, even in situations where there is an ongoing relationship, many of the assumptions underpinning responsive regulation's dialogic approach may not exist in practice. Responsible regulation assumes the communication of clear messages of posture and intent between regulator and regulatee. However, in complex regimes with multiple regulators and regulatees, those communications are apt to be missed, confused or subject to interference.[54] Responsive regulation also assumes each party to those communications is sufficiently capable and sophisticated to understand and interpret the messages being sent to by the other party. This is an especially problematic assumption in the case of small regulatees, and resource poor regulators with large, diverse and constantly evolving regulatee populations. Finally, responsive regulation assumes an ability to move up and down the pyramid in equal measure. However, a number of commentators point out that while escalation up the pyramid is relatively straightforward, moving back down again is more problematic. This is because the use of more punitive measures during periods of escalation can engender defiant, adversarial and legalistic behaviour on the part of the regulatee, thereby prejudicing the dialogic relationship between regulator and regulatee on which responsive regulation is built.[55]

Empirical evidence suggests that many regulators have responded to these limitations by modifying their application of responsive regulation.[56] Regulators who practice responsive regulation as conceived by Ayres and Braithwaite generally do so only with large and sophisticated regulatees with whom they have frequent and close contact. In other situations, the evidence suggests responsive regulation is applied differently to different regulatory tasks. With respect to administrative and support tasks, regulators tend to assume regulatees are largely virtuous and motivated to comply. As a result, their focus is on persuading and assisting regulatees to comply through the provision of information, advice and guidance. And with respect to detection tasks, responsive regulation sometimes is employed in conjunction with risk-based approaches in a manner that uses risk statistically calculated across regulatee sub-populations or segments as a proxy for individual willingness and capability to comply.[57] But when it comes to enforcement tasks, many regulators do not assume virtuosity and do not to enter at the base of the pyramid (that is, commence with persuasion and assistance). Rather, many enter the pyramid at different points determined by reference to the culpability of the regulatee, and the nature and magnitude of the risk and harm.[58] Used in this manner, the enforcement pyramid morphs into a sanctioning tool, and the regulator shifts from responding to the regulatee's motivational posture to responding to the seriousness of the non-compliance and the regulatee's culpability.[59]

Smart Regulation

Responsive regulation represented a breakthrough in regulatory thinking. One of the first significant attempts to build upon its foundations was Gunningham's and Grabosky's *Smart Regulation*.[60] Smart regulation calls for an 'imaginative, flexible, and pluralistic approach' to regulation.[61] Three core principles underpin smart regulatory design.[62] First is the use of complimentary combinations of regulatory instruments tailored to the causes and context of the specific issue. Smart regulation extols the virtues of using a mix of instruments over single instrument approaches. At the same time, however, it counsels against instrument 'smorgasboardism'. Such an approach not only is inefficient (resource intensive for the regulator; unnecessarily burdensome on the regulatee), the unthinking combination of instruments is likely to be ineffective at best and counterproductive at worst. Rather, smart regulation advocates for the use of the minimum number of instruments necessary to achieve the desired objective.[63]

Second, smart regulation recommends that governments empower non-government actors to act as surrogate or quasi-regulators. Smart regulation reconceptualises responsive regulation's single-faced pyramid into a triangular pyramid or tetrahedron whose three faces allow for escalation across three dimensions—by government as the state regulator; by professional bodies and industry associations as self-regulators; and by commercial and non-commercial third parties functioning as quasi-regulators. Co-opting third parties as quasi-regulators creates greater opportunities for innovative and flexible mixes of instruments, and frees up scarce regulatory resources to be redeployed to areas where there are no alternatives to direct government interventions.[64]

And third, smart regulation, like responsive regulation, recommends regulators (government, self and quasi) commence with the most parsimonious (least interventionist) approach, and from there escalate enforcement activity according to the regulatee's motivation and capability reflected in its compliance behaviour. Smart regulation also recommends that regulators transparently sequence their interventions and the criteria that will trigger an escalation, thereby minimising the amount of discretion in the escalation process. This, they argue, injects greater certainty and dependability into the process, and sends a powerful message to regulatees to respond positively to less interventionist forms of regulation.[65] However, more so than responsive regulation, smart regulation acknowledges there are circumstances where it is inappropriate to commence with the least interventionist approach. The first is where there is a serious risk of irreversible harm or catastrophic damage. The second is where the regulator may not have repeat interactions with the regulatee such that there is only one chance to influence its behaviour. In these circumstances, smart regulation acknowledges that a more interventionist first response may be warranted.[66]

The logic underpinning smart regulation is difficult to refute. Complimentary combinations of tools should be more effective than single tools; many heads and hands should be more effective than government acting alone; and tailoring those tools and actors to the causes and context of each issue should be more effective than a one-size-fits-all approach. The strength of its logic is matched, however, by its difficulty to implement. Effective implementation assumes regulators have the time, capability and sophistication to interpret different regulatees' compliance behaviour, and to tailor complimentary combinations of interventions to address the different motivations and capabilities reflected in those behaviours. Smart regulation also assumes regulators have the political skills to steer and direct the various surrogate and quasi-regulators it enlists into the regulatory endeavour—each of whom will have different interests in the issue being regulated—in a common direction. And further, smart regulation assumes regulators have the time and resources to combine and coordinate these interventions and actors across the spectrum of regulatees and issues for which a modern regulator is responsible. And while Gunningham's and Grabosky's prescription of smart regulation includes helpful guidance on complimentary combinations of tools and actors (and those that are not complementary), such guidance is a starting point only.[67] Whether combinations are complimentary or not is context and content specific, and cannot always be predicted in advance and in the abstract.

Problem-Based Regulation

Shortly after the publication of *Smart Regulation* came Malcolm Sparrow's *The Regulatory Craft*.[68] Whereas responsive regulation and smart regulation focus principally on instruments and actors, *The Regulatory Craft* urges that the focus remain squarely on the problem. As Sparrow explains:

> A problem-based strategy picks the most important tasks and then selects appropriate tools in each case, rather than deciding on the important tools and picking the tasks to fit. A problem-based operation organizes the tools around the work, rather than organizing the work around the tools.[69]

Sparrow defines six stages of problem-solving: nominating a potential problem for attention; defining that problem precisely; determining how to measure the impact of a solution to the problem; developing interventions that solve the problem; implementing the interventions; and monitoring, reviewing and adjusting the plan as required.[70] These steps largely mirror the stages of the regulatory policy cycle. Indeed, Sparrow's problem-based approach can be thought of as an application of the regulatory policy cycle at the micro level.

While clear on the stages of problem-solving, Sparrow has been criticised for not providing more guidance on determining what the solution should look like—whether it should be deterrent, facilitative or responsive in focus—and for not providing a menu of options and strategies from which smart regulatory mixes can be selected.[71] However, such criticisms miss a key element of Sparrow's model—that problem-solving ultimately is a matter of 'regulatory craftsmanship'. According to Sparrow, regulatory craftsmanship is a competency or, more correctly, the sum of three competencies: functional expertise, project management skills and problem-solving capacity. The latter is defined (somewhat circularly) as 'the ability to specify risk concentrations, problem areas, or patterns of non-compliance, and to design interventions that control or reduce them. In other words, to *pick important problems and fix them*' (emphasis in original).[72] The point is that regulatory craftsmanship is something that is developed, built and maintained through training and experience. It is not something that can be bestowed or reduced to a series of templates, although institutional arrangements and decision frameworks can and should be put in place to support it. In this regard, Sparrow specifies seven minimum requirements for problem-solving infrastructure. They are: a nomination system for generating issues for selection; a selection system for comparative assessment and selection of projects; a system for assigning responsibility for and allocating resources to projects; project management systems; systems that provide for management oversight and periodic review of projects; reporting systems that link projects to the regulator's overall performance measurement system; and support systems that provide access to consultants and specialists in the art of problem-solving.[73] The first of these systems—nominating and selecting problems to be addressed—is the focus of the next regulatory approach to be considered.

Risk-Based Regulation

Regulators have long used risk as a criterion for focusing their enforcement efforts. However, it was not until the 2000s that risk-based regulation came into its own. The 2005 UK Hampton Review made it government policy for all UK regulatory agencies to adopt a risk-based regulatory approach, and it has since found its way into most better regulation reforms.[74] Its rise in prominence is part of broader efforts to make regulation more rational, analytical and orderly. As Black and Baldwin observe, '[i]n its idealized form, risk-based regulation offers an evidence-based means of targeting the use of resources and of prioritizing attention to the highest risks in accordance with a transparent, systematic and defensible framework'.[75]

Advocates of risk-based regulation argue its use leads to better informed decision-making and a more efficient allocation of limited regulatory resources.[76] When used transparently, risk-based regulation also provides a rational and logical structure for explaining the basis upon which complex and difficult resource allocation decisions are made. This exposes the regulator's decisions (and decision-making processes) to public scrutiny, analysis and challenge, thereby enhancing the regulatory regime's accountability and legitimacy. Doing so, of course, admits to resource limitations and highlights those issues on which the regulator has chosen not to focus. Persons adversely affected by a decision not to focus on an issue can be expected to question and challenge that issue's exclusion. This, in turn, obliges the regulator to be able to communicate and justify its tolerance for risk.[77] While this task can be difficult and politically challenging, its transparency should be welcomed.

While risk-based approaches to regulation have proven useful, experience has revealed several challenges in their implementation.[78] First, data capture can be costly—both on the regulator and the regulatees from which it sometimes must be extracted. Risk-based approaches also can require costly and complex analytical systems. Second, risk-based regulation is not as objective and scientific as might first appear. As with cost-benefit analyses, risk methodologies are underpinned by a series of assumptions, hypotheses and judgments. These include whether to focus on specific types of risks or risk creators; whether to focus at a firm or industry level; and whether to focus on individual, composite or systemic risks.[79] An especially critical judgment is whether the analysis should be restricted to quantitative data expertly analysed, or whether it should extend to qualitative measures informed by participatory processes. Consistent with our definition of risk in Chapter 3, risk assessments should not be limited to quantitative measures alone. Community expectations and political considerations also need to be taken into account. It is therefore important that risk-based techniques incorporate participatory processes to marry expertise with experience and technical models with democratic processes. Inclusion of these participatory processes also assists to overcome two other commonly cited problems with the use of risk-based analytical techniques, namely that they are backward looking and can fail to identify new and emerging risks (by dent of their reliance on historical data), and are 'locked in' to established ways of looking at the world (a product of historical institutionalism). Participatory processes enable risk assessments to both look forward and into the shadows for risks and issues invisible to existing institutions.

The idea behind risk-based regulation is that it enables a regulator to intervene proactively to address areas of highest risk. Risk-based analytical techniques generally are well-suited to identifying those areas of high risk. What they are less adept at doing is identifying interventions to eliminate or mitigate the causes of those risks. Risk-based approaches of themselves do not shed light on whether the regulator should adopt a deterrent or facilitative approach; or whether the regulator should intervene directly, or through or with the assistance of third parties. The answer to these questions lies in the adoption of other regulatory approaches. Nor does risk-based regulation tell you what to do with low (or lower) risk areas that are not prioritised. Implicit in the model is that resources should not be directed towards them. Yet if that were the case, some regulatees within those areas might assume a licence to offend. Surely this cannot be the intention. Clearly, risk-based regulation needs to be accompanied by programs designed to ensure a base-level deterrent effect across all areas.[80] As such, it may be best to think of risk-based regulation as a targeting technique to be used in conjunction with other regulatory strategies.

Really Responsive Regulation

Really responsive regulation is both the most recent and comprehensive of the regulatory strategies considered in this chapter. It is Baldwin's and Black's attempt to build upon and address the major deficiencies of the regulatory strategies that proceeded it.[81] Baldwin and Black argue that in order for a regulator to be 'really responsive', it has to regulate in a manner that is responsive to five key elements. The first is the regulatee's attitudinal settings. This is more than the regulatee's willingness and capability to comply evidenced in its compliance behaviour. It extends to the regulatee's culture and the manner with which it functions on a daily basis. The second element is the broader institutional environment. Baldwin and Black describe this as 'a plea for institutional theories to be taken more seriously',[82] and for regulation to be responsive to the organisational, normative, cognitive, and power and resource-distribution structures, in which both regulator and regulatee are situated. Really responsive regulation emphasises the need for regulators to take into account existing state and non-state entities regulating or otherwise impacting upon the behaviour of regulatees. Third is being responsive to the different ways in which the logics of different regulatory strategies and instruments can interact. As we have observed, different strategies and instruments have different logics. Some deter and coerce; others facilitate and assist. Some assume regulatees employ rational decision-making processes; others operate on their cognitive and subconscious biases. Really responsive regulation calls on regulators to align the logics of the strategies and instruments they employ. The fourth element is the regulatory regime's own performance. To be really responsive, a regulator needs to be able to assess its own performance and to modify its strategies and instruments accordingly. And finally, regulators (and regulatory regimes) need to be responsive to change. This change might be to the government's attitude, preferences and priorities, and the regulatory objectives it sets for the regulator. Alternatively, the change might be to the composition of the regulatee population or their willingness and capability to comply. Or it might be to the regulatory space more broadly. It could be the emergence of a new and powerful actor, interest group or technology which disrupts existing power structures; or a court decision that alters the constitutional or legal environment.

Really responsive regulation calls upon regulators to be attentive and responsive to these factors in everything they do. Really responsive regulation thus is 'wedded neither to any particular strategy of enforcement nor to enforcement as the control method of first choice'.[83] Rather, really responsive regulation calls for its lessons to be taken on board with respect to each regulatory task, and to recognise that the challenges presented by each task are likely to be different and may involve trade-offs. Being sensitive to these challenges and trade-offs is another component of being really responsive.[84]

The logic of really responsive regulation, like that of smart regulation, is difficult to fault. However, even more so than smart regulation, it is very difficult to implement. Baldwin and Black refer to it as 'fairly formidable' and 'daunting', and 'question whether this is an approach that demands a level of analysis too far—whether it can be operationalized in the usual regulatory context'.[85] The answer to this question is that in most situations, it cannot. Really responsive regulation may be a regulatory strategy that is nigh on impossible to fully implement. It calls for a level of sophistication, capability and resources that few (if any) regulators possess, or are likely to possess in a world of limited government resources. As such, it might be better to think of really responsive regulation as something to which regulators should aspire, but to which they should not unduly be held to account.

Summing up Regulatory Strategy

The evolution of our thinking about regulation has produced regulatory strategies of increasing sophistication and complexity, potentially beyond our ability to put them into practice. However, one should not lose sight of the core points common to these strategies: that for regulation to be implemented effectively, the regulator needs to understand its regulatees and the regulatory space; that it has to be capable of deploying combinations of behaviour change mechanisms and tools tailored to those regulatees' motivations and capabilities; and that to do this generally involves building partnerships with other actors occupying the regulatory space with it. And despite their growing sophistication, no strategy on its own is likely to be able to meet all the demands and challenges of real world regulatory practice. Our examination of the different strategies identified circumstances in which their use in combination is more likely to produce the desired outcomes. For example, that facilitative approaches require a background deterrent element, that problem-based approaches can be buttressed by risk-regulation techniques and that both problem-based and risk-based approaches can be supplemented by a combination of deterrence, facilitative, responsive and smart regulatory strategies to deal with the problems and risks they identify. Regulatory strategy therefore should not be viewed as a choice between competing and mutually exclusive options, but as a search for synergistic combinations tailored to the context and needs of the particular situation.[86] Indeed, it is not uncommon for modern regulators to adopt strategies that are at once responsive, problem-centred and risk-based, and that seek to employ smart (tailored and proportionate) combinations of interventions and instruments.

'Street-Level' Execution

Each of the regulatory strategies discussed above assumes it will be executed consistent with its underlying logic. Responsive regulation, for example, assumes that the regulator will respond responsively according to the motivation and attitude of the regulatee, escalating up and down the pyramid in response to each regulatee's willingness and capability to comply. Smart regulation similarly assumes the regulator will use a complimentary combination of regulatory instruments tailored to the causes and context of the specific issue. But when these strategies refer to 'the regulator', they are referring not just to the organisational entity. They also are referring to persons whose job it is to make the decisions required by that strategy. These persons exist at all levels of the organisation, from senior officials making decisions that relate to larger (and more influential) regulatees, to inspectors and other less senior officials working daily on the front-line. These inspectors and other front-line officials are sometimes referred to in the literature as 'street-level' officials, workers or bureaucrats.[87] The rest of this section focuses on these street-level officials, as it has been their decision-making that has been the focus of most research.

Execution of a regulatory strategy by 'street-level' officials is not a matter of their robotically applying automated or standardised responses. Regulatory strategies (and the standards they apply) are not expressed at the level of specificity that they are able to speak to all conceivable circumstances.[88] Application of strategies and standards is a matter of individual judgement and discretion. Judgement is 'the ability to make considered decisions or to arrive at reasonable conclusions'.[89] Discretion is the autonomy of the individual decision-maker to choose from a number of legally permissible options. Discretions can be broad or narrow. Dworkin uses the analogy of the 'hole in the doughnut' to describe discretion. The hole can be large or small depending on the area left open by the restrictions that surround it.[90] The need for judgement and discretion is both inevitable and legitimate: inevitable because, as we have already observed, the complexity of contemporary issues does not always allow for rules of general application, and legitimate to balance the competing values that underpin modern regulatory practice, such as certainty with flexibility, and consistency with proportionality. As such judgement and discretion is desirable. Their arbitrary and inconsistent exercise is not.

While judgement and discretion generally are exercised individually, they also are social processes that take place within organisational structures. As Vickers observed, '[t]he mental activity and the social process are dissoluble'.[91] Black similarly observes that '[u]nderstanding discretion requires understanding decision-making, which in turn requires understanding decision processes and decision behaviours'.[92] Much effort has gone into understanding these processes and behaviours. Early theories assumed technically rational (albeit bounded) decision-making—that decisions were purposive choices made from a set of alternatives by informed and disinterested officials implementing a clear strategy in pursuit of a clear regulatory objective.[93] More recent research, however, reveals that these conditions exist in very few situations. Rather this research reveals that the exercise of individual discretion (and, therefore, the application of a regulatory strategy) is influenced or mediated by numerous personal, institutional and cultural factors, including: organisational traditions and previous experiences;[94] peer-influence and the 'routinization of practice';[95] organisational and supervisory expectations;[96] the street-level official's familiarity and frequency of contact with the regulatee (known in the literature as 'relational distance');[97] organisational controls (e.g. performance targets; approval mechanisms; work allocation; role definitions) and the level of resourcing;[98] and personal and professional preferences, values, motives and worldviews.[99] These factors are represented diagrammatically in Figure 10.3.

The existence of these factors means that the street-level official—who is at the heart of the implementation process and a key instrument through which the regulatory strategy is executed—may not always execute that strategy consistently with its underlying logic. This can give rise to perceptions of inconsistent application and disconnects between 'head-office' and the 'street'. However, to observe these inconsistencies and disconnects is not to say that street-level implementation is not patterned or predictable. It may well be, but to a broader set of factors than just the strategy's underlying logic. It is therefore incumbent on those responsible for designing and deploying the institutional and organisational arrangements through which regulation is executed to be cognisant of the personal and institutional factors that influence how street-level officials exercise their discretion and make decisions, and to seek to structure those arrangements in a manner that facilitates the consistent exercise of discretion aligned to the regulatory strategy and objective.[100]

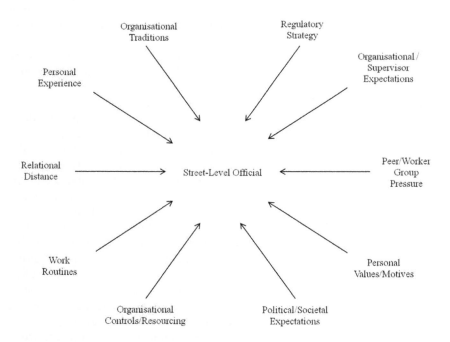

Figure 10.3 Factors Influencing Street-Level Execution of Regulatory Strategies

So how can this be done? The literature contains numerous suggestions. These include providing street-level officials with guidelines and rules to structure, focus and confine their exercise of discretion; training them in the art of decision-making consistent with those guidelines and rules; quality assurance mechanisms whereby decisions are periodically reviewed against those guidelines and rules; and accountability mechanisms whereby persons affected by a decision can seek review of it internally, or through courts and tribunals. The guidelines and rules may be specific to the organisation, or promulgated by a central government unit responsible for improving the quality of regulation more broadly.[101] They also can be found in administrative law principles that form the grounds upon which affected persons can seek to challenge a government decision. These grounds usually require decision-makers to follow fair processes, not to be biased, to take into account relevant considerations (and disregard irrelevant considerations), and to base their decision on evidence properly obtained.[102]

Of course, guidelines and rules on their own can never assure the consistent aggregate exercise of discretion. The application of the guidelines and rules themselves requires the exercise of discretion. The principles underpinning them—for example, certainty and consistency; flexibility and proportionality—do not always operate in the same direction. Judgements as to which should be prioritised and which should be compromised often are required. And as Black observes, seeking to reduce the breadth of the discretion (the size of the hole in Dworkin's doughnut) by increasing the prescription and restrictions that surround it

> . . . will not work, for all the reasons it does not work when detailed rules are used to regulate firms. For not only can rules . . . never fully control discretion, they bring their own problems. These included problems of *"rule overload"* (too many rules for the addressee to be able to absorb and remember, which means they are unlikely to comply with all of them), *rule system complexity* as detailed provisions create internal inconsistencies and contradictions, *creating loopholes* and facilitating *"creative compliance"* (emphasis in original).[103]

Recognising the broad factors that influence the exercise of discretion, Black concludes (correctly) that consistency in the exercise of street-level discretion requires 'mutuality of understanding and thus of interpretation', and that this requires engaging all actors involved in the regulatory endeavour—street-level officials, their supervisors, those who will adjudicate upon the manner with which the discretion has been exercised and the regulatees themselves—in conversation to forge a common understanding of what the regulatory standards mean and require, and when and how they should be applied.[104] And this brings us full circle to the start of the chapter—that regulation should be implemented through open and inclusive participatory processes.

Concluding Insights and Implications

In this chapter we have examined the implementation stage of the regulatory policy cycle by separately examining the processes through which regulation is first deployed, and then applied. In practice, however, deployment and application are not separate discrete activities. Nor are they always undertaken in an orderly and sequential manner. A regulator's legislative and administrative structure shapes and constrains the strategic approaches available to it and, in turn, the strategic approaches best able to achieve the regulatory objectives should influence the shape and nature of its legislative and administrative arrangements. This makes deployment and application interdependent and iterative functions.

Our discussion also has revealed that regulatory implementation is context specific. Care should be taken to avoid adopting rigid starting positions and default rules. A number of regulatory strategies commence from the proposition regulators should initially adopt the least interventionist measure and then escalate enforcement activity in response to the behaviours, motivations and capabilities of the regulatee. This logic also underpins much of the better regulation agenda. Advocates for this approach point to some obvious benefits—lower costs to government and business, less resistance and enhanced legitimacy (at least among regulatees and those whose resources and support may be required). There are dangers with this approach, however. 'Light handed', less interventionist approaches can create a regulatory environment in which risks that ought to be regulated are not, or not to the extent they ought to have been. Remember, one person's red-tape is another person's safety net. The rationale for light handed low intervention regulation also can be found wanting when *ex post* judgments of regulatory decisions are made in the face of harm. As Perez explains, the law focuses on conduct and outcomes, and less on intentions; politics focuses on blame allocation, and less on reasoned explanations; and the mass media focuses on actors (villains and victims) and avoids complexity.[105] It is no wonder that 'cover-your-arse' behaviours, defensiveness and over-cautiousness can sometimes overtake regulators (and street-level officials in particular) faced with difficult choices.

This last point highlights the important role of discretion and judgement. How regulation is deployed shapes and constrains those discretions, and the choice of regulatory strategy guides regulators and street-level officials in their exercise. But structures, systems and strategies, no matter how well designed, deployed and applied, cannot automate or replace the exercise of individual judgment. It always will remain paramount. Street-level officials, by the approach they adopt, can take perfectly reasonable laws and make them unreasonable; and can take unreasonable laws and make them feel reasonable (or at least less unreasonable).[106]

The context specific and iterative nature of regulatory implementation means getting the regulatory settings 'right' the first time is likely to be the exception rather than the rule. Regulatory settings tend to be the product of trial and adjustment. The regulatory system needs to have the built-in flexibility to be able to adjust nimbly both to data on its performance and to changes in the issue, regulatees and the broader regulatory space. Monitoring and adjusting tasks are central to this. However, in some cases, the level of performance or the nature of the change is such that a more rigorous approach is required. This brings us to the last stage of the regulatory policy cycle—evaluation.

Notes

1. Robbie W Robichau and Laurence E Lynn Jr, 'The Implementation of Public Policy: Still a Missing Link' (2009) 37 *Policy Studies Journal* 21. The title of the article reflects a perception in some public policy circles that implementation is under-researched and under-theorised. This is not the case in the regulatory field, however, where there is a rich vein of implementation research, models and approaches from which to draw.
2. Richard E Matland, 'Synthetizing the Implementation Literature: The Ambiguity-Conflict Model of Policy Implementation' (1995) 5 *Journal of Public Administration Research and Theory* 145.
3. See discussion of participation in Chapter 5, 86–90. See also: Julia Black, 'Talking about Regulation' [1998] (Spring) *Public Law* 77.
4. See Christoph Knill and Jale Tosun, *Public Policy: A New Introduction* (Palgrave Macmillan, 2012) 152–3, and the studies cited therein.
5. See Alfred D Chandler, *Strategy and Structure* (MIT Press, 1962) who is considered the pioneer of this view.
6. See, e.g., David J Hall and Maurice A Saias, 'Strategy Follows Structure!' (1980) 1 *Strategic Management Journal* 149; Henry Mintzberg, 'The Design School: Reconsidering the Basic Premises of Strategic Management' (1990) 11 *Strategic Management Journal* 171; Terry L Amburgey and Tina Dacin, 'As the Left Foot Follows the Right? The Dynamics of Strategic and Structural Change' (1994) 37 *Academy of Management Journal* 1427.
7. Regulatory legitimacy is discussed in Chapter 6.
8. See, e.g., OECD, 'The Governance of Regulators, OECD Best Practice Principles for Regulatory Policy' (OECD Publishing, 2014); Australian National Audit Office, 'Administering Regulation, Better Practice Guide' (ANAO, 2007); United Kingdom, Better Regulation Delivery Office, '"Regulators" Code' (Department for Business, Innovation and Skills, April 2014).
9. See the discussion of organisational culture at 226.
10. See Chapter 7, 145–6.
11. European Commission, 'Better Regulation "Toolbox"' (EC, 2016) 248–51 (Tool 35: Monitoring Arrangements and Indictors).
12. See, e.g., Suzanne J Piotrowski and David Rosenbloom, 'Nonmission-Based Values in Results Orientated Public Management: The Case of Freedom of Information' (2002) 62 *Public Administration Review* 643; Beryl Radin, *Challenging the Performance Movement: Accountability, Complexity and Democratic Values* (Georgetown University Press, 2006); Donald P Moynihan et al, 'Performance Regimes Amidst Governance Complexity' (2011) 21(Supp No 1) *Journal of Public Administration Research and Theory* 141.
13. For a discussion of RIAs, cost-benefit and multi-criteria analyses, see Chapter 9, 207–11.

14. Julia Black, 'The Emergence of Risk-Based Regulation and the New Public Risk Management in the United Kingdom' [2005] (Autumn) *Public Law* 512, 516. These are different to risks to society that are the focus of the regulatory regime.
15. See Chapter 5, 94–5.
16. Eric Windholz, 'The Evolution of a Modern (and More Legitimate) Regulator: A Case Study of the Victorian Environment Protection Authority' (2016) 3 *Australian Journal of Environmental Law* 17.
17. See discussion of 'street level' execution below at 242–5.
18. This adage is attributed to management consultant and academic, Peter Drucker.
19. See Chapter 6, 104.
20. Other taxonomies of regulatory tasks exist. Baldwin and Black, for example, use the anagram DREAM to refer to the tasks of detecting, responding, enforcing, assessing and modifying: Robert Baldwin and Julia Black, 'DEFRA: A Review of Enforcement Measures and an Assessment of Their Effectiveness in Terms of Risk and Outcome' (Department of Environment, Food and Rural Affairs, 2005).
21. See the discussion of regulatee motivation in Chapter 8, 169.
22. See the discussion of regulatory legitimacy (and of procedural legitimacy in particular) in Chapter 6.
23. See, e.g., Environment Protection Authority Victoria, 'Compliance and Enforcement Policy' (EPA Victoria, 2014) 19–20.
24. European Commission, 'Better Regulation "Toolbox"', above n 11, 246 (Tool 35: Monitoring Arrangements and Indicators).
25. See 224–5.
26. Employing the typology of first, second and third order changes, monitoring and adjusting generally involves first-order changes (e.g. fine-tuning existing instruments and institutional arrangements) and second-order changes (e.g. switching between, or changing the mix of, instruments that the regulator presently is empowered to use). Third-order changes such as changing objectives or replacing existing tools and approaches with new tools and approaches generally take place only after an evaluation. Baldwin, Cave and Lodge give as an example of a third-order change shifting from controlling pollution through coercive mechanisms to incentivising reductions through an emission trading scheme: Baldwin, Cave and Lodge, *Understanding Regulation*, above n 9, 256–7.
27. Robert Baldwin and Julia Black, 'Really Responsive Regulation' (2008) 71 *Modern Law Review* 59, 76.
28. See, e.g., Albert J Reiss Jr, 'Selecting Strategies of Social Control over Organizational Life' in K Hawkins and J M Thomas (eds), *Enforcing Regulation* (Kluwer Nijhoff, 1984) 23.
29. Deterrence theory can be traced to the 18th century work of Cesare Beccaria (*On Crimes and Punishments* (1764)) and Jeremy Bentham (*An Introduction to the Principles of Morals and Legislation* (1789)) who argued that the propensity to break the law is inversely related to the certainty, severity and swiftness of punishment.
30. Brent Fisse and John Braithwaite, *The Impact of Publicity on Corporate Offenders* (State University of New York Press, 1983) 247, 249. See also John Braithwaite, *Restorative Justice and Responsive Regulation* (Oxford University Press, 2002) 30–4, 106; For a more recent examination of the deterrence literature, see Arie Freiberg, *The Tools of Regulation* (Federation Press, 2010) 211–14.
31. Freiberg, *The Tools of Regulation*, above n 30, 213. Freiberg makes this statement with reference to criminal law, but it is equally applicable to regulation more broadly.

32. Prescriptive standards and coercive mechanisms are discussed in Chapter 8 at 155–7; and at 170–2 respectively.
33. Julia Black, 'Decentring Regulation: Understanding the Role of Regulation and Self-Regulation in a "Post-Regulatory" World' (2001) 54 *Current Legal Problems* 103, 105. See also Leslie M Salamon, *The Tools of Government: A Guide to the New Governance* (Oxford University Press, 2002) 8.
34. John Braithwaite and Toni Makkai, 'Trust and Compliance' (1994) 4 *Policing and Society* 1; Robert A Kagan, 'Adversarial Legalism and American Government' (1991) 10 *Journal of Policy Analysis and Management* 369.
35. Eugene Bardach and Robert A Kagan, *Going by the Book: The Problem of Regulatory Unreasonableness* (Temple University Press, 2002); Neil Gunningham, 'Prosecution for OHS Offences: Deterrent or Disincentive?' (2007) 29 *Sydney Law Review* 359.
36. See Chapter 6, 105–6.
37. See, e.g., Brent Fisse and John Braithwaite, *Corporations, Crime and Accountability* (Cambridge University Press, 1993); Neil Gunningham and Richard Johnstone, *Regulating Workplace Safety* (Oxford University Press, 1999) 215–25; Robert A Kagan and John T Scholz, 'The "Criminology of the Corporation" and Regulatory Enforcement Strategies' in K Hawkins and J M Thomas (eds), *Enforcing Regulation* (Kluwer Nijhoff Publishing, 1984) 67; Christine Parker and Vibeke Lehmann Nielsen (eds), *Explaining Compliance: Business Responses to Regulation* (Edward Elgar, 2011).
38. See generally Fiona Haines, *Corporate Regulation: Beyond 'Punish or Persuade'* (Routledge, 1997).
39. See the discussion of regulatee motivation to comply in Chapter 8, 168–9. See also: Parker and Nielsen, *Explaining Compliance*, above n 37, in particular Christine Parker and Vibeke L Nielson, 'Introduction' ch 1; Robert A Kagan, Neil Gunningham and Dorothy Thornton, 'Fear, Duty, and Regulatory Compliance: Lessons from Three Research Projects' ch 2.
40. Baldwin, Cave and Lodge, *Understanding Regulation*, above n 26, 240.
41. Neil Gunningham, 'Enforcement and Compliance Strategies' in R Baldwin, M Cave and M Lodge (eds), *Oxford Handbook of Regulation* (Oxford University Press, 2010) 120; Neil Gunningham, 'Compliance, Enforcement and Regulatory Excellence' (Paper prepared for the Penn Program on Regulation's Best-in-Class Regulator Initiative, June 2015) 3.
42. Gunningham, 'Compliance, Enforcement and Regulatory Excellence', above n 41, 2.
43. Ian Ayres and John Braithwaite, *Responsive Regulation: Transcending the Deregulation Debate* (Oxford University Press, 1992).
44. Ibid 25.
45. These examples are adaptations of Ayres' and Braithwaite's pyramids, the originals of which are in Ayres and Braithwaite, *Responsive Regulation*, above n 43, 35, 39. These adaptations reflect this book's categorisation of regulators and regulatory instruments. As such, they are illustrative only. What is important for our purposes is not the pyramid's specific content, but the ideas behind them.
46. Ayres and Braithwaite, *Responsive Regulation*, above n 43, 19.
47. Martin Lodge and Kai Wegrich, *Managing Regulation: Regulatory Analysis, Politics and Policy* (Palgrave Macmillan, 2012) 82–3.
48. For examples of its application, see Mary Ivec and Valerie Braithwaite, 'Applications of Responsive Regulatory Theory in Australia and Overseas: Update' (Regulatory Institutions Network, Australian National University, 2015). For testimonials to its influence, see: Christine Parker, 'Twenty Years of Responsive Regulation: An Appreciation and Appraisal' (2013) 7 *Regulation & Governance* 2–13; Peter Mascini, 'Why Was the Enforcement Pyramid So Influential? And What Price Was Paid?' (2013) 7 *Regulation & Governance* 48–60.

49. Responsive regulation has been criticised on policy, practical and principled grounds. See generally Baldwin and Black, 'Really Responsive Regulation', above n 27, 62–4.
50. See Chapter 3, 39–41. See also Neil Gunningham, 'Enforcing Environmental Regulation' (2011) 23 *Journal of Environmental Law* 169, 199–200.
51. An example of this are fisheries; see Baldwin and Black, 'Really Responsive Regulation', above n 27.
52. An example of this is the financial services sector; see Dimity Kingsford Smith, 'A Harder Nut to Crack? Responsive Regulation in the Financial Services Sector' (2011) 44 *University of British Columbia Law Review* 695.
53. Neil Gunningham, 'Compliance, Enforcement, and Regulatory Excellence' in C Coglianese (ed), *Achieving Regulatory Excellence* (Brookings Institution Press, 2016) 188, 190–1.
54. Baldwin and Black, 'Really Responsive Regulation', above n 27, 63.
55. Haines, *Corporate Regulation*, above n 38, 219–20; Baldwin and Black, 'Really Responsive Regulation', above n 27, 62–4.
56. For examples of different ways responsive regulation has been applied in practice, see Ivec and Braithwaite, 'Applications of Responsive Regulatory Theory in Australia and Overseas', above n 48. See also Mascini, 'Why Was the Enforcement Pyramid So Influential? And What Price Was Paid?', above n 48, 48.
57. Risk-based regulation is discussed at 239–40.
58. Gunningham and Johnstone, *Regulating Workplace Safety*, above n 37, 122–5.
59. Ibid 126–9. For an example of responsive regulation applied in this manner, see Environment Protection Authority Victoria, 'Compliance and Enforcement Policy', above n 23, 21–2; Australian National Audit Office, 'Administering Regulation, Better Practice Guide', above n 8, 64.
60. Neil Gunningham and Peter Grabosky, *Smart Regulation: Designing Environmental Policy* (Clarendon Press, 1998).
61. Ibid 4.
62. Ibid 376–7, 387–422. The authors articulate five principles; they have been distilled into three here.
63. Ibid 387–91.
64. Ibid 395–404, 408–13. See also Peter Grabosky, 'Inside the Pyramid: Towards a Conceptual Framework for the Analysis of Regulatory Systems' (1997) *International Journal of the Sociology of Law* 195.
65. Gunningham and Grabosky, *Smart Regulation*, above n 60, 391–5, 404–8.
66. Ibid 404.
67. Ibid 422–48.
68. Malcom K Sparrow, *The Regulatory Craft: Controlling Risks, Solving Problems, and Managing Compliance* (Brookings Institution Press, 2000).
69. Ibid 131.
70. Ibid ch 10.
71. Baldwin, Cave and Lodge, *Understanding Regulation*, above n 26, 268; Baldwin and Black, 'Really Responsive Regulation', above n 27, 68.
72. Sparrow, *The Regulatory Craft*, above n 68, 9.
73. Ibid ch 11. Sparrow also identified two other desirable but non-essential systems: learnings systems to share knowledge across the regulator; and reward systems that recognise team results.
74. Philip Hampton, 'Reducing Administrative Burdens' (HM Treasury, 2005).
75. Julia Black and Robert Baldwin, 'Really Responsive Risk-Based Regulation' (2010) 32 *Law & Policy* 181, 181.
76. Baldwin and Black observe that by focussing on issues of greatest risk, rather than on issues that offer the highest rate of return on investment, risk-based

regulation might lead to an inefficient allocation of resources: Baldwin and Black, 'Really Responsive Regulation', above n 27.

77. See, e.g., OECD, 'Risk and Regulatory Policy: Improving the Governance of Risk' (OECD, 2010) 193–4, 243; Black and Baldwin, 'Really Responsive Risk-Based Regulation', above n 75, 203.

78. For an overview of both risk-based regulation's utility and challenges, see the collection of papers in OECD, 'Risk and Regulatory Policy', above n 77; Black and Baldwin, 'Really Responsive Risk-Based Regulation', above n 75, 189–90; Baldwin, Cave and Lodge, *Understanding Regulation*, above n 26, ch 13.

79. The different answers to these (and other questions) mean numerous methodologies exist for identifying and scoring risks. This has resulted in considerable variability across regimes and jurisdictions in the methodologies employed. This, in turn, has made comparisons across areas difficult: Julia Black, 'Risk-Based Regulation: Choices, Practices and Lessons Being Learned' in OECD, 'Risk and Regulatory Policy', above n 77, 185; Henry Rothstein, Olivier Borraz and Michael Huber, 'Risk and the Limits of Governance: Exploring Varied Patterns of Risk-Based Governance across Europe' (2013) 7 *Regulation & Governance* 215.

80. In this regard, the UK Hampton Review recommended that all regulatory agencies adopt a risk-based approach to enforcement and also random inspections for areas not prioritised: Hampton, 'Reducing Administrative Burdens', above n 74, 27. See also Julia Back and Robert Baldwin, 'When Risk-Based Regulation Aims Low: Approaches and Challenges' (2012) 6 *Regulation & Governance* 2; Julia Black and Robert Baldwin, 'When Risk-Based Regulation Aims Low: A Strategic Framework' (2012) 6 *Regulation & Governance* 131.

81. Baldwin and Black, 'Really Responsive Regulation', above n 27. See also Black and Baldwin, 'Really Responsive Risk-Based Regulation', above n 75.

82. Baldwin and Black, 'Really Responsive Regulation', above n 27, 70. Institutional theories are discussed in Chapter 3.

83. Ibid 69.

84. Ibid 61–2.

85. Ibid 76, 93.

86. Lodge and Wegrich, *Managing Regulation*, above n 47, 99.

87. See, e.g., Janet Coble Vinzant and Lane Crothers, *Street-Level Leadership: Discretion and Legitimacy in Front-Line Public Service* (Georgetown University Press, 1998); Michael Lipsky, *Street-Level Bureaucracy: Dilemma of the Individual in Public Services* (Russell Sage Foundation, 1980); Patrick G Scott, 'Assessing Determinants of Bureaucratic Discretion: An Experiment in Street-Level Decision Making' (1997) 7 *Journal of Public Administration Research and Theory* 35; Stephen Fineman, 'Street-Level Bureaucrats and the Social Construction of Environmental Control' (1998) 19 *Organization Studies* 953; Søren C Winter, 'Explaining Street-Level Bureaucratic Behavior in Social and Regulatory Policies' (Paper prepared for the 2002 Annual Meeting of the American Political Science Association, Boston, August 2002); Marcia K Meyers and Susan Vorsanger, 'Street-Level Bureaucrats and the Implementation of Public Policy' in B G Peters and J Pierre (eds), *Handbook of Public Administration* (Sage, 2003) 245; Vibeke L Nielsen, 'Are Street-Level Bureaucrats Compelled or Enticed to Cope?' (2006) 84 *Public Administration* 861; Erica Gabrielle Foldy and Tamara R Buckley, 'Re-Creating Street-Level Practice: The Role of Routines, Work Groups, and Team Learning' (2009) 20 *Journal of Pubic Administration Research and Theory* 23.

88. Keith Hawkins, *Law as Last Resort: Prosecution Decision-Making in a Regulatory Agency* (Oxford University Press, 2002) 427.

89. *Oxford English Dictionary* (Oxford University Press, 3rd ed, 2013).

90. Ronald Dworkin, *Taking Rights Seriously* (Bloomsbury Publishing, 2013) 38–9.
91. Geoffrey Vickers, *The Art of Judgement: A Study of Policy Making* (Chapman & Hill, 1965) 15.
92. Julia Black, 'New Institutionalism and Naturalism in Socio-Legal Analysis: Institutionalist Approaches to Regulatory Decision-Making' (1997) 19 *Law & Policy* 51, 52.
93. For a discussion of rational decision-making theory and its variants, see Keith Hawkins, *The Uses of Discretion* (Clarendon Press, 1992) 20–4.
94. Winter, 'Explaining Street-Level Bureaucratic Behavior in Social and Regulatory Policies', above n 87; Keith Hawkins, 'On Legal Decision-Making' (1986) 43 *Washington and Lee Law Review* 1161.
95. Lipsky, *Street-Level Bureaucracy*, above n 87, 209; Scott, 'Assessing Determinants of Bureaucratic Discretion', above n 87; Foldy and Buckley, 'Re-Creating Street-Level Practice', above n 87.
96. Vinzant and Crothers, *Street-Level Leadership*, above n 87.
97. Donald Black, *The Behavior of Law* (Academic Press, 1976).
98. Bridget M Hutter, 'Variations in Regulatory Enforcement Styles' (1989) 11 *Law & Policy* 153.
99. Damon Alexander and Jenny M Lewis, *Making Public Policy Decisions: Expertise, Skills and Experience* (Routledge, 2014); Black, 'New Institutionalism and Naturalism in Socio-Legal Analysis', above n 92, 53; Hawkins, *Law as Last Resort*, above n 88, 4; Vinzant and Crothers, *Street-Level Leadership*, above n 87, 12; Hutter, 'Variations in Regulatory Enforcement Styles', above n 98; Winter, 'Explaining Street-Level Bureaucratic Behavior in Social and Regulatory Policies', above n 87.
100. Julia Black, 'Managing Discretion' (ALRC Conference Papers, Penalties: Policy, Principles and Practice in Government Regulation, June 2001).
101. For a discussion of these better regulation units, see Chapter 6, 110–11.
102. An example of guidelines that pull these threads together is the Australian Government Attorney-General's Department, 'Australian Administrative Law Policy Guide' (Commonwealth of Australia, 2011).
103. Black, 'Managing Discretion', above n 100, 28.
104. Ibid 28–9. See also Black, 'Talking about Regulation', above n 3.
105. Oren Perez, 'Courage, Regulatory Responsibility, and the Challenge of Higher-Order Reflexivity' (2014) 8 *Regulation & Governance* 203, 215.
106. Sparrow, *The Regulatory Craft*, above n 68, 5.

11 Evaluate

Assessment of Regulatory Policy and Regime

The final stage of the regulatory policy cycle is evaluation. Evaluation is the systematic assessment of all (or parts of) a regulatory policy and regime with the view to making recommendations for future action. Evaluation is an essential element of good policy and regulatory practice. Evaluations enable us to assess and understand the broader value of the regulatory policy and regime being evaluated, and to develop learnings to improve its performance and the performance of other like policies and regimes (current and future). There is no shortage of guides designed to assist with the evaluation of regulatory policy initiatives.[1] Nor is there a shortage of academic commentaries and frameworks for designing an evaluation process.[2] Five key elements are common to these guides and frameworks. They are: (a) the scope of the evaluation; (b) the evaluation users and the level of stakeholder (third party) participation; (c) the role of the evaluator; (d) the evaluation criteria; and (e) the evaluation strategy and methodology. These elements are interdependent: a decision with respect to one element impacts the choices available in other elements. Notwithstanding their interdependence, however, this chapter examines each element separately for analytical ease and clarity. The chapter then concludes with some observations about the manner with which evaluations impact decisions with respect to the continuation or termination of the regulatory endeavour.

Evaluation Scope

A fundamental requirement in any evaluation is to define its scope, which can be thought of in terms of its purpose or goals and the subjects to be evaluated (which are referred to in the evaluation literature as the 'evaluand'). The primary purpose of an evaluation is to determine whether to continue, modify or terminate the regulatory policy (or aspects of the policy) being evaluated. Evaluations also can have other additional purposes, for example, to assess and understand the regulatory policy's broader economic and social impact, and to develop learnings to inform the development of policies and initiatives in like areas.

The evaluand (the subject to be evaluated) usually is defined in terms of processes, outputs or outcomes. Process-focused evaluations examine the processes involved in the regulatory endeavour. These could include the processes by which the issue was diagnosed and the regulatory objectives set, alternative regimes options were designed and evaluated and the final regime chosen, and how that final regime was deployed, applied and executed. Output-focused evaluations (sometimes also referred to as process-and-results-focused evaluations) focus on the intervention's logic and outputs. They examine whether the regime has been implemented in accordance with its intervention logic, and whether the regime's outputs—its behaviour change mechanisms and instruments—have impacted on the issue's causal drivers as expected and produced the desired results (which, it will be recalled, were expressed as operational objectives). And outcome-focused evaluations focus on whether the regime has achieved its primary regulatory objectives, and is less concerned with the processes and outputs by which those outcomes and objectives were achieved.

Each of process-, output- and outcome-focused evaluations also can be defined with varying levels of specificity. Process-focused evaluations, for example, can evaluate all or some of the define, design and implement processes. Similarly, output-focused evaluations can examine all outputs (behaviour change mechanisms and instruments) or some only; and outcome-focused evaluations can be restricted to formally articulated primary objectives, or can evaluate the regime's overall regulatory impact, both intended and unintended, positive and negative—what Dye refers to as the 'policy impact'.[3] The broader the scope (purpose and evaluand), the greater are the potential benefits, but also the cost and complexity of conducting the evaluation.

Another important issue in defining the scope of the evaluation is whether it should be confined to the activities of government actors or whether it should include the activities of non-government actors co-opted or enlisted into the regulatory endeavour as co- or quasi-regulators, remembering that many regimes today are poly-centric in nature.[4] Clearly, to gain maximum benefit from an evaluation, all relevant aspects of the regime should be evaluated, including those undertaken by non-government actors. However, including non-governmental activities within the scope of the evaluation gives rise to a number of challenges. First, there is the challenge of attribution. Being able to isolate the relative impact and effectiveness of the activities undertaken by a discrete regulator (be they government, co- or quasi-) is inherently difficult. This is especially the case with output and outcome orientated evaluations where those outputs and outcomes are the product of networked activities. Second, there are legitimacy and accountability challenges. Even if impacts can be assigned to non-government actors, this does not relieve government of its responsibilities for those impacts. Governments and regulatory agencies are generally held publically and politically accountable for regulatory outcomes and, in particular, for regulatory failures, even in situations where the failure is the result of the actions or inactions of non-government actors. Scott refers to this as an accountability paradox that creates the opposite dynamic to that traditionally confronted: that is, the problem is 'NOT of too much power and too little accountability, but rather the converse—too little power and too much accountability'.[5] This makes evaluating poly-centric regimes not only difficult but also politically challenging.

The evaluation's purpose and evaluand are the key criteria for determining the parameters of the evaluation's other elements. But what criteria should be used to determine the evaluation's scope (its purpose and evaluand)? Patton argues the evaluation's scope should reflect the needs of the evaluation's primary users.[6] But this begs the question—who are those primary users and what are their needs? It also raises the question of the extent to which regulatees, those for whose benefit government regulates, the regime's co- and quasi-regulators, and other persons otherwise impacted by the regulatory endeavour (who generally are referred to in the evaluation literature as 'stakeholders') should participate in an evaluation. It is to these questions that we now turn.

Evaluation Users and Stakeholder Participation

Government actors generally are the primary users of evaluation findings. Policy analysts and officials use evaluation results to modify and improve existing regimes and to inform the design of other regulatory interventions. Other government actors may have different uses, however. Politicians, for example, may use evaluation results to laud their and their government's achievements or to deflect failures onto factors for which they are not responsible. And regulators are likely to engage in a mix of these behaviours depending on the evaluation findings, accepting the credit for what has worked and trying to learn from what has not worked while minimising any resultant damage to their legitimacy.

But government is not the only user of evaluation findings. They also are used by the host of other actors involved in, interested in or impacted by the regulatory endeavour. These stakeholders use evaluation findings to support and strengthen the positions they hold and to challenge and weaken contrary positions. We have observed that regulation frequently involves balancing different values, interests and positions, and making trade-offs between them. Evaluation findings (or more correctly, the uses to which they are put) have the potential to alter those balances and trade-offs, sometimes dramatically. The question then is should persons who hold these values, interests and positions participate in the evaluation? This is an important question. Involving stakeholders in the evaluation process offers the promise of a better informed and more robust and legitimate evaluation; however, each stakeholder may advocate for different evaluation scopes and favour the use of different criteria, processes and analytical methods. This can make the evaluation process complex and contested, and carries with it the risk of the evaluation process being captured or otherwise manipulated by these non-government stakeholders.

The nature of the regulatory regime should inform the decision about the appropriate level of stakeholder participation. In co- and poly-centric regulatory regimes where regulatees or other parties are serving as co- or quasi-regulators, their participation is near mandatory. The same also should apply to those whose resources and support have been enlisted or co-opted into it. But saying they should participate says nothing about the nature and level of that participation. There are different views as to the extent to which stakeholders should participate in an evaluation. At one end of the spectrum there is the technical approach, in which stakeholder views are but one of many inputs with the evaluator (and not the stakeholders) assessing and determining the extent to which 'success' has been achieved.[7] Then there are 'responsive evaluation' models, in which the views of the stakeholders are systematically gathered, weighed against other views and information, and subjected to collective dialogue and deliberations, but in which the evaluator remains responsible for, and the ultimate arbiter of, the evaluation.[8] And at the other end of the spectrum are approaches variously described as 'democratic deliberative', 'fourth generation' or 'empowerment' models, in which stakeholders are placed at the centre of the evaluation process, are given the tools with which to evaluate the regulatory policy themselves and assume a shared responsibility for the evaluation process.[9] The ideal under these models is for stakeholders to reach a consensus view. However, as Pawson and Tilley point out, such an expectation may be naïve. The asymmetries of power that can exist among stakeholders and the strength of their ideological differences can render consensus unrealistic.[10]

A stakeholder inclusive evaluation model recognises the political nature of the evaluation process.[11] No matter how much an evaluator may seek to be objective, neutral or purely technical in his or her approach, the process is 'heavily loaded with values, politics and power'.[12] How and by whom key decisions are made in setting up an evaluation process—who defines the scope of the evaluand, the evaluation criteria and how it is to be measured—all have the potential to profoundly influence the final outcome. The evaluator is likely to receive direction on these elements from the government agency that commissions and funds the evaluation. Their issues and concerns are, of course, important. However, they also may have a vested interest in the outcome. It is possible that they may seek to set the evaluation's terms of reference in a manner designed to maximise the prospects of a favourable evaluation. Like regulatory impact assessments, evaluations are based on assumptions and hypotheses that are susceptible to 'political adjustment'.[13] It is therefore important that the issues and concerns of other stakeholders are considered in scoping the evaluation.[14] Involving stakeholders in the evaluation process also minimises the prospect of stakeholders feeling marginalised, increases trust and confidence in the process, and reduces suspicion and alienation, thereby adding to the legitimacy of both the evaluation process and its outcomes. This, in turn, increases the prospect that the results will be accepted and effectively utilised.[15]

There are limits to a stakeholder inclusive approach though. First, there are practical and logistical limits. Not every person with an interest in the issue can always participate in the evaluation process. Second, power differentials will exist among those who participate. House and Howe, for example, recognise that power imbalances can distort an evaluation's findings;[16] and Wolf similarly notes that every public policy measure produces winners and losers, and that if the winners are better organised and represented, there is a risk of the evaluation being skewed in their favour.[17] Mertens argues that to mitigate this risk, priority should be given to groups that may be marginalised by the policy.[18] If the decision is made to have a participatory evaluation process, then every effort should be made to ensure it is as inclusive as possible, and that every stakeholder receives an equal opportunity to participate and be heard.

The Evaluator's Role

The nature and level of stakeholder participation directly impacts upon the role of the evaluator. The greater the role given to stakeholders, the more the role of the evaluator transitions from technical analysis and adjudicator of interests to negotiating and mediating; teaching and facilitating. Guba and Lincoln make the point that for the evaluation process to be truly inclusive and participatory, the evaluator needs to 'honor' the values of the various stakeholder groups. To exercise his/her judgment to prefer one set of values over another would be to dishonour those values and risk alienating one or more (or all) of the stakeholder groups.[19] Rather, the evaluator should perform the role of mediator and negotiator—collecting information about the different needs of the various stakeholders, negotiating their claims, concerns and issues, and attempting to reach agreement among them on the objectives, criteria, priorities and outcomes of the evaluation. To do this, the evaluator also needs to be a teacher and facilitator—promoting 'a pluralistic, multi-disciplinary and open exchange of knowledge'—and creating an environment in which each stakeholder has an equal opportunity to be heard and considered, is able to understand and appreciate the interests and perspectives of the other stakeholders, and is presented with information to enable it to draw its own conclusions and make its own judgments.[20]

All of this requires the evaluator to have a combination of technical, stakeholder management, communication and political skills.[21] It is rare for all these skills to be found in one person. Evaluations, therefore, often are undertaken by teams of persons with a diversity of skills, disciplines and organisational backgrounds. Bringing together these different perspectives can produce richer and better evaluations. It also guards against the evaluation being skewed by the organisational, disciplinary and personal biases of one person.[22]

Most importantly though, the evaluator (or evaluators) should be—and should be perceived to be—independent of government and any major stakeholder. When one talks of independence, one is reminded of the evaluation laws formulated by Harvard Professor James Q Wilson:

> 'First Law: All policy interventions in social problems produce the intended effect—*if* the research is carried out by those implementing the policy or their friends.
>
> Second Law: No policy intervention in social problems produces the intended effect—*if* the research is carried out by independent third parties, especially those skeptical of the policy.'[23]

But the issue of independence is more fundamental than perceived biases towards the policy being evaluated. Where regulation is heavily contested, any evaluation is likely to be 'knee-deep in values, beliefs, party politics and ideology'.[24] The independence and neutrality of the evaluator(s) in these circumstances is paramount.

The Evaluation Criteria

Central to any evaluation is the selection of the criteria to be assessed and the standards or norms of comparison. These should reflect the evaluation's purposes and the nature of the evaluand. Effectiveness and efficiency are key criteria for all evaluations. Whether the evaluation is process-, output- or outcome-focused, narrowly or broadly defined, it always is important to know if the aspect of the regime being evaluated has achieved its predetermined objectives, and whether it has done so efficiently. However, effectiveness and efficiency are malleable concepts. Both can be defined narrowly or broadly. Effectiveness, for example, can be limited to all or some of the policy's operational or primary objectives, or can extend to a consideration of unintended consequences, both positive and negative (Dye's 'policy impact'). Depending on the scope of the evaluation (process, output or outcome), the evaluation might ask: to what extent have the objectives been achieved?; what have been the (quantitative and qualitative) effects of the policy/regime?; to what extent can observed behavioural changes be credited to the policy/regime?; what other factors might have led to these changes?; and what other (unintended) effects have these changes caused?[25]

Efficiency, similarly, can be defined broadly in terms of net benefits (benefits less costs), or narrowly by reference to cost-effectiveness only. Cost-effectiveness generally tends to be measured by reference to the regulatory and compliance burden imposed on stakeholders. However, it also should include the costs to government to develop the regulatory policy and implement the regulatory regime. Typical efficiency questions might include: what are the benefits and costs of the policy/regime, and to whom have they accrued?; are the costs proportionate to the benefits?; what factors influenced the benefits and costs of the policy/regime?; and to what extent and where could the policy/regime have been implemented at lower cost?[26]

Effectiveness and efficiency are necessary but not sufficient evaluative criteria. Evaluations also should assess the policy's and regime's adherence to important legal, constitutional and democratic values.[27] These include values such as accessibility, responsiveness, certainty, consistency, accountability and transparency found in better regulation reforms' good regulation principles, and in the legal, procedural and structural dimensions of regulatory legitimacy discussed in Chapter 6. Other commentators suggest that evaluations go even further to examine regulatory initiatives against broader social values such fairness, equity, justice and human rights.[28] And in the context of collaborate enterprises such as co- and poly-centric regulatory regimes, Skelcher and Sullivan recommend that they be assessed against the core democratic values of: legitimacy (whether the institution is seen as desirable, proper and appropriate in the eyes of its legitimacy communities); consent (that the persons affected by the actions and decisions of the institution are consulted, have the right to express their views and decisions are made in a transparent manner); and accountability (that the decision-makers are selected by and accountable to the citizens).[29]

Evaluation Strategy and Methodology

The final element is the evaluation strategy and methodology. This has been left for last deliberately. The evaluation's goals and users' needs should determine strategy and methodology. The literature abounds with different evaluation strategies and methodologies. Evaluations can vary from the technical and quantitative to the descriptive and qualitative; and from preliminary 'evaluability' assessments through to intensive 'scientific' evaluations.[30] Evaluations can be 'formative' with a focus on process and activities, 'summative' with a focus on outcomes and results, or both.[31] Evaluations can employ a 'micro' perspective with the focus on the regime's structural and operational characteristics or a 'macro' perspective with its focus on the policy's political, economic and social dimensions.[32] And evaluations can be technical, responsive, democratic deliberative or empowering depending on the level and nature of stakeholder participation (see previous discussion).

There is no single 'best' method. Each has its merits. The key issue is 'fitness for purpose'—the choice of strategy and methodology should satisfy the user's needs, as reflected in the evaluation goals. This is what Patton refers to as a utilisation-focused evaluation—'an evaluation done for and with specific, intended primary users for specific, intended purposes'.[33] In the case of complex issues with a multiplicity of stakeholders each with their own interests and objectives, it is unlikely that any one strategy or methodology could satisfy the needs of all stakeholders. Rather, multiple strategies, methodologies and disciplines may need to be employed and triangulated. Not only would these assist to accommodate stakeholders' differing needs, but there is also the opportunity for the different disciplines to interact with and learn from each other, thereby producing a richer set of outputs from which to analyse and evaluate the regulatory initiative.[34]

The strategy and methodology chosen should seek to be as objective as possible—that is, to obtain measurements of performance in an objective fashion.[35] However, and as discussed above, the inherently political nature of the activity means that different stakeholders with different values and perspectives could reach different and conflicting judgments on the same factual evidence.[36] There is rarely, if ever, one objective answer. However, if one defines 'objectivity' to mean lack of bias, then that can be achieved (or, at least, any bias reduced) by involving all relevant stakeholders in the evaluation in a way that ensures their viewpoints are accurately represented and genuinely considered.[37] 'Evaluation under this philosophy, therefore, aims to ensure supporting evidence for arguments on all sides is clear and accessible'.[38]

Concluding Insights and Implications

When introducing the regulatory policy cycle in Chapter 5, we observed that evaluation is the stage most likely to be abbreviated, de-emphasised or by-passed.[39] This is regrettable. The regulatory endeavour is beset by conflict and uncertainty; decisions are made on the basis of hypotheses and assumptions; the regulatory space within which the regime operates is constantly changing; some regulatees respond to regulatory initiatives in perverse and unexpected ways; and regulators immersed in day-to-day operations can be slow to identify and respond to change.[40] A separate and dedicated evaluation stage disciplines those involved with the regulatory endeavour to reflect and assess. Evaluations should be the norm, not the exception.

Conducting a successful evaluation is both a science and an art. The 'science' is the use of systematic approaches and analytical methods. The 'artful' part is in the judgment required to successfully match each of the elements of the evaluation with the needs of the users. This chapter has sought to explain the systematic elements of an evaluation, and to make transparent those elements where judgments are crucial.

The chapter's discussion also has revealed that notwithstanding the existence of numerous evaluation guides, robust, that is, good, evaluation is not easy. The regulatory (now evaluative) space is occupied by actors with a multiplicity of objectives—some explicit, some implicit—some consistent with the regulatory policy's objectives, others potentially in conflict. This can make conducting an evaluation as complex and contested as the regulatory policy it is assessing. Moreover, these actors operate in complex poly-centric networks. This makes isolating and evaluating the impact of one regulatory intervention (and controlling for the impact of other variables, actors, instruments, etc.) very difficult. Frequently, it requires a cross-disciplinary set of skills and perspectives, and a substantial investment.

Evaluations, like RIAs, are technically rational tools. Decisions made in response to evaluations are not always as technically rational, however. As Rossi and Freeman observe:

> An evaluation is only one ingredient in a political process of balancing interests and coming to decisions. The evaluator's role is close to that of an expert witness, furnishing the best information possible under the circumstances; it is not the role of judge and jury.[41]

Consistent with the concept of the regulatory policy cycle, the evaluation takes us full circle and back to the setting of the governmental and decision agendas (see Chapter 7). The evaluation findings can act as a 'triggering mechanism' leading persons to reassess the issue or the adequacy of existing regulatory arrangements. They also can provide interested persons ('entrepreneurs and promoters') with a valuable new tool with which to impose their 'frame' on the issue. The question for government then becomes whether the issue as newly framed is such as to warrant government (again) investing its limited resources into (again) diagnosing the issue to determine whether a new policy course should be charted, or whether it should allow the regulatory policy (and regime) to continue as is or be terminated. There is one important difference at this point of time compared to the initial define stage, however. There are now persons benefiting from the regulatory regime. Some are the beneficiaries of the protections it affords, others are persons providing goods or services to it and others still are ideologically vindicated by its existence. Termination (or even modification) of the regime threatens their interests, and can lead to claims of inequity, unfairness and disadvantage should attempts be made to do so. As noted above, this makes the decision to continue, modify or terminate a political one.[42] It also means that decisions to terminate do not occur as frequently as evaluation findings would suggest.[43]

Notes

1. See, e.g., Organisation for Economic Co-Operation and Development, *OECD Framework for Regulatory Policy Evaluation* (OECD Publishing, 2014); European Commission, *Better Regulation 'Toolbox'* (European Commission, 2016) 264 (Tools #40–49); United Kingdom National Audit Office, 'Evaluation: Successfully Commissioning Toolkit' (HM Government, 2011); Government Social Research Unit, 'The Magenta Book: Guidance Notes for Policy Evaluation and Analysis' (HM Treasury, 2007).
2. See, e.g., William R Shadish, Thomas D Cook and Laura C Leviton, *Foundations of Program Evaluation: Theories of Practice* (Sage Publications, 1991); Peter H Rossi, Mark W Lipsey and Howard E Freeman, *Evaluation: A Systematic Approach* (Sage Publications, 2004); Ann Crabbé and Pieter Leroy, *The Handbook of Environmental Policy Evaluation* (Routledge, 2009); and the numerous other guides cited throughout this chapter.
3. Thomas R Dye, 'Policy Evaluation: Finding Out What Happens after a Law Is Passed' in T Miyakawa (ed), *The Science of Public Policy: Essential Readings in Policy Sciences II* (Routledge, 2000) vol 6 221, 223.

4. See Chapter 8, 164–5.
5. Colin Scott, 'Regulating Everything' (UCD Geary Institute Discussion Paper Series, No 24/2008, 26 February 2008) 2, 6 (emphasis in original).
6. Michael Q Patton, *Utilization-Focused Evaluation: The New Century Text* (Sage Publications, 1997).
7. Wayne Parsons, *Public Policy: An Introduction to the Theory and Practice of Policy Analysis* (Edward Elgar Publishing, 1995) 567–8.
8. Ernest R House, 'Responsive Evaluation (and Its Influence on Deliberative Democratic Evaluation)' (2001) 92 *New Directions for Evaluation* 23.
9. See, e.g., Egon G Guba and Yvonna S Lincoln, 'Politics and Research Methods: The Countenances of Fourth-Generation Evaluation' in D J Palumbo (ed), *The Politics of Program Evaluation* (Sage Publications, 1987) 202; Ernest R House and Kenneth R Howe, 'Deliberative Democratic Evaluation' (2000) 85 *New Directions for Evaluation* 3; David M Fetterman and Abraham Wandersman, *Empowerment Evaluation Principles in Practice* (The Guilford Press, 2005).
10. Ray Pawson and Nick Tilley, *Realistic Evaluation* (Sage Publications, 1997) 20.
11. Carol H Weiss, 'Where Politics and Evaluation Research Meet' in D J Palumbo (ed), *The Politics of Program Evaluation* (Sage Publications, 1987) 47; Pawson and Tilley, *Realistic Evaluation*, above n 10, 11–14.
12. Wayne Parsons, *Public Policy*, above n 7, 548.
13. See Chapter 9, 211.
14. Carol H Weiss, *Evaluation: Methods for Studying Programs and Policies* (Prentice Hall, 1998) 21–4.
15. Nancy R Dinkel, Charles Windle and Joan W Zinober, 'Community Participation in Evaluation' in G Stahler and W R Tash (eds), *Innovative Approaches to Mental Health Evaluation* (Academic Press, 1982) 163, 168–9; Guba and Lincoln, 'Politics and Research Methods', above n 9, 226.
16. Ernest House and Kenneth R Howe, *Values in Evaluation and Social Research* (Sage Publications, 1999).
17. Charles Wolf Jr, 'A Theory of Nonmarket Failure: Framework for Implementation Analysis' (1979) 22 *Journal of Law and Economics* 107, 129–30.
18. Donna M Mertens, 'The Inclusive View of Evaluation: Visions for the New Millennium' in S I Donaldson and M Scriven (eds), *Evaluating Social Programs and Problems: Visions for the New Millennium* (Lawrence Erlbaum Associates, 2003) 91, 103.
19. Guba and Lincoln, 'Politics and Research Methods', above n 9.
20. Parsons, *Public Policy*, above n 7, 564. See also Fetterman and Wandersman, *Empowerment Evaluation Principles in Practice*, above n 9; Graeme A Hodge, 'Reviewing Public-Private Partnerships: Some Thoughts on Evaluation' in G A Hodge, C Greve and A E Boardman (eds), *International Handbook on Public-Private Partnerships* (Edward Elgar Publishing, 2010) 81, 90.
21. Guba and Lincoln, 'Politics and Research Methods', above n 9, 223.
22. See the discussion of these biases and how they can be overcome in Chapter 7, 114–15.
23. James Wilson, 'On Pettigrew and Armor: An Afterword' (1973) 30 *Public Interest* 132, 133.
24. Parsons, *Public Policy*, above n 7, 550.
25. European Commission, *Better Regulation 'Toolbox'* (European Commission, 2016) 272 (Tool 42: Identifying the evaluation criteria and questions).
26. Ibid.
27. Julia Black, 'Critical Reflections on Regulation' (2002) 27 *Australian Journal of Legal Philosophy* 1, 27—8; Karen Yeung, *Securing Compliance: A Principled Approach* (Hart Publishing, 2004) 29; Arie Freiberg, *The Tools of Regulation* (The Federation Press, 2010) 260–8.

28. See, e.g., Julia Black, 'Critical Reflections on Regulation', above n 27, 1, 28; Freiberg, *The Tools of Regulation*, above n 27, 268.
29. Chris Skelcher and Helen Sullivan, 'Theory-Driven Approaches to Analysing Collaborative Performance' (2008) 10 *Public Management Review* 751, 756.
30. Joseph S Wholey, *Evaluation: Promise and Performance* (The Urban Institute, 1979); Hodge, 'Reviewing Public-Private Partnership', above n 20, 90–1.
31. Richard D Bingham and Claire L Felbinger, *Evaluation in Practice: A Methodological Approach* (Chatham House Publishers, 2nd ed, 2002) 5; Parsons, *Public Policy*, above n 7, 547–52. Note that Weiss uses the terms formative and summative differently (another example of the confusing and conflicting use of terminology that permeates the field). According to Weiss, formative/summative evaluations relate to the intention of the evaluator—formative designed to help improve the design and implementation of the program, and summative designed to provide information on the program's effectiveness and process/outcome evaluations relate to the phase of the program studied—process during its course and outcome at its conclusion; Weiss, *Evaluation*, above n 14, 23–6.
32. William Shadish Jr, 'Program Micro- and Macrotheories: A Guide for Social Change' (1987) 33 *New Directions for Program Evaluation* 93.
33. Patton, *Utilization-Focused Evaluation*, above n 6, 23.
34. Hodge, 'Reviewing Public-Private Partnerships', above n 20, 88.
35. Dye, 'Policy Evaluation', above n 3, 222.
36. Guba and Lincoln, 'Politics and Research Methods', above n 9, 208.
37. Mertens, 'The Inclusive View of Evaluation', above n 18, 95; House and Howe, 'Deliberative Democratic Evaluation', above n 9, 5–6. See also Chapter 7, 114–15 for processes the evaluator can employ to address his/her own biases.
38. Graeme A Hodge, 'Evaluation and the Public Interest: Public Policy, Prospects and Pointers' (Paper presented at New Global Regulatory Frontiers: Evaluating What Will Work for Nanotechnology International Workshop, Melbourne, 17 July 2006) 11.
39. See Chapter 5, 96–7 n 18.
40. See the discussion of regulatory failure in Chapter 6.
41. Rossi, Lipsey and Freeman, *Evaluation*, above n 2, 454.
42. See also Eugene Bardach, 'Policy Termination as a Political Process' (1976) 7 *Policy Sciences* 123.
43. The empirical evidence supports the proposition that terminations on the basis of evaluation results is not a frequent occurrence. Policies and programs are more often terminated for ideological reasons, such as might occur on a change of government. See Peter DeLeon, 'Public Policy Termination: An End and a Beginning' (1978) 4 *Policy Analysis* 369; Peter DeLeon, 'New Perspectives on Program Termination' (1982) 2 *Journal of Policy Analysis and Management* 108; Peter DeLeon, 'Policy Evaluation and Program Termination' (1983) 2 *Policy Studies Review* 631; Peter DeLeon, 'Policy Termination as a Political Phenomenon' in D J Palumbo (ed), *The Politics of Program Evaluation* (Sage Publications, 1987) 173; Michael Harris, 'Policy Termination: Uncovering the Ideological Dimension' (1997) 20 *International Journal of Public Administration* 2151; Andrew Jordan, Michael Bauer and Christoffer Green-Pederson, 'Policy Dismantling' (2013) 20 *Journal of European Public Policy* 795.

Part IV
Conclusion

Part C

Conclusion

12 The Future of Regulatory Governance

In Chapter 2 we explored the rise of regulatory governance. In that chapter, we explained that its rise is largely attributable to increasingly complex social and economic issues that government alone is not equipped to handle. This has seen government enlist and co-opt a range of non-state actors into the regulatory endeavour, and seen the emergence of hybrid, networked and poly-centric regulatory regimes in which these non-state actors perform a variety of regulatory roles traditionally reserved to government. In this chapter, we look forward to see what the future might hold for regulatory governance. First, we will consider likely changes in the external world. Some are continuations of megatrends already being experienced;[1] others are an extrapolation from recent events. Second, we will seek to understand the impact these changes may have on how governments govern and regulate.

A Changing, Fragmented and Demanding World

The world in which we live continues to change at an exponential rate, giving rise to new issues and challenges. Technology is the driver of much of this change. Technology has—and undoubtedly will continue to—fundamentally alter the nature of economic and social activity. From artificial intelligence, robotics and 3D printers, nanotechnology and biotechnology, through to smart phone technology and the 'internet of things'—how we work, play and rest is being changed forever. Advances in technology create new products and render existing products obsolete. Just as the CD rendered the audio cassette tape obsolete, and the Internet and mp3 is rendering the CD obsolete, so too in time (and not a lot of time) will something come along to render the mp3 obsolete. This phenomenon has repeated itself in a range of products from the film camera (made obsolete by digital technology) to floppy disks (made obsolete by flash drives), and will continue to do so with increasing frequency in the future.

Advances in communication and transportation technology continue to reduce barriers to trade and create new opportunities. Businesses, workers and capital are more mobile than ever before, and world-wide supply chains are increasingly prevalent. Local businesses increasingly compete nationally; and national businesses internationally. And this competition is not restricted to commercial enterprises. Nation states increasingly compete to attract business and investment, and the jobs and tax revenue they generate. Technology also continues to redesign the workplace. Robotics continues to replace factory workers, and in the future promises to replace taxi, bus and train drivers, and a host of other jobs. On the other hand, technology also will create new jobs yet unimagined. Researchers predict that 65% of today's grade school children will hold jobs that do not yet exist.[2]

Technology also is changing society. Communication today is near instantaneous. People today are more connected than they have ever been. Fashions and fads, ideas and innovations, spread with ever increasing speed. But so too do misinformation, hatred and hacking. With all the benefits new communications technology has brought (and there are many), it also has brought with it privacy and security risks that can threaten national security, commercial property rights and the physical and mental health of the individuals who use it.

Rapidly evolving medical technology also is having a profound impact. Improved diagnostics and new medical treatments, combined with healthier diets and environments, have seen life expectancy across OECD countries increase from 70 to 80.5 over the past 50 years.[3] Half of all babies born in industrialised countries this century can expect to live to 100![4] The ageing population places great pressure on our social welfare, pension and health care services. It also has—and will continue to—create new issues in areas ranging from workplace health and safety as older people stay in the workforce longer, to sport, recreation and fertility as they also remain active and socially engaged.

A larger population also places pressure on an environment already suffering the effects of climate change. Our changing climate will continue to be a cause of concern, giving rise to ever-more complex and challenging issues. These include water and food insecurity, rising sea levels, an increased risk of natural disasters such as floods and droughts, population displacement and an increased risk of violent conflict, to name but a few.[5]

Not all change will be technology driven, however. Globalisation has made many societies more diverse. These societies are now becoming more polarised and tribal. One only has to look at the Brexit vote and the Trump Presidency for evidence of this. However, these divisions are not only being felt at the ballot box. Societies are at once becoming more and less tolerant. Issues of refugees, immigration, marriage equality, abortion and the rights of the LBGTI community,[6] for example, are splitting liberal democratic societies, often along geographic lines (urban vs rural), demographic lines (university educated, high income vs high-school educated, low income) and faith lines (those who are religiously observant and those who are not). The increasingly polarised nature of society will make reaching consensus on important issues more difficult.

Paternalism also is likely to increase in these divided societies, as the more highly educated (and generally urbane) sectors of society consider it their role to protect the less educated from the consequences of their 'ignorance'. The belief that some people—even when fully informed—are unable to properly assess the information at their disposal and make rational decisions about which activities to undertake already underpins much lifestyle regulation (e.g. smoking, alcohol and gambling), and calls to regulate sugary foods, salt intake and junk foods.[7] It also is the foundation of the nudge techniques discussed in this book. The 'liberal' paternalism of nudge may not remain 'liberal' for long, however, especially if policy decisions are made, not on the basis of personal freedoms, but on the costs these activities impose on health care systems and the communal purse.

All of this is likely to see an increase in the number of 'wicked' problems or issues. We touched on wicked problems briefly in Chapter 7. Wicked problems are issues that are technically or morally complex and about which there is a high level of disagreement amongst relevant actors about the nature and causes of the issue, the objectives that should be set for them and the means by which those objectives should be pursued.[8] Many of the issues touched on in this chapter—refugees, immigration, marriage equality, abortion and climate change—have all the earmarks of wicked issues. The two core dimensions of wickedness—the complexity of the issue and the diversity of values and views about it—will only increase in the future.[9]

And all these changes and wicked problems will emerge in a world in which the public is more demanding and less trusting of government. The 'rights revolution' has not ended.[10] People continue to consider themselves entitled to the ever-increasing array of benefits that technological progress and higher living standards bring. And they continue to look to government to secure these benefits for them—albeit while simultaneously expecting government to minimise the fiscal and regulatory burden on them. Government also remains the first place to which the public turns to solve their problems, and to protect them from the risks of modernity. At the same time, and somewhat paradoxically, the public has become less trusting of government.[11] Governments can no longer expect the public to assume benevolence and competence on its part. Governments 'telling' the public they are doing a good job is no longer good enough. The public wants to be 'shown' the government is doing a good job and, increasingly, wants to be part of the government's decision-making processes. The public also is much less tolerant of government failure. Their displeasure is quickly seen in opinion polls, and can be brutal at the ballot box. For governments, this mix of reliance and distrust, of high expectations and low tolerance for failure, can be an explosive political cocktail.

Of course, these changes are not felt equally everywhere. They will vary from one country to another based on each country's different social, economic and political institutions. They also will vary according to each country's level of economic, social and political maturity. The BRIC countries

(Brazil, Russia, India and China), for example, are today going through changes experienced by more developed Western countries decades ago; and which countries in the so-called third world are still to go through. And it is not just economic development that is important here. The development of these countries' governance and regulatory systems frequently match those of their economic systems. And while some countries may experience these changes later than others, all will eventually experience them. That is the price of progress.

So in summary, the pace of change is likely to quicken in the future. Existing issues will continue to evolve, and new difficult issues will emerge, presenting both opportunities, problems and risks. One thing that is unlikely to change, however, is that the public will continue to place these issues at the feet of government to address—governments that themselves are not immune from the pressures these changes bring.

The Reactive World of Governance and Regulation

New technologies present governments and regulators with both challenges and opportunities. The challenges come in the form of difficult (and potentially wicked) new regulatory targets. Brownsword, for example, refers to new technologies (and new information technology in particular) creating four key regulatory challenges which he labels: regulatory prudence (the overriding responsibility of government to protect human health and safety potentially put at risk by new technologies); regulatory legitimacy (regulators employing legitimate means to pursue legitimate objectives in a regulatory space that often is fragmented into the traditional off-line world, and a new on-line world occupied by actors with strong aspirations towards self-governance and self-regulation); regulatory effectiveness (whether government is capable of designing and implementing interventions to address the challenges presented by new technologies); and regulatory connection (the challenge of regulation connecting with technologies that are not yet mature, and staying connected with them as they rapidly mature).[12]

The pace of technological change also places great pressure on government to respond equally quickly. In many areas government has been found wanting, however, closing the barn door well and truly after the horse has bolted. There is no better example of this than the manner with which Uber and Airbnb disrupted established markets and products while avoiding existing regulatory controls. The failure of governments to evolve existing regulatory arrangements in a timely manner to provide both incumbents and disrupters with certainty undermines not only the legitimacy of existing regulatory regimes, but also of government and governance under the rule of law more broadly.

The opportunity presented by new technologies comes in the form of prospective new regulatory tools with which to modify behaviours. The extent to which governments have been successful in the use of new technologies as regulatory tools is mixed, however. As Brownsword observes: 'where regulators have difficulties in controlling access to and use of modern technologies, these difficulties are, if anything, exacerbated where regulators themselves turn to the technology as a regulatory instrument'.[13] Part of the problem with regulating new technologies is a belief in some circles that what is required is regulation as innovative as the technologies it regulates.[14] This risks policy officers and regulators short-cutting the regulatory diagnostic and design processes discussed in this book and moving straight from technological problem to technological solution. As we as have observed, however, poor diagnosis and design is a recipe for regulatory failure.

More generally though, with new technologies and higher living standards comes increased expectations about the services, infrastructure and protections government can provide. These expectations often exceed government's capabilities. This is said to give rise to an 'expectation gap' between what the public believes governments should be providing, and what governments realistically can provide given the resource, political and constitutional constraints under which they operate.[15] There are three main strategies for closing the expectation gap: increasing the supply of government services, reducing demand for those services or a combination of both. Reducing demand—convincing people they no longer need a service or protection to which they are accustomed—is notoriously difficult, at least not without replacing that service or protection with something of equal or better quality. However, increasing supply often is no easier—especially in a world in which governments are under fiscal pressure. This can find governments caught between the 'rock' of increasing public demands and the 'hard place' of potential political oblivion should they seek to increase taxes to pay for them.

Governments often respond to fiscal pressure by reducing the size of the public service. However, downsizing and redundancies see the loss of institutional memory and important skills and competencies. Combine this with hiring freezes and political pressure to 'do more with less', and one does not have a recipe for sustained, high quality, failure-free government services and regulation. In this environment, the risk of mistakes and errors only increases. However, it also can be an environment that is less tolerant of those mistakes and errors. The speed and intensity with which public displeasure with government is communicated through the media and opinion polls can make politicians equally intolerant of public servants and regulators who fail to deliver in accordance with the government's expectations. It also can lead to governments increasing their level of oversight over the public sector. This has seen a proliferation of rules by which policy officers and regulators must abide, and of audit and integrity agencies to monitor their activities and hold them to account. Of this 'regulation inside government', Harlow and Rawlings observe insightfully:

> The endless official statements of regulatory principle sound well but there is a real risk of "over-juridification": regulators being hamstrung by too many rules and too much codification. The process of regulation is itself increasingly regulated. In the name of "better regulation" bureaucratic regulation is piled on bureaucratic regulation and central control is reasserted through a plethora of directions and guidance.[16]

This level of oversight (regulation inside government) only can be expected to increase as governments seek to close what some refer to as the 'governance gap' created by the megatrends of emergent wicked problems and declining public trust.[17] It also should see governments continue to experiment with new forms of poly-centric governance, thus reinforcing the trend of governance through regulation, and regulation through governance.

Regulatory decision-making also is increasingly being tested in the courts, a reflection of the increasing litigiousness of society generally and of people's frustration with systems they consider bureaucratic and unresponsive in particular.[18] This has led to the creation of a jurisprudence of administrative law (codified in some jurisdictions) that obliges regulators to ensure their decision-making processes are fair and their decisions rational (or at least not unreasonable). These requirements are both reasonable and a necessary component of the rule of law. However, if applied pedantically by a judiciary unfamiliar with the realities of day-to-day regulatory decision-making, they can impose standards that lead to defensive regulatory practices, and the imposition of a not insignificant compliance burden on regulators. This can result in limited resources being diverted away from regulatory interventions to administrative controls and compliance. It also can make regulators unduly careful and circumspect in their decision-making which can delay interventions.

Concluding Insights and Implications

So what does all this mean for regulatory governance? First, it means that the conditions that initially saw regulatory governance emerge as a distinct and important mode of governance are likely to intensify. The issues which governments are going to have to deal with will only increase in complexity. The resources at governments' disposal to deal with them will continue to be limited. This will necessitate governments continuing to co-opt and enlist third parties as surrogate or quasi-regulators into poly-centric regulatory regimes of increasing sophistication. However, the differences between these third parties are likely to become more divergent, making the task of enlisting their support, reaching consensus and agreement and building poly-centric regulatory regimes to pursue common regulatory objectives more difficult. Regulatory governance thus will become both more important and more challenging.

The increasing complexity of issues, the increasing and sometimes contradictory demands of the public, and the pressure on governments to meet those demands, will combine to make the work of those responsible for the various stages of the regulatory endeavour all the more difficult. This makes learning the lessons of the past and present all the more important. These lessons can be found throughout this book. Some of the more important are distilled in the book's conclusion, to which we now turn.

Notes

1. The term 'megatrend' is attributed to John Naisbitt and Patricia Aburdene, *Megatrends 2000: New Directions for Tomorrow* (Avon Books, 1991).
2. Cathy N Davidson, *Now You See It: How the Brain Science of Attention Will Transform the Way We Live, Work, and Learn* (Viking Penguin, 2011) 18.
3. Organisation for Economic Co-Operation and Development, 'Health at a Glance 2015: OECD Indicators' (OECD, 2015) 46.
4. Kaare Christsensen et al, 'Ageing Populations: The Challenges Ahead' (2009) 374 *Lancet* 1196.
5. Intergovernmental Panel on Climate Change, 'Climate Change 2014 Synthesis Report: Summary for Policymakers' (IPCC, 2014) 13–16.
6. LBGTI refers to people who are lesbian, gay, bisexual, trans or intesex.
7. See, e.g., Alberto Alemanno and Amandine Garde (eds), *Regulating Lifestyle Risks: The EU, Alcohol, Tobacco and Unhealthy Diets* (Cambridge University Press, 2015); Sarah Mackay, 'Food Advertising and Obesity in Australia: To What Extent Can Self-Regulation Protect the Interests of Children' (2009) 35 *Monash University Law Review* 118; Michael W Long et al, 'Cost Effectiveness of a Sugar-Sweetened Beverage Excise Tax in the US' (2015) 49 *American Journal of Preventative Medicine* 112.
8. See discussion in Chapter 7, 146–7.
9. These are the dimensions distilled by Head and Alford from the literature: Brian W Head and John Alford, 'Wicked Problems: Implications for Public Policy and Management' (2015) 47 *Administration & Society* 711.
10. Referring to Sunstein's description of the 1960s and 70s, during which people advocated for an extended concept of the rights which governments should support, discussed in Chapter 2, at 22.
11. See, e.g., Organisation for Economic Co-Operation and Development, *Government at a Glance 2013* (OECD Publishing, 2013) 40.
12. Roger Brownsword, 'The Shaping of Our On-Line Worlds: Getting the Regulatory Environment Right' (2012) 20 *International Journal of Law and Information Technology* 249. See generally, Roger Brownsword, *Rights, Regulation, and the Technological Revolution* (Oxford University Press, 2008).
13. Brownsword, *Rights, Regulation, and the Technological Revolution*, above n 12, 1–2.
14. See, e.g., Christopher Koopman, Matthew D Mitchell and Adam D Thierer, 'The Sharing Economy and Consumer Protection Regulation: The Case for Policy Change' (2015) 8(2) *The Journal of Business, Entrepreneurship & the Law* 529; Sunil Johal and Noah Zon, 'Policymaking for the Sharing Economy: Beyond Whack-A-Mole' (Mowat Centre, 2015); Vanessa Katz, 'Regulating the Sharing Economy' (2015) 30(4) *Berkeley Technology Law Journal* 1067; Sofia Ranchordás, 'Does Sharing Mean Caring? Regulating Innovation in the Sharing Economy' (2015) 16(1) *Minnesota Journal of Law, Science and Technology* 413; Hannah A Posen, 'Ridesharing in the Sharing Economy: Should Regulators

Impose Über Regulations on Uber?' (2015) 101 *Iowa Law Review* 205; Stephen R Miller, 'First Principles for Regulating the Sharing Economy' (2016) 53 *Harvard Journal on Legislation* 147.

15. See generally Matthew Flinders and Alexandra Kelso, 'Mind the Gap: Political Analysis, Public Expectations and the Parliamentary Decline Thesis' (2011) 13 *The British Journal of Politics and International Relations* 249–68.

16. Carol Harlow and Richard Rawlings, *Law and Administration* (Cambridge University Press, 3rd ed, 2009) 281. See generally, Christopher Hood et al, *Regulation inside Government: Waste Watchers, Quality Police, and Sleaze-Busters* (Oxford University Press, 1999).

17. Robert Weymouth and Janet Hartz-Karp, 'Deliberative Collaborative Governance as a Democratic Reform to Resolve Wicked Problems and Improve Trust' (2015) 17 *Journal of Economic and Social Policy* 62.

18. This is a partial reversal (one century later) of the frustrations with the court system that led governments to replace reliance on litigation with regulation as the principal means to control business. See Chapter 2, 21.

13 Conclusion

This book set out to provide readers with a series of maps and frameworks with which to navigate the phenomenon of governing through regulation. Having now been on that journey, it is time to reflect. These reflections proceed in two parts. The first part synthesises the book's various insights into several key lessons. The second part concludes with some brief final words about the book's examination of the regulatory endeavour.

Lessons

This body of work has provided numerous insights into the regulatory endeavour. This section synthesises these insights into six broad lessons. Some of these lessons reaffirm themes that have guided us in the use of the book's maps and frameworks; others challenge dominant paradigms; and others still are tips to assist those charged with the difficult task of regulating. In distilling these lessons, there is a degree of subjectivity and selectivity. Different people from different disciplines and with different perspectives will draw different lessons. There also is a degree of reductionism. Not all of the many insights could be incorporated into the lessons, and some depth and detail has been sacrificed to distil and clearly communicate them.

Lesson 1: Regulation Is Both a Complex Policy Reform and a Contested Political Project

Regulation is primarily thought of as a policy reform designed to modify people's behaviour according to defined standards to achieve specified objectives. Yet our discussion has demonstrated that regulation is as much a political project as it is a substantive policy reform. Understanding this duality—and the challenges it presents—is important. Regulatory success is measured not only in terms of policy effectiveness and efficiency but also by reference to its politics. Moreover, as a policy reform, regulation is inherently complex; as a political project, it is contested and contentious.

Regulation's complexity exists on many levels. It is found in the crowded and contested regulatory space in which issues arise. This can make defining and diagnosing those issues difficult. Actors occupying the regulatory space compete to impose their frame on the issue, and to shape the manner in which the issue is defined and diagnosed, and regulatory objectives are set. The issues themselves are often embedded in complex social, economic and political systems that make identifying their underlying causes difficult; a difficulty sometimes compounded by the fact that other causes may be buried deep in the psychology of those engaged in them. That regulatees have different attitudes, motivations and capabilities means there are no one-size-fits-all answers. This makes addressing regulatory issues and their causes all the more complex. And while modern regulators have a vast arsenal of regulatory instruments and strategies at their disposal for tackling these complex issues—a testament to the creativity and ingenuity of the public sector—carefully selecting, combining, tailoring and aligning them to the specific nature of the issue and to regulatees' different attitudes and capabilities is inherently difficult. So too is designing and deploying the institutional structures and systems to support those endeavours. Ensuring they facilitate regulation in the public interest and guard against regulation in the private interest is a constant challenge.

Navigating these complexities and challenges is an inherently political exercise. The variables of regulatory policy—whether, what and who to regulate, how, and to what standards—are, as Lasswell reminds us, political decisions.[1] They involve balancing economic, social and democratic values, and the values and interests of different actors occupying the regulatory space, often producing both winners and losers. At the same time, however, these balances need to be struck in a manner which builds coalitions in support of the regulatory reform, and maintains those coalitions throughout the reform's life. We saw that bad politics is a source of regulatory failure; and good politics an essential ingredient for its success.

The duality of regulation being both a policy reform and political project means it employs both technically rational and politically rational processes. The book's adoption of the regulatory policy cycle to navigate the regulatory endeavour is an example of the use of a technically rational process; yet the point was made that its use must be tempered by a recognition of the political forces that operate upon it. And at each stage of the regulatory policy cycle, we observed the tensions that exist between those who view regulation principally as a technically rational process employing systematic, analytical and evidence-based methods; and those for whom regulation is a political process of consensus and coalition-building employing political methods of consultation, deliberation and negotiation. We also observed that while regulatory policy has both a technical and political component, politics tends to be the master, and technical analysis the servant. This is an important lesson. All those involved with the regulatory endeavour should be alert to efforts to hide politically contentious decisions in the neutral language with which most technical approaches are described. At the same time, however, technical rationality should not be sacrificed on the altar of political rationality. Every effort should be made to place political decision-making on a more technically rational foundation.

Lesson 2: Regulation Is Both a Science and an Art; Regulatory Decision-Making a Craft

This is not so much a lesson as it is a reaffirmation and reinforcement of one of the book's key themes. The science is evident in the systematic approach of the regulatory policy cycle. Systematic approaches also formed key elements of each of the cycle's stages. These included the mapping processes of the define stage; processes for generating ideas in the design stage; regulatory impact assessments in the define stage; responsive, smart, problem-centred and risk-based approaches to guide implementation; and the various technologies that can be used to monitor and evaluate regulatory performance. We also observed the increasing use of behavioural sciences to shape more effective regulatory tools. However, these systems, tools and technologies cannot be automated or robotically applied. Their use involves the exercise of discretion and judgement. Parameters need to be set; assumptions made; and hypotheses formed. The credibility and reliability of sometimes contradictory evidence needs to be assessed, and conflicting values and interests need to be weighed, balanced and sometimes traded-off.

The making of these judgements is a craft, or an 'applied or practical art', as Goodsell refers to it.[2] Successful regulatory policy-making and implementation involves a mix of skills, knowledge and competencies—some technical and analytical; others relational and motivational; and others still interpersonal and political. And while the craft can be studied, many of the traits required of a successful practitioner, such as intuition and tacit knowledge, 'cannot be transmitted via the usual pedagogical means'.[3] As with most crafts, practice and experience is just as important as books and courses.

Lesson 3: Context Is King; Maps and Frameworks Are Useful

Another clear lesson permeating this book's examination of the regulatory endeavour is that there is no single 'best' approach. As Gunningham observes:

> The sheer variety of regulatory programs, rules, market structures, political environments, and social contexts, preclude definitive generalizations about when and to what extent any individual strategy is likely to "succeed" or "fail" in shaping the behaviour of regulated entities.[4]

Yasuda similarly observes that 'the vexing reality in regulatory governance is that context often matters more than a policy's design'.[5] Regulatory initiatives and instruments successfully employed in one context can be ineffective or even counterproductive in another context. Our discussion of ideational theories in Chapter 3 counselled against ideas being adopted uncritically. This admonishment is of general application and applies equally to the choice of any regulatory theory, instrument or strategy. As John Braithwaite, one of the authors of *Responsive Regulation*, designer of the enforcement pyramid and the father of the field in the eyes of many, observes:

> Responsive regulation asks regulators not to be dogmatic about any theory, including responsive regulation itself. Be persistently attentive to and responsive to contextual insight. . . . Responsiveness to context means not taking any theory too seriously, including the theory of the pyramid.[6]

At the same time, however, maps and frameworks for navigating the complexity of the regulatory endeavour are useful. They provide practitioners with helpful decision-making processes and procedures to assist them to carefully analyse each issue's individual context and needs, weigh and balance those needs against the benefits and costs of different options, and select the appropriate mix of regulatory policy settings accordingly. But the same caution applies to this book's maps and frameworks as they do to any others. They are intended to act as 'signposts' of better regulatory practice; not definitive instructions.[7]

Lesson 4: Regulation Is Inherently Difficult—Tolerate Mistakes; Facilitate Learning

Governing through regulation is inherently difficult. The potential causes of failure are many, as are the prescriptions for avoiding them and producing better and more legitimate regulation. Yet, as Gunningham observes, our knowledge of what works, when and in what circumstances, is tentative and incomplete, with the result that much regulation is experimental in nature.[8] Settling on the right combination of tools and approaches first time is likely to be the exception, not the rule. Moreover, regulation is designed and implemented by individuals whose rationality is bounded by organisational and resource constraints and their own cognitive limitations; who often have to work with incomplete or imperfect information; and who constantly are being buffeted by persons and groups seeking to advance their own interests and values. All of these factors 'guarantee the imperfect nature of regulation'.[9]

It follows from this that regulators (and their political overseers) need to be tolerant of mistakes and encouraging of a learning environment that enables regulatory personnel to reflect upon and respond to lessons drawn from their own experiences and from the experiences of others. Responsive regulation is an example of an approach premised on its ability to learn from its mistakes. As Braithwaite observes, responsive regulation 'assumes the strategies advanced in its name will fail very often. It is designed to learn from those failures by repairing pyramids through adding layers that cover the weaknesses of failed strategies with varieties of new or reformed strategies'.[10] Perfection is an ideal—something to aspire to—but not a benchmark against which regulators and regulatory regimes should be judged and held accountable. Things will not always go to plan; and plans will not always be right. Mistakes will happen. What is important is that we learn—individually and organisationally—from those mistakes.

Creating a learning environment is, as Black observes, both fashionable and difficult.[11] There is no shortage of methodologies (and consultants) promising to create learning organisations. These include adaptive learning technologies, 'double loop' learning and reflexive governance techniques.[12] Implementing them, however, can be challenging. First, it requires us to admit our mistakes. Such admissions expose individuals to reputational damage, and undermine confidence in the regulator and regulatory regime and their claims to legitimacy. It also is a message politicians and the public do not like to hear.

Second, it requires regulators to create the conditions conducive for self-critical learning. From an infrastructure perspective, this is relatively straightforward. We already have discussed the need for regulators to have effective monitoring, evaluation and adjustment mechanisms. Creating the right culture is less tangible and more difficult. A learning organisation requires a confident and assured workforce; one that is solution and outcome-orientated, and operates in an open, supportive, confident, decisive and accountable manner. It also needs to be an organisation open to constructive challenge. Mechanisms and structures need to be put in place to ensure existing paradigms and worldviews can be questioned. Without them, those doing the learning are apt only to see what they have been pre-programmed to see. These conditions cannot be built overnight, however. Defining and inculcating a positive and constructive culture requires time, persistence and organisational leaders who 'walk the talk' and model the behaviours they expect to see in others.

Lesson 5: Maintain a Credible Deterrent

In an era of better regulation, with its focus on using the least interventionist and burdensome techniques, there is a tendency to prefer outcome-orientated standards over prescriptive standards, and 'lighter touch' incentives, persuasion and assistance over more 'heavy handed' coercive mechanisms. However, the evidence in support of the use of these less interventionist techniques is equivocal. We observed, for example, that the current empirical research does not support broad claims that outcome-orientated standards are consistently more effective than prescriptive standards.[13] We also observed a number of recent high profile regulatory failures involving the use of outcome-orientated standards implemented with a 'light touch' that placed too much reliance on regulatees behaving responsibly and in furtherance of the regulatory objective.[14]

Viewing the issue from a different perspective, Gunningham observes that studies on what makes a high-performing workplace make no mention of the regulatory environment—positively or negatively.[15] Indeed, if one were to step back even further, one would observe that in democratic liberal capitalist societies, regulation's growth in reach and complexity has been accompanied by an increase in the living standards of the citizens of those societies. Regulation has not prevented business as a whole from flourishing. Nor has it prevented wealth creation. On the contrary, rather than operate as a brake on society, regulation in many respects has been an essential tool in securing for society the benefits of that growth—what Peltzman refers to as the rewards of 'the natural progress of opulence'.[16] Elsewhere in the book the point was made that one person's red-tape is another person's safety net. It is a point worth repeating. From this discussion, it should be clear that broad-based rejections of prescription and deterrence as regulatory tools are misplaced. Consistent with the lesson that regulation is context-dependent, there will be circumstances in which prescription and deterrence will be effective and productive, and circumstances where it will be ineffective and counterproductive.[17]

It also is clear that for regulation to be effective, there needs to be a credible deterrent—or what Kagan, Gunningham and Thornton describe as a 'regulation-induced fear of legal punishment'.[18] The fear of being detected and sanctioned is essential to generating and assuring compliance. It encourages compliance by those who otherwise might seek to avoid their obligations, provides a level-playing field for those who are complying and reassurance to those for whose benefit the regulatory regime exists that recalcitrants will be detected and sanctioned. In a world of limited resources, building and maintaining a credible deterrent has both a substantive and communicative element. Substantively, it requires the regulator to undertake a critical mass of successful enforcement actions; and communicatively, it requires the regulator to leverage those enforcement actions to create the perception that non-compliances are being detected and sanctioned with appropriate speed and severity.

Lesson 6: Regulators Must Own Their Narrative

All these insights point to the importance of regulators owning their narratives. This communicative element is central to gaining and maintaining legitimacy which, it might be recalled from our discussion in Chapter 6, is arguably a regulator's most important resource. The regulatory endeavour is difficult enough for regulators without allowing others to set the expectations against which their performance and legitimacy will be assessed. Regulators need to take responsibility for clearly articulating their role, purpose and the value of their activities. They also should be clear about how they intend to create that value, both in terms of the outputs they will produce and the manner in which they will produce them. And finally, having set appropriate expectations, regulators also should be proactive in giving an account of their performance against those expectations. In an era in which regulation and regulators are seen as political targets, regulators should be proactive in establishing in the minds of their legitimacy communities the social and economic contributions they make.

Of course, care must be taken to avoid elevating rhetoric above substance. When regulatory legitimacy is assessed by reference to perceptions, scope exists for those perceptions to be gamed by manipulation, mystification or deception.[19] The use by a regulator of strategic communications to exaggerate the extent to which it is delivering on its regulatory objectives is likely to be effective only in the short-term, and detrimental in the long-term. 'Rhetoric without action is not a recipe for success. Eventually some event or disaster will reveal if the emperor is not wearing clothes'.[20]

Final Words

This book opened by stating it is a book for its time: a time when regulation has come of age as a primary tool of governance; and a time when those charged with its formulation and implementation are facing unprecedented challenges and pressures. The book assists these persons by providing them with a series of frameworks (or maps) with which to explore and examine the regulatory endeavour without being overwhelmed by its complexity. Through these frameworks, the book has sought to demystify and make sense of the theoretical literature and to marry it with the real world of regulatory practice. This marriage of theory and practice gives the book a strong practical orientation.

The book also examines the regulatory endeavour holistically (from issue identification, through design and implementation, to evaluation), through multiple and varied lenses (including governance, public policy, law, public administration, politics and economics), and employing examples from different countries and industry sectors. As a result, its frameworks are both general enough to apply across different issues and geographies, and specific enough to provide meaningful guidance to practitioners and students of the area.

Governing through regulation is inherently complex and messy. Sometimes it fails; at other times, it may not be fully successful. Overall, however, it has operated for the benefit of society. And while there is unlikely to be a perfect regulatory regime, it is hoped that this book is an advance in that direction, and that the reader has found it both enlightening and useful.

Notes

1. Harold D Lasswell, *Politics: Who Gets What, When, How* (Whittlesey House, 1936).
2. Charles T Goodsell, 'The Public Administrator as Artisan' (1992) 52 *Public Administration Review* 246, 247 (emphasis removed). See also Malcom K Sparrow, *The Regulatory Craft: Controlling Risks, Solving Problems, and Managing Compliance* (Brookings Institute Press, 2000); Anne Tiernan, 'Craft and

Capacity in the Public Service' (2015) 74 *Australian Journal of Public Administration* 53.

3. Jos Raadschelders, 'The Study of Public Administration in the United States' (2011) 89 *Public Administration* 140, 143. See also Tiernan, 'Craft and Capacity in the Public Service', above n 2, 58.

4. Neil Gunningham, 'Compliance, Enforcement, and Regulatory Excellence' in C Coglianese (ed), *Achieving Regulatory Excellence* (Brookings Institution Press, 2016) 188, 189.

5. John Yasuda, 'Regulatory Governance' in C Ansell and J Torfing (eds), *Handbook on Theories of Governance* (Edward Elgar, 2016) 428, 431.

6. John Braithwaite, 'The Essence of Responsive Regulation' (2011) 44 *University of British Columbia Law Review* 475, 490–2.

7. To borrow the term used by Gunningham, 'Compliance, Enforcement, and Regulatory Excellence', above n 4, 189.

8. Ibid 200.

9. Barak Orbach, 'What Is Regulation?' (2012) 30 *Yale Journal on Regulation Online* 1, 10.

10. John Braithwaite, 'Relational Republican Regulation' (2013) 7 *Regulation & Governance* 124, 135.

11. Julia Black, 'Paradoxes and Failures: "New Governance" Techniques and the Financial Crisis' (2012) 75 *Modern Law Review* 1037, 1062–3.

12. See, e.g., Chris Argyris, 'Double Loop Learning in Organizations' [1977] (Sept–Oct) *Harvard Business Review* 115; Olivier De Schutter and Jacques Lenoble, *Reflexive Governance: Redefining the Public Interest in a Pluralistic World* (Hart Publishing, 2010).

13. See Chapter 8, 158–60.

14. E.g. the global financial crisis, the Deepwater Horizon oil rig disaster and the Pike River mining disaster in New Zealand. See Chapter 8, 196 n 32.

15. Neil Gunningham, 'Two Cheers for Prescription? Lessons for the Red Tape Reduction Agenda' (2015) 38 *University of New South Wales Law Journal* 936, 959 (and the studies cited therein).

16. Sam Peltzman, *Regulation and the Natural Progress of Opulence* (AEI-Brookings Joint Center for Regulatory Studies, 2005) 5.

17. Gunningham, 'Two Cheers for Prescription?', above n 15, 958.

18. Robert Kagan, Neil Gunningham and Dorothy Thornton, 'Fear, Duty and Regulatory Compliance: Lessons from Three Research Projects' in C Parker and V Lehmann Nielsen (eds), *Explaining Compliance: Business Responses to Regulation* (Edward Elgar, 2011) 37, 54.

19. See, e.g., Mark C Suchman, Managing Legitimacy: Strategic and Institutional Approaches' (1995) 20 *Academy of Management Review* 571, 591–3; Julia Black, 'Constructing and Contesting Legitimacy and Accountability in Polycentric Regulatory Regimes' (2008) 2 *Regulation & Governance* 137, 146.

20. Eric Windholz, 'The Evolution of a Modern (and More Legitimate) Regulator: A Case Study of the Victorian Environment Projection Authority' (2016) 3 *Australian Journal of Environmental Law* 17, 42.

Index

For Product Safety Concerns and Information please contact our EU
representative GPSR@taylorandfrancis.com
Taylor & Francis Verlag GmbH, Kaufingerstraße 24, 80331 München, Germany

www.ingramcontent.com/pod-product-compliance
Ingram Content Group UK Ltd.
Pitfield, Milton Keynes, MK11 3LW, UK
UKHW021606240425
457818UK00018B/416